Small Screen, Big Feels

Small Screen, Big Feels

Television and Cultural Anxiety in the Twenty-First Century

Melissa Ames

UNIVERSITY PRESS OF KENTUCKY

Scholarly publisher for the Commonwealth,
serving Bellarmine University, Berea College, Centre College of Kentucky, Eastern Kentucky University, The Filson Historical Society, Georgetown College, Kentucky Historical Society, Kentucky State University, Morehead State University, Murray State University, Northern Kentucky University, Transylvania University, University of Kentucky, University of Louisville, and Western Kentucky University.

Editorial and Sales Offices: The University Press of Kentucky
663 South Limestone Street, Lexington, Kentucky 40508-4008
www.kentuckypress.com

Library of Congress Cataloging-in-Publication Data

Names: Ames, Melissa, 1978- author.
Title: Small screen, big feels : television and cultural anxiety in the twenty first century / Melissa Ames.
Description: Lexington, Kentucky : The University Press of Kentucky, [2020] | Includes bibliographical references and index.
Identifiers: LCCN 2020022841 | ISBN 9780813180069 (hardcover) | ISBN 9780813180083 (pdf) | ISBN 9780813180090 (epub)
Subjects: LCSH: Collective memory and television—United States—History—21st century. | Television and social media—United States—History—21st century. | Television programs—Social aspects—United States. | Television programs—Psychological aspects—United States. | Anxiety on television.
Classification: LCC PN1992.8.C65 A44 2020 | DDC 791.45/655—dc23
LC record available at https://lccn.loc.gov/2020022841

This book is printed on acid-free paper meeting the requirements of the American National Standard for Permanence in Paper for Printed Library Materials.

Manufactured in the United States of America

Member of the Association of University Presses

To McKinley and Madison (and all the children in my life):
May the world you create have fewer cultural anxieties
to view through your screens.

Contents

Part III. Amplifying Affect: Twenty-first-Century Viewing Practices–From Fandom to Digital Activism and Beyond

Introduction

Watching (and Feeling) Contemporary American TV: Understanding the Relationship among Societal Conflict, Technological Advancement, and Television Programming

Twenty-first-century television has been instrumental in cultivating the shared cultural memory of emotionally charged events unfolding in the United States. Consider, for example, this nonexhaustive list of traumatic events, societal conflicts, and political milestones that most Americans witnessed through television screens: the contested Bush-Gore 2000 presidential election, the September 11 terrorist attacks, Hurricane Katrina, U.S. Navy Seals infiltrating Osama bin Laden's compound, the presidential inauguration of Barack Obama, the Occupy Wall Street movement, the Boston Marathon bombings, the Ferguson protests, the controversial Clinton-Trump 2016 presidential election, the 2017 Women's Marches, the Stoneman Douglas High School shooting, the mass imprisonment of asylum seekers at border crossings, the COVID-19 pandemic, and so on. With the proliferation of mobile technology, both the production and consumption of television have changed, which has allowed many of these events to be viewed through television coverage and video clips accessible on laptops, tablets, and smartphones. Likewise, traditional television coverage of such historical events now often comprises footage captured by everyday citizens with technological devices on hand to capture the aftermath of natural disasters and mass shootings, the real-time instances of police brutality and hate crimes, the on-the-ground experience of political rallies and social protests, and so forth.

Though television has always played a role in recording and crafting history, shaping cultural memory, and influencing public sentiment, the changing nature of the medium in the post-network era—the around-the-clock coverage enabled by countless cable stations, on-the-go accessibility granted by streaming and mobile technology, the made-for-me personalization of television playlists and ideologically specific networks—finds viewers *experiencing* and participating in this process in new ways.[1] Studying the U.S. televisual landscape of the twenty-first century, this book traces the reciprocal relationship among current events, technological shifts, and programming trends and argues that these three work together to contribute to collective national affect states.[2] While television prompts multiple—sometimes idiosyncratic—emotions in individual viewers and communities, this project focuses primarily on the ways in which twenty-first-century programming has responded to and reinforced a cultural climate grounded in fear and anxiety in the United States.[3]

Entertaining the Era of Fear: Affect in the Post-9/11, Post-Social Media Period

For those old enough to remember the September 11 terrorist attacks, their memory of the day is probably framed within a television set: an image of a plane crashing into the side of one of the World Trade Center buildings; the footage of one or both of the towers toppling to the ground; horrific panoramic scenes of New York city filled with smoke and debris, injured people, shocked bystanders, and heroic first responders.[4] Probably erased from those memories is the crawl running across the bottom of those images, the network logo displayed on the corner of the screen, or the somber commentary provided by the news anchors. As it had in past televised national tragedies, television transported viewers to the scene of this trauma, cementing the memory in their minds as readily as if they had been spectators on the ground. And, in doing so, it began broadcasting an era of fear that would grow and take on many different forms (and targets) in the following two decades.

Although the 9/11 events occurred twenty-one months after the start of the new millennium, the early decades of the twenty-first century can easily be theorized as a post-9/11 period. Many scholars have viewed the terrorist attacks as a watershed moment, "a sort of 'year zero,'" in American history.[5] For example, Walter Kalaidjian has described 9/11 as "the inaugural trauma of the twenty-first century," one that "decisively sutured globalization and disaster into the defining symptom of our times."[6] The affect theorist Brian Massumi argued that during this era "direct affect modulation" dominated over "old-style ideology" in ways more obvious than in decades past.[7] In his essay "Fear

(The Spectrum Said)," Massumi discussed the U.S. Homeland Security's use of the color-coded terrorist alert system, arguing that it is a dangerous political tool that allows the government to create a climate of controlled "affective attunement."[8] As Michael Fisher notes, "creating fear and 'moral panic'" has always been a useful tool for the elite.[9] As I will discuss in this text, however, the technological affordances of our time provide powerful tools for these elites, government officials, and entertainment moguls, as well as laypersons, to prompt such emotions.[10] Discussing the current "saturation of social space by fear," Massumi argues that mass media function as "technologies of fear."[11] Similarly, Hisham Ramadan and Jeff Shantz argue that the media play a large role in crafting and circulating "phobic constructions."[12]

It is not just public media created from above, however, that are playing this role. The rise of personally generated social media, perhaps surprisingly, can be tied to the current moment of fear as well. The post-9/11 era aligns, not inconsequently, with the post–social media era. The terrorist attacks and the rise of mobile technology both lie at the beginning of the twenty-first century's road to fear indoctrination. Whether the latter is a response to this fear culture or a catalyst to its growth (or both) is unimportant. What is important is that the new millennium quickly finds personal technological devices receiving and sending a plethora of messages that align with the collective affect state of the nation.

Though research has begun to show a connection between social media use and increased depression and jealousy among users, links between social media and anxiety (preexisting or cyber-prompted) have been slower to receive attention.[13] By design, social media seem to be associated with positive emotions—after all, we spent a decade "liking" things on Facebook before we were given other emoticon options to express negative rather than positive feelings. And Twitter's introduction of the heart symbol, which allows users to "favorite" tweets, also suggests a connection between positivity and social media. As is true of most texts we choose to engage with, we flock to social media in theory to experience positive emotion rather than negative. But besides entertaining ourselves with cute cat videos and countless pictures of artistically prepared meals and picturesque photographs of our friends' travels, why might we find the constant presence of social media feeds comforting? How might their embeddedness in our daily lives be tied to the larger cultural climate surrounding us? Richard Grusin argues that the popularity of various socially networked media can be explained by considering the historical moment in which they exist.[14] Studying the rise of social media in the post-9/11 climate, Grusin suggests that social media provide users with the illusion that they can mediatize their entire worlds; they allow users to feel a false sense of control by "producing a feeling of anywhere, anytime connectivity."[15]

This need to feel connected, as well as the fear of being isolated or divorced from the safe confines of community, may account for other technology and media trends of the early twenty-first century. Consider, for example, the rise of reality TV (which is discussed further in chapter 2). In *Liquid Fear*, Zygmunt Bauman labels reality television "modern versions of the ancient 'morality plays,'" arguing that such shows—especially the popular competition programs—focus on the "inevitability of exclusion, and the fight against being excluded."[16]

Building on the research done on twenty-first-century media and particular entertainment genres, this text looks to situate television trends—across genres—within the technological and cultural moment they occurred. Following in the steps of other influential studies of television in regard to specific periods, this book provides a snapshot of the first two decades of the twenty-first century and the ways in which television programming reflects and contributes to technological shifts and societal mind-sets.[17]

Feeling through Our Screens: Pixelated Emotions (and Academic Theory)

During the decades studied in this project, academia saw a surge in scholarship on affect, or what Patricia Clough terms "the affective turn."[18] For the majority of this period, however, "television, a medium long associated with intimacy and emotional excess," was "left on the sidelines of debates on affect in visual media."[19] Film scholars have produced various studies on the important role that affect plays in film viewership and in particular film genres.[20] The majority of the early studies on television and emotion focused on particular televisual genres, such as news broadcasting (which will be discussed shortly) and soap opera, and did not apply affect theory across televisual genres (as is attempted in this text). Where affect theory (even when the term *affect* was not specifically employed) had the most prominence in television scholarship was in regard to audience studies and fandom.[21]

The popular culture scholar Henry Jenkins discusses the importance of emotion within popular culture of all formats, arguing that "most popular culture is shaped by a logic of emotional intensification. It is less interested in making us think than it is in making us feel. Yet that distinction is too simple: popular culture, at its best, makes us think by making us feel."[22] For many of the same reasons, Carl Plantinga argues for the importance of studying film through the lens of affect—an argument that can easily be applied to television:[23]

> Strong emotions have a tendency to make a mark, leaving lasting impressions that transform our psyche and imprint our memories. For that reason alone, the means by which the movies elicit emotion are worthy of taking seriously. . . . The expression and elicitation of emotion in a film is a central element of the film experience, an experience that is worthy of study in its own right. Moreover, emotion and affect are fundamental to what makes films artistically successful, rhetorically powerful, and culturally influential. . . . The function of emotion and affect is to make film viewing powerful, rather than merely an intellectual exercise. In the long term, such experiences may burn themselves into the memories of audiences and may become templates for thinking and behavior.[24]

The idea that television programs, like film, might be "templates for thinking and behavior" is perhaps the greatest justification for studying the role that affect plays in television viewing. In a TED Talk, the television executive Lauren Zalaznick claims that "television has a conscience." She argues that "television directly reflects the moral, political, social and emotional need states of our nation—that television is how we actually disseminate our entire value system."[25] Attending to the ways in which television plays this role, especially in times of national crisis, is extremely important.

Broadcasting the Catastrophic: Scholarship on Television and Trauma

The role television plays during times of trauma has long been studied by various scholars.[26] Mary Ann Doane builds on Roland Barthes's discussion of photography, in particular its *noeme* (the essence of "*that-has-been*" or its "pastness") to argue that television offers quite a different visual experience, that of "*this-is-going-on*" or a sense of "present-ness."[27] Likewise, Jay Bolter and Richard Grusin explore the connected concept of immediacy in regard to new media. They argue not only that immediacy is a sense of transparency in which the media give off the illusion that they are *not* a mediation or a representation, and hence indicate an absence or erasure of mediation, but also that immediacy can be tied to "the viewer's feelings that the medium has disappeared and the objects are present to him, a feeling that his experience is therefore authentic."[28] News broadcasts obviously capitalize on television's claim to immediacy. The word *LIVE* appearing in the lower corner of the TV screen and the anchor's quip, "This just in," help transport the viewers to the event, giving them the feeling that they are there, that they are witnessing this event unfolding before their eyes (and allow them to ignore, should they so choose, the fact that it is being delivered to them across distance and through technology that has the potential to transform such scenes).

It is important to note that networks do exploit their power as a "live" supplier of coverage and do systematically manipulate the viewer's affective responses. The news attempts to deliver anxiety in order to enact its role of relieving it. Discussing this process, Patricia Mellencamp argues that "anxiety *is* television's affect" and suggests that when studying this medium, we should shift "our analysis from theories of pleasure to include theories of unpleasure."[29] She states, "TV envelops the shock, delivering *and* cushioning us from stimuli which it regulates in acceptable levels . . . turning news or shocks into story and tragic drama."[30] The reporter is there to inject viewers with anxiety, fear, and anger, but also to quickly administer the antidote, the assurance that everything will be just fine, and that he or she will be there to present that final happy diagnosis just as soon as it is.

The everyday news does this on a small scale, but in attending to large-scale catastrophes, this practice, which indeed predates 9/11, is all the more noticeable. Mary Ann Doane discusses these moments that disrupt "ordinary routine."[31] TV from its onset has had the capacity to capture these moments and deliver them right to viewers in their living rooms: Kennedy's assassination, the *Challenger*'s explosion, Chernobyl, the rescue of Baby Jessica, the massacre at Columbine, 9/11, the 2004 tsunami, Hurricane Katrina, the earthquake in Haiti, and countless other natural disasters (floods, tornadoes), acts of violence (bombings, wars), or unexpected death (plane crashes, fires).[32] These mediated moments not only disrupt our routine, drawing us to the screen to consume them in endless (even painful) repetition, but they also end up acting as time markers for those who witness them, epochal reference points, and they probably play a large role in a generation's structure of feeling. Doane claims that "catastrophic time stands still."[33] Hence, the event, the frozen moment in time, becomes one potentially shared with an entire generation. For example, it is likely that most people of an age to remember 9/11 could answer the question "Where were you when the Twin Towers were attacked," just as the previous generation could remember their whereabouts when they heard that Kennedy had been shot, or as the generation before that could recall where they were when they heard of the atomic bombs being dropped on Japan or the attack on Pearl Harbor. Arguably, such traumatic events—these shared generational moments—produce the shared affect that make a generation.

Focusing on media practices post-9/11, Richard Grusin theorizes "the emergence of a media logic . . . a form of medial pre-emption" he terms premediation.[34] He argues that "premediation works to prevent citizens of the global mediasphere from experiencing again the kind of systemic or traumatic shock produced by the events of 9/11 by perpetuating an almost constant, low level of fear or anxiety about another terrorist attack."[35] Grusin clarifies that premediation differs from prediction in that it "is not about getting the future right, but about proliferating multiple remediations of the future both to maintain a low level of fear in the present and to prevent a recurrence of the kind of tremendous media shock that the United States and much of the networked world experienced on 9/11."[36]

While Grusin focuses primarily on premediation in regard to the news industry, as I will discuss later in this text, similar things are happening within fictional television programming. The plethora of 9/11-related worst-case scenarios fashioned for the small screen arguably prepare viewers (at least emotionally) for a variety of future outcomes.

Guiding Principles: Central Assumptions about and Theories of Affect

This book builds on a range of—sometimes conflicting—affect theory and rests on a few key theoretical assumptions concerning affect that explain television's relationship to contemporary anxieties. This project engages with the rich pool of media scholarship focused on the way "people experience affects through entertainment products."[37] These include:

- The Mood Management Theory: the notion that we turn to certain texts to alter or maintain our emotional states (see chapters 1, 2, 3)
- The Relief or Excitation Transfer Theory: the idea that we experience positive affect through the release of negative affect (see chapters 3, 5)
- The Theory of Escapism: the belief that we turn to entertainment texts to distract ourselves from our everyday lived reality (see chapters 2, 4, 5, 6)

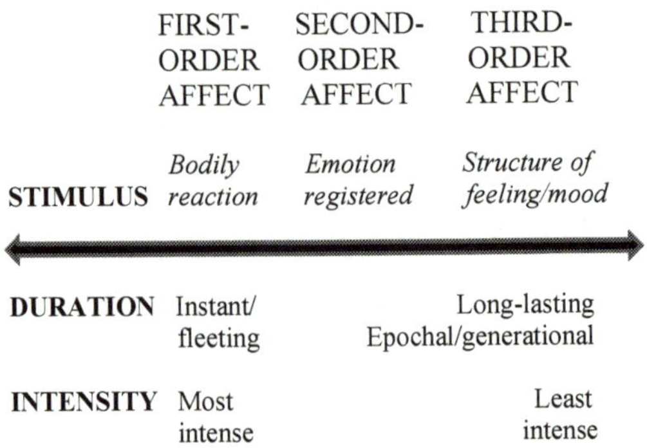

Figure 0.1. The affect continuum, or the three "orders" of affect. (Figure by the author.)

- The Empathy Theory: the explanation of the ways in which we form affective attachments to fictional characters or faux celebrities (see chapters 2, 5, 7, 8)
- The Social Comparison or Schadenfreude Theory: the argument that we consume entertainment texts in order to feel better about ourselves (see chapters 2, 8, 9, 10)
- The Uses-and-Gratifications Theory: combining all the above to a degree, the argument that we turn to media texts "for various reasons, informative, social, affective, or dispersion seeking in nature"[38]

Not particular to any of these theories specifically, this project rests on three central assumptions concerning affect. The first assumption, represented in Figure 0.1, is a nod to definitional debates in the field and explains the purposeful conflation of emotion and affect found in this project. This slippage falls into an intentionally broad conceptualization of affect.

Affect theorists have provided many useful definitions for terms such as affect, emotion, feeling, mood, sentiment, and so forth.[39] These scholarly definitions often stress the differences between such psychological and bodily states and argue for very different approaches to studying them. Consider, for example, two foundational affect scholars, Silvan Tomkins and Brian Massumi, who differ widely in their theorizations. Tomkins views the human affect system as operating like a feedback system, whereby affects are a sort of motive and humans act (unsurprisingly though not without exception) "to repeat rewarding affects and to reduce punishing" ones.[40] Tomkins uses both the terms *affect* and *emotion* in his discussion of what he sees to be the eight primary affects: interest-excitement, enjoyment-joy, surprise-startle, distress-anguish, fear-terror, shame-humiliation, contempt-disgust, and anger-rage.[41] Massumi, on the other hand, maps out a theory concerning the corporeality of affect that is based on Spinoza's definition of affect as "an impingement upon" the human body.[42] Unlike Tomkins, Massumi distinguishes sharply between affect and emotion, equating affect with intensity "embodied in purely autonomic reactions most directly manifested in the skin—at the surface of the body, at its interface with things."[43] For him affect is unconscious and is not correlated logically between content (object/image) and the bodily effect it produces, a claim Tomkins would agree with in terms of both affect and emotion.[44] Massumi argues that "it is only when the idea of the affection is doubled by an *idea of the idea of the affection* that it attains the level of conscious reflection"—and this is where he would more readily place the term *emotion*.[45]

This particular study envisions affect as an umbrella concept that represents all the more specific terms that are often used rather interchangeably outside scholarly circles.[46] As figure 0.1 shows, this conceptualization imagines affect as divided into different "levels" or "orders." This continuum can be represented in terms of temporality or duration and possibly in terms of intensity as well. On the leftmost part of the continuum is first-order affect, or bodily affect. This is the instantaneous reaction in the body to a given object or stimulus. A fear-invoking situation will result in bodily arousal: a racing heart, a sweaty brow, raised hair, and so forth. Moving along the continuum, second-order affect might be what we usually consider emotion more generally. This occurs when cognition is coupled with the bodily arousal, when the affect is realized, processed, or named. The time that separates the two orders on the left side of the range can be mere seconds, so it is often fruitless to study them as separate experiences, but it is important to acknowledge the differences between the two processes. Also, it is important to note the causality or dependence between the two: first-order affect sparks second-order affect. Or, as William James famously argued: we do not cry because we are sad; we are sad because we cry.[47] We emote in reaction to our body's instantaneous reactions to stimuli. Between second-order affect and third-order affect is a potentially large space on the continuum. This represents the temporal difference that exists between these affectual stages. On this chart third-order affect is associated with Raymond Williams's (1977) structure of feeling.[48] This concept is often used to denote a collective state of affect, the shared affect of an epoch or a generation. It is the least immediate of the affect stages and is probably the most durable. This conceptualization works on an individual level also. A sad event will register on the body temporarily (it could result, for example, in tears); the emotion of sadness can be felt for longer than the physical reaction (the tears themselves may last just minutes, whereas the emotion can last hours, maybe days); and sad events can often contribute to a milder form of lurking sadness that can linger even longer as a "mood" (shared or not). It could also be possible to argue that this continuum works when discussing the intensity of the three orders of affect: the first order being the most immediate and intensely felt in the body, the second order being sometimes slightly less striking, and the third order being the least intense of the three stages of affect as a lingering, low-level "feeling."

The second affect assumption (see figure 0.2) pertains to affect-object reciprocity, which becomes particularly relevant when discussing the relationship among texts, consumers, and producers. Obviously, certain objects cause certain affects (e.g., a sad movie can make one sad). One's emotional state, however, can also color the interpretation of an object or event (e.g., a sad mood existing before a film viewing can make one read it as sadder than it may actually be to others). This theoretical underpinning attends to the larger relationship between third-order affect—shared or collective affectual states—and textual production and reception. This process can be oversimplified into this sequence: an object triggers affect or emotion, which in turn can contribute to larger structures of feelings; those cultural moods produce certain texts that align with (or respond to) these affect states, and these texts are consumed by viewers, perpetuating the cycle. This process, of course, is not always a conscious one. Jonathan Flatley notes that "we are often ignorant of the determinative effect our moods have on the world we see and how we relate to it."[49] He details the importance of understanding the effect that structures of feelings can have, explaining that though they can be ephemeral, they can also be "just as durable and forceful as ideologies, perhaps even more so."[50] Therefore, he argues, structure of feelings should be theorized as a "full-fledged parallel to ideology," one whose function "is to narrate our relation to a social order so as to make our daily experience of that order meaningful and manageable."[51]

Thus, many of the arguments throughout this book require associating emotions with rationality (which has not always been done in scholarship), and acknowledging that emotions (affects in their second order) are not purely biological, evolutionary creations, but rather are social constructs deeply influenced by cultural situations.[52] It is not unfounded to claim that emotions are inherently rational, as in fact the argument has been made as far back as Aristotle.

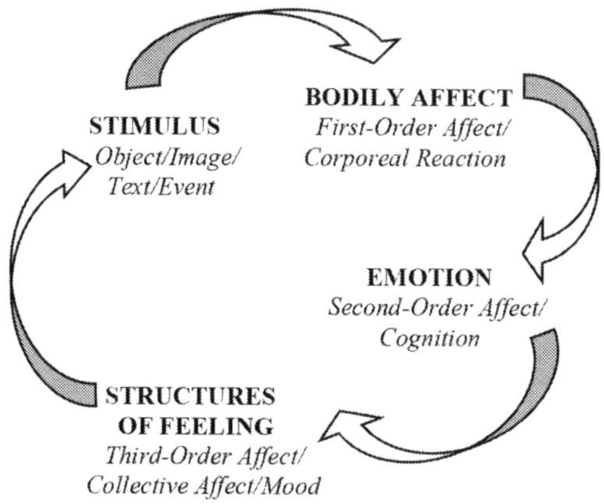

Figure 0.2. Affect-object reciprocity. (Figure by the author.)

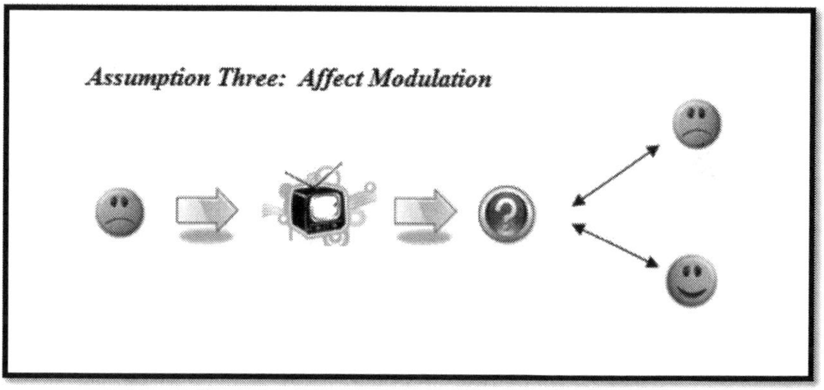

Figure 0.3. Affect modulation. (Figure by the author.)

Aristotle defined emotions as "those feelings that so change men as to affect their judgments, and that are also attended by pain or pleasure."[53] In his discussions on affect, Tomkins asserts that "the marriage of reason with affect" is what makes human beings the most complex system in nature, and he notes that "reason without affect would be impotent, affect would be blind."[54]

The final affect assumption is quite simple: people use things (texts, events, environments) to control their emotional state (see the previously mentioned Mood Management Theory). The extremely simplified chart shown in figure 0.3 applies this assumption to the causality of television viewing practices. The general argument would be that viewers often flock to

TV to manipulate or modulate their emotions. Those involved in production may attempt to use the medium for this purpose as well, as may other outside powers (e.g., politicians, corporations, activists).

Viewer agency and participation in affect modulation need to be stressed. An example could be the ways in which media outlets *and* viewers interacted with Trump's negative political discourse during and after the 2016 presidential election. As has been much discussed, Trump received more media coverage during the campaign than any of his opponents on either side of the aisle and, not inconsequently, he benefited the most from the overall negative focus of the election coverage.[55] Likewise, knowing that people could not turn away from his emotionally hyperbolic rhetoric, the news networks benefited from airing it, and hence Trump dominated the coverage. The media outlets were right: viewers tuned in, for whatever reason; they watched to be incited (joining in his fear or anger over x, y, z) or they watched because they were afraid or angry about his stances (on x, y, z). Either way—conservative supporters or liberal opposition—viewers participated in his rise to fame (and office) by tuning in. And, arguably, they tuned in knowing full well how watching his press conferences or political rallies would make them feel. Typically, we do not stumble unknowingly on our televisual texts. Their emotional triggers do not often surprise us.[56] Just as we cue up certain genres expecting emotional outcomes from them (sitcoms will make us laugh, a melodrama will make us cry, an action drama will excite us, etc.), we tune in to individual media segments knowing—often—how they will make us feel.[57] And, even when those feelings are negative, we do it anyway (something that might seem to run counter to Tomkins's claim that we look to minimize negative affect and maximize positive affect).

Figure 0.3, of course, is an oversimplification of an imperfect process. First, as Beverley Skeggs notes, as consumers we cannot always predict with absolute accuracy what emotional output a televisual text will have, and this unpredictability may actually increase its entertainment value.[58] Second, even if producers do have an intended emotional reaction in mind when crafting television programming, this is not to suggest that such is always an inevitable outcome. To buy into such an inevitability would be to duplicate the illogical premise of the hypodermic needle theory, which assumes that an intended communication or (ideological) message is directly and wholly accepted by the receiver—only in this case we would be replacing "message" with "emotion."

These three assumptions concerning affect and television consumption could easily enter into larger debates concerning technological determinism, and media determinism more specifically.[59] While this book does argue that televisual programming and technological advances in the industry have affected society (a claim that might seem to align with a determinist perspective), active viewing and audience agency—which have expanded in recent decades—ultimately suggest a relationship that is not one-directional (a belief more in line with social determinism). That said, part I of this text does touch on the consequences of televisual trends, such as the desensitization that results from repeat screenings of violent imagery or plots. Although outside the purview of this project, burgeoning research in neuroscience on plasticity (and the role that technology may play in "rewiring" the brain) could provide an entirely different (and perhaps more terrifying) perspective on television's influence on individual and societal affect states.[60]

While not a major focus in this text, many of the arguments found here would entertain previous scholars' arguments concerning the actual physical and mental effects that media products can have on us. For example, discussing the rise of cinema in the twentieth century, Walter Benjamin made the bold claim that "technology has subjected the human sensorium to a complex kind of training."[61] And in regard to television specifically, decades later Lynne Joyrich made the bold claim that "TV has begun to alter our very ways of seeing and knowing."[62] It would not be a big leap from these arguments to then consider the ways in which television may be changing the ways in which we experience and feel emotions. Grusin considers the possible influence technology may have on human affective processing, stating: "If brains and neural processing co-evolve like thumbs and video-game controllers, it then seems likely that our affective states would also co-evolve with our media and other new technologies. It is thus not unreasonable to imagine that certain affects become stronger and more muscular in different cultural and historical contexts, while others might atrophy or grow weak from disuse."[63] In fact, it may be irresponsible not to consider this particular co-evolution and the ways in which it contributes to twenty-first-century fear indoctrination.

Navigating the Times (and This Text): The Emotional Terrain of Twenty-first-Century Television

It is with the abovementioned foundational affect scholarship and grounding assumptions in mind that this book considers the ways in which national anxieties make their way into U.S. television programming across genres, and the ways in which such anxieties affect viewers and the larger cultural conversations and sentiments that surround them. Part I, "Post-9/11 Televisual Trends: Analyzing the Affectual Climate on and off the Small Screen," traces programming shifts in three specific television genres (prime-time drama, reality television, and news shows). Drawing on affect theory, these chapters discuss the proliferation and dominance of these entertainment outlets and question how emotion plays into their audience appeal and societal influence. Chapter 1 analyzes how television responded to 9/11 not only immediately after the tragedy, but also how it responded (and continues to respond) to it years later through fictionalized dramas. By studying the presence of post-9/11 motifs (e.g., salvation, justice, fear, conspiracy) in twenty-first-century fictional television narratives, this chapter argues that such programs are important sites where the terrorist attacks (and the cultural climate they sparked) are emotionally worked through. This chapter also suggests, however, that television's reluctance to revise its post-9/11 narrative in order to reflect contemporary geopolitical realities may also contribute to the perpetual fear cycle shaping national discourse. Chapter 2 turns to reality television, exploring three emotional theories that explain the rise of this televisual genre in the wake of 9/11. A study of the 2000–2010 programming schedule reveals the cultural anxieties with which producers and viewers of these shows engage—or not. Although often considered superficial, lowbrow entertainment products meant primarily for escapist purposes, reality television programs, this essay argues, grapple with important societal concerns: surveillance culture and privacy rights; the pressure of identity performance in the social media era; and shifting social, domestic, and familial expectations for men and women. Turning to one final entertainment genre, chapter 3 studies the rise in popularity of parodic infotainment news shows following the 9/11 attacks. Drawing on humor relief theory, as well as theories concerning affect mimicry and imagined communities, this essay argues that news parodies, such as Comedy Central's *The Daily Show,* satisfied various emotional needs for viewers during this traumatic period. Critics often worry that therapeutic laughter diffuses fear and anger and quells rebellious impulses, but this chapter argues that the humor provided by these programs has the potential to help viewers transform their negative emotions into action.

Part II, "Mediating Fear and Anger: How Televisual Affect Reflects and Influences Current Cultural Conflicts," moves from a discussion of larger programmatic patterns to analysis of specific television shows and subgenres that showcase the ways in which cultural fears are embedded in our entertainment. For example, ABC's *Lost* (2004–10)—the show that television scholars such as Jason Mittell have credited with starting the wave of complex television—encompasses a myriad of societal concerns and commentaries.[64] Chapter 4 focuses on just one of these: the changing status of fathers and authority figures in the twenty-first century. This chapter looks at *Lost,* and its over sixty episodes devoted to damaged or deceased dads, and it analyzes the ways in which *Lost*'s parent-child relationships comment on shifting conceptions of masculinity and, on a more metaphoric level, the eroding faith in governmental father figures in the era of the endless war on terror. Shifting from a focus on fictional fathers to fictional mothers, chapter 5 analyzes the ways in which AMC's hit show *The Walking Dead* (2010–present) critiques contemporary gender roles. Through a study of one particular character, Carol Peletier (Melissa McBride), this essay argues that the violent landscape of the zombie narrative might be an ideal space in which to interrogate conceptions of femininity more broadly, and maternity more specifically. Supernatural shows by their nature often incorporate themes such as survival, community, revenge, resurrection, and the dark side of humanity—themes that take on a new meaning in the post-9/11 period. Chapter 6 analyzes how these are incorporated into twenty-first-century vampire narratives, such as HBO's *True Blood* (2008–14), CW's *The Vampire Diaries* (2009–17), and the film adaptations of Stephenie Meyer's *Twilight Saga* (2008, 2009, 2010, 2011, 2012). Through a recurrent focus on "us versus them," these story lines bring attention to the cultural divides within the United States caused by things such as continued racial conflict, progress in the LGBTQA rights movement, and ongoing religious and political debates concerning family values. Delving into trauma theory, chapter 7 narrows its focus to one particular year of programming that featured story lines about police brutality, inequity within the criminal justice system, and the Black Lives Matter movement that has risen to speak out against both. This essay analyzes special episodes of CBS's *The Good Wife* (2009–16) and ABC's *Scandal* (2012–18)—which have been referred to by media critics as each program's respective "Ferguson episode"—and the first season of ABC's *American Crime* (2015–17), a gritty crime anthology/miniseries that unflinchingly tackled racial conflict in its debut year. While there are reasons to be wary of attempts to fictionalize current race relations, this chapter ultimately argues that series that include thoughtful, complex story lines, and televisual aesthetics that underscore the social commentary contained in the program, may allow these issues not just to be understood, but *felt.*

Returning to the three televisual genres studied more broadly in part I, the final section of the book provides three audience studies: analyses of live tweets commenting on Shonda Rhimes's drama *How to Get Away with Murder* (2014–20); ABC's long-standing reality television franchise, *The Bachelor/Bachelorette* (2002–present); and political coverage of the first 2016 presidential debate. The final chapters in "Amplifying Affect: Twenty-first-Century Viewing Practices—From Fandom to Digital Activism and Beyond" study how cultural anxieties appear within these television genres and how viewers engage with them online. As Rhimes is credited with transforming contemporary network television production and consumption practices—and having the most avid Twitter followers—it is fitting that an analysis of her hit program begins this section. Chapter 8 considers fictional television's ability to engage in public pedagogy by looking at the ways in which viewers support or undermine Rhimes's social commentary. Attending to tweets focused on the main character, the female antihero Annalise Keating (Viola Davis), reveals the warring sentiments (and different ideological camps) that still exist surrounding identity politics involving women of color, same-sex relationships, and interracial relationships. Chapter 9 builds on research concerning the ways in which reality television includes conflicting postfeminist messages that affect the contestants on the shows, as well as the viewers watching them. This chapter studies viewer reactions to a particularly controversial season of *The Bachelorette*—one that aired the star having sexual intercourse before the show's pre-scripted, approved point. The online discussions among fans on Twitter reveal the ways in which viewers resist or reinforce gender stereotypes and participate in or criticize the practice of slut-shaming. The final study presented focuses on one of the most consequential events of the twenty-first century thus far: the 2016 presidential election, which ended as it did probably in part because of a combination of the cultural fears discussed throughout the previous chapters. For example, the presidential campaign run by Trump played on post-9/11 uncertainties about homeland security and employed fear-based, divisive rhetoric about race, gender, class, and sexuality. The acceptance of this rhetoric—and his ultimate victory—may be explained by the process of phobic construction highlighted in this text. Since "phobias (of terror, crime, migration, invasion or infection, cultural decay), often involving a targeted 'other,'" create "frames by which people make sense of changing socio-political environments," it is not surprising—although it may be disheartening—that a large populace was receptive to such messages.[65] Chapter 10 analyzes the final months of the election cycle, in particular the first presidential debate between Trump and Hillary Clinton and the ways in which it stimulated conversation among viewers during the live broadcast and ongoing dialogue and activism beyond it. The conclusion, "Screening Emotion, Archiving Affect, Circulating Feelings," ends with some brief thoughts on how television and other entertainment and communication platforms act as storage houses and distribution mechanisms for personal and cultural sentiments. If the dominant affect of the twenty-first century continues to be fear, this text argues that it is more important than ever to understand and intervene in the ways in which it is circulated through media and technology.

As the summaries above reveal, this text purposely navigates between different television genres and cultural events spanning two decades, most notably those between 9/11 and the 2016 presidential election. The chapters in part I feature large-scale analyses of fictional shows, reality television, and news-related programming. In this same order, the chapters in part III provide small-scale analyses of viewer responses to specific television broadcasts from these three genres. While chapter 1 does begin with a focus on post-9/11 programming and chapter 10 closes with a focus on the 2016 election, the text does not necessarily move throughout this time period in perfect chronological order, nor does it make absolute claims about causality when it comes to the cultural anxieties discussed. It is difficult to contemplate the role television plays in shaping cultural sentiments, however, without considering how cultural events (and their televised offspring) influence one another and how cultural anxieties layer on one another over time. For example, whether explicitly or implicitly discussed, echoes of post-9/11 fears undoubtedly reverberate through every chapter. Likewise, by nature of its design, the text prompts readers to make their own connections between not only the various cultural events highlighted, but also the anxieties that connect to them.

This book also purposely draws from diverse methodological approaches, allowing for these considerations to take on different forms. Consider the different ways in which part I analyzes programming trends from across the past two decades. Chapter 1 provides quantitative data concerning thematic motifs that appear in fictional programming; chapter 2 includes a study of all reality programming throughout a ten-year period, aligning the shows' subject matter with relevant affect theories to explain television appeal; and chapter 3 situates the rise of infotainment and news parody within historical contexts and selects one sample to analyze through three particular affect theories. The chapters in part II, likewise, provide varied ways of analyzing individual television programs: chapter 4 includes tallies of particular motifs as part of its analysis; chapter 5 reads the thematic messages of a television program against the online conversation it sparked among reviewers and fans alike; chapter 6 studies a television horror subgenre alongside a popular book-and-film franchise that helped ignite the televisual trend; and chapter 7 provides a close reading of a television show down to its use of sound editing and image framing. And, finally, part III studies the live-tweeting practices of viewers—focusing on specific episodes, entire seasons, and connections to larger digital discourses. Together, these chapters aim to model the various ways in which cultural anxieties can be studied in relation to television production and consumption practices.

Part I

Post-9/11 Televisual Trends

Analyzing the Affectual Climate on and off the Small Screen

1

Screening Terror

How 9/11 Affected Twenty-First-Century Televisual Fiction

The national tragedy of 9/11 directly and indirectly influenced the cultural production within American society during the first two decades of the twenty-first century. In the years following the attacks on the World Trade Center and Pentagon, cultural products have been sites for interrogating and remediating the trauma that 9/11 caused for the citizens of a country that believed itself to be untouchable. Although these cultural concerns were played out in both nonfictional and fictional spaces across media, as I will discuss in following chapters, this chapter argues that televisual narratives provide great insight into societal concerns during the start of this century. They do this in a unique space that repackages these concerns, displacing them from reality into the safe confines of fiction, where they can be addressed time and time again with more favorable results.

In studying how the media and popular culture products responded to 9/11, in the contest of timeliness there is no debate. In general, television was quicker to respond to the tragedy than any other medium (e.g., film, print novel)—both as it was happening and in the months and years after. Quite obviously there was the real-time news broadcasting the day of the events, but special programs and documentaries also appeared in the weeks that followed. The events of 9/11, however, also seeped into the fictional worlds found in television sitcoms and dramas within only a few weeks. There were some early televisual attempts at understanding the tragedy. CNN re-aired its documentary *Beneath the Veil* and its sequel, *Unholy War*—both focused on the plight of Afghani women under the Taliban regime—in the weeks following 9/11, and to commemorate the six-month anniversary of the attacks, CBS also aired Jules and Gédéon Naudet's documentary *9/11* on March 10, 2002. The speed of this response is attributed more to television's production processes and freedoms and less to its actual desire to be the pioneers of a post-9/11 narrative. But what is more interesting, and not as theorized, is not how television responded to 9/11 immediately after the tragedy, but how it responded (and continues to respond) to it years later.

In contrast to television, Hollywood did not begin producing films inspired by or based on 9/11 until 2006, with the release of both Paul Greengrass's *United 93* and Oliver Stone's *World Trade Center.* It is this specific year—one marking the five-year anniversary of the attacks—that clearly showcases the post-9/11 affective work that would dominate televisual narratives for the coming years. When compared to the films being released now, the stories delivered through television separate themselves from the documentary-style narratives of 9/11-related film and enter the deep recesses of fiction—even into the realms of science fiction, where it is once again acceptable to be playful and perverse even while trying to work out cultural concerns lingering from a half decade earlier. But before getting to that fateful year of 2006—the year that broadcast loud and clear that the United States was a nation waiting to be saved—and the televisual trends that have lingered since, one must start at the beginning: television post-9/11 and television's history of being a cultural tool for coping with the catastrophic.

The Televisual Landscape in the Wake of 9/11

Television did not immediately begin spawning fictional narratives loosely related to the attacks. In fact, right after 9/11, television executives were quite concerned about the content of their programming, specifically any fictional narratives that might be considered disturbing, violent, or traumatic in the aftermath of the national crisis. Lynn Spigel recounts how films such as *Collateral Damage, The Siege, Lethal Weapon, Carrie,* and even *Superman* and *King Kong* were pulled from television lineups.[1] Inadvertent censorship and coverage changes also occurred during this time, however. For example, Spigel notes that the "humorists Dave Letterman, Jay Leno, Craig Kilborn, Conan O'Brien, and Jon Stewart met the late-night audience with dead seriousness" on the nights following 9/11, which caused some critics to declare "that the attacks on the Pentagon and World Trade Center had brought about the 'end of irony.'"[2] Although the industry heads were attempting to save viewers from their prepackaged violent imagery, during this period the public was actually eager to consume such depictions of trauma. Video retailers reported an increase in customer rentals of films like those pulled from the network's lineups, which suggests that the consumption of explosions, toppling buildings, and apocalyptic scenarios—at least when situated in fictionalized backdrops—was just what the doctor ordered in terms of coping strategies and escapism.[3] So it is not really a surprise that televisual narratives would pick up on these motifs in a relatively short time in the crafting of new programs and episodes.

Although much was going on in the fictional programming found on television, for the most part early media scholarship on 9/11, the U.S. attacks in Afghanistan, and the early stages of the "war on terror" focused primarily on print and television news coverage.[4] This work from the academy often attended to "the narrative and mythic 'framing' of the events; the nationalistic jingoism . . .; competing global news outlets, particularly Al Jazeera; and the institutional and commercial pressure that has led to 'infotainment.'"[5] But as Spigel states, "Despite its important achievements . . . the scholarly focus on news underestimates (indeed, it barely considers) the way the 'reality' of 9/11 was communicated across the flow of television's genres, including its so-called entertainment genres."[6] In order to accomplish the latter goal, her essay "Entertainment Wars: Television Culture after 9/11" analyzes Comedy Central's November 7, 2001, episode of *South Park* and NBC's October 3, 2001, episode of *West Wing* to showcase the various ways that television genres responded to the attacks through their narratives. Similarly, this chapter aims to fill in part of this academic void by analyzing various thematic motifs that appeared (or were amplified) in televisual fiction after 9/11 in order to prove that, indeed, these are important sites where the "'reality' of 9/11" is—even all this time later—still being worked out.

Although one might have expected television programming to grow more serious in the wake of 9/11, the opposite ultimately occurred. Some reporters, such as Louis Chunovic of *Television Week*, were hopeful that the face of television would change following the attacks: "In the wake of the terrorist attack on the United States, it's hard to believe Americans once cared who would win Big Brother 2 or whether Anne Heche is crazy. And it's hard to believe that as recently as two weeks ago, that's exactly the kind of pabulum, along with the latest celebrity/politician sex/murder/kidnapping scandal, that dominated television news. . . . We cannot afford to return to the way things were."[7]

But as Spigel notes, ironically, "the industry's post-9/11 upgrade to quality genres—especially historical documentaries—actually facilitated the return to the way things were."[8] Or, almost the way they were. If we look carefully, the ghost of the toppled towers leaves a shadowy imprint on the television programming during the remainder of the decade, suggesting that while viewers wanted to return to the comfort of "the way things were," they also were not ready to forget the tragedy that had unfolded on their home turf.

Watching Trauma Unfold on the Small Screen

In many ways, it is not surprising that fictional TV programs evolved into a space to work through cultural anxieties. After all, when many think of 9/11, their memories are of seeing the event unfold on their television screens. Also, 9/11 was framed as a trauma *to be seen* (in order to be felt), and television has long been the medium in charge of controlling feelings through the art of seeing specifically constructed imagery. For many Americans (and others across the globe), 9/11 unfolded in front of their eyes much like a Hollywood blockbuster film—almost too spectacular to believe. Slavoj Žižek writes: "When we watched the oft-repeated shot of frightened people running toward the camera ahead of the giant cloud of dust from the collapsing tower, was not the framing of the shot itself reminiscent of spectacular shots in a catastrophe movie, a special effect that outdid all others?"[9] Indeed, many survivors used the simile "it felt like a movie" to explain the experience.[10] As Susan Sontag argues, "'It felt like a movie' seems to have displaced the way survivors of a catastrophe used to express the short-term inability to assimilate what they had gone through: 'It felt like a dream.'"[11] So, is it really a surprise that the American public turned to the realm of visual culture and media to replay the event dominating their own memories? Marc Redfield argues that the phrase itself "'it was like a movie' conjures up not just an excess of event over believability, but a sense that this event *is to be mediated,* that it would have no sense, perhaps would not even have occurred, if it were not being recorded and transmitted."[12] In this explanation, the medium was needed; it was the only way that people could move from disbelief (that which they could not comprehend and some could not physically see) to belief (that which they could comprehend only through repeated seeing).

This incomprehensible tragedy of 9/11 is often classified as a cultural trauma, but it differs quite a bit from other national catastrophes. Redfield points out: "That the attacks inflicted a shock of historical scale seems clear, but the shape and scope of this wound is not. . . . If we try to conceive of trauma on a cultural level things become more ambiguous. . . . [The attacks] were not of a society-threatening scale (as warfare, genocide, famine, or natural cataclysm have been for so many human societies) and the literal damage they did to the military and commercial orders symbolized by the Pentagon and the World Trade Center was miniscule; it is of course as symbolic acts of violence that they claim culturally traumatic status."[13]

He continues to analyze the common affects of trauma and the coping process that individuals usually go through: "Trauma involves blockage: an inability to mourn, to move from repetition to working through. It is certainly plausible that hyperbolic commemorative efforts such as those on display in '9/11 discourse'. . . are in fact testimonials to blockage."[14] Redfield argues that "wherever one looks in 9/11 discourse, trauma and the warding-off of trauma blur into each other, as the event disappears into its own mediation."[15] I propose that a very similar process is at work in the televisual narratives that proliferate after 9/11; through their mediation of fictionalized scenarios they present trauma in order to do away with it, hence becoming a sort of emotional security blanket for viewers existing in an unstable post-9/11 world.

Susan Douglas posits that communications technologies "have some inherent capabilities that privilege some senses—and thus some cognitive and behavioral processes—over others."[16] I would agree and claim that these cognitive and behavioral processes relate to certain affects—the most prevalent being the affect of fear. To claim that television has this emotional power is not new, nor is the association of television with fear. In determining how television portrays 9/11 (and post-9/11 concerns), however, the association seems important. The television scholar Louise Spence observed that a year after 9/11 her students "still understood the events of 9/11 in affective and emotional terms."[17] It could be argued that almost two decades later most Americans still do. Part of this emotional understanding, and emotionally charged memory, of the event is in part due to the way it was presented through the medium of television.

Post-9/11 Thematics

In the aftermath of 9/11, two emotionally charged motifs seemed to receive this constant reinforcement in both fictional and nonfictional television programming: the rejuvenated theme of national patriotism and the fear of the "other." In the news broadcasting world, these two areas of focus seem quite interrelated. Scholars have compared this current trend of a patriotism grounded in fear to the post–World War II cold war era. Dennis Broe argues:

> The reading of the so-called war on terrorism as similar in scope and aim to the anticommunism of the former cold war is, of course, denied

> by media outlets such as the Fox News Channel, which operate in a perpetual present or in a historical moment that began on September 11, 2001. The promotion of an external enemy for the purposes of global domination and of quelling domestic dissent, coupled with the revival of a faltering economy through military spending, are characteristics in common with the Cold War. The current endless war is a global civil war fought by an apparently triumphant capitalist system against both a new, more ethnically diverse and predominantly female working class and a global anticorporate movement. At the center, this war takes the form of attacks on wages and curbs civil rights, while at the periphery, war is more openly declared against states with natural resources (oil, natural gas, water).[18]

In this sense, the media can be seen as acting the part of the man behind the curtain shouting: "Look over here, look over here. Focus on those dark, dangerous 'others' around the globe—don't think about the dark, dangerous downfalls happening right here in your own country" (e.g., the economic crisis plaguing the United States at the end of the first decade of the twenty-first century).

But regardless of the selfish motives that sparked the rhetoric for this move to national unity, waves of patriotism did flow across the country after 9/11 and flood the cultural narratives of the time. Spigel notes: "Given the political divisions that have resurfaced since 2001, it seems likely that the grand narratives of national unity that sprang up after 9/11 were for many people more performative than sincere. In other words, it is likely that many viewers really did know that all the newfound patriotism was really just a public performance staged by cameras."[19]

But as she notes, what is problematic is the fact that after 9/11 "many people found it important to 'perform' the role of citizen, which included the performance of belief in national myths of unity. And if you didn't perform this role, then somehow you were a bad American."[20]

With all this going on in supposedly nonfictional television programming, it is not surprising that these same thematic messages and cultural concerns seeped into fictional programming as well. In television shows airing in the years following the attacks, there was a sudden preoccupation with this notion of unity both at the national level and on a larger scale (themes of interconnectedness, fate, and destiny). There was also a common thematic obsession with the necessity of being "saved." The next section of this chapter turns completely to the analysis of fictional narratives on television, focusing on an overview of the programming popular in the years immediately following the September 11 attacks, the specific television season of 2006–7, which marked its five-year anniversary—concentrating most of my analysis on one specific breakout show that debuted this year, NBC's *Heroes*—and the continuation of these televisual trends at present (proving that both the narratives and viewers remain haunted by the national crisis even decades later).

Some would claim that "Americans have yearned to see current geopolitical realities portrayed in popular culture ever since the terrorist attacks of Sept. 11, 2001."[21] I would argue that Americans want to see a *version* of those realities on television. Of course, ideally this version would be one that can be brought to a neat and tidy, Hollywood-style denouement by the end of the season or series. The show that best showcases this desire is Fox's *24,* which debuted on the heels of 9/11 on November 6, 2001. Broe critiques Rupert Murdoch's news corporation, the parent entity of the Fox network, arguing that it is no surprise that *24* found a comfortable (and long) run time with this conglomerate. In fact, the show "was seen as a prestige item in the Murdoch canon."[22] Broe argues: "In *24,* the sensationalism that marks Murdoch entertainment is employed in the service of promoting and rationalizing the endless war. The emphasis on the clock, on racing against time during both the hour of the show and the show's six-month running time, keeps the audience afraid of terrorists, nuclear bombs, and viruses. Meanwhile the sympathetic vigilante ignores the legal rights and speeds rapidly ahead in his battle to save humanity (with humanity reduced to the United States only), while, as Adorno would say, fear and anxiety replace contemplation."[23]

Most definitely, the show is a hyped-up version of current events, a compressed hyperbole of many of the viewer-citizen's concerns. For example, as Stillwell argues, "the political and moral dilemmas raised by the show could be ripped straight out of the headlines. References to the Patriot Act, NSA surveillance and Guantánamo Bay figure in the show's plot. Probably the most controversial topic is Jack Bauer's [Keifer Sutherland's] propensity for torturing prisoners, particularly in cases where a 'ticking time bomb' terrorist plot is involved."[24] Although *24* might be the most blatantly obvious show broadcasting this motif of needing to be saved (specifically from an "other" in the form of a terrorist), a motif that reinforces the beliefs of the nonfictional programming surrounding it, it is not alone in exploring this televisual theme.

ABC's *Alias* actually aired over a month before *24,* on September 30, 2001. Like *24,* this show focuses on a world (read: country) in crisis needing to be saved. While Jack Bauer is part of the government's CTU (Counter Terrorist Unit), *Alias*'s main character, Sydney Bristow (Jennifer Garner), is an undercover CIA agent working to bring down SD-6, a component of the Alliance of Twelve, an international crime group wreaking havoc on the world. Some of this fictional organization's goals consist of black market weapon trading and the assembling of ancient relics that might help form a weapon of mass destruction like none existing in current times. Whereas *24* finds Bauer fighting to prevent one major national crisis per season (each season takes place over one day), *Alias* exists as a more traditional drama with plot arcs that both exist within an episode and stretch through episodes and seasons. Therefore, Bristow often has to defuse more bombs (so to speak) in one season's time. (And she is more likely to be the one tortured rather than the one doing the torturing.) Shows such as these continued to be formed even years after 9/11. In March 2006 another network decided to form its own drama centered on a governmental protection group. CBS released *The Unit,* which focuses on a top-secret military unit modeled after the real-life Delta Force.

While these dramas were maintaining popularity, another format was having varied success: dramas that focused on saving the country from the top down. From 1999 to 2006 NBC's *The West Wing* found popularity as a television drama focused on the behind-the-scenes happenings of a fictional president, his family, and his staff as they navigated particular legislative or political issues. In the seasons following 9/11, not surprisingly, plots often turned to the specter of both foreign and domestic terrorism. In 2005 ABC attempted a short-lived series, *Commander in Chief,* focusing on the presidency and familial life of the first female president of the United States, President Mackenzie Allen (Geena Davis). This show, like the others, attended to the global tension and domestic insecurity present at the start of the twenty-first century.

Although the theme of needing to be saved has been prevalent throughout all time (and throughout all narrative forms), the abundance (and popularity) of this motif on television is significant in the wake of 9/11. What can one make of the viewers' attraction to watching fictional figures do this saving (whether in the field or from the Oval Office) time and time again? And what happens when this motif of needing to be saved shifts? By 2006 television was still obsessed with this motif but not necessarily in the same ways that it had been five years earlier. Shows such as *Alias* and *West Wing* reached their close, and other programming lined up to fill the void. Salvation was still a central theme, but one would have to look more closely to see the links to the tragedy of 9/11 lurking beneath this regurgitated theme. A snapshot of a year—the television season of 2006–2007—reveals quite a bit about American society's preoccupation with this notion of being saved.

Five Years Later: An Analysis of 2006-2007 Television Programming

In the fall of 2006, one of ABC's hit dramas, *Grey's Anatomy,* launched its season with television promos and a special viewer initiation (or refresher) episode centered on The Fray's hit song, "How to Save a Life." That same fall NBC released its soon-to-be hit series, *Heroes,* with its tagline: "Save the Cheerleader, Save the World." As mentioned, although the fictional landscape of American television had been dominated by the theme of needing to be saved for much of the new twenty-first century (especially after 9/11), never before had this motif been so clearly vocalized and marketed. Doled out alongside this theme was the aforementioned focus on unity and interconnectedness. Quite often in the televisual texts of this time these two themes worked together; in fictional spaces, a world connected or a group united was one that would survive or be saved.

During this television season, twenty-nine shows ran on the four major networks, ABC, CBS, NBC, and Fox, that could fit into these categories. While some fit loosely into this grouping, like the crime dramas (CBS's *CSI: Crime Scene Investigation, CSI: Miami, CSI: NY, NCIS, Criminal Minds,* NBC's *Crossing Jordan,* Fox's *Bones, Cops,* and *America's Most Wanted: America Strikes Back*), law dramas (CBS's *Shark,* NBC's *Law & Order, Law & Order: Criminal Intent, Law & Order: Special Victims Unit,* ABC's *Boston Legal,* Fox's *Justice*), and the medical dramas (NBC's *ER,* ABC's *Grey's Anatomy,* Fox's *House*), others more obviously earn this classification because of their central preoccupation with their characters' needing to be saved from personal predicaments or national crises. This category would include shows previously discussed, such as *24* and *The Unit,* as well as similar shows: CBS's *Jericho* (concerned with the aftermath of nuclear attacks on twenty-three U.S. cities), ABC's *Traveler* (focused on the road trip of three college graduates that results in a terrorist attack on a museum), and Fox's *Standoff* (about an FBI Crisis Negotiation Unit). This group also includes shows that discuss needing to be saved in different ways: ABC's *Lost* and NBC's *Heroes* (both of which will be analyzed in greater depth), as well as Fox's *Prison Break* (which focuses on a governmental conspiracy that sends a man to death row for a crime he did not commit) and ABC's *Day Break* (a *Groundhog Day*–type series replaying one day in the life of a detective accused of murdering an assistant district attorney). And still other programs fall into this group owing to their focus on interconnectivity: ABC's *The Nine* (which follows the lives of nine strangers who survive a hostage crisis) and *Six Degrees* (as evidenced in the title, this show plays on the theme that everyone is connected to one another in some way).

Although many of these shows did not enjoy a long run time, the fact that these themes were so prevalent is quite telling. Even more intriguing is the central affect that all these shows share: fear. Logically, it makes sense that each of these shows would foreground this human emotion. In situations where individuals need rescuing or redemption, fear is often the affect that drives them. And just as nonfiction television programming operates, these narratives exist to deliver this fear so that they can alleviate it. At first thought, it might seem that consuming this constant array of fear-evoking, life-threatening situations might make viewers more fearful in their everyday lives. However, "the quotidian fare of violence, disaster, and death that TV audiences consume [actually] nourishes fantasies of invulnerability" and, hence, diminishes fear.[25] As I discussed in the introduction, the habitual consumption of these fictional series, like the regular consumption of serial news broadcasts, operates like Tomkins's weak negative affect theory: repressing societal fears through narratives of salvation.

Not surprisingly, however, many of these narratives grounded their installations of fear in a problematic us-versus-them binary. Although this opposition has long been used to stimulate dramatic conflict, its possible tie to the media rhetoric of 9/11 is hard to overlook. In discussing this common binary, Michael Bader explains that the "feelings of insecurity and disconnectedness that plague us in our personal and social lives" are often "blamed on the actions of some 'other' who is then demeaned and attacked."[26] As in the case of the political powers that be after 9/11, "this process of projection is deliberately used by conservatives to solidify their base. By creating an imaginary 'us' and 'them,' they can then promise satisfaction of deep and legitimate longings for a community safe from both real and illusory threats posed from the outside."[27] This us-versus-them binary also exists to nurture a superiority complex common to citizens of the United States.

In analyzing the responses of her students in the wake of the national disaster, Spence noted: "The idea that the greatest power in the world might not also be the greatest country seemed to be too much for the students to handle. As a matter of fact, for some, the only way of explaining the 'why' of the attacks was that 'they' hated 'us' because of our freedoms and affluence, because 'we' are so great. They wanted so much to believe in our goodness and innocence that they ignored everything they had 'learned' about the banality of evil."[28]

This sort of mind-set, beyond solidifying this dangerous (and hierarchical) binary, also resulted in the "sentimentalizing of 9/11"—again showcasing how emotion is deeply intertwined in the (mediated) events of September 11.[29] To prove that this emotional fixation was not short-lived and played out in narratives long after the attacks, I now turn to one specific hit debut show of 2006: NBC's *Heroes.* Its narrative uses fear amplification, the us-versus-them binary, and motifs of unity, fate, and interconnectedness to subtly tease out this theme of a nation needing to be saved.

NBC's *Heroes* (2006–2010): Season 1

The main premise of *Heroes* involves a plot in which seemingly ordinary individuals realize they have extraordinary powers. Throughout the first season of this series, these main characters begin a physical odyssey that forces their paths to cross with those of the other "heroes" and a spiritual odyssey that forces them to come to terms with the responsibility that comes along with their special talents or abilities. The inner conflict these characters face symbolizes larger societal conflicts: when does one step up, when does one speak up, when does one strike back, when does one actively play the role of the hero, and when does one passively lie back and wait to be saved? In their analysis of the show, Lynnette Porter, David Lavery, and Hillary Robson pick up on this cultural conflict: "If heroes can be (or are, according to the series) genetically enhanced, then the rest of us regular mortals are off the hook as far as trying to save humanity collectively or one person at a time. Not everyone can be a hero. Heroism becomes a genetic imperative of the few, who can then wield their power as they see fit."[30] But although the show's foundation does in part enable a mind-set of passing the proverbial buck, its use of everyday individuals aligning themselves for a common altruistic goal does tap into the shared longing to be part of the larger scheme of things, to make a difference, to be one of the good guys. *Heroes* encourages "viewers to think about what makes a modern hero and how each person might be called upon to do something extraordinary. Because *Heroes* deals with life-or-death events and presents so many characters facing crisis points in their lives it quite naturally provides a more philosophical framework for thinking—at least sometimes—about life's larger themes."[31] And some of these larger themes become more important to viewers in the wake of a national tragedy.

This being so, one of the major themes of the show comprises the previous themes of interconnectedness, fate, and destiny. In fact, in the final episode of season 1, "How to Stop an Exploding Man," Mohinder Suresh's (Sendhil Ramamurthy's) voiceover states this directly: "So much struggle for meaning and purpose, and in the end, we find it only in each other, our shared experience of the fantastic and the mundane."[32] Of course, it is the shared experience of the fantastic that dominates the show. In this final episode, all the characters' paths, their destinies, have crossed so that they are all in one shared point in time where they can prevent a national tragedy, one foreshadowed throughout the season's run, from occurring.

Returning to the previous discussion of censorship after 9/11: this apocalyptic story line changed quite a bit between its original creation and its eventual airing. Tim Kring, the creator of *Heroes,* recounts the revamping of the explosion story line:

> The bomb that ultimately goes off or is prevented from going off in New York was actually attached to a terrorist story and at the heart of that terrorist story was a very sympathetic character, a Middle Eastern engineer. A young, very brilliant engineer who had become disillusioned and disenfranchised and finds himself involved with a terrorist cell and is basically the architect of the bomb. That character could actually generate and emit a tremendous amount of radioactivity through his hands. That character became Ted on our show once we moved away from the terrorist story. The terrorist story was actually shot and beautifully finished, but it never saw the light of day. It didn't make it past the screening at the network.[33]

Changed or not, a terrorism-like disaster did end up bringing all the characters together at the close of season 1. When we analyze the tragedy that motivates them to join forces, the allusions to 9/11 should not be overlooked.

The first mention of this pending disaster within the show, and hence the first allusion to 9/11, comes in the form of Isaac's painting on the floor of his art studio—a vision of a New York cityscape in flames.[34] This disaster finally becomes "reality" toward the end of the season when, "in 'Five Years Gone,' *Heroes* presents an alternative future vision not only of the characters' world but also of the series itself. In terms of the season's story line, the episode reveals a dystopia that is yet to come."[35] The echoes of 9/11 are not all that subtle, as Porter, Lavery, and Robson note: "Rather than opaquely addressed, references to terrorism are hammered home. After the introduction of the Linderman Act, Homeland Security is called upon to clamp down on attackers 'acting against America's interests.'"[36] In this episode, as the president speaks to a sober crowd in the ruins of the city, beneath a banner reading "America Remembers," the scene is reminiscent of memorials stationed at Ground Zero years after September 11.

This episode highlights our fascination with the theme of the "do-over."[37] Viewers are shown this post-explosion scene in order to hope (along with the main characters) that it can still be prevented. Television scholars suggest that "a deeper reason" behind our love of this theme

> might be that since 9/11, we are perhaps collectively foreseeing a terrible future and shuddering at the view. Now the kaleidoscope turns into a mirror, and in "Five Years Gone" we are suddenly looking at a distorted image of ourselves, at what we could become in the aftermath of 9/11. Viewers experience a shock of recognition when President Nathan Petrelli (actually Sylar) appears in front of a devastated New York landscape to speak inspirational platitudes designed to unite Americans and prevent another disaster. The scene is a slightly twisted reflection of ceremonies upon the fifth anniversary of September 11, 2001.[38]

As Porter, Lavery, and Robson note, the timing of this episode is important. The disaster viewers are shown is *five years* in the future. During this episode, if the characters could go back in time *just five years* (and some do have this power) and alter events, an explosion would not hit New York and forever change the world. When viewers are watching this episode full of longing to rewrite the past, it is not unimportantly five years after the attacks of September 11, 2001.

These visual images of the fictionalized ground zero are quite stirring and interesting from an ideological standpoint. Redfield analyzes the term *Ground Zero,* which "emerged quasi-spontaneously as a proper name in American mass media immediately after the attacks. As a proper name, uncontextualized and capitalized, it refers to the site formerly occupied by the World Trade Center towers."[39] He explains that "as an idiom in more general use, it refers to the impact point of a bomb or the exact locus of an explosion. The term was military jargon when it was used at the Trinity site during the development and testing of the atom bomb; after the bombing of Hiroshima and Nagasaki, it entered the American sociolect and is now commonly used to describe centers of devastation, natural or man-made."[40] The term "both calls up and wards off ghosts of Hiroshima, remembering that other scene of destruction while also distancing or demoting it by rendering it an *other* ground zero."[41] Redfield claims "just as 'Ground Zero' appropriates and effaces the past, it appropriates and effaces the future. Invoking the nuclear threat, it imagines the future *as* past, and as imaginable. The hammer-blow has fallen: Ground Zero itself has appeared in the world—and yet we have survived. Thus 'the worst,' in Derrida's phrasing (or at least a version of the worst), is at once conjured up and conjured away."[42]

Therefore, I would argue that remediated fictionalized images of ground zero, like that seen in *Heroes,* reassure viewers that they can survive the worst—that humans can and will save themselves.

Although that analysis may suggest the scene is comforting, in truth the viewer's first exposure to it is probably somewhat disturbing. It is not necessarily the image of this fictionalized ground zero that is so chilling, however, but, rather, the rationalization given within the narrative for allowing it to come to be. It is a justification grounded in the affect of fear. In ".07%," Daniel Linderman, one of the key "villains," offers this justification to an up-and-coming politician, Nathan Petrelli, for allowing the explosion to occur: "I said people needed hope but they trust fear. This tragedy will be a catalyst for good, for change. Out of the ashes, humans will find a common goal. A united sense of hope couched in a united sense of fear. And it is your destiny, Nathan, to be the leader who uses this event to rally a city, a nation, a world."[43] When Nathan objects to the plan, stating that half of New York will be lost, Linderman states that it will amount to *only* a .07% decrease in the total world population—an acceptable loss.[44] The importance here is again the amplification, the manipulation, of fear.

This idea of capitalizing on fear surfaces one episode later, when Claire speaks to Sylar, the principal bad guy of season 1, as he disguised himself as Nathan: "You made everyone afraid of us."[45] He responds, "I made everyone aware of us, fear is just a natural response."[46] Again, fear is stressed but this time the focus is the fear that arises out of a societal structure founded on the us-versus-them binary, as they are now living in a world where "normal" humans are terrified of the "heroes" because of their special powers.

The Continuation of a Televisual Trend

Although *Heroes* reveals the cultural anxieties prevalent during its time of production, the sort of narrative "working through" evident across programs in the 2006–7 television season continues at present. Although this list is not exhaustive, consider these few examples. During the 2008–9 television season, Fox launched another narrative, *Fringe* (2008–13), which explores the concerns of a nation forever battling an invisible enemy called "terror." Created by J. J. Abrams, Alex Kurtzman, and Roberto Orc, this science fiction program focuses its plot on the FBI "Fringe Division," agents operating under the supervision of Homeland Security. At the heart of this show lies an eclectic team headed by Olivia Dunham (Anna Torv), an FBI agent with enhanced supernatural skills left over from being part of a childhood experiment; Dr. Walter Bishop (John Noble), a mad-scientist figure and former government researcher who understands the capabilities existing on the periphery of science; and his son, Peter Bishop (Joshua Jackson), an eventual love interest of Olivia and investigative sidekick. Originally the program was concerned with investigating "the pattern"—a series of unexplainable and often catastrophic events caused by fringe-science attacks. The perils from which the characters save society hint at mass concerns about the possible use of biological warfare and new technology. Like *Heroes,* this program ended its first season with an obvious moment of wish fulfillment when it presented viewers with a parallel universe in which the Twin Towers had not been destroyed on 9/11.[47] This story line is continued in its later seasons.

Although not as popular, as indicated by their early cancellations, similar programs have been featured in each subsequent year. In 2009 ABC premiered its new drama *FlashForward* (2009–10), a program hinted to be the replacement for the soon-to-depart *Lost.* Brannan Braga and David Goya adapted Robert J. Sawyer's 1999 science fiction novel to create this program about a mysterious event that causes a blackout whereby the entire human population loses consciousness for two minutes and seventeen seconds. During this brief period, all unconscious persons have visions of their lives six months later. A team of Los Angeles FBI agents assemble the Mosaic, a database system that compiles the visions of all who have volunteered what they saw through a website. These tentative future visions lay the foundation for their investigation as they attempt to discover not only how this event was possible but also how it can be prevented in the future. This program, airing for only one season, both began and finished its run with a catastrophic terrorist attack that was loosely reminiscent of 9/11. The following year NBC tried its own hand at a new post-9/11 drama, promising (even more directly than ABC did with *FlashForward*) that this would be the show to fill the void left by the popular culture juggernaut *Lost. The Event* (2010–11) opens with a terrorist attack in which not only is the U.S. government the target (specifically the president), but the weapon of choice is an airplane. Created by Nick Wauters, the drama is decidedly science fiction, focusing on a group of extraterrestrials who have been trapped on Earth (some detained by the American government) for sixty-six years. As the one-season program progressed, this group begins mounting escalating attacks (first on the United States alone and then on a wider scale) in an attempt to deplete the human population so that its members can occupy Earth. As is true of the majority of the post-9/11-themed shows, it is up to a small group of people (mostly government officials) to attempt to save the day . . . the nation . . . the world.

The televisual landscape from 2010 to 2019 further revealed lingering post-9/11 trends. The salvation motif remained in a variety of post-apocalyptic programs, such as NBC's *Revolution* (2012–14) and AMC's *The Walking Dead* (2010–present). And a proliferation of supernatural/fantasy programs—such as CW's *The Vampire Diaries* (2009–17), ABC's *Once upon a Time* (2011–18), NBC's *Grimm* (2011–17), Fox's *Sleepy Hollow* (2013–17), and ABC's *Agents of S.H.I.E.L.D.* (2013–present)—often found the "good-versus-evil" theme common to these shows reading as loose 9/11 allegories. The prevalence of government-focused programs continued, and with subsequent releases the political critique found within such shows escalated: Showtime's *Homeland* (2011–20), CBS's *Person of Interest* (2011–16), ABC's *Scandal* (2012–18), Netflix's *House of Cards* (2013–18), NBC's *The Blacklist* (2013–present), FX's *The Americans* (2013–18), CBS's *Madam Secretary* (2014–19), NBC's *State of Affairs* (2014–15), NBC's *Blindspot* (2015–present), ABC's *Quantico* (2015–18), ABC's *Designated Survivor* (2016–18), and CBS's *SEAL Team* (2017–present). Redemption was a central theme of one of the few programs to tackle 9/11 directly. A major story line of NBC's *The Village* (2019) featured Nick Porter, a former army ranger who returns from Afghanistan in 2019 after losing his right leg during an attack that killed the rest of his unit. The character suffers from post-traumatic stress disorder, which viewers assume to be from his experiences in the war. As the season progresses, however, viewers learn that Nick enlisted because he was an eighteen-year-old New York firefighter during the September 11 attacks. He slowly deals with repressed memories of losing colleagues during both the terrorist attack and the ensuing war.

To more systematically analyze the prevalence of specific post-9/11 motifs, I also investigated fifteen years of television programming, from 2000 to 2014, coding shows for thematic content that aligned with various post-9/11 themes, as well as for new, emerging genre trends, such as the increase in post-apocalyptic or dystopian programming. Across genres, 262 debut programs were tagged as being associated with post-9/11 themes during this period. Whereas in 2001 a total of only twenty shows (ten of them new) had such focus, in subsequent years these numbers increased significantly: most years featured forty to sixty shows (ten to twenty of them new each year) preoccupied with these themes. In the thirteen years after the attacks, yearly averages for programs containing particular motifs were as follows: twenty-six shows per season included story lines related to justice, ten to terrorism, eighteen to government, seventeen to salvation, twenty to vengeance, ten to conspiracy, and sixteen to fear. Analyzing the prevalence of certain themes throughout the extended decade also showed a spike across the board in debuting shows with post-9/11 themes around the five-year anniversary of the attacks, which aligned with my previous analysis of the 2006–7 television season.

Slowly Shifting Representations of Terrorism

While the prevalence of these themes in television may allow viewers to *work through* some of the cultural anxieties lingering from the September 11 attacks, this steady stream of fear-based programming actually helps *create* and *sustain* those very same anxieties—especially those anxieties concerning another potential terrorist attack on home soil. Ultimately, this barrage of programming both reflects and helps cultivate a national climate of fear. Interestingly, these fear-based narratives do not always align with the most imminent global threats. For example, there are relatively few representations of, or references to, ISIS in twenty-first-century television shows. This review of television programming suggests that throughout the last decade TV shows have often ignored the shifting geopolitical landscape (or have been slow to depict it). For example, such narratives often fail to address the ways in which the threat posed by ISIS today differs from those presented by al-Qaeda in the years immediately following 9/11. The medium's continued role in post-9/11 affect modulation may explain this phenomenon.

Even a casual television viewer may notice that some things have shifted in TV programs that take on terrorism story lines specifically. There has been an effort to stray away from the stereotype of Arabic or Muslim terrorists by developing plots that offer up another global threat (e.g., *Homeland, Madam Secretary,* and *Designated Survivor* all included story lines focused on Russian cyberattacks, which are a present threat to U.S. national security). When the typical Arab- or Muslim-as-terrorist plot is in place, it is usually accompanied by Arab or Muslim characters intended to counter such stereotypes. Unfortunately, as scholars are quick to point out, this move often simply results in crafting a new type of clichéd character. Evelyn Alsultany, former director of Arab and Muslim American Studies at the University of Michigan, has documented the new TV trend wherein "if there is a terrorist theme with a Muslim or Arab as a terrorist, the writers and producers will typically throw in another Arab or Muslim character to try and defuse the stereotype."[48] These characters tend to be depicted as extremely patriotic American citizens or "an innocent Arab-American who's been victimized by post-9/11 hate."[49]

The most notable shift in representations of fictional terrorism on television has been the increasing instance of plots that feature terrorist actions and threats that stem from within the United States. Recent seasons of *Designated Survivor* and *Quantico,* for example, have had story lines in which American citizens—often holding positions within government—are responsible for (or complicit in) large-scale terrorist attacks that have occurred on U.S. soil. This turn toward the terrorist-within story line aligns to some extent with the political critique found in many contemporary shows. This may reveal the continued distrust of government officials that was amplified after 9/11.

As I noted above, the one change that did not occur on a large scale throughout the last two decades, as one might have expected, is reconfigured terrorist story lines that refer to or allegorize the contemporary threat of ISIS rather than al-Qaeda. Though ISIS-related plots do occur in a few shows, their overall absence (despite the fact that terrorism story lines remain prevalent) seems telling. Like many programs, *Madam Secretary,* a TV show depicting the behind-the-scenes work of Secretary of State (and later President) Elizabeth McCord (Téa Leoni), focuses most of its terrorist story lines on a fictional group (in this case, Hizb al-Shahid). The common practice of creating a fictional terrorist organization may be a tactic to protect a program's shelf life, allowing it to have a universal appeal even years after its release. When fictional terrorists are embedded in story lines, as opposed to fictionalizations of real terrorist groups, they can serve as stand-ins for any terrorist group that may be at large when a viewer is watching the episode. It also serves to distance fictional narratives ever so slightly from the reality viewers may be trying to escape. Although most of its terrorism-themed episodes focus on its fictional terrorist group, *Madam Secretary* has also included multiple references to ISIS, including a story line that suggests a link between Hizb al-Shahid and ISIS. It has also aired one particular episode specifically centered on ISIS. Despite its overt focus on this real-life terrorist group, this episode showcases how contemporary television seems reluctant to move away from the America-in-peril motif found in post-9/11 narratives.

Season 2, episode 6, "Catch and Release," opens with chilling footage that remediates the ISIS-caused deaths of the American civilian journalists James Foley and Steven Joel, whose videotaped beheadings were broadcast globally in August and September 2014.[50] The first moments of this episode include a video of an American aid worker accused of being a spy kneeling beside an ISIS leader. The American captive is forced to read a script about how the United States' interference in Syria is responsible for his pending death by beheading. The remainder of the episode focuses on the government's investigation and response to this murder. Governmental officials determine that the terrorist leader shown in the video is American-born (and, importantly, not of Arabic decent); this man also happens to be the son of a State Department worker. The fact that *Madam Secretary*'s most comprehensive story line tackling ISIS results in a plot focused on an estranged American family is telling, as it again places the United States at the center of a narrative that had the potential to delve into wider-reaching geopolitical concerns. Assuming current televisual texts are still being used to modulate lingering post-9/11 fears, this episode serves as an example of the how such programming seems to require a continued depiction of the United States as the center of attention (and likely target) of the war on terror.

The lack of realistic representations of ISIS on television, however, might simply align with the United States' slow comprehension of this threat or the ways in which it differs from its predecessor (or both). Writing for the *Atlantic*, Graeme Wood explains how many Americans—and even, at least initially, government officials—misunderstand the nature of ISIS because they "tend to see jihadism as monolithic" and, hence, "apply the logic of al-Qaeda to an organization that has decisively eclipsed it."[51] Wood details the ideological differences between ISIS and al-Qaeda and the ways in which they affect the focus of their terrorist actions: "The humanitarian cost of the Islamic State's existence is high. But its threat to the United States is smaller than its all too frequent conflation with al-Qaeda would suggest. Al-Qaeda's core is rare among jihadist groups for its focus on the 'far enemy' (the West); most jihadist groups' main concerns lie closer to home. That's especially true of the Islamic State, precisely because of its ideology. It sees enemies everywhere around it, and while its leadership wishes ill on the United States, the application of Sharia in the caliphate and the expansion to contiguous lands are paramount."[52]

So, regardless of whether television shows rely on the United States–in–peril motif as part of the continued post-9/11 trends, or whether these hyperbolic plots simply reflect Americentrism, which is common in U.S. popular culture, it is clear that integrating realistic story lines related to ISIS would result in an incongruity with the typical television mythology concerning terrorism. More realistic fictional portrayals of ISIS could help Americans better understand the threat this group poses and, as a result, move past some unnecessary lingering post-9/11 fears about the likelihood of another 9/11-like terrorist attack on U.S. soil. To its credit, *Madam Secretary*'s story line discussing ISIS in relation to its fictional terrorist organization may provide this sort of cultural education. In the scene that introduces this story line, the secretary of state's husband, a religious scholar, Henry McCord (Tim Daly), questions the possibility of Hizb al-Shahid and ISIS working together because of their ideological differences. Should the television program delve into this in greater detail, it might help counter the misconception that there is some commonality among all jihadist terrorist groups.

The television program that has provided the most realistic ISIS-related story lines to date is Showtime's *Homeland*. In fact, sadly, its fifth season premediated the terrorist attacks in Europe that soon followed. (The season was almost completely filmed before the coordinated terrorist attacks that occurred in Paris on November 13, 2015, killing over one hundred people.) Fans may have anticipated a departure from story lines focusing on Muslim terrorists during a season in which the main characters relocated from the Middle East to Europe. And while the season does delve into other threats (with attention paid to Russian cyber terrorism, for example), the focus on Muslim terrorism continues to be a central aspect of the show.[53] The show can be praised for pointing out real problems in the U.S. approach to combating ISIS, highlighting one speech in particular, which appeared in the season 5 opener, "Separation Anxiety."[54] During a CIA debriefing, a main character, Peter Quinn (Rupert Friend), an agent who spent two years in Syria, is asked whether the United States' strategy is working, to which he replies:

> What strategy? Tell me what the strategy is. I'll tell you if it's working.
> [Silence]

> See, that right there is the problem. Because they, they have a strategy. They're gathering right now in Raqqa by the tens of thousands. Hidden in the civilian population. Cleaning their weapons. And they know exactly why they're there. Why is that? They call it the end times. What do you think the beheadings are about? The crucifixions in Deir Hafer? The revival of slavery? You think they make this shit up? It's all in the book. Their fucking book. The only book they ever read. They read it all the time. They never stop. They're there for one reason and one reason only. To die for the caliphate and usher in a world without infidels. That's their strategy. And it's been that way since the seventh century. So, do you really think that a few special forces teams are gonna put a dent in that?[55]

When asked for suggestions for how to proceed, Quinn recommends "200,000 troops on the ground indefinitely to provide security and support for an equal number of doctors and elementary school teachers."[56] He is, of course, told this is impossible. This fictional CIA agent's assessment of his government's inability to effectively combat ISIS realistically delves into the difficult predicament the United States finds itself in concerning the real-world fight against them.

With thoughtfully crafted story lines, fictional television has the potential to critique U.S. military practices and to help inform citizens about geopolitical issues. As we saw in the discussion of post-9/11 fictional programming on the air, however, it also had the potential to maintain cultural anxieties that have dominated the United States for two decades. Furthermore, when story lines fail to align realistically with real-world conditions, television may end up manufacturing unfounded fears. The continued attention to 9/11 (or at the very least post-9/11 televisual themes evident in this study) neglects contemporary threats and perpetuates a fear cycle from which viewers have very little chance of breaking free.

2

Escaping Reality by Watching Reality TV?

Voyeurism, Schadenfreude, and Other Coping Mechanisms for Avoiding or Engaging in Societal Reflection

While the contemporary televisual fiction landscape contains programming that forces viewers to confront lingering cultural fears, at first glance the bevy of reality programs on the air suggests a desire to avoid addressing those very fears. As chapter 1 discussed, in the immediate aftermath of 9/11 media critics predicted a turn toward serious programming and increased dedication to global news coverage. Yet, instead, entertainment and social media trends indicate that Americans retreated into themselves on a microscopic level. This turn toward the self is evident in the explosion of reality television programs that focus on the minutia of everyday life, on the individual rather than the community, and—in most cases—on American lives and locales.

The media critic Susan Douglas analyzed the post-9/11 news programming and determined that, contrary to hopeful expectations for more coverage of international news, "attention to the rest of the world was fleeting," and by 2004 the "percentage of stories about foreign affairs on the commercial nightly news broadcasts was lower than it had been in 1997."[1] The era of around-the-clock coverage and international media collaboration allowed for a greater focus on global issues, but, apparently, that was not what Americans wanted or, at least, it was not what they were given. Douglas reflects on Marshall McLuhan's infamous (and idealistic) notion that advanced technology could unite us all within one global village; she argued that in the United States "new communication technologies have not created a global village but have, ironically, led to a fusion of ethnocentrism and narcissism, best cast as a 'turn within.'"[2] Thus, it is not surprising that escapist television genres fit right into this cultural turn.

Analyzing the popularity of reality television in the early years of the twenty-first century, Douglas argues: "If television news, in particular, bears especial responsibility for squandering its ability to enhance a global awareness despite its ever-augmented capabilities to do so, reality TV, colonizing television as it did between 2001 and 2005, insisted that the most productive way to use communications technologies was to focus them on individual Americans in confined and controlled spaces hermetically sealed from foreign peoples and culture."[3]

Those most critical of this television genre—or at least the timing of its popularity—argue that it reveals a problematic moment of cultural narcissism in the Unitized States. William Hudson opines: "While more than five thousand American soldiers lost their lives fighting in Iraq and Afghanistan and thousands of others suffered severe wounds, most Americans felt little direct involvement in their nation's endeavors and were only mildly inconvenienced —mainly by waiting in long lines for airport security checks—by the challenges the country faced. The post-9/11 period featured instead the rise of 'reality TV' programs pitting individuals against one another on desert islands or in Donald Trump's boardroom to see who would emerge as 'No. 1.' In the end, radical individualism triumphed over 'United We Stand.'"[4] Studying this massively expanding genre continues to be important today since, according to Nielsen analytics, reality television has significantly changed the makeup of the prime-time viewing block.[5] By 2010 "15 of the top 20 highest-rated programs among" young adults were reality television programs.[6]

The affective affordances of this genre can partially explain its popularity.[7] In the early years of the twenty-first century, these shows—drastically divorced from current geopolitical realities—arguably provided emotional comfort and an escape from cultural anxieties that stemmed from the September 11 terrorist attacks. When the content of this supposed lowbrow, escapist fare is analyzed in greater depth, however, it becomes clear that these television shows are not as isolated from contemporary anxieties as they might at first glance appear. Although their Americentric focus primes them to avoid commentary on larger geopolitical issues, they do grapple with a variety of societal concerns on a smaller, often more domestic level. This chapter lays out three emotional theories—schadenfreude, vicarious affect, and voyeurism—that explain the draw of reality television; it looks at examples of programming that fit each and explores how such shows reveal the cultural anxieties with which producers and viewers engage and disengage.

The History and Popularity of Reality TV

To be clear, though its massive popularity and presence may be new, the reality television program has been part of the televisual makeup for over four decades. The first reality program debuted in 1973 with PBS's *An American Family,* a show dealing with the Loud family in all its public so-called dysfunction and disintegration.[8] But, as Mark Andrejevic chronicles, the reality television trend did not become "a full-fledged media phenomenon" until the late 1980s and early 1990s.[9] Around that time, shows such as *America's Funniest Home Videos* and *Cops* rose to popularity, and, more important, MTV took the stage as the procreator of the type of reality TV that would follow with their hit programs, *The Real World* and *Road Rules.*[10] Now, in the new millennium, reality shows have become one of the most popular genres of TV entertainment, offering programs on many often incredible subjects: *Extreme Makeover, Celebrity Fit Club, The Ugly Duckling* (plastic surgery, diet, and makeover shows about how all can be beautiful with just a little help), *The Amazing Race, Survivor, Big Brother* (competitive game shows often centered on prize money), *Fear Factor, Jackass* (the gross-out shows that capture people doing unimaginable feats), *The Osbournes, The Surreal Life, The Simple Life* (offering a glimpse into the private lives of stars, many of whom have already been forgotten), *American Idol, Dancing with the Stars, The Voice* (interactive talent competitions where stars are born or wannabes flop), *Temptation Island, The Bachelor/Bachelorette,* and *Date My Mom* (romance, dating, relationship counseling shows selling the age-old idea that everyone has a soul mate and sometimes he or she can be found on national television). With each passing year, more reality television programs aired and more subgenres formed, which led critics to attempt to determine what sparked and sustained this televisual trend. (An analysis of television programming from 2000 to 2010 shows an increase of almost 300 reality television shows, from fewer than 25 on the air in 2000 to just under 350 by 2010.)

Various industry factors can explain the rise of reality television. For example, the financial struggles that producers face in the post-network era easily explain this genre's dominance. At a time when less money is coming in from advertising sponsors, reality TV shows are beneficial additions to network lineups because they are less expensive to produce.[11] Such shows proliferated as helpful network lifelines during the 2007 Writers Guild strike: the production of reality shows continued even when "media production work in more traditional sectors came to an abrupt halt."[12]

While this approach to programming was obviously logical from an industry standpoint, many have questioned why viewers would fall in line and tune in to such programs. Followers of such shows have often been ridiculed for watching something labeled "reality" when much of it seems manufactured and anything but real.[13] As Andrejevic points out, however, viewers have "proved themselves savvy enough to understand that the contrived fare they were watching functioned more as escapist entertainment than immersion in brute reality. Fans were no more duped by the promise of access to an unmediated spectacle than the self-consciously savvy pundits."[14] In fact, the genre itself quickly capitalized on the real that is not-so-real by creating reality shows that were "self-conscious parodies of their original premise of access to the unscripted interactions of people who are not professional entertainers."[15] One example would be *Joe Millionaire*, an obvious spoof on dating shows like *The Bachelor*, in which a group of beautiful women flocked to Paris under false pretense only to fall in love with a man hugging the poverty line rather than a silver spoon.

The tension between the real and the performative elements of reality television programs is, arguably, part of its draw. The ways in which reality television contestants construct their onscreen identities mirror the "performance demands" that everyday individuals face in "a preponderance of social and psychic spaces" where they are asked to "play themselves" and watch others do the same.[16] The genre's popularity also probably reflects the increasing—although definitely not new—attention to celebrity culture. Reality television provides one of the entertainment industry's easiest means for everyday persons to earn their fifteen minutes of fame. Laura Grindstaff argues that reality TV provides "the opportunity for acquiring celebrity cafeteria-style: it enables ordinary people to walk in and serve themselves to celebrity status without the bother of extensive training, formal credentials, or even much in the way of talent, because performances are already strongly shaped by underlying cultural assumptions about particular character types and by carefully assembled frameworks of action."[17]

The genre has appeal for those not necessarily chasing the cult of fame as well. Quite simply, these shows—like any successful entertainment product—are emotionally provoking. Michael Hirschorn argues that reality television programs have "the visceral impact of documentary reportage without the self-importance and general lugubriousness. Where documentaries must construct their narratives from found matter, reality TV can place real people in artificial surroundings designed for *maximum emotional impact.*"[18] It is this aspect of the genre—the ways in which it strives for "maximum emotional impact"—that this chapter explores.[19] The popularity of this genre arguably can be tied to the ways in which reality television caters to our hidden human passion for schadenfreude (rejoicing in the humiliation and misery of others),[20] vicarious affect (living through the experience and emotion of others), and voyeurism (gaining pleasure from invading the private, emotional moments of others).

The Emotional Draw of Reality Television: Three Affect Theories

In order to map out the emotional appeal of the genre, reality television programs airing between 2000 and 2010 were coded according to the affect theories that were most likely to explain why viewers watched such programming. Figure 2.1 shows the shifts in the emotional draws for reality television programming as well as general programming trends. For example, the jump in overall reality television offerings following the 2007 Writers Guild strike is easily seen. Also, as reality television programs and subgenres began to proliferate around this time, the programs that began to air were more likely to tap into viewers' desire for vicarious or voyeuristic experiences rather than the initially popular schadenfreude-based shows that were appealing (perhaps owing to their novelty rather than anything else).

In examining the middle of the decade—the same 2006 television season explored in chapter 1—it also becomes clear that it is often impossible to determine simply one emotional theory that explains why viewers may tune in to a particular reality television program. During this year, 176 reality television programs aired, 67 of them for the first time. The three affect theories were split relatively uniformly across the board: 76 programs were coded for schadenfreude, 85 for voyeurism, and 98 for vicarious affect. Forty percent of the programs (70 shows) were coded as being aligned with two different affect theories and 6 shows were coded as aligning with all three. Of the 100 programs that were coded as aligning with only a single affect theory, schadenfreude came in as the lowest category (only 19 programs were tagged as being watched largely for this emotional draw), whereas the remaining two had virtually equal draws (41 programs were coded solely for the vicarious affect theory and 40 programs for voyeurism). But what does all this mean and why does it matter? To unpack this data further, we will look at examples from each category individually and discuss the ways in which these shows—and the emotional impetus for watching them—reflect societal concerns that are being worked through or avoided.

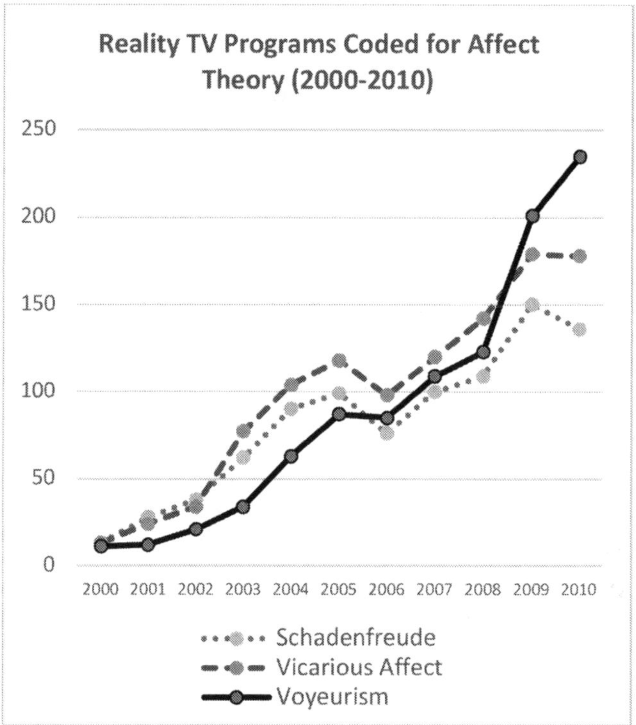

Figure 2.1. Selection of reality television shows coded for affect theory, 2000–2001. (Figure by the author.)

Schadenfreude: Disengagement and Antipathy as a Coping Mechanism?

When people think of reality television—at least its origins—the shows aligned with the schadenfreude theory are often among the first that spring to mind. This theory explains why millions of viewers have tuned into various gross-out shows like *Fear Factor* and taken pleasure in watching the catfights unfold on *The Bachelor*, or why some people tune into *American Idol* during the audition episodes, when thousands of wannabe vocalists often embarrass themselves, but then do not watch the formal competitive performance episodes that follow. Arguably, and perhaps counterintuitively, these shows spark positive affect (enjoyment, amusement) in viewers through their consumption of the negative affect (humiliation, heartbreak) of those on the screen. Viewers can chuckle at the mortified contestants and think, "At least that's not me." Atte Oksanen explains how this works, arguing that in reality television the narrative simply "creates a frame that enables the input of affective material."[21] She argues that "participants become vehicles for the expression of affects. Affects overrun confessions. The characters are at the mercy of the camera and confessions become shocking affective statements that enable the full portrayal of bodily expressions. Reality television tries to capture emotional expressions such as tears and weeping."[22] Producers bank on these scenes because they are—as Laura Grindstaff, borrowing terminology from pornography, puts it—the "money shot" of reality television.

The emotional exploitation of the contestants is not the sole amusement for viewers. The genre's predictable staples provide entertainment as well. (Chapter 9 provides an instance of what happens when programs deviate from this predictability.) For example, the ways in which contestants quickly morph—or are edited—into stock characters allow viewers to laugh at such obvious televised self-performances. Researchers have found that sincerity, or lack thereof, is one of the tropes that surface most frequently in conversations about reality television stars.[23] Viewers simply do not trust that the contestants are being sincere, and, therefore, the impulse to criticize or laugh at them seems justifiable.[24] Although it may seem a strange place to wrestle with questions concerning morality, scholars have argued that the genre can be considered a modern iteration of "the ancient 'morality plays,'" as it allows viewers to contemplate "the limits of permissible behavior."[25] Many reality television programs place contestants in stressful situations that trigger objectionable behavior.[26] Annette Hill argues that ethics is actually "at the heart of reality programming. Rights to privacy, rights to fair treatment, good and bad moral conduct, and taste and decency are just some of the ethical issues that arise when examining the reality genre."[27] That this genre rose to popularity during a time when viewers were exposed to ethical debates concerning the ways in which the United States chose to protect citizens (e.g., the Patriot Act) or battle the War on Terror (e.g., enhanced interrogation methods) is then not surprising. Concerns about ethical behavior on a large scale were traded in for small-scale ethical concerns where the stakes were much lower.

The genre can also be seen addressing more personal, domestic anxieties that surfaced in the twenty-first century—anxieties that have nothing to do with the terrorist attacks. Consider, for example, the reality television subgenres focusing on crises within individual homes, marriages, and families that became popular during this time. Two of the first shows of this kind were ABC's *Wife Swap* (2004–13) and Fox's *Trading Spouses* (2004–present). Both shows follow two families as each of the wives—who are usually polar opposites when it comes to personality and background and face quite different household challenges—is dropped into the home of the other. Viewers then watch "each woman as she performs her counterpart's routine, exposing the dirty laundry (literally) and zooming in on quirky behavior, small cruelties and moments of quiet despair."[28] The entertainment within these shows tends "to reduce the women and their families to types, pitting slobs against control freaks, spendthrifts against killjoys, and hardworking Cinderellas against spoiled heiresses" to create the desired viewer-enticing conflict.[29] They offer up the same formulaic crisis week after week, so what's the appeal?

Catherine Orenstein argues that these shows are popular because they engage with societal anxieties concerning the changing domestic landscape in the United States:

> According to the most recent U.S. census, just over half of American households consist of married couples, and less than a fourth of American households are made up of nuclear families (down from 39 percent in 1990). More than half of American marriages will end in divorce (52 percent), the number of single mothers has shot up, and the number of children born out of wedlock has reached 33 percent—up from just 4 percent in 1950. Women now marry on average five years later than they did in the mid-20th century (now it's at age 25) and, in part because of delayed marriage, over a quarter of households now consist of singles living alone. Finally, between 1990 and 2000, the number of unmarried couples—straight and same-sex—living together out of wedlock rose by 72 percent.[30]

Marriage today simply looks different and comes with different challenges, and these reality shows—in all their hyperbolic glory—capitalize on these challenges. Viewers at home can laugh at these exaggerated portrayals of household problems they may be struggling with, watching them neatly resolved by each episode's end. With their focus on unruly wives, these shows also reflect shifting expectations for males and females when it comes to marital and child-rearing responsibilities. Their hyperbolic marital conflicts and reinforcement of gender stereotypes both bring attention to these shifting (or not shifting enough) expectations for men and women. (Chapters 4 and 5 will discuss how societal anxieties about masculinity and femininity and changing family dynamics have influenced fictional programming as well.)

These two networks also offered two other programs that feature families in distress, but this time the distress is linked directly to parenting: Fox's *Nanny 911* (2004–present) and ABC's *Supernanny* (2005–12). Both programs, which star a child-care expert sent to fix all the problems the flailing parents cannot, have been heavily criticized. Experts have chimed in to point out that the advice given on the shows is often overly simplistic or questionable.[31] But more problematic is the fact that all the families, and their problems, are extreme examples of parenting struggles rather than realistic ones faced everyday by families in general.[32] By focusing on sensational topics and exploiting parental mistakes (often those made by mothers), these shows perpetuate negative stereotypes and highlight poor parenting practices rather than healthy ones.[33]

So what is the appeal of these reality television programs that showcase not-so-real parenting problems? As exaggerated as they may be, they do diverge from the age-old portrayal of perfect familial bliss that was common in television programming for decades. Arguably, viewers can take comfort in watching parents falter and fail (often in outrageous fashion) because this makes them feel better about their own parenting missteps. And while the direct advice stemming from the nannies' mouths might be overly didactic or unsound, the programs—taken as a whole—do offer subtle "lessons on the hazards of parenting in an age of instant gratification and endless digital diversion."[34]

These scenarios of viewers taking pleasure in the pain of husbands, wives, fathers, and mothers may suggest that it is not just the ethics explored in the reality television programs that we should be focusing on, but the ethics of watching such scenes in the first place. This has, in fact, been one of the major criticisms of the genre, the fact that "it highlights people's weaknesses and the bad side of people," allowing viewers "to see people at their worst."[35] The attention to "people who are thrown off the island, or the guy who doesn't get the date, or people who have to eat bugs, people making a fool of themselves"—the "losers" of any individual series or episode—have been viewed by many as problematic.[36] The good news is that researchers have found that, generally, viewers prefer to see contestants succeed rather than fail.[37] Perhaps, then, this explains the decrease of reality programs watched primarily for schadenfreude.

Vicarious Affect: Escaping into the Worlds and Feelings of Others

The finding that viewers tend to want a more positive outcome for the reality contestants they follow aligns with the vicarious affect theory. This theory suggests viewers identify with the participants and cheer them on as they tackle "uncommon (wilderness survival, international travel) and common (dating, home redecorating) tasks."[38] In the case of the former—watching common people tackle uncommon tasks—viewers arguably tune in to these programs to escape into a world that is unlike their own, to experience adventures and interactions that they are unlikely to have in their own lives.[39] To return to previous examples, this is the viewer who watches a season of a competitive reality program like *American Idol* through to its end (rather than just watching the audition sequences): following the performances, investing in the rising stars, living vicariously through their excitement and dreams of fortune and fame, rooting them on, and perhaps even picking up the phone or jumping online to vote for them. Likewise, this is the fan of a dating elimination show like *The Bachelor/Bachelorette* who watches not to see the catfights or dating faux pas, but to virtually tag along on dream dates and exotic vacations, to root for true love to succeed, to speculate on which contestants will go home, and to hope for certain ones to win.

But it is not all about escapism. Many of the uncommon tasks these common people are assigned unfold in extreme, even dangerous, conditions. Consider, for example, the show that many credit with launching the reality television craze, CBS's *Survivor* (2000–present). Constants are shipwrecked in exotic locations with a group of strangers who are all competing to be the last one standing at the end of the season. Before 9/11 this program would seem, like the above examples, to be simply escapist fare. But after 9/11 its popularity grew throughout the decade, which suggests that the show is also appealing to viewers on an allegorical level where the contestants fighting to survive in their constructed setting stand in for citizens who are struggling to survive in the post-9/11 cultural climate. (The ways in which this survival motif infiltrates fictional television is explored more in chapters 1 and 5). John Timpane writes, "What if the undeniable horrors of 9/11 drove the arts more toward reality? And yet at the same time pushed them more toward fantasy? What if we were simultaneously running away from the world" and toward it?[40] Michael Hirschorn argues that "post-9/11, *Survivor* became less a fantasy and more a metaphor for an imagined postapocalyptic future. What happens on these shows might be a Technicolor version of how we behave in real life, but so is most fiction. Creative endeavors—written, scripted, or produced—should be measured not by how literally they replicate actual life but by how effectively they render emotional truths."[41]

In this case, *Survivor* (and reality television programs like it) may be tapping into unresolved emotions and unaddressed anxieties that still linger years after the terrorist attacks. Viewers who watch the show cathartically get to experience survival, safety, and the other side of trauma—albeit vicariously through an extremely mediated version of reality.

There are, of course, alternative explanations for what these competitive reality television programs reveal about our societal values. For example, David Grazian has argued that competitive reality shows "celebrate the radical right-wing values championed especially by the free market Republican" and that "the sociological underpinnings of reality programming [are] a product of its recent historical context, the George W. Bush era," and the rise of neoliberalism.[42] Looking at reality television programs focused on the more common life struggles, Hirschorn reads the "intensely emotional tales" captured by home improvement shows like ABC's *Extreme Makeover: Home Edition* (2003–12) as pointing toward the "people who have fallen through the cracks of Bush-era America—often blue-collar families ravaged by disease, health-care costs, insurance loopholes, layoffs, and so forth."[43] Regardless of the subgenre, these programs give "viewers the chance to compare and contrast their own lives with those of the show's" protagonists, allowing them to register the onscreen emotions of the participants and reflect on their own emotions as well.[44]

Voyeurism: I See, Therefore I Feel

There is one final theory that explains the mass consumption of reality programming: the thrill that viewers get when they peek behind the closed doors of everyday people and celebrities, peering into the private and the taboo alike. Psychologists have determined, perhaps as would be expected, that people with voyeuristic tendencies are more likely to watch reality programming.[45] But as a cultural group, Americans have always tended toward the voyeuristic side when it comes to entertainment. The increased access to celebrities in the era of social media has simply amplified this. Arthur Cassidy, a "social media and celebrity psychologist," argues, "Our need for celebrities as icons and Idols has created a nation of tele addicts where we have forged an unconscious attachment to particular celebrities. Our insatiable need for them as idols has created a celebrity obsessed society of reality television dependency."[46] And the entertainment industry capitalizes on this dependency. Some studies have shown that our celebrity addiction might not be all bad. In fact, our connections to celebrities may even increase our self-worth. Michael Levy, author of *Celebrity and Entertainment Obsession,* explains, "Knowing what takes place in the [lives] of the most popular people in the world" and feeling a part of their world can cause viewers to regard themselves more highly.[47]

While research, and our long history of cult celebrity culture, explains why reality television programs featuring celebrities are so popular, these same interpretations might not explain why viewers tune into watch pseudo-celebrities, everyday persons seeking their fifteen minutes of fame and instant stardom, on the screen. In fact, in this age of increased surveillance, one might think that televisual spying on a bunch of average people (who admittedly signed up for it) may hit too close to home. Antonio Lopez observes that "post 9/11 our society has become increasingly one of surveillance. Additionally, more and more people have personal capturing devices, such as cell phones, PDAs and digital cameras that make anyone vulnerable to having their image seized by strangers."[48] This has become our lived reality, and with it come real, justifiable anxieties about how to navigate through spaces that are more and more embedded with technology.[49] Watching reality television puts the viewers in a position they do not usually occupy: they become the ones doing the surveilling. And networks capitalize on the pleasure this voyeuristic empowerment brings to fans. For example, devotees can pay a fee to see twenty-four-hour online footage of the housemates competing on CBS's hit show *Big Brother* (2000–present).

As I discussed earlier, reality television by its nature brings attention to the performative ways in which we all construct our identities. But it also draws attention to the ways in which this is amplified now with advanced technology and social media. Watching the contestants craft personas fit for media consumption speaks to the ways in which we all navigate our own "identities as technologically mediated people."[50] Competition shows like *Big Brother* and *Survivor* situate their "contestants in a media constructed space with specific rules and parameters," and viewers get to watch to see who succeeds within them.[51] These shows then allow viewers to see contestants publicly embodying a social anxiety they are forced to address daily.

The Marriage of Reality Television and the Internet: The Circulation of Affect

So far, this chapter has explored the various emotional appeals of the reality television genre and the ways in which various subgenres may reflect cultural anxieties. But it is important to note that viewers are not only gaining pleasure by watching these shows, they are gaining pleasure by interacting with them. Although television has been inspiring fan activity for decades, the reality television genre has produced a plethora of programs that depend on viewer interactivity—for example, casting votes through telephone calls or online submissions. This tradition is not new. The first interactive television experience of this nature was July 1999's *Dateline* episode in which "the program urged viewers to log on to the Internet in order to cast 'guilty' or 'innocent' votes in response to the television coverage of a murder trial."[52] Since then viewers have been logging on to vote on not-so-life-and-death matters, although their passion for doing so sometimes makes it appear otherwise. Competitive talent programs like *Dancing with the Stars* (ABC, 2005–present) and *American Idol* (ABC, 2002–2016; 2018–present), for example, require audience participation (i.e., votes).

Like other genres, successful reality television programs inspire creation of various online sites for viewer interaction. For example, followers of *The Bachelor/Bachelorette* can log on to The Bachelor Nation Fan Wiki, which houses details on over twenty seasons of the franchise's various series (e.g., *The Bachelor Pad, Bachelor in Paradise*). Fans can participate in online fantasy leagues where they compete to see if they can correctly predict the winner of the season. They can also continue their voyeurism on sites that encourage sleuthing—collecting and commenting on the social media posts of participants, recording spottings (sometimes accompanied with pictures) of them in public—in a spoiler-ridden effort to discover the results of the shows before the season ends.

Reality television also inspires live tweeting—the act of commenting about the program, as it unfolds, on Twitter. While this happens to some extent in all television (as chapters 8, 9, and 10 will discuss), the phenomenon is particularly interesting when it comes to reality television programs where viewers are commenting on contestants' behaviors or performances and the contestants themselves, in an extension of their performances onscreen, can directly engage with such conversations. If reality television is a form of mood modulator, if—as studies have found—it increases positive affect in viewers, then live tweeting reality television shows seems to circulate and amplify that positive affect. Imagine a viewer taking pleasure in making fun of someone behaving badly onscreen. Now that viewer can post a humorous tweet and then take pleasure as that tweet is liked, retweeted, or responded to. Twitter—and other social media sites—then become a repository, a storage house of the emotions that various television programs have prompted in viewers.

Conclusion

This chapter has explored some of the emotional appeals of the reality television genre and the ways in which this genre reflects cultural anxieties. This discussion cannot end without contemplating one of the potential consequences of living in an age in which reality television is rampant. Consider again the aforementioned argument that reality television is designed for "maximum emotional impact." What effect does consuming an endless array of emotionally exploitative television programming have on viewing audiences? Arguably, it develops a preference, and perhaps even a demand, for emotionally charged narratives and personalities. Some have gone as far as crediting the reality television genre with producing America's first reality television election and president.

The rise of Donald Trump—and the societal fears that factored into his rise—will be discussed in greater detail in chapter 10, but let us for a moment consider the possibility that an entertainment trend did, in fact, help create a cultural climate that led to this particular political outcome. Media scholars have argued that Trump mastered the skills needed to win over the American public in the course of his 2016 presidential campaign during his time starring on his reality television show, *The Apprentice*.[53] In an article for the *Chronicle of Higher Education*, Kelly Field interviewed scholars of reality television to determine which reality television strategies Trump translated into political maneuvering. It turns out quite a few reality TV tactics may have been at play. For example, Trump learned that "outrage equals attention," which provided him with a strategy with which to dominate the news cycle.[54] Producing reality television taught him that "only the most outrageous statements and actions get past the cutting-room floor," so in order "to survive editing," one has to grab attention through shocking or extreme behavior.[55] These lessons culminated in his middle-of-the-night tweets; Trump knew that "if he says something outrageous, it will be on the morning news show."[56]

Arguably then, his random Twitter rants may be much less random, and much more strategic, than people give him credit for.[57] His election techniques proved the adage that there is no such thing as bad publicity: ultimately, it is all about screen time and dominating the narrative.[58] And master screen time he did. According to a study by the Shorenstein Center at Harvard, Trump received 15 percent more media coverage than Clinton leading up to the 2016 election.[59] Also, long before his administration would coin the phrase "alternative facts," Trump learned that reality need only look real, and that what looks real is "in fact often scripted or at least highly planned."[60] He also learned that he can shape reality, "control the script," by bypassing the traditional news media and speaking directly to the American public on Twitter.[61] Trump's political pageantry was dependent on skewed visions of reality. Reality television draws on powerful archetypes and stock characters; so too did Trump's campaign rhetoric: "He cast Hillary as the crook archetype, and himself as the savior who is going to save us from bad hombres."[62] Trump's language—with a major focus on competition and winning, as Trump consistently titled himself (both before and after the election) as the inevitable winner—also aligned with the ways in which we speak about reality television scenarios and contestants.[63]

While we will never be able to truly prove that the twenty-first-century reality television craze—and not a slew of other factors—set the stage for the forty-fifth U.S. president, the mere suggestion points toward the importance of considering the influence of emotionally charged television.

3

Performing and Experiencing Anger (through Humor)

Infotainment's Increased Visibility and Political Effect

In the days following the September 11 attacks, a variety of people—such as Graydon Carter, the editor of *Vanity Fair,* and Roger Rosenblatt of *Time*—lined up to declare the end of the age of irony.[1] With the smoke from the towers still hanging in the air, their predictions that we would abandon our era of detachment in order to fully grapple with our newly realized geopolitical realities seemed likely. But this did not occur. Contrary to their proclamations, irony—criticized as it often is for its political inefficiency—cemented itself within our cultural landscape and became a tool for the masses to critique the contemporary moment.

This chapter studies the rise in popularity of parodic infotainment news shows following the September 11 attacks. Drawing on the humor relief theory, as well as theories concerning affect mimicry and imagined communities, this chapter argues that news parody shows, such as Comedy Central's *The Daily Show,* satisfied various emotional needs for their viewers during this traumatic time. Though critics often worry that therapeutic laughter diffuses fear and anger and quells rebellious impulses, this chapter suggests that the humor provided by these programs helps viewers transform their negative emotions into action. For some viewers, these comedic critiques of the news industry inspired political engagement and critical thinking and helped reframe problematic cultural sentiments. To understand how we have arrived at our current televisual landscape rich with emotionally charged news alternatives, we must first trace the slow decline and transformation of the traditional news industry, the history of news parody genres that predate our contemporary ones, and understand how the post-9/11 climate allowed popular satirists like Jon Stewart, Stephen Colbert, Trevor Noah, Jon Oliver, and Samantha Bee to become influential political critics.

Once upon a Time There Was News on the News

To anyone paying attention, the changes in the news industry over the past half century are quite noticeable, even if they occurred gradually. Although television news once appeared to be strongly dedicated to upholding journalistic standards and committed to public service—despite the bottom line—many feel this is no longer the case. Barbara Matusow, the author of *The Evening Stars,* explains how financial issues prompted many of the changes in the news industry. For decades the broadcast network news divisions failed to make profits and, in fact, lost money on a large scale.[2] For example, in 1962 NBC lost $12 million and CBS lost $5 million, but nobody within those news organizations seemed concerned about going over their budgets.[3] In the twenty-first century, this willingness to ignore the bottom line is no longer the case, and the most dominant news suppliers have begun strategically integrating features from the entertainment industries into the news as a way to raise profits and attempt to slow dwindling viewership. The term *infotainment* emerged as a catchy buzzword to capture and critique this phenomenon.[4] This televisual genre would continue to rise in popularity well into the twenty-first century, and with it the face of traditional news broadcasting would be forever altered; the news began to lure in viewers "with Hollywood-star looks, provocative lead-ins, snappy editing, and sensational, often titillating stories."[5]

As the media critic Jeffrey Jones notes, the "artificial separation between politics and popular culture" started to dissipate with the rise of the cable news networks in the post-network era.[6] It further began to erode as the "Big Five" corporations making up the network oligopoly cemented their presence in mainstream news broadcasting. In the era of 24/7 news coverage, with a proliferation of news stations at our disposal, it is easy to assume we are getting better coverage today than in earlier years. What we are really getting, however, is simply a very different type of news coverage crafted by a few powerhouse companies. Today's media reach more Americans than ever before, but they are controlled by a frighteningly small number of owners.[7] In the 1980s, over fifty media corporations controlled the news industry; today that number has shrunk to five.[8] In fact, the top five U.S. programmers—Viacom-Paramount/CBS, Disney/ABC, NBC Universal/Comcast, WarnerMedia, and

News Corporation/Fox—now control more than 75 percent of *all* prime-time programming. Since these companies are heavily involved in the world of entertainment, it is not surprising that their news coverage has been influenced by their dual interests. Stories about celebrities now often get precedence in news coverage in a way that strengthens these corporate synergies and act as a means (often unsubtle) of company promotion.[9] Although there have been efforts to limit the reach of these conglomerates, they have been unsuccessful, and legislation has allowed the Big Five to increase (rather than decrease) their scope over the past two decades. Laws that have attempted to regulate the consolidation of media ownership have been ruled as violating the First Amendment.[10] Such rulings have suggested that if companies like Comcast and WarnerMedia own the broadband networks, then it is a violation of their free speech rights to compel them to carry any content on these networks that they would prefer to censor or omit. Corporate free speech is thus rapidly "becoming synonymous with the right of one monolithic media corporation to dominate any given market."[11]

Daya Kishan Thussu argues that of the powerful Big Five, the biggest changes in television news in the United States can be attributed to the rise of Fox News as the most popular news provider.[12] Part of its success is due to how it managed to cater to a homogeneous audience in terms of ideological beliefs. As early as 2006, reports from the Pew Research Center began showing this dominance. Surveys indicated that nearly one-quarter of Americans (23 percent) said they regularly watched Fox News and that the majority of these viewers self-identified as being right-wing Republicans.[13] Fox has also led the way in allowing focus-group data and audience polls to help determine the news they package. Audience surveys indicate that "Fox is giving the conservative audience what they want to hear—spinning news to benefit Republicans and others who share their conservative political views," and this tactic is working to their great advantage in terms of ratings.[14] News coverage has never been without bias, but it used to be more common that every news story was a slight reflection of the reporter telling the story.[15] In today's news market, however, it would be more accurate to declare that every news story is a (more than slight) reflection of the network broadcasting it. This shift in the news industry has many long-standing journalists very much concerned. A former NBC senior vice president and producer of *NBC Nightly News* contemplates how these current practices—if in place decades earlier—could have altered events as we know them: "I shudder to think about what would have happened if there were consultants back during the civil rights coverage, when we got calls saying NBC News are 'nigger lovers' and 'we'll never watch this network again.' Consultants would have said ease off, you're making people uncomfortable, don't do these stories. And that's the unfortunate thing happening in all news media, because people are avoiding stories that make people uncomfortable because they don't want to lose viewers and readers. That's not good for democracy."[16]

These concerns, now over a decade old, were not unfounded. Many blame the trend of news networks taking on a determinedly liberal or conservative bias and not broadcasting fair and balanced coverage to account for the current environment wherein we all exist primarily in echo chambers (reading and watching news and interacting with people on social media) that reinforce our ideological beliefs.[17] Cultural critics have blamed this echo chamber effect for the outcome of—and people's reactions to—the 2016 presidential election.

Though the move to fashion news toward an ideologically homogeneous viewer base has motivated many of the shifts in the news industry, the quest for increased audience ratings has also played a role and further influenced news consumption practices. During the past half century, U.S. audiences for peak-time network news bulletins have steadily declined.[18] Numbers are down substantially, from 85 percent in 1969 to 29 percent in 2005,[19] and by 2013 this figure had plummeted further: only 11 percent of American viewers tune in to traditional prime-time news programming.[20] Although numerous factors have played into these decreased viewing statistics, many believe that they are the result of Americans, especially those in younger demographics, opting for online or alternative new sources.[21]

Despite this decrease in viewership, news programs have, contrary to logic, proliferated.[22] The reason behind this is financial: news programs are cheaper to produce than other television genres. According to *Forbes,* an average half hour of sitcom costs $1.3 million to produce, scripted television shows cost between $2 million and $3 million an hour, and reality shows, touted as the cheapest of all forms of programming on the air, generally cost between $1 million and $3 million per season to produce.[23] News programming, however, beats even reality television in terms of cost: production of a typical hour-long show averages only $500,000 or less.[24] Even though these programs are cheaper to produce, the attention to the network's bottom line still affects the genre's public service role. Unsurprisingly, the shift to "ratings-conscious" television, coupled with a continued dependence on corporate advertising, ultimately influences the news agendas set by networks.[25]

The increased commercialization of television has forced the news industry further into the entertainment business, which has resulted in a more informal communication forum that emphasizes "personalities, style, storytelling skills and spectacles" over content.[26] The result is a tabloid-style approach to news broadcasting that blends fact with fiction and circulates often meaningless trivia unrelated to important current affairs.[27] News networks have also begun integrating tactics that leave ample room for attacking their credibility. For example, more common than ever before is the use of "look lives" or "live on tapes," footage shot and delivered on-delay under the guise of real-time, live-event coverage, as well as reenactments that trick viewers into believing that they are seeing real events as they unfold.[28] Other arguable missteps include inappropriate attempts to make news coverage comical or entertaining. One example would be the decision made by CNN during a financial report on Viagra stock to have the reporter relay stock information while a track of Frank Sinatra singing "Makin' Whoopee" played in the background.[29] Perhaps the most frightening trend is the industry's overall focus on *appearing* like a dominant news force, rather than being one. Bonnie Anderson, a veteran journalist and former vice president of recruiting at CNN, recounts an email she received from Garth Ancier, the new head of programming for all Turner Broadcasting networks at the time: "We need younger, more *attractive* anchors (male and female) who *project credibility.*"[30] In her book, *News Flash: Journalism, Infotainment, and the Bottom-Line Business of Broadcast News,* Anderson notes how this trend toward the star anchor or reporter led to the proliferation of underskilled news correspondents and dangerous reporting environments, and less emphasis on journalistic integrity.

Many media scholars have attempted to determine a definitive start date for the realm of news-entertainment hybridity. Some point to the political climate of the 1980s and 1990s, when the mixing of celebrity and politics was first noticeable.[31] For example, some argue the election and popularity of Ronald Reagan during the 1980s can be seen as predicting the news trends that would follow.[32] Still others credit the news scandals of the 1990s—particularly the O. J. Simpson trial and the Monica Lewinski–Bill Clinton affair—with forever changing the news landscape.[33] The 1990s also saw the first use of talk shows as popular sites for presidential hopefuls. For example, during the 1992 presidential campaign, many candidates appeared on programs such as the *Larry King Live* show—occurrences that today are commonplace for politicians rather than noteworthy.[34] Critics of the time saw this "'entertainmentization' of politics" as "a degradation of the electoral process"; but, despite their original outcries, the trend would continue and multiply in the coming decades.[35] For example, by the time Arnold Schwarzenegger announced his candidacy for governor of California on NBC's *Tonight Show with Jay Leno* in 2003, no one objected. Comparing this case of a celebrity-turned-politician to that of his predecessor, Ronald Reagan, Anderson argues that if Reagan "had announced his candidacy for the 1966 California governor's race while sitting in a studio next to Johnny Carson, he would never have been taken seriously. But for Schwarzenegger, it was a brilliant move."[36] And that became a move that would be repeated and expected for all politicians who would follow. In 2007 Senator John Edwards announced his run for the presidential election on *The Daily Show with Jon Stewart* and the 2008, 2012, and 2016 elections saw all the candidates making regular appearances on various talk shows.[37] Some scholars embrace this new forum for politics, arguing that "popular culture has become one of the more open and free-flowing arenas for communication about politics," especially in comparison to the ideologically slanted news coverage being delivered by the standard networks.[38] Others, however, are more critical of the role popular media and celebrity culture play in politics. For example, many have argued that the election of Donald Trump as the forty-fifth president of the United States can be blamed on citizens' obsession with entertainment and celebrities.[39] Further, many worry that Trump's post-election practices—holding televised victory rallies and posting his informal political musings on Twitter—may be forever changing political protocol.[40]

All the shifts in the news industry have led to pessimistic predictions about its future. Neil Postman's *Amusing Ourselves to Death* (1985), one of the earlier texts to highlight how public discourse in the United States was assuming the form of entertainment, sparked academic conversations about the shifts in the news industry. Decades later, scholars are criticizing the same infotainment trends, arguing that they are dangerous "not just for journalism, but for American society as a whole."[41] Reese Schonfeld, CNN's first president, succinctly sums up the problem, noting that in today's television network world everything "has become worldwide and skin deep. . . . Coverage splashes over everything and saturates nothing."[42] In even harsher criticism, John Simpson, a veteran BBC correspondent, commented that "thanks to the diminishing effects of appealing to the lowest common denominator," the United States "is turning into an Alzheimer nation, unaware of its own or anyone else's past, ignorant of its own or anyone else's present."[43] Their criticism echoes Postman's claim: "Americans are the best entertained and quite likely the least well-informed people in the Western world."[44] Andrew Marr attributes this to the fact that the idea of the news itself has altered: "It stopped being essentially information and became something designed to produce—at all costs, always—an emotional reaction, the more extreme the better."[45] And the most common complaint from all critics of the news industry is that "the trivial has triumphed over the weighty; the intimate relationships of celebrities from soap operas, the world of sport or the royal family, are judged more 'newsworthy' than the reporting of significant issues and events of international consequence."[46]

With so many critical of the shifts, one would hope that the changes in the industry were at least successfully leading to the increased viewership they were intended to secure. But, in all actuality, the news-as-infotainment is not actually drawing in more viewers. In fact, the opposite may be occurring. As early as 2003, more than half of the people polled by the Pew Research Center for the People and the Press noted that they felt that the persons in charge of determining news content are out of touch with the general public.[47] This seems to be even more the case in younger demographics, which I will discuss later in this chapter. But while traditional news viewership continues to decline, another genre has steadily risen: the news parody show.

Politics as Entertainment: The Rise of Infotainment across Televisual Genres

As the news industry continues to suffer blows to its economic bottom line and its professional integrity, entertainment genres have risen as "alternative forums for political discussion, information, and critique."[48] In today's television lineups, political coverage looks quite different from how it did in earlier decades. Sketch comedy, news parody shows, and even reality programming have begun to overshadow the political coverage appearing in more traditional news genres.[49] Amber Day, author of *Satire and Dissent: Interventions in Contemporary Political Debate,* suggests that these programs are contributing to a renaissance that is taking place in the realm of political satire.[50] She argues that the political discourse occurring within such satiric genres is more vibrant than that occurring through traditional outlets devoted to serious political dialogue.[51] Others agree and argue that this new type of quasi-political programming may be the best tool to renew political interest among the disengaged youths of America. Studies of college students find that young adults today are consuming very little traditional news and are disconnected from traditional sources of political information.[52] Thussu explains that "soft news media," which she defines as "entertainment-orientated, quasi news and information" programs, have "had the unintended effect of increasing the likelihood that a foreign policy crisis will receive public attention, particularly among" young adults who are "not typically interested in politics or foreign policy."[53] For example, Jody Baumgartner and Jonathan Morris's 2006 study of *The Daily Show with Jon Stewart* found that the program—especially popular among young American viewers—was exceptionally influential during both the 2000 and 2004 presidential elections.[54] Skeptical of the genre's actual influence on young voters, Cass Sunstein suggests that the popularity of such programming may simply reflect this generation's preference for a self-selected diet of news information and cautions that the genre may merely reinforce preexisting opinions.[55] This criticism directed at the popular news-entertainment shows, however, actually does not differ much from the criticisms aimed at the traditional news industry.

For instance, Jones points to the alarmist titles of books like *Remote and Controlled*, *Seducing America*, and *The Sound Bite Society* that critique the move toward sensational news coverage.[56] He sums up three types of arguments made against the merging of politics and entertainment. For some the "problem with television is ontological—citizens have forgotten the importance of social connections and the benefits those connections have in producing a rich, democratic polity because we have divorced ourselves from each other through our isolated acts of watching entertainment television."[57] For others, "the problem is epistemological—television is an inferior (even dangerous) means of knowing the arena of politics. Due to the technological biases of electronic communication . . . , television offers little more than amusement, entertainment, and distraction because the medium is incapable of helping us think in any other way."[58] And for others still, "the problem is phenomenological—television is a cynical medium that may encourage us to feel engaged or empowered politically, but ultimately such feelings are false and temporal, certainly not residual or behavioral."[59] As Jones points out, these criticisms are faulty on several different levels: there has always been a long history of engagement between entertainment and politics, politics itself relies on drama to a degree and has always had an entertainment value for participants, politicians are often groomed to be showmen, and politics is crafted specifically through (and for) media spectatorship, which often relies on entertainment.[60] Likewise, Thussu notes that "news as entertainment has a long and venerable tradition, from the broadside ballad to the yellow and tabloid press, from cinema newsreels to television."[61] The fear that infotainment is dumbing down the populace has been present since the dawn of mass media.[62] Although much of the discussion (and criticism) of contemporary political entertainment programs hinges on its role in the current historical moment, many fail to recognize its long history, which reveals that the contemporary infotainment programs are simply a new iteration of something that has been present for decades.

The News Parody Program: A Brief Overview of Its History and Criticism

News entertainment programs have existed since television's onset: programming such as NBC's *Meet the Press* (1947–present) and CBS's *Face the Nation* (1954–present) have served as predecessors of today's pundit talk shows. Similarly, fake news and news parody programs have roots that trace back to early print journalism.[63] Consider, for instance, Benjamin Franklin, who wrote fake news stories under pseudonyms centuries before our current media-saturated moment.[64] The genre became increasingly popular during the twentieth century as publications such as *Mad Magazine* and *The Onion* carried on Franklin's spirit of "constructive irony."[65] During this time news parody shows on television experienced similar success. These programs, which are framed like traditional news programs but understood by viewers to be a mock-up of the format, began proliferating in the 1990s and have since appeared in media markets around the globe: *That Was the Week That Was* (BBC, NBC, 1962–63, 1964–65); *This Hour Has Seven Days* (CBC, 1964–66); *Not Necessarily the News* (HBO, 1983–90); *This Hour Has 22 Minutes* (CBC, 1993–present); *TV Nation* (NBC, Fox, 1994, 1995); *The Day Today* (BBC, 1994); *The Daily Show* (Comedy Central, 1996–present); *The 11 O'Clock Show* (Channel 4, 1998–2000); *Da Ali G Show* (Channel 4, HBO, 2000, 2003–4); *Have I Got News for You* (BBC, 1990–present); *The Rick Mercer Report* (CBC, 2004–present); *The Colbert Report* (Comedy Central, 2005–14); *The ½ Hour News Hour* (Fox, 2007); *Chocolate News* (Comedy Central, 2008); *D. L. Hughley Breaks the News* (CNN, 2008–9); *This Week Thus Far* (CBC, 2011–present); *Last Week Tonight with John Oliver* (HBO, 2014–present); *Full Frontal with Samantha Bee* (TBS, 2016–present).[66]

Although the massive popularity of these news parody programs might be new, the format itself has existed in various forms for decades. For example, faux news reports have commonly appeared in variety and sketch television programs. One of the most well known is probably *Saturday Night Live*'s (1975–present) "Weekend Update," an ongoing segment of NBC's late-night sketch comedy show.[67] Outside the comedy realm, although often hosted by comedians, elements of the genre have also influenced late-night political talk shows, such as *Politically Incorrect* (Comedy Central, ABC, 1993–97, 1997–2002); *Dennis Miller Live* (HBO, 1994–2002); *The Chris Rock Show* (HBO, 1997–2000); *Real Time with Bill Maher* (HBO, 2003–present); *The Nightly Show with Larry Wilmore* (Comedy Central, 2015–16).

Despite their longevity, contemporary news parody programs often face age-old critiques related to the political utility of satire and irony. While some critics celebrate modern media satirists as "legitimate players in serious political dialogue," others question whether they should hold such influence.[68] Some question the merger of comedy and politics and point out the difficulty of determining the point when comedy turns into critique. Other skeptics question the efficacy of this form of satiric engagement and its power to shape the political mediascape in any meaningful fashion. And, most cynically, some suggest that such programs may simply reinforce the status quo and dominant norms.[69] Drawing on criticism of satire more generally, many fear that for all their passion and rage, these programs may—contrary to their intention—defuse anger and rebellious impulse.[70]

Those holding more idealistic theories of satire—those who see "irony as a potential antidote to cynicism and disengagement"—have more faith in the genre's potential.[71] Supporters are quick to point out the evolution of the genre and the ways that it more closely aligns with serious news programming today. For example, contemporary news parodies contain little to no fictionalized material and impersonations, but instead include "deconstructions of real news events, improvisational pranks, and ambushes of public figures" to comment on current affairs.[72] These shows discuss politics in a vernacular common to the regular viewer, providing an important introduction to politics for some viewers.[73] In this way, these new political television programs provide an entryway into active citizenship.

The Rise of News Parodies after 9/11

So what prompted this inclination to be more politically active or the desire for a more digestible form of political coverage? Research would suggest that the September 11 terrorist attacks—and the polarization of traditional news networks that occurred in the following decade—catapulted this genre into mass popularity, making it "the comic trope" of our times.[74] Studies have found that "the exponential growth in satiric offerings in the United States in particular roughly coincided with the eight years of George W. Bush's tenure as president."[75] This is perhaps unsurprising: his administration "produced an atmosphere in which the mainstream press was reticent to appear adversarial, meaning that much official language and policies went unchallenged, particularly in the lead-up to the Iraq war."[76] Many argue that "the Bush administration took advantage of patriotic fervor to advance an aggressive and questionable (if not also illegal) series of domestic and foreign policy initiatives," and that news alternatives rose to meet the needs of those pulling away from news outlets that were moving from the realm of journalism into "propagandist marketing."[77] Consider for a moment the visual aesthetics of news broadcasts in the months following 9/11: "Banners were unfurled, inevitably in red, white, and blue, along the crawl space at the bottom of the television screen announcing 'America at War,' or 'America under Attack' as if the story were about a basketball or football tournament. News anchors appeared . . . with flags pinned to jackets, and patriotism, long banished from television, was unhappily rediscovered."[78]

Objectivity was missing from the news landscape during this time, which seemingly demanded the performance of patriotism. More problematic, though, was the role the government played in determining the content of the news. Statistical analysis of new programming from the immediate post-9/11 period indicates that approximately three-quarters of the content of most news broadcasts stemmed directly from government statements and press releases.[79] This eventually caused "the traditional news media to lose its credibility as a legitimate source of information."[80] At this time news parodies "stepped into the political-comedic void, providing more than just needed laughter to a nation traumatized by such brazen actions."[81] Fake news programs "became the perfect format for questioning the faux 'reality' that was increasingly being created through the manipulations, distortions, and outright lying of the Bush administration and a compliant, sloppy, and sensationalistic news media."[82] Since many felt the news media had abandoned their role as "watchdogs"—monitoring government and corporate abuse—and had morphed into "an uncritical conduit of powerful institutions to spread their messages, the time period was ripe for a takeover by the news parody programs."[83]

An Example of Post-9/11 TV Political Satire: The Influence of *The Daily Show with Jon Stewart*

Undoubtedly, the most popular news parody program of the twenty-first century—one that paved the way for many other successful shows—is *The Daily Show,* which premiered on Comedy Central in 1996, hosted by Craig Kilborn. Although it was similar in format to today's show, the program did not gain its political edge until Jon Stewart took over in 1999, and its popularity increased after 9/11.[84] Marketed first and foremost as a comedy, the program has always been intended to amuse the audience, but as the years passed it became dedicated more and more to addressing the biases of so-called straight news coverage. The basic formula for the show is not unlike those of some of its predecessors: "a mixture of cheeky renditions of the day's news headlines, on-location reports of bizarre stories, and celebrity interviews."[85] Its host interrogates—sometimes humorously and sometimes seriously—the content of the daily news.[86] This commentary is punctuated by special reports from "senior correspondents" (comedians posing as experts).[87] These segments, shot "on location," showcase one of *The Daily Show*'s staff members posed in front of an obvious green screen claiming to be relaying factual information from the steps of the Capitol, the distant shores of foreign countries, and so forth, while the live studio audience sees that they are positioned just feet away from the host's desk, and the knowing audience member at home understands this to be the case. As Aaron McKain notes, through these parodic segments "the show mocks and deconstructs the news media's longstanding practice of sending reporters to read statements in front of the White House or at the scene of a crime, a convention that aims to create the illusion of immediacy and construct the news media as a (falsely) transparent medium that enables viewers to experience the reality of a situation."[88]

These same correspondents also carry out ambush interviews or special interest segments by interacting with people in the field—sometimes concerning strange, trivial, or local non-mainstream news stories, but other times covering surprisingly serious topics being overlooked by other news outlets. Each episode then ends with a consensual interview filmed before the live audience. Guests typically include celebrities (actors, musicians, fellow comedians) and often politicians or political experts (quite frequently academics and published authors).

Stewart's name became synonymous with the show, which he hosted from 1999 to 2015, and he was often the subject of attention and critique.

Although Stewart consistently insisted that he was not a journalist, social reformist, or media critic, but, rather, "a comedian who has the pleasure of writing jokes about things that [he] actually care[s] about," many began regarding him as a legitimate player in the political sphere.[89] Under his tenure, *The Daily Show* was recognized as leading "the social critique and satire of the modern news industry."[90] *Newsweek* described the show as "fearless social satire," crediting Stewart himself as "battling pomposity and misinformation" at every turn.[91] A bit more understated, Stewart explained the show's goals: "What we try to do is point out the artifice of things; that there's a guy behind the curtain pulling levers."[92]

Academics studying Stewart's role as a media critic often point to one particular moment that transformed him from mere comedian into a social critic who successfully prompted change in the news industry. In October 2004 Stewart appeared on CNN's *Crossfire* and criticized the hosts for their "partisan hackery," which, he argued, was hurting Americans.[93] Stewart's political clout was only heightened when—following his criticism of the show—CNN decided to cancel *Crossfire*.[94] In the years that followed, Stewart's critiques of the contemporary mediascape earned him "a Television Critics Association award, not for comedy, but for outstanding achievement in news and information," as well as "two Peabody Awards for its election coverage."[95] He also won the respect of Americans for his integrity. A variety of polls ranked him among the most prestigious journalists. In a 2008 Pew Research Report, Stewart "tied with Dan Rather, Tom Brokaw, Anderson Cooper, and Brian Williams as the most admired and trusted journalist in America." And in 2006 *Television Week* ranked Stewart as the fifth-most powerful person in television news.[96] A 2009 online poll conducted by *Time* magazine determined that Stewart was the most trusted televised newscaster since Walter Cronkite, beating out other reputable newscasters such as Katie Couric, Charles Gibson, and Brian Williams for the title.[97] The following year, *People* titled him the "most influential man of 2010."[98] Beyond the attention Stewart received for his influence on political journalism, the show was also revered as a popular comedy program, winning multiple Emmy Awards and drawing in an average audience of 1.6 million viewers.[99]

No one would question Stewart's comedic talent, but it was his media literacy efforts that continually placed him in the national spotlight. *The Daily Show* repeatedly showed politicians contradicting themselves and demonstrated how seldom television news organizations fact-check their own coverage, even though they have "the evidence and means to do so."[100] Stewart attended to more than just sloppy journalistic practices, pointing out the often unethical (or biased) actions of mainstream journalists and network pundits as well. For example, during the 2004 presidential campaign, the reporter Ed Helms appeared on *The Daily Show* for an interview. When Stewart asked him about the debate scheduled for the following day, Helms proceeded to read the report he intended to file—a report written a full day before the event was to occur.[101] Stewart, seemingly shocked, asked about his writing process, carefully clarifying: "You write your stories in advance and then put them in past tense?"[102] Helms claimed that all reporters "write stories in advance based on conventional wisdom" and then make the actual events fit the article they wrote.[103] When Stewart pressed him to explain why reporters would do this, Helms answered, "We're lazy? Lazy thinkers?"[104]

Another big moment when the show highlighted unethical journalism occurred five years later. Fox News's Sean Hannity reported on Republican Congresswoman Michele Bachmann's November 5, 2009, Tea Party rally against the Democratic Health Care Reform. During Hannity's follow-up interview with Bachmann, "footage" of the demonstration played in the background as Bachmann noted that she estimated that 20,000 to 45,000 people were in attendance. (The *Washington Post* estimated that 10,000 people attended the event.) Hannity, musing at those numbers, and the impressive footage of a packed crowd, noted that it was a great turnout for a Thursday. On November 10, 2009, Stewart critiqued the footage on his show, pointing out that Hannity showed two different clips during his interview with Bachmann: one (of the actual event) briefly shown at the beginning of the interview (showcasing bright, clear blue skies, fall coloring on the trees, and—not unimportantly—fewer people in attendance) and another, which played for the majority of the interview, containing different footage—footage not from Bachmann's demonstration, but from Fox News pundit Glenn Beck's 9–12 Rally months earlier (evident not only by the larger—Saturday—crowd size, but by the cloudy sky and green foliage). Attending to this purposeful manipulation of footage is just one of the ways that *The Daily Show* teaches its viewers the importance of being a critical consumer of news.

Stewart's fight against media corruption eventually led to work offscreen. On October 30, 2010, he and Stephen Colbert, host then of *The Colbert Report*, held a political rally: the Rally to Restore Sanity. Although originally concocted to satirize a "Restoring Honor" Rally put on by Glenn Beck, Comedy Central's event was viewed by many as a serious political demonstration. Over a quarter million people turned out at the Washington Mall to hear

Stewart speak out against the media's failure to adequately monitor political action.[105] The event proved that the audiences of news parodies are—or can be—politically active, and that they do not necessarily just sit at home passively laughing at the political critiques unfolding on their screens.

While all this sounds quite positive, scholars have questioned whether *The Daily Show* is actually having a *positive* political influence. For example, Jody Baumgartner and Jonathan Morris conducted a study during the 2004 presidential election on the effect the program had on the political attitudes of regular viewers. They determined that participants who watched the program were more distrustful of the political system and held negative opinions of the media. They concluded that "exposure to *The Daily Show*'s brand of political humor influenced young Americans by lowering support for both presidential candidates and increasing cynicism."[106] Critiquing their findings, Michels and Ventimiglia note that though viewing *The Daily Show* might foster skepticism, "it can just as easily lead to action as apathy."[107] Their study found that although viewers reported increased cynicism, they also reported increased "confidence in their ability to understand the complicated world of politics."[108] Critical of the notion that a satirist could be considered "more credible than 'real' news anchors" when they are not "obliged to adhere to the [same] ethical standards," Robert Spicer analyzed the "ambiguous" space that comedians like Steward occupy.[109] Ultimately, he suggests, it might be the in-between-ness of Stewart's position—"his place as 'just a comedian'"—that affords him "the political cover to do [the] things that 'real' journalists might be afraid to do or are prevented from doing by their corporate media owners or the standards of journalism that would" view them as lacking objectivity.[110]

The debate will most certainly go on concerning whether news parody programs and comedians should have such an influence in the political awareness of citizens, but it is hard to argue that Stewart did not play an instrumental role during the early decades of the twenty-first century. An article in *USA Today* called Stewart not just "a TV phenomenon but also a cultural force, if not a hero, influencing discourse at the dinner table and in the college dorms and even, some believe, turnout at the polls."[111] The program—during Stewart's tenure and after, with Trevor Noah as host—sparks a "serious demand for fact, accountability, and reason in political discourse," making it arguably one of the most crucial media literacy programs on television today.[112] Moreover, it set the bar—and often provided the talent—for the successful shows that would follow (e.g., HBO's *Last Week Tonight with John Oliver,* TBS's *Full Frontal with Samantha Bee*).

Affect Modulation: Three Theories of Emotion That May Explain *The Daily Show*'s Appeal

Although the political influence of news parody programs like *The Daily Show* has been well studied, what has been less well theorized is the emotional effect these programs have on viewers. Though it is, of course, impossible to claim that *all* viewers watch news parodies for the same reasons, or experience them in the same way, various theories of emotion offer potential explanations for the popularity of this genre in the post-9/11 era. As chapter 1 discussed, the terrorist attacks can be considered a national trauma, one that was felt on a cultural level—to varying extents—by those living in the United States at that time. A common response to trauma is alexithymia, a form of psychic numbing wherein feelings are blocked because experiencing them would be overwhelming. The popularity of news parodies during this time indicates that viewers were, indeed, anxious to *feel* things in the aftermath of the attack, although—as one of the humor theories suggests—perhaps not the negative emotions associated with the trauma.

From a psychological perspective, people often get to a point when they can experience those negative emotions only after working through the trauma. This process often entails repeated discussion of or reflection on the traumatic events. John Ellis argues that television viewing can function as a form of working through, helping viewers process their feelings until they no longer need to avoid them.[113] Television, including the news parody genre, is known for its predictability and repetitive formats. Regular viewers of *The Daily Show,* for example, come to expect certain stylistics, certain delivery, and—perhaps more important—certain content. The familiar topics and critiques, many related to the post-9/11 government and media, provide viewers with the opportunity to digest information and media literacy strategies in short daily segments and, perhaps, to process their own emotions about living in these tumultuous times. Once realized, one way that negative emotions are combatted is through the process of catharsis. Satire has long been argued to be cathartic; it brings about pleasure by providing an opportunity to express or release negative emotions. John W. Self explains how this works in terms of *The Daily Show*'s political commentary: "A straightforward argument against the establishment can build anger and tension in an audience that subscribes to the same value system, developing a sense of being wronged. An ironic and satirical argument, if presented adeptly, can *stir* the audience. It can *stoke* the fire of anger, but at the same time, it can *release* the pressure."[114]

Self's overview points toward the potential benefits and consequences of cathartic release: it can lead viewers to experience, even amplify, their negative emotions (which could lead to social action), or it could allow those to dissipate (which could lead to apathy or inaction). The three theories presented next serve as possible explanations for *The Daily Show*'s post-9/11 popularity; they also showcase these different viewing outcomes.

Humor Relief Theory

One of the most prominent explanations for why humans are drawn to humor is very much tied to the above-mentioned notion of cathartic release: the humor relief theory. Psychologists have previously suggested that humor is a defense mechanism that provides relief from one's fears. Arguably, humor serves as a defense mechanism against all negative affects, providing relief from a range of emotions, such as anger, disgust, and sadness. A recent study conducted by Stanford University supports this. People were shown a series of photographs coded according to their emotional content. After being exposed to disturbing pictures (e.g., corpses, car accidents, dental offices), participants were asked to record the intensity of the positive or negative emotions sparked by these scenes. Other subjects were asked to improvise jokes that were based on the photographs before rating their emotional reactions to the original pictures. Participants who were able to formulate jokes related to the pictures they were exposed to experienced higher levels of positive emotions and lower levels of negative emotions.[115] The study suggests that part of humor's power results from its ability to initiate a change in perspective.[116] This aligns with the humor relief theories of Herbert Spencer and Sigmund Freud, which both "describe humor along the lines of a tension-release model."[117] This popularly adapted theory suggests that laughter has the power to convert negative affect into positive affect. By extension, this means that comedic texts have the ability to act as affectual registers—altering emotional states at the consumer's will. The strategic consumption of certain comedic televisual genres could be considered a coping mechanism whereby viewers choose—even if unconsciously—to engage in humor to rid themselves of negative emotions.

Consider how this works through *The Daily Show*'s visual aesthetic. Viewers are presented with images from the mainstream media that may spark fear, anger, disgust, and so forth (e.g., lying politicians, manipulative media outlets, corrupt corporations, bigoted citizens). These images are delivered in a satiric fashion (often compared to other clips to point out absurdities and inconsistencies within the content and argument being covered), they are sandwiched between the host's comedic commentary, and they are preceded and followed by a humorous still image and pun-filled caption that boils the news story down to one witty punch line. The negative affect that might have resulted from the original media imagery is replaced with positive affect as the laughter created from its new delivery form defuses and displaces the original negative emotion. Take, for example, the still images portrayed in images 3.1 and 3.2. In these segments Jon Stewart is discussing two serious global and domestic issues, North Korea's nuclear program and continued Wall Street corruption, respectively. One might assume that—if delivered without comedic spin—the former might spark fear and the latter might produce anger. But the image panel that accompanies Stewart's discussion of the issues disrupts those negative affects, replacing them with pleasurable ones as the audience laughs at the pop culture puns referenced in the captions. The juxtaposition of Kim Jong-un with the caption "Nuke Kid on the Block"—a reference to the 1990s boy band New Kids on the Block—generates humor in place of, or in addition to, fear. In the other example, Stewart's report on continued banking corruption is lightened by the caption "the Big Bank Theory," which uses the font and coloring, and all but one letter, of the title of the popular sitcom *The Big Bang Theory*. Again, while viewers still may be angry about the material being relayed, their bodily reaction is altered as they register the joke and potentially react to it by laughter or smiling.

A similar practice is in place in the segments shown in images 3.3 and 3.4. In the first, Stewart is critiquing Fox News's inconsistent stances on political issues, referring to them as the "Mighty Morphin Position Changers," a play on the Mighty Morphin Power Rangers franchise. As image 3.4 shows, humor-provoking captions do not always require a punny pop culture reference. In this clip Stewart is critiquing the ways that Secretary of State Hillary Clinton and Vice President Joe Biden exaggerated their economically disadvantaged upbringings. In the onscreen visual displayed during Stewart's commentary, their heads appear peeking out of barrels with the phrase "Poor-Off" placed between them. The imagery highlights the way they—and many politicians—compete to seem like the more relatable average Joe or Jane, often spinning their own backstories to do so. A cynical viewer may get irritated by seeing this familiar political move, but the combined imagery potentially mollifies those negative emotions as the viewer instead smirks, rather than scowls, at the the repurposed profiles of the two prominent political figures.

Image 3.1. *The Daily Show*'s nuclear threat pun.

Image 3.2. *The Daily Show*'s bank corruption pun.

Image 3.3. *The Daily Show*'s critique of news bias.

Image 3.4. *The Daily Show* on political pandering.

The idea of news parody viewing as affect modulation may seem to suggest a viewer consciously attempting to change his or her emotional state by tuning into a particular television program. Though certainly this occurs, it should be noted that this process is often unconscious. We are not always aware of the ways in which we use cultural texts to modify our moods.

The Affect Mimicry Theory

While the first theory showcases the ways in which news parody programs may reduce viewers' levels of negative affect, the next theory reveals how such viewing may actually amplify negative affect. The affect mimicry theory suggests that we often mirror the affects that we come in contact with. We smile when others smile. In fact, we often put ourselves into positive social situations in order to "catch" positive moods.[118] Film research posits that this empathetic process occurs with onscreen fictional characters as well. In *Engaging Characters: Fiction, Emotion, and the Cinema,* Murray Smith describes two specific levels of emotional engagement that are at work when one views a film. The first, which he terms "*alignment,* concerns the way a film gives us access to the actions, thoughts, and feelings of characters. The second, *allegiance,* concerns the way a film attempts to marshal our sympathies for or against the various characters in the world of fiction."[119]

If all this is true of fictional film characters, it would make sense that watching a real person (in performance mode or not) display anger (in farcical or serious ways) on television would trigger some of that same emotion being broadcast. In the case of *The Daily Show,* scholars have argued that "the emotional core of the show might well be considered restrained anger at injustice and hypocrisy."[120] The range of Stewart's expressions of anger on the show depended on the topic being reported on. Most of his satire was delivered with a level of "intellectual detachment," but sometimes he would perform angry rants, perhaps exaggerating his anger for comedic purposes. The issues that enraged Stewart the most seemingly received the greatest amount of airtime and often were the targets of his most amplified performances of affect.

An example of this would be the song-and-dance number titled "Fox News, Go Fuck Yourselves," which he did after a back-and-forth media war with the Fox News pundit Bernard Goldberg. Goldberg went on air telling Stewart: "If you just want to be a funny man, who talks to an audience that will laugh at anything you say, that's okay with me, no problem. But if clearly you want to be a social commentator, more than just a comedian and if you want to be a good one, you better find some guts. . . . You are not nearly as edgy as you think you are."[121]

Goldberg was criticizing Stewart for not being as hard on his liberal guests as he was, allegedly, on Fox News and their conservative base. Stewart clearly wanted to respond to this criticism: the response took the form of an eleven-minute musical number (complete with a full gospel choir). Skits like this aim to grab viewers' attention—getting them to attend not just to the comical performance but also to the issue at hand that has inspired it. But at times, the comedy and performance aspects of the show drop away and viewers see a moment of nonperformative, real anger from the host. In these rare times, when he is truly enraged and visibly angry, his straight-man persona drops, and he often addresses the camera in fiery earnest. Examples of this include his rage against conservatives trying to escape blame during Hurricane Katrina and the politicians who delayed the passing of the 9/11 First Responders Bill.[122]

Witnessing these varying levels of anger has the potential to produce comparable levels of anger among the viewers at home who empathize with Stewart. Arguably, this is what the host and the producers desire. Therefore, the affect mimicry theory suggests that while some may turn to *The Daily Show* and other news parody programs to be distracted from their fear or anger—to rid themselves of such negative affect—some may very well turn to the program in order to *feel* these negative emotions. At first this idea might seem counterintuitive, and it would, in fact, directly contradict Silvan Tomkins's claim that humans are hardwired to act in ways that increase positive affect and decrease negative affect.[123] But in a time when the constant bombardment of negative imagery and fearful rhetoric are leading to desensitization, viewers may turn to a show like *The Daily Show* in order to be enticed to feel anything at all. They may be drawn to the program in the hope that they will encounter moments of such real anger; they may long to find someone expressing the anger that they are not, and that maybe—just maybe—that will prompt them to express such emotions just as freely.

And is this positive thing? In an interview the affect theorist Brian Massumi talked about both laughter's and anger's ability to "reconfigure" a situation: "Affective expressions like anger and laughter are perhaps the most powerful because they interrupt a situation. They are negative in that sense. They interrupt the flow of meaning that's taking place. . . . Anger, for example, forces the situation to attention, it forces a pause filled with an intensity that is often too extreme to be expressed in words."[124]

Arguably, these extreme moments of anger that news parody programs broadcast to viewers—inviting them to share in their outrage—are present for just this reason: to force "the situation to attention."

Imagined Communities

The desire to surround ourselves with like-minded people who feel the same way about social issues connects to the third theory that might explain what viewers get out of news parody programs. Benedict Anderson's notion of imagined communities was originally conceived to explain the sense of comradeship among citizens that helped sustain the nation-state. He considers various cultural tools that help foster this sense of interconnectedness among strangers. Anderson argues that daily print newspapers did this type of work, connecting people through "empty time."[125] People would pick up the newspaper and know that somewhere in their country, millions of others were participating in that particular moment, in the shared experience of reading that same newspaper edition, with the same date staring back at them from the corner.

Arguably, television viewers today may similarly imagine communities that are tied to them through the consumption of the same popular culture products. (This is especially the case for those watching programs live, as I will discuss in the part III of this book.) In the case of *The Daily Show,* viewers can imagine a mass viewing audience of like-minded individuals (probably liberal-leaning Democrats skewing younger in age). They expect that the viewership will share their own opinions (and those of the host) and that their emotional reactions to issues will be similar. Part of the draw of watching a program such as this—and perhaps any program, more so if it has a certain level of renown and cultural capital—is being part of a specific in-group. In particularly trying times, this sense of interconnectedness can help rid viewers of negative emotions linked to feelings of isolation. Of course, unlike Anderson's readers, who were all reading the newspaper at relatively the same time, *The Daily Show*'s viewers are not necessarily watching at the same time or even through the same medium (many will watch the show on delay on their DVRs, or download it from Comedy Central's own website, or view it in segments as YouTube clips). Still, they can imagine someone else sitting somewhere (before a flat-screen television, a laptop, an iPad, or a smartphone), viewing the same material, laughing at the same imagery, and being enraged by the same issues.

The ways in which *The Daily Show,* like many contemporary television programs, capitalizes on Internet paratexts furthers this type of imagined camaraderie. Building on Anderson's concept, Arjun Appadurai considers the ways in which technology plays a part in this type of community building. Focusing largely on Internet interactions, Appadurai conceives of "imagined worlds" and, later, "*virtual neighborhoods.*"[126] In the new global era, he claims that the people are able to imagine, visualize, and internalize an interconnectedness within the world as never before. This is easily seen through the ways that active television audiences engage with other viewers of their preferred shows (e.g., live tweeting about their favorite shows, getting involved on fan sites). *The Daily Show* presents multiple opportunities for viewers to engage with the program outside the traditional viewing time and, in fact, provides an opportunity for them to actually enter the space of the show itself. For example, in 2017 and 2018 *The Daily Show with Trevor Noah* set up an online voting system so that viewers could vote on Donald Trump's "greatest" tweets. (In this case *greatest* was probably interpreted as the most horrifying, outrageous, or ironic tweet.) Mirroring the format of the familiar NCAA March Madness brackets, their 2017 Third Month Mania bracket featured sixty-four of Trump's most infamous tweets broken into four categories, or conferences: Celebs, Enemies, Gov't Affairs, and WTF. Following the progression of the NCAA tournament, the sixty-four tweets were paired into thirty-two matches and viewers could vote for their favorite within each twosome. This process continued through various rounds (similar to the NCAA's Sweet Sixteen, Elite Eight, Final Four, and Final rounds) until a winning tweet—based on viewer votes—was determined. *The Daily Show* included segments in various episodes in March in which the correspondents, parodying sports broadcasters, discussed the matchups and revealed the winners. *The Daily Show*'s 2017 semifinals included tweets from each category. Representing the winning tweet in the Celebs category was "Sorry, @Rosie is a mentally sick woman, a bully, a dummy and above all, a loser. Other than that, she is just wonderful!" Coming in at the top of the Enemies category was "Nothing ever happened with any of these women. Totally made up nonsense to steal the election. Nobody has more respect for women than me!" The finalist for the WTF category was "I would like to extend my best wishes to all, even the haters and losers, on this special date, September 11th." And the victor of the Gov't Affairs category (and the ultimate winner of the entire online contest) was the tweet "Are you allowed to impeach a president for gross incompetence?"[127]

The Daily Show's online contest, which made the target of the ongoing joke the sitting Republican president, clearly reveals the expected viewership of the show: people would hold similar ideological beliefs, share similar views about the current president, and—perhaps—have a similar sense of humor. The shared viewing material sets the stage for viewers to form these imagined communities, and the opportunities to actually engage with fellow viewers then further solidifies them.[128]

This chapter suggests an imagined community for the show that is liberal, but this is often true of the television news parody genre as a whole. In her 2012 book, *A Conservative Walks into a Bar,* Alison Dagnes discusses how political humor in general has an inherently liberal bias.[129] As chapter 10 shows, however, this is not always the case in online spaces, such as sites like 4chan, where conservative satire proliferates.[130] The structure of this chapter purposely mirrors the framework of this book, moving from analyses of episodes that aired in the years after 9/11 to examinations of those that surrounded the 2016 election. As a result, the episodes do focus more on critiques of Republican administrations. This is due partly to the intended audience of the show, but it is also the case because President Obama was not targeted in mainstream political satire during his presidency at the same rates as the presidents who preceded and followed him. Media critics have discussed the various reasons behind this, suggesting a hesitancy to avoid humor that might have a racial connotation, as well as aspects of Obama's personality and communication style that did not lend themselves to parody.[131]

Conclusion: I Laugh, Therefore I Think (Humor as a Tool for Critical Thinking)

Shared viewing experiences and shared online exchanges are important in terms of community building, but what may be even more crucial to this process is the shared laughter those various experiences and exchanges prompt. It may be that the laughter, above all else, is doing powerful—and consequential—emotional work. In *All Joking Aside: American Humor and Its Discontents,* Rebecca Krefting argues that charged humor—which satire depends on—builds community and enacts a form of "cultural citizenship" that allows people to question the social order.[132] So in this view, the laughter prompted by *The Daily Show* sparks more than just imagined bonds but also a shared form of critical thinking necessary for social reform.

Although Neil Postman once famously quipped that "thinking doesn't play well on TV," others have argued to the contrary.[133] In his book titled *Thinking through Television,* Ron Lembo argues that television helps form cultural attitudes and opinions that affect viewers' daily lives.[134] Since studies on comedy reveal that humor is a powerful tool for memory formation, it is not unreasonable to claim that televisual comedy may be having a major influence on the solidification of cultural sentiments.[135] Writing specifically about news parody programs, Terrance MacMullan argues that they make viewers think *while* they laugh.[136] Rachel Sotos cautiously notes that while programs like *The Daily Show* do not always endorse "reason over emotion," through their critiques of media rhetoric they do encourage "awareness of the way our emotions are manipulated and distorted."[137] Now that we have supposedly entered into a post-truth era, in which facts are unimportant, political beliefs are readily influenced by the media, and emotion plays a key role in people's voting practices, perhaps these types of televisual lessons in media literacy training are more important than ever before.[138]

Part II

Mediating Fear and Anger

How Televisual Affect Reflects and Influences Current Cultural Conflicts

4

"All the Best Cowboys Have Daddy Issues"

A Psychoanalytic Reading of the Father-Child Relationships on ABC's Lost

It is commonplace in cultural studies to claim that everything is constructed. Therefore, to state with an air of certainty that fatherhood is a constructed role formed from the images and expectations of any given society at any given time would hardly surprise many. In fact, the argument itself is not new. Luigi Zoja, the former president of the International Association for Analytical Psychology, has studied the figure of the father and argued that the father's underlying image, at least in the Western world, has been profoundly shaped by Greek mythology, Roman law, Christianity, and both the French and Industrial revolutions.[1] As a Jungian psychologist, Zoja contends that there is more to the formation of father imagery than just historical and contemporary forces aligning to assist in its construction. Part of that construction runs much deeper, exists on a subconscious level, and is archetypal. So, despite the shifting parental trends occurring in the twenty-first century—the change in the father's role as head of the household, for example—part of the image of the father figure remains static and unchanging, the product of centuries of solidification. Thus, it is no surprise, as I will discuss in this chapter, that this long-standing construct can be seen airing regularly on television. But why is it important to consider the influence of these societal scripts on, and fictional depictions of, fathers?

Jungian psychologists in particular are fascinated with what they call "the collective aspects of man's nature."[2] Andrew Samuels explains that this part of human makeup is "formed from collective material such as myth, legends, and recorded/observed patterns."[3] In studying the father in particular, he explains that "behind the personal father whom we know and to whom we relate, lies an innate psychological structure which influences the way we experience him."[4] Therefore, beneath one's images of one's father is a combination of "archetypally and culturally determined expectations . . . and the personal, historical experience of the idiosyncrasies of a particular man. The flavour of one's image of 'father' depends upon the personal father's mediation of the archetypal father."[5] The reason psychologists from all schools of thought have spent much time theorizing this particular role is the stock they place in the father's overall ability to affect the psychological maturation of their patients, making him "a powerful inner agent in the emotional life of" his offspring.[6] Even Carl Jung himself cautioned that "parents should always be conscious of the fact that they themselves are the principal causes of neurosis in their children."[7] Many times this stems from parents placing their personal baggage, and projecting missed opportunities, on their children in an attempt to live vicariously through them. Jung wrote: "What usually has the strongest psychic effect on the child is the life which the parents (and ancestors too, . . .) have not lived."[8] Jung explained further: "Generally speaking, all the life which the parents could have lived but of which they thwarted themselves for artificial motives is passed onto the children in substitute form. That is to say, the children are driven unconsciously in a direction that is intended to compensate for everything that was unfulfilled in the lives of their parents."[9]

According to Ralph Layland, fathers who sidestep this common pitfall would be in Jung's category of "the loving father"—one "who can accept that it is the [child's] right to bring to him all its needs, wishes, fantasies and feelings, but does not expect the [child] to deal with his own mainly unconscious needs, wishes, fantasies or feelings that are inappropriate to that relationship."[10] Quite obviously, the personal father's influence on his child—good or bad—is not one that should be underestimated.

The father figure remains more than just a representative of the personal father, the individual man known to his son or daughter. This figure also becomes a symbol standing in for all authority figures, for order, law, and government. Michael Bader argues that the nation, an ultimate authority for many, is often viewed as "a metaphor for a family" and that "we project onto ever-expanding forms of social authority the longings originally satisfied by parents" in our childhood.[11] He continues that "on a symbolic level, we look to our leaders to provide the protection and strength usually associated with fathers."[12] Even the terminology used for government heads—phrases such as "the Founding Fathers"—reveals this conflation.[13] With this dual layer to the father figure, it should not be surprising that narratives across popular culture are ripe with complex father figures and offer up a multitude of telling father issues. In contemporary American texts at least, this bombardment may be the result of two completely unrelated conditions: the changing status of the father in the twenty-first century and the national crisis in authority and security after the 9/11 attacks.

This first motivating force means that fictional fathers stand in for real fathers and that the narratives in which they appear are trying to work through problems of domesticity and patriarchy in the family—private-zone issues transferred to the public space of mediated mass entertainment. For example, the past century has seen a rethinking of the role of the father and traditional male expectations in general. Samuels credits the 1970s women's movement for assisting in this re-visioning.[14] Psychologists now report seeing a "new kind of man" with new kinds of problems: "He is a loving and attentive father to his children, a sensitive and committed marital partner, concerned with world peace and the state of the environment; he may be vegetarian. Often, he will announce himself as a feminist. He is, in fact, a wholly laudable person. But he is not happy—and bids fair to stay miserable until either the world adjusts to him or he manages truly to *integrate* his behavioural and rôle changes at a level of psychological depth."[15]

Part of this adjustment the father has had to make, one that conflicts with centuries of cultural training, stems from a shift that has occurred within the past few decades from viewing the father as "the head of the family" to viewing him as a "co-parent."[16] And, in more and more families, with the father's financial responsibility as the head of the family becoming less necessary and divorce becoming more common, "it has been said that the father is becoming a luxury."[17] Zoja explains that the father's "traditional psychological functions are exercised to an ever slighter degree. His material tasks are conferred to mothers or institutions. His erosion as a psychological figure is often now accompanied by physical disappearance."[18] Studies have tracked this trend of the disappearing father in the United States throughout the last decades of the twentieth century and into the twenty-first. Although this disappearance is often physical, in many cases it is simply emotional. It has been reported that American fathers "spend an average of seven minutes a day with their children."[19] This lack of quality time shared by father and child is viewed by many as a failure to fulfill the parental role.

The personal father is not the only authority figure being accused of failing to live up to his obligations, however. The second motivating force behind the plethora of failed father figures plaguing fictional narratives might be indicative of other, larger authorial failures: for example, governmental failures after 9/11. This would mean that these fictional fathers are allegorical in nature, and that these story lines are working through problems of national concern. ABC's groundbreaking television drama *Lost* (2004–10) offers a multitude of father figures that suggest not only a crisis concerning the role of the father in the twenty-first century but also the crisis of national security experienced by Americans after the attacks. In particular, the program showcases three specific types of troubled father-child relationships: those in which the father is absent or dead, those in which the father is portrayed as abusive or evil, and those in which the father and child are estranged or their relationship is severely damaged.

The Importance of "Dead" Dads in Narratives across Media

Scholars have long been fascinated with the problematized father-child relationship and its portrayal in narrative works. Often of particular interest is the representation of the absent or dead father. Roland Barthes boldly suggests that the absent father is almost a prerequisite to narrative success, stating, "Every narrative (every unveiling of the truth) is a staging of the absent, hidden or hypostatized father."[20] Other scholars have agreed that for both narrative and character development to happen, fathers must be absent. Jason Bainbridge, for example, argues that "for a great variety of stories, from *Oedipus Rex* to *Harry Potter* to *Equus* to *Dexter* to any of the Pixar movies, it is the absence of the father that initiates the narrative and, in many cases, forces the protagonist to assume the role of the hero."[21] I should caution, however, that for the absent father to really have a narrative effect, he must be more than simply absent and missing from the story line; "he must be alluded to, represented (often metonymically), and affect the action."[22]

This figure of the dead father is often analyzed through a Freudian or Jungian lens. One common way that academics read such narratives is through Freud's discussion of father-murder and father-rescue—the theory that children long simultaneously to bring about their fathers' downfall and to be the cause of their salvation. Michael Zeitlin analyzes Donald Barthelme's *Dead Father* (1975), claiming it is involved in a complex (and direct) commentary on this Freudian notion.[23] Zeitlin draws attention to this moment within the text: "On the rescue of fathers. . . . When you have rescued a father from whatever terrible threat menaces him, then you feel, for a moment, that you are the father and he is not. For a moment. This is the only moment in your life you will feel this way."[24] In this passage Zeitlin claims that "Barthelme is following and reiterating the original Freudian explication of the rescue fantasy: 'All [the son's] instincts, those of tenderness, gratitude, lustfulness, defiance and independence, find satisfaction in the single wish *to be his own father.*'"[25] Barthelme's novel explicitly addresses Freud's belief that many children long for the death of the father as much as they wish to be his savior in passages such as this one: "We *want* the Dead Father to be dead. We sit with tears in our eyes wanting the Dead Father to be dead."[26]

In a Jungian reading, there might be a valid reason to "want" the father dead. Only in that ideal form, it seems, can the father ever reach his full potential. As Barbara Greenfield explains, for Jung the father is "a mental, spiritual principle that is 'above' and 'beyond' the material world, . . . a sort of divine perfection . . . beyond the reach of mortals still tied to the physical world."[27] When he is portrayed as bodiless, as a deceased father would be, he can represent more than he was; he can stand for the law, for the idea of authority, for the symbolic realm as a whole. Bainbridge analyzes villainous father figures in popular culture, reading them against the theories of fatherhood proposed by Freud and Jung, theories that he finds problematic in nature.[28] He concludes that these narratives "evince a desire to return their bad fathers to this Jungian state;" and that in doing so "they all become literally bodiless, leaving [their] physical trappings . . . (along with the blame for their crimes) to become truly Jungian-like and redeemed."[29] Bainbridge argues that only in absence, in death, moreover, can "the good father . . . be truly made present again" after he has fallen from that pedestal of perfection within narrative spaces.[30]

Getting the Picture on the Small Screen: Televisual Critiques of Failed Fathers

ABC's *Lost* is unique in its extensive, critical portrayal of multiple father figures. Other contemporary television programs have included similar critiques of fathers, but these have existed on a much smaller scale. In *Masculinity and Popular Television,* Rebecca Feasey analyzes a variety of late twentieth- and early twenty-first-century television programs for the ways they portray male characters. Her comprehensive project covers much ground: representations of gay men on sitcoms; gender bending in science fiction; and masculinity as defined by sports media, reality television, and advertising. Most relevant, however, are the moments when she focuses on television fathers. For example, in studying the soap opera, Feasey notes that the recurrent theme of unknown paternity currently challenges the importance of the fatherly role.[31] Her discussion of the failed father figures found on contemporary adult animated sitcoms—such as *The Simpsons, King of the Hill,* and *The Family Guy*—can be related to *Lost.* Feasey argues that these programs make it clear that the principal male characters—portrayed regularly as incompetent family men—are not to be viewed as upstanding "role model[s] of masculinity, fatherhood or parenting."[32] Although without a doubt ineffectual, the fathers in these programs differ greatly from those on *Lost.* Their parenting practices may occasionally qualify as neglectful, but they are rarely depicted as purposefully abusive, and, unlike the majority of the fathers on *Lost,* they remain in the household as members of relatively traditional nuclear families.

Although many popular culture texts, televisual and otherwise, have housed problematic fathers, no narrative to date has showcased as many flawed father figures as *Lost.* The program offers a running commentary on father-child relationships; this focus even appears in episode titles such as "All the Best Cowboys Have Daddy Issues."[33] Perhaps this focus on the father can be attributed partially to the show's use of character backstory—its flashback-heavy narrative form that pairs events from the present with crucial scenes from the past. In fact, these story lines may be necessary because "stress between parents and children drives many of the personal histories of the characters on *Lost,* and is the reason many of these people were on Oceanic 815," the flight that landed them on the island where the narrative unfolds.[34] But, whatever the reason for this plethora of father-child story lines, their purposeful inclusion is hard to miss. In season 1, eighteen episodes included references to father-child relationships. In season 2, thirteen episodes developed such story lines. Season 3 included thirteen episodes with this focus. Season 4, a shortened season because of the 2007 writers' strike, had eight of fourteen episodes touching on this motif. In season 5, almost all the episodes—twelve of sixteen—further developed father-child conflicts or introduced new ones. And in season 6, even as the series reached its close, *Lost* continued its steadfast commitment to father-child story lines by expanding on existing relationships and debuting new ones in nine of its final sixteen episodes.

Fathers Who "Lost" Their Lives: Murder, Mayhem, and Magic

Lost offers viewers story lines that fall within the most outrageous of this category: fathers who died at their children's hands. Three story lines are devoted to the murder of evil fathers on the program: John Locke, who arranges for the murder of his con man father, Anthony Cooper; Benjamin Linus, who murders his abusive and neglectful father, Roger Linus, and leaves his body unburied; and Kate Austin, who murders her father, Wayne Janssen, in an attempt to save her mother from his perpetual physical abuse. While the deaths of these men and their physical absence from their children's lives are important, more important is the influence they wield from beyond. These murdered men are alluded to frequently in the series, appearing in the memories of their children through flashbacks and ultimately influencing their actions (and therefore the plot more broadly). One such example of the dead father's lingering presence can be seen in the story line devoted to Kate and Wayne Janssen. Kate is haunted, quite literally, by the memory of murdering her father. He appears in visions in the form of another character on the island and in the unlikely form of an unexplained horse that wanders around the tropical landscape. This notion of father haunting carries over, becoming a reoccurring plotline for a major father-child relationship arc on the show—that of the relationship between Jack and Christian Shephard. The relationship between Jack and his father results in regular visions, or seeming hallucinations, of the dead man on the island and later, after the rescue, off the island as well.

Lost's focus on the past might seem to conflict with a Jungian reading or, more accurately, Jungian analytical practices that emphasize the here and now rather than the patient's past. The flashbacks (or memories) and hallucinations found in *Lost,* however, are very much a part of the characters' "here and now." And it is largely through these memories—and, more important, the hallucinations—that the characters work through their father issues. This is significant because Jung saw value in hallucinations. One criticism that Jung had of Freud was that he made too great a distinction between hallucination and reality.[35] Jung's work was concerned with "psychological reality *as experienced by individuals* as opposed to what Freud termed 'actual reality.'"[36] The program often leads viewers to ponder the question "What is reality?"; this leaves them with an answer close to Jung's—that reality is variable and individualized. Jung did not view the unconscious as an enemy to be thwarted but as a potentially empowering, creative, and helpful force within individuals.[37] Therefore, the characters' hallucinations on the show can be read as therapeutic and self-healing rather than as detrimental to their mental stability.

Not all the characters, however, work through their father issues. Although *Lost* does provide detailed story lines devoted to the dead or murdered father, it offers up more examples of partially developed story lines hinting at the negative effects of the absent (although not always dead) father. This category would include numerous characters, such as Claire, Hurley, Anna Lucia, Sawyer, Eco, Desmond, and Miles. These absent fathers inadvertently affect the narrative through their children. For example, Claire's lack of a father (both her own father as well as her child's father) results in her insecurity in raising the child she gives birth to on the island. This child and its well-being become a recurrent focus of the show. Another character with absent father issues is Sawyer. The suicide of his father drives most of his pre-island existence and shapes his renegade personality both on and off the island. And the absence of other characters' fathers simply leaves them with personal problems that they must resolve even after the crash of Oceanic 815. For example, Hurley's flashbacks indicate that his compulsive eating disorder stems from the day his father abandoned Hurley's family. In their analysis of paternal failures on *Lost*, Holly Hassel and Nancy Chick note another set of characters that would fit loosely into this group: Jacob and the Man in Black. They argue that since these twins are "at the heart of the island's origin story," their fatherless childhood is quite important because they then have "no model of fatherhood, or even manhood."[38] They claim that this "fatherless origin story retroactively explains the inadequacies of fathers on the show."[39]

Not all absent fathers influence their children in such negative ways, however. As Bainbridge's analysis of popular culture texts suggests, more often the absent father exists within a narrative to force the protagonist into the hero's role.[40] *Lost* highlights this narrative function of the absent father in an early episode of season 1 devoted to the central father-child dynamic of Jack and Christian Shephard. In this episode a flashback reveals a confrontation between a ten-year-old Jack and his father after Jack has been severely beaten during his failed attempt to defend a school friend from bullies.[41] Of his failure his father remarks: "You don't want to be a hero; you don't want to save everyone, because when you fail you just don't have what it takes."[42] As is usual on the program, the flashback is relevant to the present happenings on the island: Jack is being called to the hero's role by the episode's end. In this episode, Jack's hallucinations start and he begins seeing his deceased father walking about on the island. He ultimately follows this supposed figment of his imagination through the jungle and ends up discovering a cove with drinkable springwater—something of which he and the other survivors are in desperate need. He returns with the good news and, despite his father's childhood warnings, rises as a leader with his infamous speech: "If we can't live together, we're going to die alone."[43] Jack's words unite the survivors, and for the rest of the series he remains cast as its central hero.

Lost Souls: The Scars of the Evil or Abusive Father

When *Lost* does offer a father who remains in his child's life, it is often a father the character could have done without. These depictions would include Sun's father, Mr. Paik, a corrupt businessman with mob connections; Penelope Widmore and Daniel Faraday's father, Charles Widmore, who systematically destroys his children's happiness; and Alex's father, the already mentioned Benjamin Linus, who becomes her surrogate father only after stealing Alex from her birth mother. Charles Widmore and Benjamin Linus both eventually contribute to the deaths of their children, making them fall easily into the classification *evil.* Charles Widmore quite directly sends his son, Daniel, to his death by ordering that he travel to the island on a scientific expedition, knowing that he will be murdered once there. And, in a much more shocking scene, Benjamin Linus stands by and watches a mercenary shoot his daughter, Alex, in the head after attempting to call the man's bluff during a hostage situation. The last words Alex would have heard were: "She's not my daughter. I stole her from a crazy woman when she was a baby. She's a pawn. She means nothing to me. I'm not coming out there, so if you want to kill her, go ahead and do it."[44]

What is interesting to note is that all the "evil" fathers on the show occupy leadership positions: Both Benjamin and Charles are the leaders of the island at different times, and both Charles and Paik are corporate powers off the island. Each of these men's political or business success comes at the expense of their children's happiness or lives. In this way the series echoes the claims that Feasey makes in *Masculinity and Popular Television* concerning medical heroes, like those found in *ER* and *House,* and crime heroes, like those found in *24* and *Spooks,* who all sacrifice family for career accomplishments.[45] There does remain a noteworthy difference, however: the characters of Feasey's analysis all work in fields in which their sacrifice ultimately is for the greater good of others; this is not the case for the powerful fathers portrayed on *Lost.* Also, in choosing the most powerful men to be the most evil fathers, *Lost* sets up an interesting analogy: the abusive, evil father as the corrupt, failed governmental leader.

The Estranged or Strained Father-Child Relationships

While many of the fathers on *Lost* cause their children serious emotional and physical damage, others exist to show less dramatized examples of strained father-child relationships. The motif of the estranged father-child relationship began in the very first episode of the show, when viewers were introduced to Michael Dawson and his son, Walt Lloyd, arguably one of the most important father-son dynamics the show offers, after Jack and Christian. Their fellow survivors on the island witnessed their struggle to cope with becoming father and son after years apart, and they often engaged in an ongoing commentary about their relationship struggles. Although Michael ultimately goes to extreme lengths to see that his son is able to leave the island, his initial frustration and discomfort with fatherhood are noted by his fellow castaways. In one episode devoted to this father-son duo, a passing comment from Hurley to Jack showcases this fact: "He seems to hate it, doesn't he? Being a dad."[46] Though Michael and Walt's relationship sparks the earliest conversations on the show concerning this theme, other characters refer to their strained father-child relationships as the series progresses. This list would include Charlie, Sayid, Claire, Tom, Miles, and Ilana. Of all the estranged father-child relationships on the show, the only one that nears repair is that of Hurley and David Reyes—a father who abandoned his child for seventeen years only to reappear when his son won the lottery. One additional relationship that hints at a father-child reconciliation is that of Miles and his father, Dr. Pierre Chang. It turns out that Chang did not abandon his child for selfish reasons but sacrificed his relationship with him (and perhaps his life) to save both him and his mother. This revelation in season 5 potentially shifts his father from this category and into the next to be discussed, the suffering good father. With *Lost*'s plethora of absentee fathers, its familial depictions mirror realistic societal patterns. In many ways these fictional fathers align with Zoja's research concerning the disappearing role of the father in American society during the twenty-first century and studies concerning the current crisis of masculinity. Regarding the latter, David Magill argues that, indeed, *Lost* is "a meditation on masculinity."[47] He also reads the show's "narrative of wounded white masculinity" as symbolizing "the wounds of war" felt by America after 9/11.[48] In this way, his analysis of the show hints at the way *Lost*'s fathers represent post-9/11 fears.

One final father-child relationship that could be classified as estranged is one that is also an anomaly since the father was actually, for the majority of the character's life, a caring, consistent presence in his child's life. Jin was raised by Mr. Kwon, a fisherman in a poor village. Jin is so ashamed of his background that he lies to everyone, even his wife, about his past, claiming that his parents are dead. Viewers are unaware of what type of father Kwon was until Sun, Jin's wife, learns of his existence and visits him. He explains to her that he had been involved with a prostitute who left Jin in his care as an infant. Although Kwon never knew for sure that the child was actually his, he raised him as his son.[49] Quite obviously, against the backdrop of horrific father figures, Kwon represents one of the few good fathers that *Lost* depicts. He also aligns with most of these good fathers in an interesting way: most of them are not fathers by the traditional definition. Most of the positive paternal figures are father stand-ins—stepfathers or surrogate fathers. Another example is Sam Austen, Kate's stepfather. Sam raised Kate as his own, concealing that the abusive, alcoholic Wayne Janssen is her biological father—a fact that he knew would hurt her. Although much of Kate's past is linked to pain, she and Sam had a very positive relationship during her childhood, and she looks back on it fondly during her time on the island.

The Price of Playing the "Good" Father

While *Lost* makes such positive representations few and far between, it also combines them with a surprising narrative twist. Most of the good father figures are punished or meet their untimely demise. Two key examples are Charlie and Jin. Charlie had struggled throughout his early years with various problems. He often played a fatherly role to his drug-addicted brother, Liam, resolving the problems Liam caused during their early years spent playing together in their band, Drive Shaft. The roles eventually switch, however, when Liam goes through rehabilitation and becomes a functioning family man and Charlie takes over his role as a heroin addict. In the first few seasons of the show, Charlie constantly struggles to believe that he will ever be good enough to take care of someone other than himself. His friendship with a fellow castaway, the pregnant Claire, however, eventually develops into a romantic relationship wherein he becomes a surrogate father for her son, Aaron. Although the path is not problem-free for the three of them in their island quasi family, Charlie assumes the role of a good father. But his duration in that role is short-lived, as he soon becomes aware that he is destined to die soon. Rather than trying to dodge fate, he gives in to it when he realizes that his death can save all his friends on the island—most important, Claire and Aaron. In a touching scene before he dives to the ocean bottom to willingly enter his watery tomb, he takes off his ring, a family heirloom, and places it in Aaron's crib.[50] This coupling of death with acts of fatherly protection is not isolated. Another character who shows the price a good father pays is Jin. Although he is only presumed dead (during a cliff-hanger break between seasons 4 and 5), his act of dying in an effort to stop a freighter from exploding, after ensuring that his wife and child make it to safety, again shows that no rewards are given to the fathers who act in the best interest of their children.

Many questions arise from these few story lines. Why not let these positive father representations exist as foils for the numerous negative ones? After all, most narratives rely on such good-versus-evil character pairings. What exactly is the show suggesting by allowing these visions of the good father to be fleeting? What does it mean that these characters' efforts to protect their children result in their downfall and death? The answer may lie in the parallels that can be made between the fathers or leaders on the show and the figureheads or leaders of American culture. The answer may be that *Lost* is simply not interested in depicting positive father figures because the program is much more concerned with the negative ones existing both within and outside its narrative constraints.

The Paternal Hand of Fate

With seventy-three episodes devoted to developing father-child story lines and twenty-three characters with "daddy" issues, this is not an accidental motif but a purposefully developed theme. But the question remains: Why? Why would a complex show like *Lost* devote so much of its narrative material to father-child dynamics? Such motivations may tie into its devotion to character development.

With its flashbacks, and later flash-forwards and flash-sideways, the program intentionally allows viewers to parse the characters' motives for their actions and the experiences that shape their personalities. Some of the most influential experiences that shape an individual's life are those of father-child interactions, and the father's influence is tied to the child's fate. On this, Jung wrote: "If we normal people examine our lives, we too perceive how a mighty hand guides us without fail to our destiny, and not always is this hand a kindly one. Often we call it the hand of God or of the devil, thereby expressing, unconsciously but correctly, a highly important psychological fact: that the power which shapes the life of the psyche has the character of an autonomous personality. . . . The personification of this source goes back in the first place to the father."[51]

For Jung, the actual, physical father may not have this all-powerful influence, but the father figure often becomes a symbolic representative of this imagined force. Sometimes, however, the actual, physical father does act in this direct role. For example, the majority of the program's fathers (the absent or dead fathers) would fall into Jung's category of the "nonexistent" father. In his studies, Jung found that "without the father's emotional support . . . it becomes almost insurmountably difficult for a child to be properly born and confirmed in his own identity."[52] Since many of the characters on *Lost* struggle with identity issues, the father issues are in place to account for these problems. Although the show's writers and producers may be as well versed in psychology as they are in philosophy and physics, an alternative explanation for their focus on the father figure exists.

Searching for a Savior

Like the programs discussed in chapter 1, *Lost* is a show with salvation as a central theme. All the characters are physically awaiting rescue from the island and are constantly in need of salvation from mysterious forces, outside threats, and communal disturbances; often they need to be saved from themselves (or their pasts). Symbolically, the figure who most often plays the role of savior in a person's life is a parent or, more stereotypically, a father.

Part of the cultural myth of the father is that he should be a strong, empowering force, able to protect and improve his family. According to psychological theory, when this cultural myth plays out correctly, the child's developmental process is a more positive one. When fathers fail to protect their children (by absence, neglect, or abuse), these children grow up in a perpetual search for safety, mistrusting themselves and others. This is clearly seen in a host of characters on the show.

With the focus on these failed fathers, however, they must represent more than just a gathering of poor parents. Thus, the question arises: What do fathers represent or for what is fatherhood a symbol? Bainbridge argues that "the existence of fatherhood as a cultural construction . . . permits fathers to exist as father figures for a much wider group of people than just their biological offspring."[53] Therefore, father figures, persons not related to individuals by blood and perhaps not even connected to them, can take on the father's symbolic role and wield psychological power. This echoes Bader's argument that the nation, through its leader, takes on the symbolic role of a father and is sought for protection and strength.[54] Assuming this transference to the national father is happening on *Lost,* the program is not simply critiquing individual fathers. As a cultural product of post-9/11 America, the show is instead making a more indirect statement about the "father" figures of the country.

Lost as a Product of the American Post-9/11 Cultural Climate

Cultural artifacts are often the product of their time, and *Lost* is the product of a "bad dad." It was written and produced when failing government and weak figureheads prevailed. President George Walker Bush was, arguably, a man with his own "daddy issues." The Bush administration had ulterior motives for entering into the 2003 war against Iraq, and an address President Bush made six months before that associates these motives with fatherly influences. Before the war, when addressing the Senate on homeland security issues in 2002, Bush discussed the threat posed by Saddam Hussein. In this list he included Saddam's failure to comply with United Nations' regulations; his advancement of chemical, biological, and nuclear weapons programs; and his hatred toward the United States.[55] In an aside, Bush said, "After all, this is the guy who tried to kill my dad."[56] Bush was referring to the alleged assassination attempt of former President Bush while he was visiting Kuwait during the Clinton administration.[57] Revenge was not the primary motive for the Bush administration's declaration of war, but this affect-driven presidential afterthought is intriguing nonetheless. Zoja argues that "there is a relationship between the feelings that a leader awakens in his country's citizens and those which a father, in the same country and period, awakens in his children."[58] The most prominent feeling awakened in the United States during the Bush administration was fear—to such an extent that it was the shared national affect in the first decade of the twenty-first century (if not longer). Reflecting this fear, *Lost*'s fathers provoke responses of fear and insecurity in their children on the small screen.

Lost remediates many post-9/11 fears throughout its run, discussing topics ranging from torture to biological warfare to the threat of governmental surveillance. In *Living Lost: Why We're All Stuck on the Island,* J. Wood explains how *Lost* accomplishes this:

> What *Lost* does so successfully is take these very real concerns straight off the front pages, abstract them into their psychological impression, and then crystallize that sense back into the framework of the narrative. These characters aren't being threatened by otherworldly aliens or vampires, creatures normally only seen on the

> screen or in pulp fiction; this situation involves the psychodynamics of terrorism that the contemporary audience experiences in the everyday world and plays it out on television 24 times a year. As such, *Lost* performs a very necessary function: It gives a narrative (and a safely distant context) to a real-felt sense of trauma. By giving these abstract ideas a tangible narrative with a beginning and ending each week, that sense of terror is contained by the show, and thus becomes something that might actually be manageable.[59]

In Wood's reading, "the show abstracts and co-opts our very real concerns over the War on Terror" and becomes a sort of "repository for the sense of distress that has been generated, rightly or wrongly, through our media, government, and the collective cultural response to such voices."[60] As Sarah Burcon aptly points out, the program also acts as a sort of wish fulfillment, showcasing viewers' desire to return to a pre-9/11 state.[61]

In this way, the series explores the notion of post-trauma survival. Wood notes that what the fictional survivors on *Lost* have that most Americans do not is membership in a "group that has all survived the same unbelievable trauma," one that supports "both the individual and the individual's need to be part of the group. . . . This aspect of the psychology of the show shouldn't look unfamiliar because it's what most people think happened after our own big plane crashes on September 11, 2001. But that kind of response doesn't just automatically" occur.[62] Wood compares the sacrifices made following WWII to those of 9/11:

> [The same] things didn't really happen after September 11th, as we were told that our comfy lifestyles would not have to change and no sacrifices beyond simple symbolic gestures were necessary—just think of all the flags posted on gas-guzzling cars in the months after September 11th, while next to nothing was done to lessen U.S. dependence on a fossil fuel economy and its crazy market fluctuations due to events in the places that provide a good deal of those fossil fuels. In its own manner, *Lost* became a model for how we could have responded as a group after a trauma, but weren't able to or chose not to.[63]

Although *Lost* does offer a community united, it also delivers fear through narrative moments grounded in the problematic us-versus-them binary. Although this opposition has long been used to stimulate dramatic conflict, in *Lost* it is tied to the media rhetoric of 9/11. Bader explains that the "feelings of insecurity and disconnectedness that plague us in our personal and social lives" are often "blamed on the actions of some 'other' who is then demeaned and attacked."[64] This problematic practice of "projection is deliberately used by conservatives to solidify their base. By creating an imaginary 'us' and 'them,' they can then promise satisfaction of deep and legitimate longings for a community safe from both real and illusory threats posed from the outside."[65] This us-versus-them binary also exists to nurture a superiority complex common to U.S. citizens.

In *Lost* the us-versus-them binary showcases itself within the community of survivors but also externally between the community and "the Others." The inner group conflict begins in the second part of the pilot episode when Sawyer accuses Sayid of being a terrorist and having caused the plane to crash, simply because of his middle-Eastern background.[66] But the mysterious "Others" exist as the dangerous "them" that spark fear in the survivors throughout the first few seasons of the show. In fact, the island leaders sometimes capitalize on this fear to condone unethical behavior. For example, as the unofficial leader of the castaways, Jack allows Sayid to torture a captured "Other" (Ben) in order to extract information from him. And on the other side of the island, both Widmore and Linus (each a temporary leader of the "Others") participate in massacres to ensure their community's survival.

The term *Other* is packed with cultural baggage, but, in a post-9/11 American cultural context, does it necessarily mean "terrorist"? Wood answers this question directly: "Are the Others terrorists? Not exactly, not in the popular sense: Terrorists need to be dehumanized in the rhetoric used to describe them in order to reinforce their difference from us. This often comes in the form of turning them into animals and monsters. The Others don't use the same tactics we've come to associate with terrorism, like beheadings and suicide bombings."[67] Michael Newbury likewise distances the behaviors of the Others on the program from those of terrorists in the real world. In his view, the Others behave like cold-war nation-states, relying on the technological superiority of their military and surveillance systems.[68] Overall, many scholars caution against simple readings of the show. Jesse Kavadlo argues that reading "*Lost* as a political parable risks reducing the show to a cardboard morality play."[69] Likewise, Wood clarifies: "It's not as if *Lost*'s writers and producers actively set out to create some sort of allegory of the times. When you're steeped in the culture (as an artist or consumer), some kind of reaction to events and circumstances will exercise itself through a work, whether directly, obliquely, or actively ignoring those circumstances."[70] Wood suggests that we are "stuck in a state of unconscious distress because we don't have any clear grasp on what it is we're supposed to be afraid of" and, therefore, "can't really confront that distress directly [because] we just don't know enough about it."[71] As a result, the fear we feel as a nation after the attacks unconsciously resurfaces and seeks resolution in narrative spaces through repetition. And, in the case of *Lost,* this repetition often comes in the form of quite telling father-child conflicts. Regardless, whether inadvertently or purposefully, the program ultimately reminds viewers of the source of their fears: the post-9/11 rhetoric concerning terrorism and the hyperbolic depictions of terrorists made readily available by government figures in the wake of the September 11 attacks. With its direct attention to "othering," *Lost* asks its viewers to contemplate the consequences of this practice and invites critiques of those who perpetuate it: governmental "fathers."

Conclusion

Twenty-first-century fictional narratives such as *Lost* are full of flailing father figures whose prevalence is indicative of cultural problems outside those fictive realms. For decades scholars have been analyzing televised portrayals of fathers as simple familial symbols—the fictional representatives of cultural norms, or, more accurately, cultural desires. And though these characters may represent our societal wish list for a perfect family (as they may have in the days of *Father Knows Best* and *Leave It to Beaver*), and though some may exist to work through current cultural concerns about shifting familial structures (as in the declining presence and importance of fathers in the twenty-first century), today these fictional constructs may represent much more. Somewhere along the line there may have been an evolution from fatherly portrayals as familial symbols to fatherly portrayals as signifiers of national affective states. A cigar may be just a cigar, but it seems that in twenty-first-century narratives a "father" is no longer just a father.

5

The Trauma of Post-Apocalyptic Motherhood

The Walking Dead's *Social Commentary on Contemporary Gender Roles*

Television shows featuring plane crashes, toppling buildings, and governmental crises broadcast their post-9/11 influences loudly and clearly. The proliferation of post-apocalyptic and supernatural narratives that rose to popularity during the early decades of the twenty-first century, however, also reveal cultural anxieties that linger years after the terrorist attacks. One such example is AMC's *The Walking Dead* (2010–present), a program about a core group of survivors fighting to stay alive through a zombie apocalypse. Originally centered on a former Georgia-based sheriff, Rick Grimes (Andrew Lincoln), and his family, the narrative continues on to showcase how strangers from all walks of life can form familial relations, community, and friendship even in the direst circumstances. Despite this one hopeful theme that weaves itself throughout the various seasons of the show, the program is undeniably dark and—like the post-9/11 television programs discussed in chapter 1—often presents fear-based story lines centered on similar themes: survival, community, justice, revenge, resurrection, and the dark side of humanity. Zombie narratives (much like their sister narratives, vampire tales, which will be discussed in chapter 6) also highlight an us-versus-them binary—a fear of a dangerous "other" lurking in the shadows ready to tear apart communities. Like chapter 4 in its analysis of *Lost,* this chapter reads this program as one that is working through cultural concerns lingering from the terrorist attacks, but also as one that reveals anxieties related to shifting gender norms—some of which stem from the rhetoric that surfaced immediately after 9/11.

In regard to the latter, *The Walking Dead* both conforms to and rejects the stereotype of "the emotional woman" as well as the association of women with nurture more generally and motherhood specifically. The program's main characters include a prominent father-son duo, but as the seasons stretch on it is almost devoid of any mother-child relationships—although it is not lacking in terms of children who mourn mothers and vice versa.[1] As part of its complicated critique of twenty-first-century gender roles, *The Walking Dead* presents motherhood as both horrific and traumatic. This chapter analyzes the ways in which the show uses one particular character, Carol Peletier (Melissa McBride), to carry out its gender commentary. As she progresses from the role of the emotional woman (an abused wife and mourning mother) to that of the hardened female (an exiled group leader and child killer at various intervals), she eventually pays the price for deviating from expected gendered behavior, and then—surprisingly—transcends such punishment (at least temporarily). This chapter eventually turns to reactions from fans and critics concerning one particular scene from season 5—deemed by media critics as one of the most horrific, disturbing, and shocking moments of fictional television—wherein Carol, a surrogate mother figure, is forced to assassinate the child she was tasked with caring for. One might assume that the emotional reactions viewers had to this plot twist would indicate that various societal expectations for women are so ingrained in our culture that even post-apocalyptic programs about hordes of zombies are expected to conform to them. Analyzing fan commentary concerning this character—much of which celebrates her deviance from traditional gender norms—suggests, however, that the violent landscape of the zombie narrative might be an ideal space in which to interrogate conceptions of femininity more broadly, and maternity more specifically.

When a Zombie Isn't Just a Zombie

Zombies have long served as metaphors within fictional narratives, allowing the horrific flesh-eating undead to represent a host of societal concerns. In "Go On: Bring a Zombie to Life," Jonathan Maberry discusses how authors use zombies as a tool to establish a threat that then motivates the characters who are faced with surviving it.[2] Like many dystopian or post-apocalyptic story lines, the zombie narrative allows the author almost to skip the exposition, letting him or her off the hook for crafting a backstory that fully explains how the societal downfall came to be. In many of these tales, the zombies simply get to exist unquestioned, standing in for any number of threats ailing contemporary society, allowing the writer "to explore the dynamic of ordinary humans facing a shared crisis and how that crisis impacts them."[3] For example, the familiar figure of the zombie "participates in narratives of the body, of life and death, of good and evil," gesturing "to alterity, racism, [and] species-ism."[4] In their most literal readings, of course, zombie narratives, like other plague narratives, can be read as revealing cultural concerns about "contemporary illnesses such as AIDS, SARS, or H1N1."[5] Many of these texts, however, reveal anxieties ranging from economic and national security worries to concerns focusing on environmental and domestic issues. It is perhaps the wide range of concerns simultaneously affecting society—particularly in the United States—that has led to the increasing popularity of this genre in the twenty-first century. In his article "Why Are Zombies So Popular," Dan Birlew points to the various issues afflicting the United States in the new millennium as being likely inspirations for this genre revival: "Things have been pretty rough for Americans . . . : hijackers are flying passengers into the sides of buildings; the economy has crashed not just once, but a few times; people who've worked extremely hard their entire lives are now out of jobs; everyone's getting paid half or less of what they used to; people have invested their life savings into homes that are now more valuable as scrap."[6]

But, to be fair, scholars were attending to the allegorical nature of the zombie narrative well before the onset of the twenty-first century.[7]

Perhaps unsurprisingly, for decades scholars have read zombie narratives as providing commentary on cultural consumption, capitalism, and related issues. Adam Baker reads contemporary apocalyptic fiction like the zombie narrative as representing "our fear of poverty, our dread of downward mobility."[8] In "We *Are* the Walking Dead," Gerry Canavan argues that zombies exist as a capitalistic critique, since they "leave nothing in their wake besides endless copies of themselves, making [them] the perfect metaphor not only for how capitalism transforms its subjects but also for its relentless and devastating virologic march across the globe."[9] Similarly, in his essay "Zombie Geographies and the Undead City," Jeff May views the zombie narrative as one that critiques urbanization and communities' increasing codependency on cities.[10] In related commentary, Michael Newbury argues that zombie narratives address environmental concerns and the potential collapse of the agricultural industry.[11]

Like all creatures at the center of a horror narrative, however, the zombie also shines a light on identity-centered conflicts.[12] For example, Jon Stratton discusses how the language used in zombie fiction mirrors the fear-based language used in Western communities to discuss displaced people. Analyzing

European newspaper reports, he highlights articles that refer to "hordes," "floods," or "tides" of Kurdish refugees (or "aliens") "storming" Europe in "mass exodus."[13] Drawing parallels between the rhetoric used to discuss the asylum seekers and the language used to describe zombie invasions in popular fiction, Stratton argues that the latter serves to point out the dehumanization of the former.[14] This can be seen in U.S. anti-immigration rhetoric during the 2010s as well. For example, in the lead-up to the 2018 midterm elections, President Trump frequently used words such as *invasion* to discuss the "caravan" of Central Americans crossing over the Mexican border to seek refuge in the United States.[15]

With a long history of the zombie standing in for a host of real-world "othered" people, it was only to be expected that the genre would be called on to work through concerns related to terrorism in the twenty-first century. Many scholars have analyzed the popularity of *The Walking Dead,* and the recent zombie craze more generally, as a product of the September 11 terrorist attacks in particular and the ways in which the United States responded to them.[16] In his article "Are Zombies the Guilty Conscience of Post-9/11 America," Will Nixon suggests that "the zombie renaissance" represents American's reactions "to 9/11 and the mess" the government has made of global relations ever since the attacks.[17] Similarly, Andrea Peyser suggests that *The Walking Dead* and its prequel, *Fear the Walking Dead,* can be considered "allegories of governmental paralysis and official incompetence."[18]

The Walking Dead's Exploration of Survival and Community after Tragedy

The Walking Dead rests on a central post-9/11-related question: Where do we go from here? Zombie narratives often highlight two possible ways to deal with the post-apocalyptic world: survive or rebuild. Story lines that focus on surviving often showcase central characters on the run doing anything possible to survive on a daily basis—even if it means a lone existence. Story lines that focus on rebuilding highlight the importance of community, structure, and group cohesiveness; they include central characters who (sometimes) place limits on what they are willing to do to survive, which, for the most part, include not being willing to exist alone. *The Walking Dead* showcases both of these survival mind-sets throughout various characters who make the transition from lone survival to group living (e.g., Michonne, Bob, Gabriel, Enid) and various central conflicts that ground the individual seasons.

The third season of *The Walking Dead* highlights these two warring mind-sets—survival versus community—through the parallel story lines unfolding: the core group held up at the prison and the inhabitants of the gated community of Woodbury. The group that viewers have come to know and love (Rick's crew) hold a bit of both mind-sets: they are a community of sorts, a surrogate family system, but they find themselves primarily on the run playing the role of survivor.[19] They keep attempting momentary respites that could be viewed as community building (e.g., life on the farm in season 2; life at the prison in season 3; life in Alexandria in seasons 5 and 6), but these are always abandoned when their main goal must again be to simply survive. They do have limits on what they will do to achieve this goal, but viewers have seen these get stretched thin over time.

One of the primary settings of season 3 is Woodbury, a town led by the Governor (David Morrissey). Woodbury exists as a faux utopia showing how there is a chance for normalcy and life after tragedy. At least, that is what it seems to be at first glance. It is a seemingly normal town (quaint even, a throwback to yesteryear), and the residents seem safe and happy—no one is on the run and, before recent events, there had not been a death among them in quite some time. But viewers quickly learn (if they did not guess immediately) that things are not quite what they seem in this happy town. The Governor is willing to go to great extremes to ensure their safety, including murder. But his motivation is not purely altruistic: his scientific projects (experiments on captured zombies) are in place because he longs to cure his infected daughter (whom he has kept locked away in his living quarters), and all his actions really seem to be aimed at ensuring his place as a leader and a father figure to this new generation of survivors.

Usually those existing on the "community" side of the community-survivor continuum are portrayed as the more morally sound; after all, they have the betterment of society on their side. *The Walking Dead* flips this notion on its head. In analyzing this particular season, many have asked: Is it too much of a stretch to read the Governor, who gives his charismatic speeches about community, freedom, and the future of humanity, as an allegory for George W. Bush? Was the hypocrisy of the Woodbury leadership meant to be a metaphor for the politics of the Bush administration? Can we read the staged fight scenes (between humans and zombies whose teeth had been removed) as alluding to the smoke-and-mirrors media spectacles of the post-9/11 era?

Media critics have specifically pointed out the episode "Made to Suffer," wherein the Governor calls Rick and his group terrorists, not once but twice.[20]

The story line with the Governor highlights the show's commentary on the war on terror and the position Americans have been placed in after 9/11: they have been asked to sacrifice constitutional freedoms for the sake of national security.[21] As a roundtable discussion of *The Walking Dead* pointed out: "The Governor has earned the unwavering loyalty of the Woodbury residents by offering them the security and the semblance of the lives they used to have. They live in actual houses, have an ample supply of food and alcohol, and walk down zombie-free streets. In return, they agree to give up certain freedoms, and don't ask too many questions about how the Governor ensures their security."[22]

Further, the language used by the Governor mirrors the post-9/11 rhetoric circulated by the Bush administration. He not only labels the main characters as terrorists but instills fear in his community by claiming that the newcomers want to "destroy" them and their way of life. The fact that the Woodbury residents are in the dark about why Rick's group actually invaded the town—to rescue their captured friends—points toward the ways in which the secrecy surrounding the government's war on terror "may be dulling our moral sense."[23] DJ Pangburn analyzes the scene that best underscores these parallels:

> At Woodbury's makeshift arena, where militia members have fought surrounded by chained, de-jawed zombies (no doubt a nod to Rome's violent gladiatorial games and imperial dictatorship), the Governor makes a speech. It is, in a sense, a speech made thousands of times in human history: demagoguery crafted to whip plebeians into fearful, patriotic automatons. . . . In the Governor's speech one hears the echoes of Marc Antony's eulogy for Caesar, saying Brutus and Cassius' assassination plot was an attack on Rome itself. And, of course, we hear the echoes still ranging the American landscape of Bush's post-9/11 speeches, such as the oft-repeated phrase "They hate our freedoms."[24]

The Governor eventually is thwarted, but other figures rise to fill the role he played in posing moral dilemmas about the costs of survival.

As the series continues on, it is obvious that the show is purposely casting post-apocalypse communities as surviving only through extreme measures and questionable ethical decisions that reveal the potentially horrific side of our human nature. Outside the group, this theme is found in season 4, when the morals of the "good" survivor group are contrasted with those of the "bad" residents of Terminus. Terminus is a railway community that originally attempted to act as a sanctuary for all survivors but—after having been repaid by invaders who stole, tortured, and killed them—turned just as vicious as those who inflicted such injuries on them. They survive by luring unsuspecting refugees into their camp, only to take their positions and then literally consume them, having resorted to cannibalism to survive. Season 5 offers yet another variation of this motif when it pits the main cast against the survivors in Atlanta's Grady Memorial Hospital, where the medical facility exists in a sort of police state as the powers that be save only enough people from the local area to help sustain their existence and turn a blind eye to the abuse of patients and staff alike. Season 6 offers not one but two groups that pose as human threats to the main characters: the Wolves and the Saviors, who both attempt to undermine the group's security within their gated community in Alexandria through manipulation and acts of extreme violence. Seasons 7 and 8 offer up a plethora of communities that have formed diverse survival groups representing a range of social structures and moral codes. Some of these end up working together to fight, arguably, the show's most extreme villain: Negan (Jeffery Dean Morgan), the leader of the Saviors.

The theme of dehumanization is highlighted by conflicts within the main core of characters as well. The return of Morgan Jones (Lennie James) in season 5 allows for him to be positioned as the moral compass, in contrast to the changing leadership of both Carol and Rick. (Carol's escalating acts of violence in seasons 4, 5, and 6 will be discussed later in this chapter.) Conversations between long-term survivors address the danger of losing one's humanity in the face of great adversity. As the series progresses, Rick is transformed into "a wartime leader, trained by dark experience to be ever vigilant, ruthless toward outsiders and trustful of almost no one."[25] When Rick's paranoia finds him dangerously close to crossing ethical lines, Glenn notes: "I want us to be safe, too, but I can't give up everything else." It is in moments like these that Rick, perhaps surprisingly, becomes a different iteration of the Governor, acting as a "metaphor for the post-9/11 American security state" or perhaps the paranoid citizens that it has created.[26] Philip Simpson analyzes Rick's struggle to assimilate into the domestic setting of Alexandria during seasons 5 and 6 as representing the struggles many viewers at home have while watching the show: "We have feared and fought each other and much of the world for far too long and we're no longer sure how to live peacefully even if the opportunity is handed to us."[27]

The Walking Dead continually points toward the horrors of surviving at any cost, suggesting—at least during the first half of the series—that protecting one's community from "invaders" through any means is immoral. That the fictional events of the show's early seasons unfolded against the backdrop of real-world debates about Homeland Security practices, foreign policies, and horrific accounts of the lengths our own country went through in its efforts to be safe (e.g., "enhanced interrogation techniques") is no coincidence. This show, along with so many others, offers viewers a chance to wrestle with the ethical dilemmas faced by fictional communities in peril in order to provide social commentary on the ways in which our real communities deal with their own conflicts. There is something horrific about imagining a world plagued by zombies, but there is something even more horrific about realizing that, in some ways, the world we are living in might be just as horrible.

The Walking Dead's Post-Apocalyptic Gender Portrayals

Though characters like the Governor and Rick serve as interesting fictional figures to study as metaphors representing real moral dilemmas, their positions as male leaders afford them privileges not always granted to the females in similar circumstances. Carol serves as the best example of a female character who serves a similar narrative role, but the ways in which her character is gendered at different points during the series complicate the social commentary her acts are intended to reveal. Her characterization, however, also ultimately serves to critique traditional gender roles in important ways. One of the more notable ways in which Carol draws attention to stereotypical gender expectations involves the age-old problematic binary that associates men with reason and women with emotion (privileging the former over the latter, of course).

Different historical moments often resurrect or repurpose gendered portrayals of emotion for particular reasons. That the post-9/11 moment has done this is not surprising. In *The Terror Dream: Fear and Fantasy in Post-9/11 America,* Susan Faludi convincingly showcases how feminism was attacked in the aftermath of 9/11 as one of the supposed reasons for the vulnerability of the United States. In the days following 9/11, Faludi herself was bombarded by calls from various journalists who wanted her opinion on how "9/11 pushed feminism off the map" or sounded its "death knell."[28] Reporters asked for her opinion on phenomena such as "the return of the manly man" and the trend of women becoming "more feminine" after 9/11 (and, therefore, in their opinions, less feminist).[29] There was an oddly celebratory nature to some journalistic articles that predicted the death of feminism after the attacks. For example, in a piece titled "Hooray for Men," Mona Charen wrote: "Perhaps the new climate of danger . . . will quiet the anti-male agitation we've endured for so long."[30] And, in an attack on specific feminists, such as Susan Sontag, articles went to press such as Ann Coulter's "Women We'd Like to See . . . in Burkas."[31]

And, in the weeks and months after 9/11, it was not just self-identified feminists who felt the effects of this cultural shift. Faludi notes: "Soon after the World Trade Center vaporized into two biblical plumes of smoke, another vanishing act occurred on television sets and newspaper pages across the country. Women began disappearing. . . . Three weeks after 9/11, the number of opinion pieces written by female writers at *The New York Times* had dropped from 22 percent to 9 percent and women's representation on Sunday news talk shows plummeted, decreasing by nearly 40 percent."[32]

When women were featured in the media, it was not the strong women of earlier days being showcased. Women who garnered the most attention needed to fit the script of the moment; they needed to be vulnerable and in need of male protection. The 9/11 widows fit well into this narrative and, therefore, became the focus of the media frenzy. These women were desirable because "they weren't ambitious careerists trading commodities on the eighty-fourth floor [of the World Trade Center]. They were at home that day tending to the hearth, models of all-American housewifery."[33] Along with these images of women in need of saving were, of course, those who could do the saving: men. Some of the most iconic images associated with 9/11 are of first responders who became symbolic representations of the nation's courage and resilience.

Years later it seems that some cultural representations still want to depict the two genders along these affective lines, and Carol's character oscillates between reinforcing and rejecting this stereotype. Her early story lines focused on her status as an abused wife and later a grieving mother. As the seasons progress, this emotionality slowly recedes as she is portrayed as more emotionally hardened. She is depicted as a strong, perhaps even masculine character gaining a leadership role in the survivors' camp. When she first acts in ways that evoke a sense of masculine power and autonomy, however, she is punished for it.

In season 3, for example, Carol begins training the children of this community in survival tactics, which causes some of her fellow survivors to question her position as a role model. This season also finds Carol making the call to kill two fellow survivors who are infected by a plague that threatens to wipe out the entire group. Despite the fact that the group's leader, Rick, has previously made morally questionable, unilateral decisions on behalf of the community, he casts Carol out as a punishment for her action. In this example, Carol, who grows away from her status as emotional woman and into a symbolic stand-in for the rational man—making the cold and calculating but logical call to protect the group—is punished for not behaving according to social norms.

This sexist plot development was completely in line with the show's gender bias, as many have noted the program's "patriarchal problem."[34] For example, one critic applied the comic book writer Gail Simone's notion of *fridging* to the show. Simone coined the phrase "women in refrigerators" to refer to the array of female characters who were "depowered, raped, or cut up and stuck in the refrigerator" in popular comics.[35] Since then, feminist comic book fans have adopted the term *fridging* to note the pointless death of a female character in order to fuel a male character's pain and narrative action.[36] This happens repeatedly on *The Walking Dead*. Along these lines, Sara Century, a media reviewer for *Bitch* magazine, notes the shows problematic portrayals of weak women, asking: "Does someone want to do a tally of how many women in *The Walking Dead* attempt suicide, go insane, or give up their authority by deferring to men? Because every single female character does at least one of those things. Just giving you a head's up."[37] In a piece for *Dame* magazine, Laura Bogart analyzes the show's lack of gender complexity, examining the ways in which the show undoes even its strongest female characters. For example, "The . . . formidable female warrior, Michonne, is treated like a dreadlocked, katana-wielding Man With No Name—until a rather bland, predictable attempt to humanize, or, rather, feminize her. Of course, [viewers discover she lost] a young child in the apocalypse. Of course, after the loss of her child, she ceases to feel like a person. Of course, the only way for her to heal is to bond with the hero's baby daughter."[38]

Considering the show's general treatment of women (at least in its early seasons), when Carol was punished for not toeing the gender line, it was not a surprise. What was surprising, though, was what happened when she returned from exile.

The Evolution of Carol: *The Walking Dead* Undergoes a Patriarchal Shift

Carol's ejection from the group is not permanent, and when she returns the patriarchal center of the show begins to shift. In season 4, she reunites with part of the community after they have all been forced (once again) on the run. She ends up joining one other adult survivor, Tyreese (Chad Coleman), who has ended up traveling with two sisters, Lizzie (Brighton Sharbino) and Mika (Kyla Kendey), and Rick's infant daughter, Judith. Despite Carol's having progressed far from her original matronly characterization, these episodes in which she travels with this set forces her back into playing the role of maternal stand-in for the children she is protecting. Her role as surrogate mother to this trio of girls is terminated in season 4's episode "The Grove," which aired on March 16, 2014.[39]

An oversimplified summary of the episode would be as follows: Carol and Tyreese find temporary shelter in an idyllic cottage in the woods. Carol works to continue developing survival skills in the two sisters: the gentle Mika is resistant to killing anything (she refuses to shoot a deer, commenting that they could just eat peaches instead), and the troubled Lizzie (who suffers from an unspecified emotional disorder) refuses to believe that the walkers are not human (the opening scene of the episode foreshadows a moment when she attempts to play tag with an attacking walker). Even after a group of zombies attack them and they are all forced to defend themselves, Lizzie holds fast to her belief that the walkers are not necessarily dangerous. So sure is she of her worldview that she decides to stab her younger sister to death in order to prove to the adults that Mika could change into a zombie and not be a threat. Viewers are privy only to the aftermath of this violent act, as they discover this incident just as Carol and Tyreese do, returning to the property to find Lizzie in front her sister's dead body, still holding a knife, and baby Judith within reach and apparently next for the kill. They manage to lure Lizzie away from the scene, Carol is forced to stab Mika in the head—an act that prevents humans from transforming into zombies—to prevent the change Lizzie so desperately wanted to witness, and a decision is made. Carol tells Tyreese that Lizzie can't be around other people, and then she takes the girl out to the field, tells her to "look at the flowers," raises a gun to the back of her head, and kills her.[40]

Fan reaction to the episode was pretty consistent; those live tweeting the episode noted how shocking, sad, and horrifying it was, but when Carol's role in Lizzie's death was specifically mentioned, most voiced sympathy for the difficult situation she was placed in. For example, one Twitter user wrote, "Did not see that coming but so good & love Carol even more" (@Craig_ing). Another wrote, "Those poor girls, but I'd do the same as Carol" (@solsbeary). And others celebrated Carol's survivalist instincts, seemingly less fazed by the death of the children: "She plays no games. Carol will take out any threat at any age" (@RedSocialite).

Normally a scene involving a woman killing a child would evoke massive negative reactions (probably directed at the female character and sometimes the actress who plays her), but the fans of *The Walking Dead*—either because they already have an abnormally high tolerance for violence or because the post-apocalyptic setting recalibrates moral compasses—did not produce an onslaught of blaming tweets. In fact, the line "look at the flowers" became a recurrent hashtag associated with Carol in the seasons that followed, used not to signify a horribly sad incident but instead to celebrate Carol's status as a badass.

The program continued to put Carol in situations that show her acting against so-called normal maternal impulses. In season 5, the reunited group finds shelter within the previously mentioned gated community just outside Alexandria. Carol reinvents herself as a domesticated den mother, baking casseroles and cookies and sporting knit sweaters and floral shirts. The show makes it quite clear that this feminine persona is an intelligent masquerade, intended to make the residents underestimate her.[41] As one television reviewer notes, Carol's performance points out "how gender is something that we do": "It's a *performative* activity that we have to continuously work at because it's a socially constructed idea. Carol *performs* this weak embodiment of women in order to be able to sneak around the community and do as she wishes. At one point Carol even remarks to Rick, 'You know what's great about this place? I get to be invisible again.' Carol challenges the innateness of gender by not only being an extremely strong, capable female survivor, but also by masquerading as the opposite kind of woman she has become now."[42]

Nowhere is this performance more stressed than in "Remember," in which members of the core group are shown being interviewed on camera by the leader of the Alexandria community in order to be granted permission to remain in their midst. If Carol's appearance has not already cued viewers to her act, her speech—packed full of lies and delivered with overly feminine linguistic features like hedging—soon reveals her new facade. When asked about her life before and her recent contributions to the group, Carol responds meekly: "I did laundry, gardened, um. Always had dinner on the table for Ed when he came home. Um. I miss that stupid, wonderful man every day. You know, I didn't have much to offer this group, so I think I just sort of became their den mother. And they've been nice enough to protect me."[43] Analyzing this scene, Rikke Schubart argues that Carol purposefully plays the stereotypical angel of the house in order to mask her strengths.[44] Fans embraced Carol's impersonation of the goodly housewife, just as they did her evolution away from that very same role. They celebrated her even when, once established in Alexandria, she threatens to kill another child—not to protect others, but to protect herself.

A young boy, Sam, discovers Carol breaking into the gun repository, which reveals her facade. In a moment of chilling dialogue, Carol threatens the boy, detailing what she will do to him if he tells anyone what he has seen:

> If you [tell], one morning you will wake up and you won't be in your bed. You will be outside the walls, far, far away, tied to a tree. You will scream and scream because you will be so afraid and no one will come to help because no one will hear you. Well, something will hear you. The monsters will come. . . . They will tear you apart and eat you all up while you are still alive. All while you can still feel it. Then afterwards your mom will never know what happened to you. Or you can promise not ever to tell anyone what you saw here and then nothing will happen and you will get cookies, lots of cookies. I know what I think you should do.[45]

In many ways this scene is more disturbing than the one wherein Carol is forced to kill Lizzie, but, yet again, no fan outrage surfaced in the Twitterverse. In fact, fans jokingly posted tweets such as "You're not her first kid, Sam. Watch yourself #Lookattheflowers" (@TheNomad83).

In the end, the Alexandria residents benefit from the faux housewife in their midst; when their walls are breeched by violent infiltrators, the Wolves, it is Carol who saves the day, trading in one costume for another. She strips off her matronly attire, puts on the clothing of a deceased assassin, smears blood across her face (copying their distasteful war paint), and systematically kills the invaders off one by one, shattering the illusion she has crafted for herself in order to save many community members.

What makes *The Walking Dead*'s character development of Carol fascinating is that it is not a tidy, straight trajectory wherein she seamlessly is transformed from a stereotypical feminine character into a masculine one—from an emotional maternal figure to one (seemingly) unaffected by the deaths of children. Season 6 finds Carol struggling to come to terms with the woman she has become, specifically the number of human lives that have been lost at her hands. Despite having just saved Alexandria from an attack by the human invaders, she finds herself haunted by her actions, keeping a running list of how many people she has had to kill in order to protect herself and those close to her. In "Not Yet Tomorrow," viewers find Carol sitting on her porch smoking a cigarette on the eve of another battle against a human threat (the Saviors). Although she is reluctant to spill more blood, she is unwilling to risk her friends' lives by not accompanying them to attack the dangerous group. While Carol feels guilt over both the lives she has taken and the ones she predicts she will take the following day, her newly situated love interest, Tobin (Jason Douglas), reframes her skills in an interesting way. When he admits that she "can do things that—that just terrify [him]," Carol responds by asking him how he thinks she is able to do those things.[46] His response can be read as a statement about motherhood more generally:

> Tobin: You're a mom.
> Carol: I was.
> Tobin: You are. It—it—it's not the cookies or the smiles. It's—it's the hard stuff. The scary stuff. It's how you can do it. It's strength. You're a mom to most of the people here.
> Carol: To you, too?
> Tobin: No. You're something else to me.[47]

In a sometimes hyperbolic fashion, *The Walking Dead* often paints motherhood as being scary. Consider, for example, the horrific scene early in the series wherein Lori (Sarah Wayne Callies), Rick's wife, dies during an emergency C-section and her own young son has to shoot her in the head so she will not turn into a zombie.[48] Or consider the moment when a mother of two, Jessie (Alexandra Breckenridge), watches her younger son, Sam, get eaten by zombie and her screams doom her to the same fate.[49] Or when tragedy falls on one of the show's main couples—and original characters—as Maggie (Lauren Cohan) is forced to watch Glenn (Steven Yeun), the father of her unborn child, beaten to death before her eyes.[50] But Tobin's aside about motherhood being "hard" and "scary"—a role that requires "strength"—seems to be a direct moment of commentary wherein the program makes a statement about motherhood outside the fictional landscape. By specifically drawing attention to the fact that motherhood is not simply all about "the cookies or the smiles," the work, challenges, and sacrifice of motherhood are alluded to quite plainly.

If this moment of dialogue existed in isolation it could be dismissed as not of much importance. The surrounding episodes, however, continue to focus on Carol's conflicted emotions about not only herself, but the role that her fellow longtime group survivor, Maggie, should play in the group's protection now that she herself is an expectant mother. Despite Carol's specifically wanting to keep Maggie safely out of harm's way in their battle against the Saviors, the two women get captured. Carol reprises her role as the pathetic woman, performing weakness in order to be underestimated by their captors, and ultimately outsmarts them. Not unimportantly, the two slaughter their imprisoners and fight their way free well before they can be rescued by the rest of their (predominantly male) group. Tobin's comment about the scary lengths that a mother will go to to protect her own then serves as foreshadowing for the acts these two female characters are forced into in "The Same Boat."[51] Still, Carol is unable to see this as a victory—or to see her ability to kill as a strength—and by the season's end she has exiled herself once again from the group, hoping that if she is out on her own that she can avoid murdering any more humans.

Why We Hate the Housewife but Love the Female Badass

Since Carol the Badass became a fan favorite, whereas the original Carol the housewife was rarely a passing thought in viewers' minds, fans' impatience with her role as a quasi pacifist was not surprising. Critics, likewise, pointed out the problematic ways in which her most recent characterization was plotted. For example, in "Taking the Teeth Out of Carol," one blogger notes that focusing on Carol's self-crisis as a result of PTSD rather than grounding it so heavily in her relationship to motherhood would have been a better idea.[52] For example, another character, Glenn, is showcased as reluctant to slaughter the Saviors, but his reluctance is not connected to his role as an expectant father.[53] For the most part, however, Carol's character has been extremely well received, and the question might be: Why is she so popular and what does her popularity reveal about the current gender landscape?

Perhaps viewers embrace Carol because of her very divergence from the conventional portrayals of television mothers. After all, Carol's character becomes "richer, more complex and formidable when she is liberated from parenting."[54] Bogart writes: "Carol's transformation from battered wife to one-woman assault squad is . . . radical: She is only able to become her better, stronger self after her child is killed by zombies. . . . Nothing in her characterization now is expressly tied to her identity as a mother."[55] Perhaps fans do not balk when Carol shoots a young girl or threatens to feed a young boy to the zombies because women living in post-apocalyptic settings "are exempt from the expectations of unfailing, uncomplaining maternal devotion, because in the hells they inhabit, there are no PTA bake sales that demand slaved-over cupcakes."[56] What this suggests is that such narratives provide opportunities for critiques of motherhood that may be resisted in other settings. Bogart writes:

> One of the primary appeals of horror-based entertainment like *The Walking Dead* . . . is that it offers us catharsis; the chance to see our most brutal . . . impulses enacted onscreen. It makes sense, then, that [shows like this] would feature characters that can embody and express attitudes towards motherhood that most women could never feel truly safe admitting. After all, motherhood is often referred to as the toughest job on the planet; but it may be the only job where any random internet commenter or nosy-pants in the grocery store thinks that she or he qualifies as a supervisor, full of "constructive criticism" and "helpful feedback." And women who fall short of the maternal ideal (or, worst of all, opt out of having children altogether) are made into monsters. This makes women like Carol so essential: They can blast those monsters back to oblivion.[57]

As media products always have a reciprocal relationship to the cultural climates that spawn them, it is not difficult to read *The Walking Dead* as attempting to work through the cultural anxieties fixated on women as mothers, among others. The decades following 9/11 have been rife with hyperbolic rhetoric concerning the supposed crisis facing masculinity in the twenty-first century and conservative calls to put "family values" back at the center of the national fabric, so it only makes sense that contemporary zombie narratives would reflect this rhetoric.[58]

The Zombie Narrative as an Ideal Genre for Gender Critique

While certain genres like dystopia, science fiction, and horror are always ideal spaces for doing such work (and providing cultural commentary on social issues more generally), perhaps the zombie narrative is particularly primed to be a site where debates concerning femininity and maternity are battled out. As a horror subgenre it stems from the gothic tradition that often associates motherhood with monstrosity.[59] Gothic narratives often focus on the displacement or death of the mother or the erasure of her physical body.[60] Though male figures have often been the focus of horror narratives, there has been a notable spike in females taking center stage in horror story lines, particularly in recent Hollywood horror films.[61] What is worth noting, though, is that anxieties concerning motherhood play out differently in zombie narratives than they do in other horror narratives. The classic horrific mother tends to be depicted as one who harms or abandons her children; she represents a "destructive and dysfunctional" force in their lives.[62] This same motif is not present in zombie narratives: mothers are no more likely to be turned than any other character. In *The Walking Dead* particularly, mothers are almost never shown as walkers posing a threat to the children they have left behind. If horror films represent external societal concerns about motherhood, the zombie narrative may actually represent internalized concerns that mothers have—concerns that may be the product of all those external pressures.

Further, when zombies appear in contemporary media they are—for all intents and purposes—viewed as ungendered, sexless bodies. Once they become "walkers"—a term that purposely dehumanizes them—they no longer are divided into socially constructed categories like man and woman. (No one refers to them as female versus male walkers, for example.) This is not the case in other horror or supernatural genres that depend on highly gendered others that thwart human communities (e.g., witches, vampires). Consider for a moment how often the plot of vampire narratives is tied to the gender and sexuality of the main vampires or to their romantic or sexual relationships with human characters. Like other horror genres, zombie narratives give us the classic human-versus-other conflict, but the other is not often gendered as female (even if in a particular scene the zombie threat happens to represent a body that may have originally been female). This may seem like a minor point of difference, but it does change the potential underlying message. Battles involving humans and zombies do not then prompt readings wherein we see female humans in conflict with an other that is seen as a distorted mirror vision of herself (representing, as might be the case in vampire narratives, a fallen version of herself) or a metaphorical representation of her patriarchal other (i.e., man). A zombie, in this way, is simply a zombie.

That is not to say, however, that the zombie itself is not coded in a way that draws attention to important gender-specific critiques. After all, by nature such plots draw attention to the body, subtly attending to debates concerning what qualifies as "life" and focusing explicitly on the actual invasion and transformation of human bodies.[63] These foci have led scholars to argue that zombie narratives are ideal sites in which to imagine and construct gender and sexual identities differently through their reconstituted social worlds.[64] Other academics have argued that continual focus on families in peril in zombie narratives like *The Walking Dead* provides commentary on issues such as the decay of the modern family.[65] And still others have read consumption in zombie narratives through a feminist lens, suggesting that they nod toward the time pressures and constraints of Western culture—pressures felt even more forcibly by women and mothers.[66] If we can look through the melodramatic plots and gratuitous gore, programs like *The Walking Dead* actually reveal important cultural sentiments—and potential correctives—concerning expectations for contemporary women.

Zombified Feelings: What Zombie Narratives Do Affectively for Viewers

Like all social critique presented metaphorically, zombie narratives do run the risk of placing too much distance between viewers and the social problems they aim to draw attention to.[67] *The Walking Dead*'s aesthetic structure, however, often prevents it from at least falling into the catharsis trap that other horror narratives fall into. Most of the post-9/11 television shows analyzed in this book (with the exception of perhaps *American Crime,* which will be discussed in chapter 7), offer regular, tidy, happy denouements, releasing viewers from the negative affect they inspire, but *The Walking Dead* refuses to provide sustained relief from terror. Happy moments on the program are fleeting at best. So why is the show so popular, or as Shaunna Murphy puts it, "Why do millions upon millions of people tune in to watch a group of characters they've grown to love go through all sorts of hell week after week, with no respite in sight?"[68] Murphy tackles this question in an interview with Dr. Travis Langley, the editor of *The Walking Dead Psychology: Psych of the Living Dead.*[69] Langley sees the zombie boom as a response to recent trying times and argues that, from a psychological perspective, consuming these dark tales might be doing viewers some good.[70] He details a laundry list of potential benefits that could be gained from watching a program like *The Walking Dead:* "learning empathy for unlikable characters . . . , psychologically getting used to the feeling of finding hope in terrible situations," and being exposed to the "racial and gender equalizing that can happen onscreen once most of humanity has been wiped out."[71] Concerning the last, Langley explains the importance of how traditional social roles quickly dropped away during the early seasons of *The Walking Dead:* "Everybody has to be involved in survival, everybody has to have all these different skills. . . . You don't even necessarily think about race [anymore]. Daryl went on a mission looking for medicine, and all three other people in the car were African-American. The fans didn't even *think* about race in that situation. It had become a non-issue; a common humanity was pulling them together. We've got a big, scary undead 'them' out there, we need to stop thinking about the superficial sorts of 'them' that used to worry us."[72]

While shows like *The Walking Dead* may act as positive social training tools, responding positively to the fear-based climates that spawn them, some suggest their popularity may actually indicate our desensitization to fear. In a piece for *Rolling Stone,* Joshua Rothkopf discusses how zombies moved from fringe culture to mainstream popular culture as a response to "our era of shapeless fear."[73] He quips: "AMC's new spinoff show tells us to *Fear the Walking Dead,* but perhaps that emotion is an afterthought."[74] This brings us back to one of the assumptions made in the beginning of this book about how television shows engage with affective climates. While individual texts and genres may rise to popularity in attempts to respond to or critique cultural anxieties, even some of the best attempts may end up inadvertently reinforcing those very same anxieties or numbing us to them in ways that might limit the influence of their social commentary.

6

A Country (Still) Divided

How Recent Vampire Series Use Nostalgia to Comment on Current Issues Related to Gender, Race, and Sexuality

Vampire narratives from *Dracula* to the present-day offerings have been analyzed (and allegorized) in terms of race and cultural conflict, allowing the fictional figures in such texts often to represent much more than mere mythical creatures. For example, scholars have read Bram Stoker's text as reflecting the fears that spawned the eugenics movement during the early twentieth century—fears of blood contamination and interracial marriage.[1] Scholarly analyses of vampire texts at the close of the twentieth century have read such narratives as alluding to other cultural concerns, such as terrorism—fears of "the other," who can hide among us and attack without provocation.[2] In *Our Vampires, Ourselves,* Nina Auerbach argues that every age embraces its own particular kind of vampire—a cultural archetype that plays out the societal concerns from which it derives.[3] Similarly, in the American post-9/11 cultural climate, the various vampire fictions represent the current cultural fears. One of the devices they use to do this, however, actually turns attention away from the contemporary moment, transporting viewers to a previous era of conflict. Recently, some of the most popular vampire texts have remediated a past historical event—the Civil War—to bring attention to the cultural divides currently plaguing the United States, such as continued racial conflict, recent progress in the LGBTQA rights movement, and ongoing debates concerning family values and gender roles. Since vampire texts throughout the centuries have attended to racial tensions and cultural rifts, the evocation of the Civil War is, in many ways, not surprising. What is surprising is the specific ways that vampire crossover texts are integrating this historical event into their narratives. This chapter analyzes three vampire series that have crossed mediated divides, revising narrative content from print collections to fit the serialized small screen and the Hollywood big screen: HBO's *True*

Blood (2008–14), CW's *The Vampire Diaries* (2009–17), and the film adaptations of Stephenie Meyer's *Twilight Saga* (2008, 2009, 2010, 2011, 2012).

HBO's hit drama derived from Charlaine Harris's popular novel series, *The Southern Vampire Mysteries* (2001–present). One of the main vampire figures in this series (in both print and televised versions) is Bill Compton (Stephen Moyer), a vampire whose human life as a soldier and family man ended during the Civil War. Although the primary focus of the series is often the romantic relationship between Bill and the main protagonist, Sookie Stackhouse (Anna Paquin), the social commentary surrounding this melodramatic focus is often more noteworthy. The first season of *True Blood* actively draws on Bill's historical past, one that prompts main characters to criticize the racial inequity of the nineteenth century. This attention to race is expected from the series' onset. In fact, the very first moments in the program's opening credits house controversial scenes from the racially divided American south of the 1960s (e.g., an image of a child in Ku Klux Klan attire). Although this focus on race relations often slips into the background as the series progresses, Bill Compton exists to remind viewers of the divided state of the country both in the 1800s and at present; moreover, the juxtaposition of these time periods suggest that society has not progressed all that far. *True Blood* also uses its narrative to critique other issues that divide the United States in the twenty-first century. The show focuses heavily on diverse sexualities, allowing the discrimination the vampire characters experience on the show to parallel discrimination experienced by homosexuals, for example, in present-day America. As the series was released in 2008, during the height of the outrage over Proposition 8 (the California Marriage Protection Act), a short-lived state constitutional amendment that ruled that only a marriage between a man and a woman would be legally recognized, it was primed to be a text that transferred societal debates over the role of the family and the sanctity of marriage into the fictional confines of the vampire-infused world in a way that critiqued the current political landscape.

Released a year after *True Blood, The Vampire Diaries* also draws on the Civil War to highlight contemporary concerns, although more subtly. The CW's teen drama brought renewed attention to L. J. Smith's 1991 trilogy of the same name. Probably inspired by the success of Meyer's *Twilight* series, Smith took advantage of the resurgent popularity of vampire narratives, expanding her print series after almost two decades and accepting a television deal that would take her original story line in a vastly different direction. Smith's original series focused on a love triangle between two vampire brothers and their human love interest, Elena Gilbert (Nina Dobrev). This remained the tie that bound the two versions together for the majority of the adaptation's run. Although much could be contrasted between the television series and the original trilogy, for the purposes of this chapter the most significant change relates to the backstory of the two brothers. Smith's novel series portrayed the two male characters, Damon (Ian Somerhalder) and Stefan Salvatore (Paul Wesley), as brothers born during the Italian Renaissance. The CW series alters their pasts, recasting them as young men who met their demise on American soil during the Civil War era. The television series devotes much more of its narrative contents to the past than did its textual predecessor. For its first five seasons it also segregated vampires and witches along racial lines; for example, Elena's friend Bonnie Bennett (Kat Graham) is an African American descendant of slaves in the CW series but not in the original novels. The racial segregation of the vampires and witches will be discussed later in this chapter.

Unlike the previous two examples, the adapted *Twilight* films remain closer to their ancestor texts, focusing primarily on the romantic relationship between a human, Bella Swan (Kristen Stewart), and a vampire, Edward Cullen (Robert Pattinson). The Civil War connection within this series is the origin story of Jasper Cullen, who was a major in the Confederate Army when he was turned. Though this plot element is rather minor, this series is perhaps the most obvious of the three in the way that it expresses nostalgia for a past era through the characterization of the main male characters. All the series use the Civil War as a way to anchor their stories in an American past that is sometimes romanticized.

The Civil War era shares with the twenty-first century a societal resurgence of patriotism—patriotism that comes in a form so strong that it can divide a nation. In fact, some critics have drawn parallels between the Tea Party movement of the early 2000s and the Civil War Confederacy.[4] The protagonist vampires from these series associated with the Civil War epoch are also useful to analyze in that they do not exist as vampires traditionally do. They are not depicted as an "other" to be feared (which might be expected from post-9/11 texts). They exist instead as heroic characters who work alongside their human partners to thwart evil in various forms—evil that threatens to terrorize their communities. But these narratives still depict dark, dangerous others in a way that calls out for a post-9/11 reading. In these texts, all the good vampires are American and (at least initially) all the bad vampires are foreign. Some examples of the evil non-American vampires from these series include Aro Volturi in *Twilight,* Russell Edgington in *True Blood,* and Niklaus (Klaus) Mikaelson in *The Vampire Diaries.* As I will discuss shortly, this is not an entirely new phenomenon, but it is certainly one that has been amplified in the post-9/11 moment.

The characterization of the main male characters in these series is also noteworthy. Especially in the case of Bill Compton, Stefan Salvatore, and Edward Cullen, these characters represent traditional American values; they are polite, old-fashioned, and chivalrous. Their depictions, therefore, are much different from those of vampires in past narratives and may be a product of shifting conceptualizations of masculinity or the conservative rhetoric concerning family values that dominated the early and mid-2000s. For example, in the *Twilight* series, Edward's refusal to have sexual intercourse with Bella until marriage is often read as aligning with the abstinence-only education movement popular during this time period.[5]

This chapter aims to explore the fascination that recent vampire narratives have with the Civil War period and the so-called traditional values associated with that bygone era. Ultimately it suggests that this historical backdrop functions to redirect viewers' attention to the cultural divides that trouble the country *at present* in regard to issues including politics, religion, race, gender, and sexuality. This tie to the Civil War, however, also reflects the nostalgia for a past era and the current trend of heightened patriotism or nationalism being expressed by subsections of the American public. Thus, these television and film vampire tales continue to function as their ancestor texts have: they embody the cultural concerns and fears of the time in which they are created and offer up fascinating critiques in the guise of fiction.

Same Fangs, Different Story: How Contemporary Vampires Differ from Those of the Past

Although vampire tales have historically served a double purpose—entertainment and social commentary—the characterizations of the main players have changed quite drastically. The popular culture scholar Robert Thompson credits Anne Rice's *Interview with a Vampire* with the broadening of the vampire genre, calling her text the "ground zero of the modern iteration of the vampire"—one that expanded "the mythology into its modern iteration."[6] According to Thompson, "before Rice, the vampire story was a costume drama with limited literary scope," but today we are presented with a "modernized and domesticated" vampire; these tales rip "away the traditional narrative from the black-caped, thickly Euro-accented terror guy you run from, to the handsome, seductive bad-boy next door you want to sleep with."[7] Part of this alteration is practical; after all, there are more potential story lines if vampires can suddenly be cast as romantic heroes as well as evil creatures. Thompson argues, "Once you can let vampires next to us, and with us in our bedrooms, that opens up an extraordinary amount of narrative territory that we didn't have before."[8] The result of this change is a more complicated vampire than that of previous generations. As the male lead and the heroine's love interest, the vampire "has transformed into an alluring combination of danger and sensitivity, a handsome romantic hero haunted by his lust for blood and his guilt for the humans he killed in the past. No bats, no capes, and perhaps just a touch of white pallor to provide a whiff of the grave . . . and so much the better if he shimmers in the manner of *Twilight*'s Edward and resembles an Armani model. He's often courtly, too, in the fashion of another age—the age, in fact, when he was born and lived as a human before 'being made.'"[9]

This new-age vampire is one often riddled with guilt, trying to overcome his bloodlust through self-control.[10] His story is that of a "man struggling to master his worst impulses—perhaps even his essential nature—through whatever means necessary."[11] In *The Vampire Diaries* and *Twilight* this results in some "vegetarian" vampires that feed on animals rather than humans, and in *True Blood* it finds some vampires relying on synthetic blood rather than actual human blood. Although this evolution of the vampire is part marketing ploy—allowing vampire tales to morph into romance novels, films, or television shows to attract a wider audience—it is probably as much a response to the contemporary climate.

The Twenty-first Century Vamp: Explaining the Post-9/11 Popularity of Vampire Narratives

In an era that has found Americans afraid of the potential terrorist hiding next door, the vampire story line has joined the ranks of zombie tales, and dystopian narratives of all kinds, in their ability to work through the cultural fears lingering in the years after the September 11 attacks. Many have argued that vampires, and even their werewolf companions, serve as an analogy of American views of post-9/11 terrorism and the pervasive anxiety and trauma that continue to exist during the resulting geopolitical and financial crises.[12] The vampire scholar Rebecca Housel explains: "Similar to the post 9–11 surge in superhero films, people are looking for escapist entertainment that reclaims some sense of agency and power over the impermanence in life that's been so exaggerated in recent years with things like the situation in the Middle East, the uncertain global economy, and widespread unemployment in the States."[13]

As the post-9/11 years stretch on, the initial fear of foreign attack has, at times, been replaced by other fears: declining confidence in the government's ability to morally protect its citizens and an awakening sense of guilt associated with an awareness of the role the United States played in the global circumstances that led to 9/11. In this regard, Amy Jenkins suggests that vampires point toward the parts of ourselves that we are afraid of, and perhaps this can be expanded to include how we feel about our status as American citizens as well: "We look around us and we see all the wonderful things that have been achieved, but also that we're greedy and murderous still. There's undeniably evil 'out there,' but we're all human and what does that say about the deeply ungovernable parts of ourselves? After 9/11 we identified a new enemy without but the vampire cult isn't just about the enemy without—it's also about the enemy within."[14] Regardless of whether they represent the enemy within or without, what do we make of the fact that contemporary vampires do not seem all that *evil* anymore?

Though the vampire may be a handy metaphor for terrorists hiding in plain sight or our own cultural corruption, the recent transformation of the vampire into a tame, lovable creature of the night points toward our need to feel safe—even from archetypes that would previously have been associated with anything but safety. Laura Westengard argues that contemporary vampires "reconfigure the post-9/11 decade from a time of traumatic uncertainty into one of idealized fantasy by serving as screens upon which the American public projects the illusion of a more perfect, more coherent reality, thereby eliding the fragmentary trauma of 9/11 and its aftermath."[15] As I have noted, today's primary vampire protagonists are more likely to refrain from murder, be depicted as a romantic protector, and, therefore, to take on the role of the hero rather than villain. None of these vampire tales, however, is free of villains—or villainous portrayals of vampires.

The Americanization of the Vampire: The "Other" as Terrorist in Contemporary Vampire Stories

Of course, it is no surprise that vampire stories would have at least one character depicted as a dark, dangerous "other" to be feared. What might be surprising, however, is how consistent the criteria for good versus bad vampires have been in recent history. With increasing frequency, the good vampires are American and the bad vampires are foreigners (in keeping with traditional vampire lore, usually of European decent).

This modern trend of American vampire as virtuous and European vampire as evil has roots that go back to the last few decades of the twentieth century. In "Foreign Fangs, Domestic Defenders: The Americanization of the Vampire in the Contemporary Novel," Candace Benefiel details how "the vampire, transplanted from the Old World to the fertile soil of the New, has been reinvented in a variety of ways to reflect his essential Americanness."[16] She lists ABC's gothic soap opera *Dark Shadows* (1966–71) and Stephen King's novel *Salem's Lot* (1975) as some of the earliest examples of this phenomenon. As such narratives proliferated throughout the remainder of the century, Benefiel argues that the vampire was quickly transformed "from dangerous European invader into an American icon."[17]

The consistency of this characterization into the twenty-first century could also be explained as more than just the continued evolution of a genre. The shifting representations of vampires could very well be a response to the post-9/11 climate. Vampires are a handy metaphor for terrorists—they attack innocent communities from within without provocation. And while the modern vampires are not being cast in a way that would make this symbolic representation obvious—narratives are thankfully not suddenly spawning a slew of Middle Eastern vampires—these story lines still can be read as reacting to the contemporary moment with their insistence that the heroic vampires be American and their antagonists be foreign. The tactics of these othered vampires also occasionally conjure up associations with terrorists. In the season 4 finale of *The Vampire Diaries,* "Graduation," multiple scenes underscore this connection. Kol Mikaelson (Nathaniel Buzolic), one of the original vampires, returns from the dead and organizes a group of other resurrected supernatural creatures to punish the humans responsible for their deaths. In this scene he appears standing in the midst of a high school graduation seating area and threatens one of the main characters, Elena's best friend, Bonnie Bennett, informing her that if she does not ensure his renewed ghostly immortality, then the town will pay.[18] The camera then pans across the other faces in the crowd and viewers realize, along with Bonnie, that he is the ringleader of a much larger group of dangerous creatures.[19] Though Kol is not threatening a specific act of violence that would point toward terrorist connections, the depiction of a violent group of people lying in wait at a public event certainly does.

Another scene in this episode also finds an ancient supernatural creature tormenting others. Alexander, a vampire hunter from the 1100s, threatens Rebekah Mikaelson (Claire Holt), his former lover and also another original vampire, and her new love interest, the very human Matt Donovan (Zach Roerig). Alexander has rigged a parking lot with explosives, and Matt ends up frozen in place, standing on a pressure-switch bomb. Quite obviously, the inclusion of landmines brings to mind the guerilla war tactics of al-Qaeda. In a parallel scene, another vampire hunter, Connor Jordan (Todd Williams), is holding the patrons of a local restaurant, The Grille, hostage. Although it is Connor who ends up strapped to C-4 explosives, this encounter again seems to cast the supernatural bad guys as terrorists.[20]

Since the main players in these staged acts of terror are very old supernatural creatures, their origin stories tie them to homelands in places far from the United States. This is important primarily because of the choice of the writers of the series to change the origin story of the Salvatore brothers, making them younger American vampires born during the antebellum period instead of during the Italian Renaissance. In purposefully recasting the main characters as American, writers of this vampire adaptation reinforce the narrative trend of separating good and evil across national divides.

Vampires of a Divided Nation: Analyzing the Civil War Vampire Origin Story

The Civil War origin story common to *The Vampire Diaries, True Blood,* and *Twilight* series does more than simply help bolster this "American equals good, foreigner equals bad" equation. As the Civil War was a historical period rife with national conflict, the focus within these narratives—however prominent or fleeting—can be read as mirroring present-day national divisions.

These three series are not the first or the most recent to use the Civil War era as a backdrop for vampire narratives. Timur Bekmambetov's film *Abraham Lincoln: Vampire Hunter* (2012), is, quite obviously, set in this period.[21] In this narrative, all American vampires descend from a plantation owner in New Orleans. This choice of the New Orleans settings is probably connected to Rice's *Interview with a Vampire.* Just as the novel is credited with being the "ground zero" for the domestication of the vampire, it is also responsible for the trend of setting vampire tales in the South during the pre–Civil War era. In Rice's story the main character, Louis de Pointe du Lac, is an indigo plantation owner in 1791 New Orleans when he is turned by Lestat, a vampire who feeds on the slaves of local plantations. In this vampire narrative and others, "a strong correlation is implied between the vampire's use of humans as unwilling food sources, and slavery as practiced in the antebellum South."[22] While all the series discussed here are set in the twenty-first century, they all point backward in time to the years surrounding the Civil War with similar moments of cultural critique. Though *Twilight* nods toward this period only ever so slightly, both *The Vampire Diaries* and *True Blood* do so with more frequency and purpose.

Just as *The Vampire Diaries* purposely altered the Salvatores' backstory, the television series makes major changes to the character of Bonnie Bennett—changes that include her name, race, and ethnicity. In L. J. Smith's original series, the character is Bonnie McCullough, a Scottish American descendent of the ancient Celtic druids. In the CW series, Bonnie is an African American whose lineage dates back to Salem, Massachusetts, during the witch hunt. Her family relocated to Mystic Falls, the show's main setting, in 1692. Her ancestor Emily Bennett was Katherine Pierce's "handmaiden" in the series at the time that Katherine (Elena's doppelganger and archenemy for most of the series) turned Damon and Stefan into vampires. Given that the year is 1864 and that the fictional town of Mystic Falls is in Virginia, it is likely that Emily, euphemistically and ambiguously labeled a handmaiden, is actually Katherine's slave. Therefore, the television series links witchcraft to slavery rather than ancient Celtic traditions, making the black characters othered on many fronts: race, religion, and species (if witches are read as nonhuman).

As is true of the alteration of the Salvatores' origin story, the changes applied to Bonnie are not accidental or inconsequential. The revision of Bonnie's character is part of a larger choice made by the writers of the television series. For quite some time, the supernatural creatures on the program are divided overtly by race. Until the sixth season, all the witches on the program are black, whereas the vampires and werewolves are white.[23] Since the series depicts witches and vampires as perpetual enemies—the witches are tasked with maintaining the Earth's natural balance, and the vampires disrupt that balance in their immortality—this racialization is somewhat problematic, as it places characters in a stereotypical black-versus-white conflict. And while other vampire series use the vampire to explore contemporary race relations, *The Vampire Diaries* does not enter into this social commentary and, in fact, may unproblematically endorse strict racial divisions.

True Blood's use of the Civil War past is quite different from that of *The Vampire Diaries,* as are its overall dealings with race. Sabrina Boyer analyzes the Confederacy imagery found in *True Blood*, arguing that most of it is tied to the character Bill Compton, a Confederate soldier who was turned into a vampire when he was making his way home to his family at the close of the Civil War.[24] Returning to his hometown of Bon Temps, Louisiana, in the twenty-first century, he is presented with a cultural climate that, at times, does not differ much from the Jim Crow era he has already lived through. The only difference is that now the targets of segregation are vampires. Boyer analyzes one of the opening scenes in the series, explaining:

> There are places where vampires can and can't go. These places are not labeled spaces, but they are clearly marked. For example, as Bill enters into Merlotte's and meets Sookie for the first time, he orders wine [since Sam, the owner, does not carry True Blood, the synthetic blood substitute], in order to fit in. He understands that to be accepted within the restaurant, he must obey the behavioral rules a bar dictates. As a vampire and other in a Southern bar, he is the recipient of a "racist" ideology, one that is prejudiced against the vampire race.[25]

This connection between vampire discrimination and historical racial discrimination is again touched on when, later that season, Sookie's grandmother is murdered by a vampire-hater after taking Bill to speak at a meeting of the Glorious Descendants of the Dead—an organization comprising persons whose ancestors had fought in the Civil War.[26] Another incident that depicts vampire hate crimes as an evolution of the racial hate crimes that predated them involves a "group of stereotypical Southern 'rednecks' [who] collectively decide to set fire to a house on the outskirts of town that is said to house a vampire clan. They do so, and destroy the vampires inside."[27] Through scenes such as these the series uses the figure of the vampire to reflect past and present race relations in American society.

Cultural Critiques: What These Vampire Fictions Reveal about Twenty-first-Century Racial Ideologies

Vampire narratives have a long history of providing subtle social commentary on dominant racial ideologies, but, like many cultural texts, sometimes these narratives fail in their attempts to critique racial discourse. As a result, scholars have both praised and criticized *True Blood* and *Twilight* for their depictions of race. Like *The Vampire Diaries, Twilight* constructs race through a white-nonwhite binary.[28] Most critics of the series have found problems in the way it portrays the werewolves (as being of Native American decent), not the vampires, as other. Natalie Wilson argues that in this series:

> Whiteness is . . . idealized in its racial associations. Edward is constructed as a white, godlike vampire, and the color white is associated with purity, beauty, and heroism. The non-white is rendered inferior, with the Quileute shape-shifting werewolves portrayed as not as good or heroic as the white vampires, and their russet-colored skin, black hair, and dark eyes are associated with violence, danger, and savagery. . . . In the series, being a vampire accords one all sorts of privileges that echo real-world white privilege, or the social capital afforded to those with white skin. For example, The Cullens' beauty, wealth, and intellect are linked to their whiteness.[29]

In stark contrast, the Quileute characters—such as Jacob Black (Taylor Lautner), Edward's romantic rival—are depicted "as literally and figuratively darker," their animality emphasized.[30] Even Jacob's last name, Black, points toward his status as racial other. Further, "the series also features a number of other characters whose villainy is either associated with non-white skin and/or their black hair and clothing," which reinforces the problematic symbolism that equates white with good and black with evil.[31] The vampire and werewolf characterizations throughout the series are also classed. As Natalie Wilson highlights, the Cullen family is portrayed as wealthy while the members of the Quileute tribe are depicted as poor.[32] Edward and his family reside in an ornate mansion, but Jacob's house is small and tumbledown.[33] *True Blood* also portrays its werewolves as representing the lower socioeconomic level. In the program the werewolves—with the exception of Alcide Herveaux, another of Sookie's male suitors—are presented as white-trash, drug-addicted bikers. *The Vampire Diaries* deviates from this association of werewolves with poverty. The most prominent werewolf of the series is Tyler Lockwood, a member of one of the wealthy founding families of Mystic Falls. And though all three series play on the long-lasting feud that pits vampire against werewolf, *The Vampire Diaries* complicates this simplistic us-versus-them conflict in the creation of a hybrid race of the two supernatural creatures.

All the series, however, ultimately present the werewolves as subservient to the vampires. In *Twilight* the werewolves choose to align themselves with the good vampires in order to protect common loved ones, but in *The Vampire Diaries* and *True Blood* the werewolves quite literally play the roles of servants doing the biddings of vampire overlords. This story line is introduced in the third season of *True Blood* when Russell Edgington uses werewolves as protectors and warriors in his battle against his enemies. In *The Vampire Diaries* the hybrids, which conceptually could be seen as a progressive narrative inclusion, are ultimately just slaves to their creator, Klaus. Because of a sire bond, the hybrids are forced to unquestioningly carry out Klaus's bidding, even when it results in their deaths.

Of the three series, *True Blood* is often the most highly praised in terms of how it deals with race, but it also receives its fair share of criticism. Amy Jenkins claims that the vampires of *True Blood* work to express racial anxieties, which allows the show to articulate "the continuing challenges of diversity and mixed-race relationships."[34] The depiction of vampires as "ungovernable, unknowable, predatory and exotic," however, still points to the age-old fear that "foreigners are going to come and steal our women."[35]

Some read *True Blood* as responding to post-race ideology. Nicole Rabin argues that *True Blood*, like many new vampire narratives, promotes "a society 'beyond' race."[36] She reads the social interactions in the show as playing into this mind-set:

> The society of the show is encapsulated within the local bar Merlotte's in the fictional town of Bon Temps, where the entire cast of main characters work, and are joined daily by all the other locals in their community. This society includes Caucasian and African American characters of varying social classes, both heterosexual and openly homosexual. All the characters are friends despite their racial, class, and sexual differences; the society of the Bon Temps epitomizes the politics of multiculturalism where differences are accepted as a means for maintaining the status quo. In conjunction with the politics of multiculturalism comes the link between the multiracial phenomenon and post-race ideology/color blindness: multiracials and interracial marriage are used as examples of having reached this idyllic state beyond race.[37]

One of the main premises of the show, however, undermines this utopian vision of race relations. "The preoccupation with blood and lineage works against the show's presentation of multiculturalism critiquing a post-race ideology. From the very beginning the show's title, *True Blood,* declares the relevance of blood purity to its viewers, and immediately begs the question as to whose blood is true or what blood is true?"[38]

Rabin argues that the vampires in *True Blood* are symbols of multiraciality and therefore are able to mirror the real-world experiences of multiracial individuals, such as the experience of "passing."[39] In the pilot episode of *True Blood,* viewers hear a speech from the American Vampire League in which the spokesperson argues that the invention of synthetic blood, called True Blood, means that "there is no reason for anyone to fear" vampires, arguing that they "just want to be part of mainstream society."[40] Before the marketing of True Blood, if vampires wanted to interact in mainstream society, they had to mask their status as vampires and pass as humans. The spokesperson points out that with this new substitute, the main reason for humans to fear vampires has been eliminated: "The defining line of the boundary between these races—that vampires would drink [humans'] blood—was their main point of difference; but, . . . this difference is no longer an issue because the synthetic blood allows vampires to forgo this need and 'pass' in the mainstream human society."[41] By featuring this speech so early on in the program, *True Blood* is pointedly directing viewers' attention to the struggles that racial minorities face in mainstream society.

The show regularly included commercials for the American Vampire League, short interview segments and speeches advocating equality for vampires. These clips extended beyond the confines of the program itself: HBO ran them as faux news reports to promote the series. These segments were fashioned after those of real equality-seeking organizations. The series eventually devoted a season to exploring the Vampire League's opposition, an anti–vampire rights group, the Fellowship of the Sun. This organization also used the mass media to spread its agenda and encouraged "humans to join in the fight against vampires" with language that mirrored the anti-immigration, antiterrorist rhetoric circulating at the time.[42] In portraying the Fellowship members in ways that "are reminiscent of Ku Klux Klan imagery and tactics," *True Blood* reveals its larger political stances. In making the Fellowship members all white, in the midst of a racially diverse cast, the show makes a decision that is interesting and unusual when compared to other post-9/11 narratives. In this instance, the bad guys—the ones engaged in suicide bombings and guerilla war tactics—are white Americans, not foreign others.[43] In a decade that saw terrorist attacks on American soil because of religious fundamentalism, *True Blood* forces viewers to recognize that such extremism does not stem only from far-off regions or specific religions (such as Islam). As this is not a popular point to acknowledge, in its own way the program is acknowledging an issue that has caused divided sentiments in the minds of Americans during the first decades of the twenty-first century.

Allegorize This: Vampire Narratives' Commentary on the Sexual Politics of the New Millennium

Race relations, of course, were not the only issue dominating the media discourse at the start of the new millennium. Vampire narratives of this time often broke with the tradition of allegorizing racial difference and began to use the vampire as a figure that symbolized a sexualized other. Vampires could always be read in a way that points toward so-called nonnormative sexuality, but specific plots indicate a purposeful desire to engage in the cultural debates occurring over sexual orientation and gay rights at this time.

As J. M. Tyree notes, *True Blood* owes much to Rice's vision of vampires: "the bayou mansion setting," "the sexed-up vamping of Southern aristocrats," and the embracing of "gay relationships and open bisexuality among vampires."[44] But *True Blood* moves beyond Rice's legacy in pointedly invoking contemporary debates about sexuality. In an interview, Rebecca Housel notes the obvious "parallels between the vampires living as citizens after 'coming out of the coffin'" and "the struggle for gay rights, like legalizing gay marriage."[45] Although the Fellowship of the Sun, the anti-vampire group, can be read as a shadow of the Ku Klux Klan, it also mimics the rhetoric of fundamentalist Christianity circulating at the start of the century.[46] The "God hates fangs" sign featured in the opening credits brings to mind the bigoted claims of "God hates fags" heard "at Prop 8 activist gatherings, or notably as used by the Westboro Baptist Church."[47]

Arguably, the *True Blood* character that draws the most attention to the series' progressive stance is Lafayette Reynolds (Nelsan Ellis). As a flamboyant "queer man of color in a white 'redneck town,'" he regularly "has to defend himself against stereotypes concerning gay men. One instance in the series has Lafayette jumping over his stove to argue with a group of white men who sent their burgers back because they 'don't want no AIDS burger.'"[48] Tyree argues that Lafayette's characterization—as an intelligent, "unpredictable, irrepressible, and impish figure, a short-order cook, male prostitute, and drug dealer"—upends "any neat parable of assimilation" that the show might otherwise suggest with the integration of the vampires into human society post–True Blood manufacturing.[49] Although there are many things to celebrate in the program's attention to sexual politics, it does not avoid criticism in this area. Tyree argues, "*True Blood*'s tones often clash, using the vocabulary of gay rights to serve a central heterosexual love affair."[50] And some of the plots that draw attention to the discrimination faced by homosexuals are quite problematic. In "Vamp Stamp: What Is *True Blood* Saying about Women and Sex?" James Brady Ryan discusses the story line devoted to the hate crimes against "fangbangers." In season 1 women who slept with vampires, derogatorily termed fangbangers, were murdered by a serial killer. Although the perpetrator was portrayed as villainous, in having women "punished for their sexual activity," the show reinforced the age-old narrative trope of punishing women for being anything but chaste.[51] Considering the conservative rhetoric dominating the early 2000s, this story line is actually not surprising.

Conservative Vampires? How the Family Values Campaigns of the Early 2000s Infiltrated Fiction

The vampire series that often gets the most attention in terms of being affected by the family values campaigns of the early twenty-first century is *Twilight*.[52] Like *True Blood*, the *Twilight* saga sets up the troubling equation wherein sexual attraction is coupled with violence and the loss of female innocence adds up to death.[53] Carrie Anne Platt argues that *Twilight*'s main story line, "a passionate yet chaste romantic relationship between an immortal vampire and a human woman," is ultimately an "unabashedly pro-abstinence" tale "based on a steadfast denial of the (multiple) pleasures of the flesh."[54] She argues that "Meyer employs conservative social values like the policing of female desire, the protection of female virtue from ruin, the importance of marriage, and the sanctity of life as key plot devices" to create "a world in which vulnerable women need to be protected at all times, both from external forces and their own desires."[55] And who gets to protect women (from themselves)? Men. Vampire men, no less. In *Twilight*, it is Edward who is cast as Bella's protector (along with Jacob from time to time). Edward's role as protector is deeply problematic, however, as the means he uses to accomplish that duty are quite extreme. Critics of the series often focus on Edward's escalating stalker-ish behavior.[56] Platt describes the main love story as "essentially a controlling and abusive relationship," and Gina Dalfonzo describes Edward as "one of modern fiction's best candidates for a restraining order."[57] The series hyperbolically represents the belief—one possibly heightened during the Republican-controlled early years of the twenty-first century—that it is men's responsibility to protect women, even from themselves.

Twilight's cohorts, *True Blood* and *The Vampire Diaries,* do not fall into the same trap in terms of policing female sexuality. They do not shy away from sexualizing women, and, in fact, it is hard to find a chaste character (male or female) in either series. Although *True Blood* does initially highlight Sookie's innocent nature through her costuming—she is dressed in white for all of season 1—it is not long into the series before she is sexually involved with her vampire lover (and is, arguably, interested in another). And while one might expect *The Vampire Diaries,* a network television show aimed at adolescents, to be a bit more reserved than *True Blood,* it features sex scenes quite regularly (although not as explicitly). Whereas *Twilight* seemed to be channeling the ideology of Bush-era conservatism, *True Blood* and *The Vampire Diaries* seem to reflect a more modern view of female sexuality in which sexual activity is not demonized. Despite this fact, all three series align in that their female protagonists are constantly portrayed as being in need of rescuing by their big, strong, chivalrous (vampire) men—characters that can be viewed as echoes from the past.

Chivalry Lives On (If You're Over One Hundred Years Old): Male Vampires Embody Nostalgia

Just as all these series rely on Civil War origin stories, they all contain similar male protagonists. The principal vampire love interests in these tales are depicted as morally sound, polite, and gallant creatures. These characterizations may point toward the shifting expectations concerning masculinity at the end of the twentieth century and the start of the twenty-first. In *Twilight,* Edward is determined to protect Bella's virtue by forcing her to remain a virgin until she is married. In this series, he abides by moral codes from a century earlier, despite their mismatch with today's practices and Bella's own desires. Similarly, in *The Vampire Diaries,* Stefan is obsessed with preserving Elena's mortal innocence—in not allowing her to become a vampire and, later, when that fails, in returning her to her human state at any cost.

All the male protagonists of these vampire series are cast as protectors. In *Twilight,* Edward plays this role to an extreme. At certain points in the series he determines where she can go, whom she can see, and what she can do. (He even goes as far as disconnecting her car's battery so she cannot leave her house.) Edward operates under the outdated notion that men know best and that it is his duty to keep her safe, even when such efforts are not wanted. Although not as extreme, Bill plays a similar role in *True Blood*—constantly claiming to know what is in Sookie's best interests and thwarting her freedom when she does not agree. It is because of this shared trait that many scholars have been concerned that audiences, comprising mostly young girls and women, may "see Edward Cullen as the perfect boyfriend or life partner" and Bill Compton "as the ultimate Southern gentleman . . . with fangs."[58]

Unlike *Twilight* and *True Blood, The Vampire Diaries* offers up not one but two very different characters who engage in extreme acts of chivalry. At a glance, it might seem that Stefan Salvatore and Edward Cullen are almost replicas of one another—from their onscreen appearances (disheveled brown hair, pale skin, and dark, haunted eyes) to their behaviors (soft-spoken speeches, passionate moral stances, and sweet romantic gestures). What links the two most directly is their conflicted relationship toward vampirism: while both enjoy some of the benefits of their vampiric existence and immortality, both suffer from immense guilt over their past killings and strive to live as "vegetarians" feasting only on animal blood or human blood stolen from local blood banks.

In "Chivalry Is Undead: Bad Boy/Nice Guy Dichotomies in *The Vampire Diaries* or, What Does Elena Want?" however, Tarah Scalzo makes a compelling argument for analyzing Stefan's brother, Damon, as the more chivalrous character on the show, arguing that the different ways in which the boys struggle to integrate chivalry into the twenty-first century speaks to the conflicting expectations set for contemporary masculinity. In an interesting comparison between *Twilight* and *The Vampire Diaries,* Scalzo reads Damon and Edward as "bad boys" representing old-fashioned chivalry and masculinity and Stefan and Jacob as "good guys" representing modern-day masculinity and sensibilities (i.e., sensitive, feminine, brooding). Like Edward, Damon goes against Elena's wishes in order to protect her, while "Stefan frequently defers to Elena's wishes rather than asserting his own," even when it costs her her human life, and Jacob simply worships endlessly at the altar of Bella, willing to do almost anything to please her.[59] Focusing primarily on *The Vampire Diaries,* Scalzo analyzes the many ways in which Elena is confused about which character—and which type of masculinity—she should find desirable. While she is drawn to the "confident and sexual dominance of Damon," she is ambivalent "about what it would mean to succumb to this attraction" and, therefore, she continually returns "to the sensitive, more submissive Salvatore, Stefan"—the choice she feels she *should* make.[60] Scalzo argues that the characterization of Damon and Stefan point toward the many

> representational changes that certain facets of our culture are trying to make in terms of defining masculinity. For the last twenty years, it seems like we've been overhauled with girl power (Spice Girls, Buffy), but now, it seems the factor to manipulate is the place and role of boys (and by extension, men). The bad-boy/nice-guy dichotomy has never been so important in literature, and . . . fictional women have been plagued by this type of indecision for more than a hundred years. . . . Now, more than ever, young women are confused as to what they *should* desire in a mate vs. what they actually *do* desire. Meaning: What qualities *should* be attractive in terms of masculinity vs. what qualities actually *are* attractive, and who's setting these standards?[61]

Therefore, is it really a surprise that *The Vampire Diaries* presents viewers with the conflicted Elena Gilbert, who is torn between two very different representations of masculinity?

Scalzo suggests that these representations of masculinity, particularly the rise of the sensitive man (as seen through Stefan's character), are the unintended results of the women's movement, but the feminist scholar Susan Faludi (as discussed in the previous chapter) offers a different—yet related—explanation for the depictions of masculinity circulating today.[62] In *The Terror Dream: Fear and Fantasy in Post-9/11 America,* Faludi analyzes the rise of the "manly man" after 9/11 (of which Damon could be an example) as a result of a renewed feminist backlash fueled during the weeks following the attacks. She documents an array of problematic responses to 9/11, such as "the denigration of capable women, the magnification of manly men, the heightened call for domesticity, [and] the search for and sanctification of helpless girls" in the media.[63] She determined that these unexpected aftereffects of the attacks constitute a national fantasy, one "in which we are deeply invested."[64] In terms of sentiments related to gender roles, she argues that September 11 did not *do* anything to anyone, it did not *cause* specific emotional reactions, but, rather, it revealed emotions and beliefs buried beneath the surface of the national fabric. Therefore, these vampire narratives—packed full of female characters in perpetual danger and heroic men lying in wait to save the day—could be read as a product of the current cultural moment, one in which gender expectations are again in flux.

Conclusion

As a typical CW high school melodrama, *The Vampire Diaries,* perhaps unsurprisingly, houses the fewest moments of overt social commentary in this triad. It is not politically progressive like HBO's *True Blood,* and it does not seem to be as influenced by the political climate as was Meyer's *Twilight* saga. With story lines about proms, parental conflict, friendship spats, and boyfriend problems, *The Vampire Diaries* sometimes seems to be a narrative that resists a post-9/11 reading. As this chapter highlights, however, moments arise that pull it into the larger trends of vampire narratives—trends that can be viewed as resulting from recent national events. The Civil War trope that surfaces in all three series acts as an interesting allegory for the post-9/11 moment, and the characterization of good old American-born vampire heroes saving humans from terrorist-like attacks suggests that this series—despite its ample moments of adolescent angst and predictable young adult plots—is, like other contemporary vampire series, a product of its time, seeking out its own idiosyncratic way of working through this twenty-first-century age of terror and divided political sentiment.

7

Fictionalizing Ferguson in Prime-Time Dramas

Interrogating the Potentialities and Consequences of Remediating Events That Are Still in Progress

Though television programs from the early years of the twenty-first century featured fictional narratives that focused on global threats, and the years that followed spawned a range of programs about the supernatural that sometimes alluded to those threats, recently the televisual tides have turned. Lately there has been a notable rise in fictional programming focused on the domestic threats faced by citizens of the United States. Recent televisual attempts to remediate the race-related conflicts unfolding across the country suggest that television is once again using fictional narratives to reflect societal concerns. The 2010s saw a wave of programs with story lines concerning police brutality, inequity within the criminal justice system, and the Black Lives Matter movement, which has risen to speak out against both. Shows across televisual genres have tackled these issues (e.g., *Being Mary Jane, Black-ish, Blue Bloods, Brooklyn Nine-Nine, CSI: Cyber, Law and Order: SVU, Orange Is the New Black, South Park, The Carmichael Show, UnREAL*), and media critics have begun debating their efficacy as tools for social critique.[1] This chapter analyzes specific episodes of CBS's *The Good Wife* (2009–16) and ABC's *Scandal* (2012–18)—which have been referred to by media critics as each program's respective "Ferguson episode"—and the first season of ABC's *American Crime* (2015–17), a gritty crime anthology miniseries that unflinchingly tackled racial conflict in its debut year. There are reasons to be wary of attempts to fictionalize current race relations, but this chapter ultimately argues that series that include thoughtful, complex story lines, as well as televisual aesthetics that underscore the social commentary contained within the program, may allow these issues to be not just understood, but *felt*.

In analyzing the missteps and successes of the television programs that tackle this subject matter, this chapter considers the arguments of trauma theorists who problematize the goal of inducing empathy for marginalized or victimized persons through fictional accounts. Carolyn Steedman argues that consuming stories of pain, loss, and suffering—if not done critically—can lead to emotional exploitation: "In those moments of vibrating reception, when the heart throbs in sympathy and we are sublimely aware of the harmony of our reactions with those of the person we are sympathizing with . . . he or she who tells the harrowing tale, is diminished by having that story to tell; and is subordinated in the act of telling."[2] Although some trauma narratives may prompt a "more passive form of voyeuristic spectatorship," it is important to conceptualize consumers as active, with agency and the ability to identify with multiple perspectives.[3] This merger of critical thinking and feeling allows for "self-reflexive empathy" and "empathetic unsettlement."[4] Jill Bennett argues that art, "by virtue of its specific affective capacities," can escape the trappings of "crude empathy" and capitalize on "embodied perception in order to promote forms of critical inquiry."[5] The final program analyzed in this chapter serves as a successful example of televisual witnessing—one that can prompt a more productive, self-conscious form of empathy.

Television and Race: Why TV Is Not, and Should Not Be, Color-Blind

Television's role in shaping racial ideology has been well studied by academics, and the vast majority of the scholarship focuses on portrayals of African Americans. Ample studies have highlighted the ways in which black men, women, and families have been represented in fictional television, and how racial stereotypes surface across the various television genres.[6] Scholars have also studied the influence of these portrayals—the ways in which racialized television imagery actually affects viewers.[7] Television's role at crucial moments of racial conflict has also been stressed. For example, in *Black, White, and in Color: Television and Black Civil Rights,* Sasha Torres discusses the ways in which television influenced American's perception of the social, political, and ethical issues raised by the Civil Rights movement.[8] Since the consensus among scholars is that television is "a powerful instrument capable of favorably or unfavorably shaping U.S. racial politics," it is no surprise that many are turning a discerning eye to the recent explorations of the Black Lives Matter movement on television.[9]

Of course, attention to television's efforts (or lack thereof) to attend to the racial inequities of the criminal justice system predates the Black Lives Matter movement. Unsurprisingly, even some of the best televisual attempts to tackle these issues have been met with skepticism. For example, FX's critically acclaimed show *The Shield* (2008–12), which has been praised for exploring the ways in which issues concerning law and justice play "out along the fault lines of race, ethnicity, and gender," has nevertheless received criticism for reasserting "a conservative vision of the white male hero as the ultimate guarantor of social order."[10] Some scholars have suggested that the limits of the police procedural—the genre that has traditionally integrated such story lines—might be to blame.[11] Although crime shows are not alone in frequently casting African Americans in criminal roles, their tendency to do so, combined with their role in mythologizing violence, means that they "have the potential for doing harm by reinforcing enduring racial stereotypes and white fears about urban black criminality."[12] Specific contemporary crime shows that have been blamed for doing so include CBS's *Blue Bloods* (2010–present), which has been accused of sustaining "a racist world view" and Fox's *Shots Fired* (2017), which presents a pointed reversal of the Black Lives Matter movement with story lines such as one focused on "the shooting of an unarmed white man shot by a Black cop" who verbalizes a racist agenda.[13]

Two Recent Televisual Critiques of the Criminal Justice System

The majority of the recent explorations of the Black Lives Matter movement have stemmed from genres outside the police procedural, although some—but not all—often have regular story lines relating to the criminal justice system. Of this analysis, the first two examples—*The Good Wife* and *Scandal*—are shows that focus on politics and law within the scope of their larger melodramatic foci. *The Good Wife* follows the life of Alicia Florrick (Julianna Margulies), a partner at a major Chicago law firm, and her husband, Peter Florrick (Chris Noth), a governor in the perpetual spotlight for various scandals. *Scandal* focuses primarily on the professional feats of a high-profile Washington, D.C., political adviser and "fixer," Olivia Pope (Kerry Washington), and her on-again-off-again love affair with the president of the United States, Fitgzerald Grant (Tony Goldwyn).

The Good Wife: *A Failed Attempt at Social Commentary*

The least well received of the three examples analyzed in this chapter was the first to air: the season 6, episode 12, of *The Good Wife,* titled "The Debate," which was broadcast on January 11, 2015. It began by projecting two disclaimers across the screen: (1) "This episode was written and filmed prior to the grand jury decisions in Ferguson and Staten Island," and (2) "All mentions of 'Ferguson' are in reference to the events in August 2014 after the shooting death of Michael Brown."[14] Directly after these two screens, the episode cut away to apparent camera-phone footage of a black character, Cole Willis, being shot and killed by two mall police officers.[15] The faux footage, as the media critic Simon Howell notes, is "very Eric Garner-esque" and, therefore, carries with it some of the same emotional resonance.[16] Through these allusions, within the opening minutes of the episode viewers were immediately aware that the fictional story line they were about to watch was directly related to recent real-life events—most pointedly the deaths of Michael Brown and Eric Garner and the resulting turmoil that their respective communities in Ferguson, Missouri, and Staten Island, New York, endured.

Although most of the actual references in the show were to Ferguson, and therefore to the tragic death of Brown, the fictionalized murder in *The Good Wife* appears as a strategic merger of the events that occurred in both cities. On July 17, 2014, Garner, a forty-three-year-old black man approached by law enforcement for selling illegal cigarettes, died as the result of a chokehold placed on him by a white New York City police officer. His death was captured on cellphone video, and his final words, "I can't breathe," became a battle cry for protesters in the years that followed. Brown, an unarmed black teenager, was shot and killed only weeks later, on August 9, 2014, by a white police officer in a suburb of St. Louis. The shooting, similar to far too many earlier ones, prompted protests that continued for weeks. Months later, when the grand jury decided not to indict the officer who had killed Brown, the city erupted again into another wave of protests.

Although the episode begins with imagery of a death resulting from a police shooting, the tragedy is not the main focus of the one-hour narrative. The main story line concerns Alicia Florrick's televised debate for the Cook County state's attorney election against her opponent, Frank Prady (David Hyde Pierce). The debate is interrupted within minutes when the jury comes back with a not-guilty verdict exonerating the police officers involved in the murder showcased in the opening scenes. A protest takes place, police arrive in riot gear, politicians squabble about how to manage the situation, and the fictional dialogue is punctuated with a lot of references to real-world protests (how this could be "another Ferguson" or how the situation could go "full Ferguson" if not handled correctly).[17]

Media critics found plenty to criticize in this episode, such as a string of scenes that unfold in the kitchen of a hotel where the debate had been held. The two political opponents hold an impromptu, off-camera debate in front of the kitchen staff, many of whom are working-class minorities. They discuss "issues in the justice systems that make tragedies like this one commonplace" as "a group of young men of color (hotel workers) slowly drift in and act as a Greek chorus, pointing out how ridiculous it is seeing two white people who are running for office arguing about how more people of color need to hold political offices."[18] Writing for *Vulture,* Lauren Hoffman states that their asides work to some extent to acknowledge "the fact that this story is coming from a television show with an overwhelmingly white cast and creative team."[19] Others, however, issued strong objections to the ways in which this scene and episode played out. In an article for the *Atlantic,* David Sims wrote, "It felt patronizing, to say the very least, and like the show was trying to acknowledge recent events while admitting it lacks the authority to really dig into them."[20] In regard to the debate scene in particular, others called it "an embarrassing episode of 'white-splaining' from a show that is usually more nuanced when it comes to political matters."[21]

Whereas the kitchen scene received the most attention by critics, the ending has also been criticized as being overly "tidy": Alicia's husband, Peter, arrives at the scene of the protest in his capacity as the governor with the victim's widow, both of them urging the crowd to remain peaceful—which, of course, they do.[22]

Some have suggested that perhaps it was just "too soon" to have an episode like this, but others have argued the flaws were all in how the episode was executed.[23] The episode spent only a fraction of its time really delving into race, doing so as it bounced between other melodramatic story lines.[24] But some critics did think it had its moment of worthy critique, for example, showing that canned political statements—like those spouted by Alicia and Prady in the kitchen—do little to improve real-world racial justice.[25]

Scandal: *An Effort at Cultural Critique That Was Met with Mixed Reviews*

Compared to *The Good Wife* episode, Shonda Rhimes's attempt to respond to current race-related events though *Scandal* was better received, although not unanimously embraced. As mainstream media have noted, despite Rhimes's huge influence on cultural representation on television, before the season 4, episode 13, airing of "The Lawn Chair," race had been overtly mentioned in the show's dialogue only twice: "When Olivia told the president she was feeling kind of 'Sally Hemmings [*sic*]/Thomas Jefferson' about their affair, and when Olivia's father delivered a ferocious lecture . . . telling her, 'You have to be twice as good as them to get half of what they have.'"[26]

Coincidentally, "The Lawn Chair" aired on March 5, 2015, "the same week that the Justice Department released its scathing report on the Ferguson Police Department," delivering a story that seemed directly—rather than more tangentially, as was the case with *The Good Wife*'s episode—inspired by the murder of Michael Brown.[27] In the episode, Olivia is hired "by the Washington Metropolitan Police Department to help minimize the backlash (the 'optics,' as the chief put it) after a black 17-year-old was shot and killed by a white cop four blocks from the Capitol."[28] The situation escalates when, within minutes of Olivia's arrival on the scene, the dead teen's father arrives with a shotgun in hand demanding to see the cop who has killed his son. As the episode stretches on, Olivia finds "herself in conflict both with the police who'd hired her, and a neighborhood activist, Marcus, who condemned her for being on the wrong side. 'Helping . . . *and* cashing a check from the Washington Metro Police?' he said. 'Impressive. What's the going rate for playing both sides?'"[29]

As Aisha Harris notes in a piece for *Slate,* in this episode, Olivia is finally "forced to fully grapple with her complicated role as a black woman serving the mostly white federal government. . . . It's not often that *Scandal* addresses how complicated Olivia's role is as a black woman with so much and yet so little power, and how it affects her."[30] These critiques surface primarily in Olivia's onscreen interactions with Marcus, who later in the series becomes one of her infamous "warriors." He taunts her "for being on the wrong side; for arriving in an impoverished neighborhood with her Prada bag and thinking she could make things right when she was almost as removed from the reality of the situation as the MPD police chief appeared to be. 'Your black card's not getting validated today,' he [tells] her."[31]

Following this exchange, she argues with the police chief, who refers to the increasing group of African American protesters on-site as an angry mob, stating, "The fact that they stand in groups and say things you don't like doesn't make them a mob . . . it makes them Americans."[32] Then she joins the protesters behind the barricade, abandoning her loyalties to her police department client. The shot of Olivia in the midst of the crowd, her face and voice aligned with theirs in anger, is a powerful moment for the episode. In placing the show's heroine—the character viewers are most likely to empathize and identify with—in the protest, the program is inviting viewers to metaphorically cross the police barrier as well, to experience the emotion of the outraged crowd along with her.

Another powerful moment in the show is when Olivia addresses the attorney general, David Rosen, who is failing to help resolve the situation before it escalates further: "You talk about fairness and justice like it's available to everyone."[33] Her words crystalize the message of the show: the criminal justice system does not treat all citizens equally. Trying to get Rosen to empathize with the father, who now envisions an outcome in which he ends up in jail or the morgue, she tells him to imagine what it would be like to live in fear every day of his life.[34] This theme punctuates the episode to spark social reflection. For example, at one point the grieving single father reveals the lengths that African American parents go to in order to keep their children safe, telling her that he "stuck a University of Maryland sticker" on "his truck so cops who pulled Brandon over wouldn't think he was 'just a thug without a future.'"[35]

Ultimately, the events of the murder are revealed. Brandon Parker, the deceased young man, was stopped by Officer Newton while he was walking home because he apparently matched the description of someone who had stolen a cellphone. When Parker reached into his pocket to show the officer a receipt for a cellphone he had purchased legally, Newton fired his weapon, fearing that the boy was reaching for a gun. At first the officer plays up his remorse, noting that as a father he can't imagine how he "would be feeling now if [he] were that boy's father." But as the story line continues, Olivia reveals that Newton has planted evidence at the crime scene—a knife by the body to make the shooting seem more justified. In an overly neat ending, the guilty officer is arrested, but not before delivering a blatantly racist rant to Olivia in front of a shocked squad room of onlookers: "[You people are] taught to question me, to disobey me . . . and somehow I'm the animal."[36] Newton's diatribe continues as he claims the boy's blood is not on his hands but rather is the fault of a community that has been taught to question a cop's authority.[37] As Sophie Gilbert notes, this "horrifying statement of privilege" is one "echoed in the [actual] Ferguson report"; many Ferguson officials mentioned "a lack of 'personal responsibility' among African-American members of the Ferguson community that causes African Americans to experience disproportionate harm under Ferguson's approach to law enforcement." Or, as Newton says it in the episode, "They didn't teach him the right values. They didn't teach him respect."[38]

Many praised the episode. Gilbert, writing for the *Atlantic,* called the episode "a lesson in how to thoughtfully model fiction around real-life tragedy." Despite the fact that "the timing of the episode was eerie: days after the anniversary of Trayvon Martin's death coupled with the release of the Ferguson report," many critics commended *Scandal* for its attempt to "tackle police brutality and institutionalized racism."[39] Others appreciated the episode as one that sought to narrativize Rhimes's own thoughts on the racial injustice experienced across the country. Gilbert notes that though critics often problematically "interpret Rhimesian characters as avatars for their co-creator," in this case it is "hard not to perceive Olivia's taking a stand as being representative of the show doing the same." (And *Scandal* actors and Rhimes herself have confirmed this to be the case.)[40] Gilbert continues: "Maybe *Scandal* wanted to be a show that wasn't about race—a show that was simply an addictive, outrageous drama about a brilliant career woman with a complicated personal life who just happened to be black. Maybe it hoped never to have to be in this situation. But the events of the past year seem to have merited a response, and it's to the series's credit that the delivery was so graceful, and so utterly sad."[41]

As was true of *The Good Wife,* some criticized *Scandal* for its overly optimistic ending. In the end, Olivia and her team save the day, and despite the fact that he disturbed a crime scene (firearm in hand), the grieving father is not arrested. Instead, he is personally escorted to the White House, where he cries on the president's shoulder. Harris criticizes this lack of realism and the fact that the program didn't push itself far enough. She asks:

> Why did Brandon have to be a standup kid in the end, who *didn't* steal a cellphone? And why did Officer Newton have to be an undoubtedly dirty cop? Most cases of this nature are not so easily defined—racism and prejudice are often much more covert than that. When Michael Brown, Eric Garner, and many other unarmed people of color are killed by the police, the first thing many defenders will say is that they were 'asking for it' by robbing a corner store or selling loose cigarettes, or, oh I don't know, *carrying around a fake gun in an open and carry state.* Such viewpoints allow people to avoid empathy and see people of color as less than.[42]

Writing for *Paste Magazine,* Shannon Houston spoke out along similar lines: "*Scandal* did not need to give its huge audience an imaginary world where justice is served because, unfortunately, many people believe that such a world *is* the America we live in. If you're going to make a 'race' episode, why support those delusions?"[43] Similarly, Michael Arceneaux of VH1 notes: "In reality, no way would a Black man who grabbed his shotgun to seize control of the crime scene involving his son be allowed to walk away from all of that with not only no arrest, but the opportunity to both meet and cry on the president's shoulder."[44] But Arceneaux forgives the show this moment of unreality, saying: "I feel like we needed to see this lie this week. It's a fantasy, but it's great that we were allowed to see a place where Black lives, grief, and anger matter."[45]

Not all critics abhorred the ending. Gilbert, in fact, argues that it was emotionally delivered and thoughtfully crafted: "From the music that accompanied two of the episode's most poignant scenes (Marvin Gaye's 'What's Going On' and Nina Simone's 'I Shall Be Released') to the way the camera lingered on visual details (Olivia's shaking hand after a confrontation with Clarence, her obviously conflicted expression on the sidelines, a portrait of John F. Kennedy in the White House, the final shot of a beautiful face in a body bag), it was an extraordinary hour of television."[46]

Gilbert also draws attention to the significance of the episode's last line of dialogue: "'My son's name was Brandon,' Clarence Parker told the president, right before he finally broke down. His name mattered. His life mattered."[47] Rhimes admitted that *Scandal*'s creative team spent a lot of time debating how to end the episode, specifically whether it should end hopefully or not.[48] On the night the episode aired, Rhimes discussed this on social media, tweeting: "In the end, we went with showing what fulfilling the dream should mean. The idea of possibility. And [not] the despair we feel now."[49]

Just as media critics were divided on the episode, so, too, were fans. Some applauded the episode (e.g.: "It's almost like having diverse voices in TV leads to interesting commentaries on the world around us or something"; "The discussion that has been sparked in my house over #Scandal tonight! Thank you @shondarhimes"; "Tonight's episode @ScandalABC will stay with me. Deeply powerful, moving, soul-stirring work"). Some felt that it could help white viewers become more empathetic (e.g.: "I wonder if non-Black viewers actually feel our pain after seeing this episode. Shonda slapped you in the face with OUR reality"; "Between Nina Simone and actually showing the body being zipped into a body bag, Shonda Rhimes wants her viewers to FEEL OUR

PAIN! Thank you"; "Let's be clear, tonight's episode of #Scandal should have made you feel some type of way. Now be a part of the change you wish to see"). But others felt TV should be escapism that does not delve into this type of reality (e.g.: "For me, #Scandal is fun campy entertainment. A storyline around a black boy being killed by the police . . . that's too real for me"; "The timing of that speech from the cop and this movement. . . . It wasn't appropriate"; "These stories make me sick. And watching them fictionalized makes me sick too apparently"; "Looks like Scandal has everyone fake caring about police brutality again"). And still others noted that they felt sad after viewing the episode because such justice seems possible only within the confines of a fictional television show (e.g.: "It's sad we can only get justice when we write it into fiction"; "What did I say? A nice and tidy ending that shows that justice will be served in America. Don't have time"; "Mixed feelings because this is how we wished things would've been resolved in real life"; "If only 'justice' moved as swiftly as on #Scandal").[50]

The mixed reactions among the fans of *Scandal* were to be expected. In an interview with *Flavorwire,* Eric Haywood, the writer and producer for Fox's popular show *Empire* (2015–20), discusses the catch-22 shows are faced with when they decide to write an episode focused on a black man or woman dying at the hands of law enforcement:

> What happens any time any show tries to touch on anything that is both current and controversial, [is that] the response from the audience is immediate and also completely varied. . . . Responses from the audience . . . [are] almost always split right down the middle. Half of the audience says, 'I'm so glad that this show that I love is taking on this topic, because it needs to be discussed.' The other half immediately says that, 'I really don't tune in to my favorite show to see these grim topics. I can watch the news if I wanted that. I just want to be entertained.' And so it leaves you in a position of, well, what do you do? Do you completely ignore what's going on in the world so you don't ruffle people's feathers and risk being accused of being either out of touch or ignoring the most important topics of the day? Or, do you try to address them and risk being accused of pandering, or do you risk turning off the segment of the audience who openly admit they just want to turn their brain off and be entertained? So there's really no one right answer.[51]

The jarring nature of these ripped-from-the-headlines episodes guarantees strong reactions from viewers and critics alike, but those strong reactions are not going to be uniform.

As for the negative critical reactions these shows faced, some of them stem from the fact that quite obviously a stand-alone episode focused on racial injustice is always going to fall short and not do *enough*. "There's nothing wrong with the 'race' episode, per se, and there are ways they can be done well," Houston notes. "The 'race' episode doesn't have to be synonymous with the 'urban riot' episode. So-called everyday racism is just as compelling, and offers just as much drama as martial law. And maybe if we had more of those, we wouldn't need the 'race/riot/oh yeah, racism is a big issue in America' episode."[52]

While stand-alone episodes like these are useful because they invite viewers to think about racial issues that might not be on their minds all the time, Houston argues that it is problematic when television programs deliver "their New Important Timely Episode Which Will Tackle The American Race Problem, and then spend the rest of the season ignoring these problems altogether." This, she claims, "speaks volumes about the real problem of American race relations, where consistent, realistic, public, ongoing dialogue is still not happening."[53]

Debates Concerning Television's Ability to Address the Black Lives Matter Movement

Episodes like these from *Scandal* and *The Good Wife* have found media critics questioning whether—despite its past success in engaging with civil rights—television is the right tool for taking on these critiques. Like Houston, Joshua Alston was skeptical of the effect that stand-alone episodes in a series can have: "The 'very special episode' once had the power to spark national conversations, back when *Maude* was wrestling with an unwanted pregnancy or Arnold and Dudley were being groomed by a pedophile on *Diff'rent Strokes.* Scripted television is no longer in the position to lead the conversation around social issues, and as a result, the benefit to delving into those issues less frequently outweighs the risk of salting an open wound."[54]

Other critics are less pessimistic about television's potential to spark critical reflection and social change, but they do realize the challenge of crafting the television series or episode that effectively prompts such reflection and change. They pose important questions, such as: "How does a fictional TV show accurately depict" serious issues like racial inequality "without trivializing or offending?" "Does fictionalizing it bring more harm than good to the movement?" "Is there a 'correct' way to handle police brutality in a . . . television show?"[55]

Overall, there was consensus among critics that these episodes cannot be created to check off a social justice box (i.e., we did our Black Lives Matter episode), or—even worse—in the hopes of seeing a spike in ratings or social media mentions.[56] There was, however, debate on who should participate in their creation. As I noted earlier, much of the criticism wielded at *The Good Wife*'s episode touched on the fact that it was written and directed by white people and featured predominantly white characters. As a result, it was, unsurprisingly, "clumsy," as one critic wrote, probably because "there was no one around with a personal connection to the issue to provide some much-needed nuance and direction."[57] This seems to suggest that only programs with diverse producers and actors are equipped to deliver such story lines, but not all critics agree. Houston, for example, argues that if "a predominantly white cast takes on the issue of race with boldness and nuance . . . it can be even more exciting to watch—that is to say a 'race' episode on *The Good Wife* can send an even stronger message than, say, racial dialogue on a show like *Empire* or *Black-ish,* where such themes are partly anticipated."[58] But not everyone can agree—regardless of the program's makeup—that even a "nuanced" story line is going to have the desired effect. *Scandal,* which features a more diverse production team and cast, was praised by viewers for crafting a more multifaceted story line, showing how police shootings affect not only the victim's family and community, but also those in law enforcement. Some critics suggest, however, that the quest for delivering the all-encompassing episode that addresses all sides of the issue might be part of the problem. According to Alston, "Scripted stories about police-involved shootings of black people have to show the impact of the events on everyone around them, even though they affect everyone's lives differently. Therefore, any scripted take on BLM is bound to look like *All Lives Matter: The TV Show.*"[59]

If shows really want to delve into "all" sides of the issue—and perhaps this is not the ideal—more narrative space is required than what is provided in a single episode. This might be the reason that of all the shows explicitly tackling story lines relating to the Black Lives Matter movement, Netflix's *Orange Is the New Black* (2013–17) has received the most uniform praise. As a show that regularly attends to "the dysfunction of the criminal justice system," its narrative framework was a logical space to explore police brutality and racial inequality, which it did through a tragic story line in its fourth season.[60]

American Crime: An Example of How Televisual Aesthetics Can Affectively Critique Racial Politics

Of course, as I previously noted, the special "race" episode featuring large-scale riots is not television's only avenue toward bringing attention to such inequalities and the emotional toil they take on people. More powerful are explorations of "everyday racism."[61] *American Crime* focused on just this—over the course of an entire series—and was, arguably, more successful than many of the other televisual attempts to bring attention to recent racial concerns. But it was not just that its narrative space—eleven episodes—allowed for a "more nuanced portrait of race," but also that the show's particular aesthetics allowed its social commentary to have a greater emotional influence.[62]

American Crime premiered the same day as *Scandal*'s "Lawn Chair" episode aired. Like the other shows, *American Crime* was influenced by recent events. In an interview with the *Los Angeles Times,* the show's creator, John Ridley, best known for his Academy Award–winning screenplay for *12 Years a Slave,* commented on this: "The sad reality is that, unfortunately, these events remain cyclical in our country. It was never our desire to exploit any of these things, and it's not my desire to just merely say things. I really want people to *feel things,* to reexamine the world around them."[63]

American Crime features interlocking story lines in which seemingly unconnected characters are connected through one violent event: "In this case, it's the horrific assault of a white couple living in the bedroom community of Modesto, Calif.—an attack that leaves the husband, military veteran Matt Skokie, dead, and his wife, Gwen, a former beauty queen, in critical condition. The suspects arrested and charged with the crime are all minorities," and so the crime prompts a critical examination of race and prejudice (between and within racial groups).[64]

As Cory Barker notes, the show purposely begins the story after the attack, forcing viewers to "sympathize with the characters before [they] truly begin to understand the role they may or may not have played in the heinous offense." What is also noteworthy is that none of the characters is particularly likable; viewers are forced to identify with characters who embody various biases that they may see (or wish not to see) in themselves.[65] While there is a central mystery to solve—who actually committed the crime—the show really draws viewers' attention to the range of "casual racism on display, where characters offhandedly reveal their prejudice, or where established institutions express their inherent racism."[66] The mother of the murdered military veteran, Barb Hanlon (Felicity Huffman), is one of the more overtly racist characters, although she struggles to acknowledge her biases against people of color. Her more overt racism is contrasted with the complicated racial viewpoints of other characters. For example, Aliyah Shadeed (Regina King), the black Muslim sister of one of the men arrested for the crime, regularly expresses her anger and distrust of white people and the system that provides them with their various privileges. And, smartly, the show also showcases internalized racism as well. The best example is a Mexican-American, Alonzo Gutiérrez (Benito Martinez), the father of one of the young men accused of being an accomplice in the crime, who angers his own community by speaking out against illegal immigrants. Discussing the importance of his character's storyline, Martinez commented: "It throws back this curtain where people within their own culture say things that they would not say out loud among others. It's that level of honesty that I hope leads to open discussions that we rarely have."[67]

Despite the fact that the victims of the central crime are white and the suspects are all minorities—which in and of itself provides commentary on the criminal justice system—the program systematically dissolves racial stereotypes. In particular it works to shatter illusions concerning white victimhood. As the investigation unfolds, information is slowly revealed that indicates that the attacked couple were not the upstanding citizens their families believed them to be, but, rather, were involved in the sale of drugs and engaged in illicit sex with multiple people. Similarly, the story line involving the star-crossed lovers, the meth addicts Aubry Taylor (Caitlin Gerard) and Carter Nix (Elvis Nolasco), slowly establishes Aubry—a young white woman from an upper-middle-class foster family—as the negative influence on Carter, a young black man estranged from his devoutly religious family.

While the complicated characterizations and multilayered story lines have been applauded, what makes *American Crime* truly exceptional is its televisual stylistics. Whereas the other programs analyzed here—*The Good Wife* and *Scandal*—probably shared Ridley's goal of trying to get audiences to "feel things," specifically things related to racial inequality, *American Crime* was unique in that its overall aesthetic seemed devoted to this goal. The show's very filmic audiovisual techniques often reinforced the social critique it was trying to unfold, allowing that commentary to be more *felt*.

Image 7.1. Café scene with divided booths from *American Crime*.

Many scholars have pointed out *American Crime*'s "visual dexterity" and its "stylized" nature.[68] All the aesthetic choices concerning the audio and visual compilation of the program are purposeful and underscore the show's themes. For example, one visual motif that appears throughout the season is one of division (see image 7.1). Unlike traditional television staging, the series' characters are often placed so that barriers exist between them and other characters, or so that even when they exist as the only character onscreen, they are not centrally located, which suggests feelings of imbalance or isolation (see image 7.2).

Another common visual element *American Crime* uses is the extreme close-up when two people are in dialogue. In traditional filming both parties in a conversation are visible at some point throughout the dialogue; both parties are often visible in the same frame or through alternating shots between the two participants. *American Crime,* however, consistently shoots entire conversations with only one speaker fully visible. Often the back of the second person's head can be seen in these scenes, or the second party is present but is purposefully blurred so that his or her figure can barely be made out (see image 7.3). Arguably, these stylized techniques reinforce themes such as othering, segregation, and breakdown in communication.

Image 7.2. The physical barriers of a visiting room in *American Crime.*

Along with these visual tactics, various editing and audio elements contributed to the emotional resonance of the show. Returning to the show's use of one-on-one conversations, the audio editing was purposely uneven so that dialogue was often out of sync with the visual of the actor speaking the lines, creating a jarring effect wherein viewers are always struggling to get their eyes or ears to catch up, or sync up, with the onscreen image or sound. There are also regular scenes in which characters "speak over and across one another," which makes it hard to follow the conversation.[69] The show also strategically uses silence. Although it is filled with many quick edits in which scenes are abruptly interrupted (creating a sense of "nervy energy"), there are many lingering shots in which characters (or parts of their bodies) are shown for extended amounts of time, allowing for prolonged moments of viewer contemplation.[70]

On top of the unique televisual aesthetics *American Crime* brought to its narrative, it differed from the other two examples studied here in one important way: it lacked narrative closure. *The Good Wife* ended conveniently with the governor and the widow of the victim calming a protesting crowd, and *Scandal* ended with the unrealistic scene of the grieving father sobbing on

Image 7.3. Close-up shot of Aliyah Shadeed (Regina King) on *American Crime.*

the president's shoulder, but *American Crime* did not provide an ending packed with wish fulfillment, and it sidestepped the normal requirement to wrap up all narrative loose ends. The show concludes on a decidedly unhappy note, with more deaths than it began with. Three main characters die in the final hour of programming: one by homicide and two by suicide. Most of the lives of the surviving main characters are still in ruins when the series ends. For example, Alonzo's family is contemplating exile, considering moving away from Modesto so they can start anew, and Barb is left with only her relationship with her estranged son and his fiancé (although her final scene could suggest that her redemption is still possible). A descriptor that might be fitting for the series as a whole is *hopeless,* as the stark realities of social inequity are never viewed through rose-colored glasses. Yet, ironically, the final unspoken word of the first season is the word *hope.*

The one story line that does surprisingly end on a positive note is Hector Tontz's (Richard Cabral), the heavily tattooed Mexican gang member illegally residing in the United States. After being deported and narrowly escaping trial in Mexico, Hector ends up on a job interview, hoping he can secure a position and help support his young daughter and her mother. While it seems initially as if his criminal past will prevent him from securing the position, he delivers an impassioned speech that—it seems—sways the interviewer's mind (the end of this scene is not overtly shown).

> My girlfriend, right? See, she asked me if I was tired of my life, getting cut up, getting shot. I'll tell you for real: I'm not tired of my life, I'm worn out. See, I know people come in here all the time asking you to take a chance on them, tell you how they changed. See, I don't know from other people what makes them do how they do. But I'm twenty-six years old, and all I got to show for my life is a limp and a [scar] and a five-year-old girl who needs her daddy to live straight. I'm not part of nothing anymore, I'm just trying to get a job.[71]

The final scene is of Hector getting into his girlfriend's car after the interview and her asking how he feels. Hector, who seems visibly relieved and happy, answers: "I feel . . ." and the then season ends without that last word spoken. The unspoken word seems to be hope—that for the first time he is hopeful for his future—but it is important that the show does not actually allow it to be delivered.

Other critics read the show as ending on a more positive note. Writing for *Entertainment Weekly,* Keertana Sastry focuses on the motif of forgiveness that is woven throughout the final episode. Sastry argues that "it's the most important yet least utilized word in *American Crime*'s season finale," pointing out that it is woven into "three different church services attended by three different families all connected by the titular violent act."[72] And one of the most poignant scenes comes when Aubry's foster mother and Aliyah share an emotional embrace after Carter's and Aubry's deaths. Whether they are forgiving each other—and the role their family member had played in their own loved one's death—or themselves is unclear, but it is one of the few empathetic moments the show provides between characters across racial lines.

Despite the few thematic nods toward forgiveness and hope, the lack of perfect narrative closure provided by *American Crime* aligns with the social commentary the show is attempting. As Braxton notes, the program "touches on bigotry, stereotypes and racial profiling within a context that does not offer convenient explanations or resolution."[73] These are issues that are not reaching tidy closure in real life; therefore, it is fitting that individual narratives presented in the show are also resolution-free. Libby Hill agrees, writing:

> So at the close of *American Crime*'s first season, there's really only one fate left to be determined: that of the audience. But even that seems pretty clear. An audience tunes in to see the resolution of a conflict, in this case, the murder and attack on Matt and Gwen Skokie. People were accused and released, someone confessed, though one could never be certain she was telling the truth, and many people ended up dead. But was there justice for the crime perpetrated? Was there an answer we can stand by and feel a sense of closure to? No. Not really. But maybe that's the point. Maybe in America crime is not [an] open and closed story, no matter what *Law & Order* might have you believe. It's merely a tale that spins itself out, pulling ever more people into its web, before spitting them back into the world half-digested or worse.[74]

As chapter 5 discussed, the majority of television programs or episodes that directly or indirectly engage with cultural anxieties end with positive denouements, providing viewers with happy closure, or at least temporary relief from their fear and anger. Most government-themed programs feature brave CIA and FBI agents or dutiful political leaders saving the nation from peril. Passengers stranded on mysterious islands get rescued. Good thwarts evil, even if the good guys are vampires and werewolves. Although chapter 5 highlighted *The Walking Dead*'s bleakness, even it occasionally (although such instances become increasingly rare) shows the group of survivors experiencing momentary respites from suffering. *American Crime,* in this case, is darker than even the zombie apocalypse because it remains entirely grounded in reality and almost entirely hopeless (besides its final line of silent dialogue). Importantly, its only moment of hope is left for the viewer to insert into the program for himself or herself.

The Consequences of Remediating In-Progress Cultural Conflicts

The two subsets of television that I have attended to in part II—the post-9/11-themed shows and the recent programs concerned with contemporary race relations—might seem like an odd coupling, but they do similar emotional work (with perhaps different consequences). As is probably evident, remediations of 9/11 and shows working through post-9/11 anxieties are not going anywhere. One reason may be that they are a relatively easy story to tell. As chapter 1 discussed, viewers like their danger packaged as a free-floating, outside threat. Perhaps it is easier to enjoy such fears because on some level we realize the unlikelihood of those 9/11-related fears being actualized. The spectacular dangers we see in most of these post-9/11 dramas are only slightly more real than the threat of the zombies and vampires and other apocalyptic wonders that we often see in narratives that serve as allegories for those fears.

Remediations of domestic tragedies like the murder of Michael Brown or Eric Garner (or too many others to list here), are *not* easy to tell. And so most television shows will not tell these stories, or, as I've discussed in this chapter, will not tell them well. In many ways, because the threat they fictionalize is much more real and *present* than the terrorist-themed dangers presented in the 9/11-related shows, these shows have greater power to influence viewers. These shows have the power to do good and the power to do more damage.

In many respects, 9/11 is an event completed. Though the larger threat of terrorism is ever-present, the actual event of 9/11, while still reverberating in our cultural operations, is one that has reached closure. But unlike 9/11, Ferguson (serving as a representation of systemic racial injustice in the United States more broadly) is still very much an event-in-progress. Despite individual rulings and reports, Ferguson is not over. It is not over because, unlike 9/11, which stands as an isolated incident of sorts, the events surrounding Ferguson are very much linked to a string of similar, cyclical incidents.

Fictionalizations of the racial conflict afflicting the nation do prompt many questions concerning the ethics of crafting narratives that attempt to remediate these domestic tragedies-in-progress. We might ask any of the following: What does it mean to remediate a cultural tragedy that is *still in motion?* In what way does the affect-reciprocity cycle discussed in the introduction change when the cultural events are unfolding *simultaneously* with the cultural fictions being spawned to remediate them? What kind of affectual *power* does this give to these parallel, fictional narratives? Can they heal, influence the cultural climate, refine public sentiment? As television scholars have questioned concerning fictional explorations of other social issues, does watching these narratives actually act to *defuse* activist impulses rather than stimulate them?

Consider again Alston's overall pessimism concerning television's capabilities to adequately address the Black Lives Matter movement. Leaving room for some hope that the medium could tackle these issues, he wrote: "Television still has the power, albeit diminished, to shape the public discourse. But the only way scripted shows can effectively present the problem is for the audience to first agree that the problem exists."[75] I would argue that the only way to get people to "agree that the problem exists" is to *show* them that it exists. While in theory real-world examples should very well do this, there is power in fictional narratives that transport viewers into conflicts that they would not usually experience or witness. There can be potential benefits to allowing viewers—especially white viewers—to empathize and identify with characters of color who are experiencing racial inequality. Likewise, viewers of color can gain some comfort in seeing their stories of racial injustice told—if told well. Furthermore, the cultivation theory would suggest that "television images inform public opinion about the social world."[76] Therefore, these fictionalizations can help get viewers to "agree that the problem exists." Moreover, if done well—as I argued was the case with *American Crime*—it can get viewers not just to contemplate this social inequity, but to *feel* it.[77] And it might be that added affective element that will help television be a powerful ally in the fight for racial justice.

Part III

Amplifying Affect

Twenty-first-Century Viewing Practices—From Fandom to Digital Activism and Beyond

8

Live Tweets as Social Commentary?

Analyzing How Gender, Race, and Sexuality Play into Conceptions of Morality in How to Get Away with Murder

We are living in an alarmist age in which tirades about society's eroding ethics are abundant, and the media often act as a convenient scapegoat for those who fear our cultural values are disintegrating before our very eyes. For decades, critics have cast blame at television for contributing to our so-called moral decline.[1] Television has been framed as a bad role model for youths and adults alike, and scholars have contemplated the effect that television viewing across genres has on the audience—citing, for example, the debaucherous behavior featured on reality television, the narcissism present in celebrity programming, and the excessive violence featured in fictional drama. Recently, such fearmongering has even turned from concerns about the content of television programming to worries about the negative consequences related to twenty-first-century television viewing practices. For instance, studies have been released arguing that binge-watching television might lead to antisocial dispositions, depression, or immorality.[2] Online behavior, which is increasingly tied to media consumption, is also a target for panicked proclamations about our inevitable indoctrination into immorality. Social media have shouldered the weight of this blame, being credited with prompting increased levels of depression, jealousy, and apathy, and for creating a generation of narcissists.[3] Television viewing today often entails double screening—wherein viewers are not only engaging with the content on their television screens, but also commenting on that content through social media. Recent studies find that 43 percent of tablet and smartphone owners report using their devices while watching television every day.[4] In particular, research indicates that 95 percent of the conversation occurring on social media concerning television is taking place on Twitter, making it an ideal site of study to determine exactly what viewers are doing with their double screens.[5]

When these data concerning media conversion are read alongside the alarmist rhetoric about the negative effect technology is having on cultural ethics, one might come to the conclusion that this tag team of Twitter and television is bound to destroy humanity as we know it. Or not. Unsurprisingly, actual studies of online television fandom indicate that audience engagement with television programming—even programs packed full of scandalous story lines—are much more complicated than any simplistic fearmongering or causality theory might imply.

When Nielson released a study in August 2015 reporting which television programs had the most active fans on social media, it was not shocking that two of Shonda Rhimes's shows—*Scandal* (ABC, 2012–18) and *How to Get Away with Murder* (ABC, 2014–20)—made the top-ten list.[6] Media critics within and outside academia have analyzed how Rhimes's social media practices, as well as those of her fans, have transformed contemporary network television production and consumption practices.[7] While the post-network era in general has resulted in more fragmented and noncollective viewing experiences, Rhimes's three-hour block of television programming (*Grey's Anatomy, Scandal, How to Get away with Murder*) actually prompted a return to live television watching—and, more important, live television commentary. Capitalizing on the must-see nature of her "fan-obsessed TV dramas" and the "Twitter activism" they inspire, Rhimes has evolved into a "savvy media mogul" who has changed prime-time viewing practices, cultivating practices wherein viewers, show actors, and show producers engage in synchronous online dialogue during her programs on a weekly basis.[8] Eager to follow the success of the Shondaland shows, now virtually every television program has its own hashtag, and networks are eager to promote them. Considering the influence Rhimes has had on contemporary viewing practices, her shows make ideal sites for studying the potential consequences and benefits of such active viewing practices—viewing practices that are often quite emotionally charged. Moreover, considering Rhimes's self-stated agenda for her own programming—to use her fictional texts to carry out work related to social justice—studying these viewing practices allows us to determine the ways in which they support or undermine attempts from shows' producers to engage in a form of public pedagogy.

How to Get Away with Murder's Brand of Morality

Rhimes's hit television drama *How to Get Away with Murder* (*HTGAWM*) forefronts tenuous societal debates concerning the morality and immortality of the current U.S. justice system. Mirroring recent headlines regarding college gang rapes, peer-pressure-motivated murder, and child abduction, the show merges real-world criminal cases with its fictional narratives, thereby providing insight into the ways in which the legal system does not always provide an easy path toward justice. This melodrama's complicated, interlocking plots showcase a slew of sudsy story lines—backstabbing, betrayal, blackmail, and, of course, adultery—that tackle morality in terms of romantic relationships, family power dynamics, and educational competition. Weekly, fans of *HTGAWM* storm Twitter to extend their interaction with the show by live-tweeting their viewing experiences, critically engaging with the fictional morality tales and debating the real-world ethical implications of Rhimes's narratives. Questions of morality have always been a thread running through Rhimes's programming, such as the explorations of medical ethics in *Grey's Anatomy* and *Private Practice* and political ethics in *Scandal.* In the case of *HTGAWM,* morality appears to be the heartbeat of the show. Taken collectively, her programming clearly situates itself as a form of public pedagogy—a means in which to educate, develop citizenship, challenge dominant cultural discourses, foster public intellectualism, and prompt social activism by using informal institutions, public spaces, and popular culture.[9] Therefore, studying audience reactions conveyed on Twitter provides insight into how viewers are reacting to her weekly "lessons." This analysis also suggests—contrary to alarmist rhetoric concerning the detrimental effects of our current screen-centric lifestyles—that these various media platforms are serving as pedagogical tools for engaging in important cultural education.

How to Get Away with Murder is centered on Annalise Keating (Viola Davis), a middle-aged African American legal professor, and her five up-and-coming ambitious law students, but it is Annalise who draws the most audience attention for her peculiar scruples. For example, critics often note her "ambiguous" morals and some have even gone as far as claiming she operates in accordance with "a Machiavellian moral compass," which suggests that she acts in duplicitous, cynical, and self-serving ways.[10] The show's pilot encourages such readings, as it immediately underscores the moral gray area that the characters operate within. During Annalise's opening lecture to her students—featured prominently in the original promos for the show—she says: "The question I'm asked most often as a defense attorney is whether I can tell if my clients are innocent or guilty. And my answer is always the same: I don't care."[11]

Viola Davis is often asked to chime in about her character's sense of right and wrong. In an interview she observed, "I think we're all morally questionable. . . . I think that we . . . act on nature and not on morals. I [find] her to be a realistic protagonist. I find her to be very human, as we all are, in that we have grey areas."[12] Along the same lines, Peter Nowalk, the show's creator, argued that Annalise's personalized form of justice could be seen as a response to a system that is stacked in favor of some rather than others: "It's not so black and white to her. . . . Justice is very complicated, and the justice system is much more corrupt than you would think it would be. . . . I think Annalise feels like she's being moral. She's standing up for the people who don't get stood up for a lot."[13]

Rhimes's critiques of the criminal justice system within the show are not surprising; they are aligned with the social commentary she weaves into all her television programs—much of which is intended to debunk the myth that we are living in a post-identity society in which everyone exists on an even playing field. For example, early seasons of *Grey's Anatomy* featured story lines related to the gender discrimination Isobel "Izzy" Stevens (Katherine Heigl) faced in the medical profession because she was an attractive woman and the ways in which motherhood challenged the trajectory of female doctors, such as Miranda Bailey (Chandra Wilson) and, later, Meredith Grey (Ellen Pompeo). Likewise, *Scandal* explored the ways in which high-profile figures felt the need to remain closeted to ensure career success—most notably, Cyrus Beene (Jeff Perry). While Rhimes is certainly not alone in combating insinuations that the United States is post-identity, and particularly post-racial, she has been at center stage since racial inequality in Hollywood, a long-standing systemic problem, has recently garnered prolific media attention.[14] For instance, the 2015–16 awards cycle brought increased attention to the lack of diversity in the entertainment industry. Two events that helped reignite this conversation were Viola Davis becoming the first African American female to win a Best Actress Emmy in 2015 for her role on *How to Get Away with Murder* and the massive outcry that followed the 2016 announcement—for the second year in a row—of an all-white slate of Oscar nominees.[15] During her 2016 acceptance speech for the Producers Guild's Norman Lear Award for Achievement in Television, Rhimes told the audience, in a somewhat tongue-in-cheek manner, "I completely deserve this. . . . I have against the odds, courageously pioneered the art of writing for people of color as if they were human beings."[16] She then continued more seriously to explain why it is quite sad that in the twenty-first century her practices could be viewed as revolutionary:

> It's not trailblazing to write the world as it actually is. Women are smart and strong. They are not sex toys or damsels in distress. People of color are not sassy or dangerous or wise. And, believe me, people of color are never anybody's sidekick in real life. . . . I created the content that I wanted to see and I created what I know is normal. So basically, you are just giving me an award for being me, in which case I totally deserve it. Really, I am honored to receive it. The respect of this award does mean the world. It just makes me a little bit sad. First of all, strong women and three-dimensional people of color is something Norman [Lear] was doing 40-something years ago. So how come it has to be done all over again? What are we waiting for?[17]

This speech underscores Rhimes's commitment to social equality—and her belief that media representation factors heavily into this. This chapter analyzes Rhimes's efforts to broadcast her public pedagogy through her television shows by highlighting some of the social commentary present in *HTGAWM*. To study how her "lessons" are being received by her massive viewing audiences, this chapter analyzes the live-tweeting practices of *HTGAWM* fans. As Twitter use is rapidly increasing—over 500 million users generate approximately 340 million tweets a day—the social media site is steadily attracting academic analysis.[18] Building on previous scholarship, this study examines how viewers of fictional programming turn to Twitter as a medium in which to engage with important societal critiques, and how such live-tweeting practices may constitute a form of digital activism. By focusing in part on tweets responding to the morality of the main character, this chapter also investigates to what extent live tweets pertaining to television dramas reflect larger cultural anxieties concerning gender, sexuality, and other issues affecting identity construction and how they might reveal the ways in which moral frameworks are influenced by identity politics.

She Did a Bad, Bad Thing: The Rise of the Antihero on Television

Television scholars have long suggested that television programming reflects societal values.[19] If television acts as a cultural mirror of sorts, the rapid rise of the antihero on the small screen—a classification that Annalise Keating arguably belongs to—might be seen as disconcerting. Alarmists would posit that the increasing number of shows featuring dark and twisty, morally compromised antiheroes points toward a weakening ethical landscape in American culture, but this is not likely the case.

The antihero has existed as a character archetype since the early Greek comedies and tragedies, and its popularity often resurfaces at distinct points in history.[20] Hypothesizing the causes behind this recent resurgence, Jonathan Michael notes: "If we consider the 21st century so far—9/11 terrorist attacks, the Iraq War, Enron, Hurricane Katrina, the economic recession, Hurricane Sandy, the Newtown shootings, the Boston Marathon attacks—there's been a steady stream of terrible events to shake our faith in humanity."[21] Although it might seem counterintuitive, research indicates, as chapter 1 notes, that in dark times we actually want to surround ourselves in even darker narratives. As a result, the beginning of the twenty-first century provided us with a golden age of television drama filled with antiheroes like Tony Soprano (*The Sopranos*), Walter White (*Breaking Bad*), Dexter Morgan (*Dexter*), Jack Bauer (*24*), Don Draper (*Mad Men*), and Gregory House (*House*), who offered escapism and relief from our real-world evils by transporting us into their ethically compromised fictional worlds.[22] As this list of prominent antiheroes reveals, they often share a defining feature: they're all men. As Meghan Gallagher notes, "It seems that edgy, complicated characters who stray from the path of morality, are incredibly popular, as long as they embody stereotypes of patriarchal masculinity."[23] Despite the overwhelming popularity of male antiheroes, female antiheroes have been slow to gain entrance into the bad boy club until recently. The televisual tides have been turning with female characters like *UnREAL*'s Rachel Goldberg, *Nurse Jackie*'s Jackie Peyton, *Weeds*'s Nancy Botwin, *The Americans*' Elizabeth Jennings, and *Homeland*'s Carrie Mathison fighting their way into the category, suggesting that women, like men, can be "morally bereft *and* relatable at the same time."[24]

Scholars claim that part of the appeal of watching characters who cross the lines of acceptable morality is that we can see ourselves (or our potential selves) in such characters, and can glimpse a "relatable version of a good self that has gone bad."[25] The typical formula of an antihero narrative helps make these characters palatable. For example, nearly all the programs featuring antiheroes include a backstory that allows us to forgive, or at least explain, the character's moral transgressions. Annalise's backstory falls in line with this expectation: she is scripted with a narrative past that includes childhood trauma and spousal abuse.[26]

Research indicates that viewers also seem to gain pleasure from the cognitive dissonance created by characters who are not purely good or evil. Jason

Steward notes this phenomenon in his analysis of *Nurse Jackie*'s antiheroine: "Jackie is an adulterous, drug-sniffing, domineering, devious super nurse, who, at times, also displays the unwavering moral compass of a burning Catholic saint. From show to show, we see her juggle such contradictions as giving free medical care to cash strapped patients while also robbing an epileptic of their OxyContin stash during a seizure."[27]

Alongside internal conflicts as part of antihero characters' appeal, others argue that it is a character's sinful side that lures us in. Jonathan Michael contends that shows featuring antiheroes tap into our scariest fantasies—the ones lurking, often unacknowledged, within the human psyche.[28] Scholars studying our fascination with such characters have drawn on Freud's psychoanalytic theory to explain how "watching or reading about violence, sex, or other taboo behaviors provides a sense of catharsis and serves as an outlet for a human's aggressive tendencies or needs."[29] Similarly, Sophie Janicke and Arthur Raney argue that though we "are constantly self-regulating in order to meet the demands and expectations of society, books and television allow us to 'violate our own typical standards of morality' by enjoying and relating to the anti-hero character."[30]

This cathartic relationship between antiheroes and viewers contextualizes the large fan following of *HTGAWM*'s Frank Delfino (Chris Weber), Annalise's assistant and ethically unbound "fixer." Chris Weber calls him "a hit man with a heart of gold" but clarifies that he does not consider him to be an antihero, noting that he is a cold-blooded killer who "enjoys it."[31] But despite the fact that he drowns undergraduate students, stuffs corpses into suitcases, and sends people to jail for crimes they did not commit, fans do not react as harshly to his immoral behavior as they do to Annalise's (as I will discuss later). Arguably, the differing reactions these two characters draw stems from the double standards that exist for male versus female fictional characters generally and are further complicated by the racial dynamic presented in the Annalise-Frank pairing.[32] One might ask: Would Frank be beloved among fans as a "hit man with a heart of gold" if he were represented by an actor of color? The latter half of the second season features flashbacks to help explain how both Annalise and Frank arrived at their current compromised ethics. It is important to note, however, that the scenes devoted to Frank's downfall toward immorality cast Annalise as the catalyst for his initial moral lapse. This narrative inclusion conjures up the trope of the female temptress and problematically presents a black character as the corrupting force over a white character.[33] Although individual story lines ultimately find Frank's level of immorality trumping Annalise's (for example, she is one of the few characters who has not been directly responsible for a murder), the addition of their backstories highlights the ways in which moral superiority is often granted by default to white men.

While male characters who walk on the dark side are easily labeled as antiheroes and are often well received, similar female characters—whether they are classified as antiheroes or not—are typically described as "'off-putting' and 'obnoxious'" or, more commonly, they get tagged with the all-too-popular buzzword *unlikable*.[34] Countless critics have addressed the gendered "double-standard of likability" and its influence on how "we process fictional women."[35] The result, as Lauren Duca explains, is that "there are infinitely more obstacles faced by leading ladies making morally questionable choices."[36] For example, Michelle Juergen discusses the recent backlash that antiheroines like *Girls*'s Hannah Horvath, *Orange Is the New Black*'s Piper Chapman, *Enlightened*'s Amy Jellicoe, and *Nashville*'s Juliette Barnes have faced. Juergen writes: "Viewers and critics have no problem cheering on *Breaking Bad*'s Walter White or the blood spatter pattern analyst/serial killer Dexter Morgan as they sell drugs and slice up bad guys, but they find it difficult to watch the awkward and uncomfortable real-life situations that *Girls* [for example] addresses, and instead see its women as 'annoying, selfish and entitled.'"[37]

Juergen argues that "we're not used to being served up unpalatable women," and, therefore, when we are faced with "women who act in a way we're used to seeing only male characters act," it's "alienating" and we unfairly brand them as "unlikable rather than well-crafted and complex."[38] Female characters—like their real-world counterparts—are punished for projecting masculine-coded traits like ambition, aggression, or strength.[39] In turn, this often affects the authors—across media and genres—who craft such characters.

A *New York Times* best-selling author, Roxane Gay, discusses this practice of critics dismissing a female character on the basis of her perceived unlikability—her failure to live up to "a very elaborate lie, a performance, a code of dictating the proper way to be."[40] Similarly, Claire Messud, author of *The Woman Upstairs,* angrily responded to the notion that her female protagonist was unlikable. After an interviewer commented that she would not want to be friends with Nora, the main character, Messud responded:

> For heaven's sake, what kind of question is that? Would you want to be friends with Humbert Humbert? Would you want to be friends with Mickey Sabbath? Saleem Sinai? Hamlet? Krapp? Oedipus?

> Oscar Wao? Antigone? Raskolnikov? Any of the characters in *The Corrections*? Any of the characters in *Infinite Jest*? Any of the characters in anything Pynchon has ever written? Or Martin Amis? Or Orhan Pamuk? Or Alice Munro, for that matter? If you're reading to find friends, you're in deep trouble. We read to find life, in all its possibilities. The relevant question isn't "is this a potential friend for me?" but "is this character alive?"[41]

Sadly, the criticism female antihero characters are facing mirrors what they would encounter if they were actually alive. As Jessica Valenti notes, "Women's likability is something feminists use as proof of inequity—he's a boss, she's a bitch. . . . The implications of likability are long-lasting and serious. Women adjust their behavior to be likable and as a result have less power in the world."[42]

It is not surprising, then, that these gendered power dynamics play out so frequently on the small screen. E. Keating notes: "Women leaders in television are portrayed as icy, heartless, manipulative, and vindictive. Take a look at Jessica Pearson from *Suits,* Annalise Keating from *How to Get Away with Murder,* C. J. Cregg on *The West Wing,* Emily Thorne on *Revenge,* and Olivia Pope and Mellie Grant from *Scandal* just to name a few. This sets a dangerous precedent about assumptions of women in power today, and as an audience, society should demand more strong women characters they can respect, instead of love to hate."[43]

The question, of course, is whether audiences read these female characters as critiquing this double standard or—intentionally or unintentionally—reinforcing it.

Shondaland's female characters are arguably meant to elicit awareness of such gendered double standards. The compromised morals of her two most prominent leading female characters—*Scandal*'s Olivia Pope and *HTGAWM*'s Annalise Keating—further complicate this, however, because they are deemed unlikable not simply because they do not fit the traditional female mold but also because of their regular moral transgressions. Of the two black female characters, mainstream media criticism suggests that Annalise is more likely to be referred to as unlikable and to receive the harsher criticisms for her wrongdoings. Meghan Gallagher calls Olivia Pope an "effective antihero" for mastering the art of being "both likable and unethical."[44] She writes: "This is likely due to Olivia's motivations for her immoral behavior. It is partially her own determination to do good which leads Olivia to unforgivable transgressions, making those crimes easier for audiences to swallow. Olivia Pope struggles constantly with her own sense of right and wrong, wanting desperately to do what is ethical, but more often than not failing in this quest. This is discussed within the context of the show as 'wearing the white hat,' a phrase Olivia uses to assert that she is on the side fighting for good instead of evil."[45]

Critics have observed that there are no white hat tropes in *HTGAWM*, which might account for the harsher criticism directed at Annalise.[46] In an interview for the *Hollywood Reporter*, Nowalk confirms that Annalise was meant to stand in contradistinction from Olivia: "Olivia believes in the White Hat, and there's no hat for Annalise; there's reality and justice. I don't think she thinks there is justice; it's kind of whoever plays the game the best."[47] Critics such as Brian Cantor have read Annalise in the same light, noting that she "does not offer a compelling justification for her behavior. She, in fact, ridicules the application of moral righteousness to the legal system. Her job is to get her client off—not get her client off *because* she is innocent or *because* the legal system requires perfection from the defense and prosecution in order to promote the best sense of justice."[48] Cantor argues that Annalise is more realistic than the typical antihero: "[She] emerges as a disillusioned, fundamentally imperfect but infinitely pragmatic realist. She knows she cannot individually change the world. And she has no interest in [defusing] situations with clever, witty wordplay. Her answer to any strife, challenge or adversity is to overcome it—for no other reason than because it needs to be overcome."[49]

Because of her status as a highly debated female antihero, Annalise makes for a fascinating case study for analyzing how fans react on social media to complex fictional characters embroiled in complicated ethical situations.

Twitter as Morality Police? An Analysis of Live-Tweeting Practices

Research Questions and Methodology

To examine live tweets from the show through the lens of morality, attending to debates concerning cultural values and ethics, this study focused on tweets that "critiqued" the show in one way or another to answer the following research questions:

> RQ 1. Do the majority of live tweets posted by viewers of *HTGAWM* focus on the show's portrayal of the justice system or on its various melodramatic subplots?

RQ 2. Do the live tweets posted by viewers of *HTGAWM* reflect the research on gendered ethics, especially in terms of responses to so-called female antiheroes or "unlikable" characters?

RQ 3. How useful is Twitter as a means of gauging cultural sentiments, particularly in regard to societal expectations for moral behavior?

RQ 4. In what ways do the live tweets posted by viewers of *HTGAWM* engage with Rhimes's social commentary or demonstrate that live-tweeting fictional television programs could be a form of digital activism?

Twitter data were collected from September 24 through November 19, 2015, spanning nine episodes from the season 2 debut of *HTGAWM* until its mid-season hiatus. Live tweets associated with the hashtag #HowToGetAwayWithMurder were scraped (i.e., collected) weekly using NodeXL—a program that gathers all tweets associated with a specific hashtag and transfers them to Excel.[50] To narrow the data pool, only tweets that were posted from 8:00 P.M. EST to 9:01 P.M. EST during the one-hour original broadcast of the program that would have aired in the Eastern and Central time zones were analyzed. Because the study focused on live-tweeting practices, the data were limited to the initial one-hour period; this would increase the likelihood that the tweets posted corresponded with the particular episode airing that evening. The data pool was further reduced by limiting analysis to content that was posted in English and to original posts (i.e., retweets and replies were not included). The resulting data pool consisted of 18,439 tweets.

The data were then coded to highlight "critiquing" tweets.[51] The criteria for critiquing tweets was broken down into two large categories, each with various subcategories: (1) small-scale critiques, including subcategories such as personal opinions and media criticism concerning characters, actors, show creators, writing, plot, and so on; and (2) large-scale critiques, including subcategories such as posts engaging with the law- and justice-related story lines presented on the show, or posts engaging with the social commentary Rhimes embedded in such story lines. The tweets included in the analysis below were selected from this narrowed data set because they were representative of the posts or sentiments appearing most frequently on the feed. There is much debate across fields at present concerning the ethics of studying, and specifically citing, tweets for academic purposes.[52] Siding with scholars who argue that "publicly visible Twitter messages are guaranteed to have been published to the Internet at large," this study aligns with the belief that archiving and analyzing such tweets for academic research is within ethical research practices.[53]

Discussion of Findings

RQ 1. Do the majority of live tweets posted by viewers of HTGAWM focus on the show's portrayal of the justice system or on its various melodramatic subplots?

Since *HTGAWM* is, in part, a legal drama, it was expected that many critiques of the show would focus on its depiction of the justice system and on the illegal actions of the central cast of lawyers. While these critiques were present, this focus was rather minimal. (Note that all comments in the figures in this chapter and the following two chapters are presented exactly as they were originally typed by Twitter users.)

It was anticipated that, as the main character, Annalise would often be the focus of the critiques found on Twitter, but again expectation was that these would focus primarily on her compromised professional ethics—especially since the cliff-hanger between seasons 1 and 2 predicted that she would be involved in yet another murder cover-up. While Annalise was the character most often targeted by name as the main topic of a tweet, her personal rather than professional actions were more often the focus of critiques. Of the 18,439 tweets, Annalise was directly mentioned in 2,463 (and indirectly referenced in many more), making her account for 13.36 percent of the discussion unfolding under the #HowToGetAwayWithMurder hashtag.[54] Exemplary of how her personal actions were critiqued were numerous tweets that framed her as a skilled liar, a bully, or a two-timing romantic player. By comparison, her professional ethics were mentioned only occasionally. For example, on September 25, 2015, @dawniebgood87 wrote, "Annalise plays dirty just like the justice system." And on October 15, 2015, a conversation unfolded on the feed debating whether Connor or Annalise was correct in dealing with evidence proving that their teenage client was guilty of homicide. Rachel Romanczuk (@RachelER22) wrote, after Annalise sided with protecting the client while Connor actively worked toward getting her convicted: "I'm with Connor. Annalise only cares about money and winning."

Annalise, however, was more often the topic of more superficial critiques focused on various aspects of the show ranging from costuming and acting to characterization and plot.[55] The latter types of comments were the most frequent; the majority of the tweets critiqued the character's personality and actions. For example, many negative tweets focused on Annalise's drinking. On October 8, 2015, Vale Váz (@valeria13201422) wrote, "She is pissy drunk." Even more tweets focused on her adulterous relationship with Nate. On October 15, 2015, Maria Nkata (@CrackHeadJemi) posted: "'What kind of woman sleeps with a man who's wife is dying?' The Annalise kind who doesn't give a F@&$$." And some tweets even attended to Annalise's own position of privilege. For example, on October 8, 2015, @_therealmami wrote, "Annalise walks like she owns a cotton gin"—a tweet that associates Annalise with slavery but complicates her empowered positionality by comparing her to a slave owner. Users also praised her for behavior they viewed as positive. One example occurred when Annalise refused to commit euthanasia by providing Nate's dying wife with drugs so that she could kill herself. On October 16, 2015, Hajarah Mamman Nassi (@Hajmannas) posted, "Proud of you Annalise, really thought she was gonna help Nate's wife, glad she didn't."

The fact that tweets more often engaged with superficial aspects of the show rather than the underlying story lines suggests that *HTGAWM*'s melodramatic stylistics and overarching plot often overshadowed its more episodic focus on weekly legal cases. These findings support the media critic Jessica Rawden's criticism of the show's employment of legal motifs: "The actual courtroom drama is mostly . . . used more as a device to show off the talents of the law school students."[56] She argued that other legal dramas, such as *The Good Wife,* more effectively use their legal story lines "to look at the complexities of. . . politics and moral ambiguities" involved in practicing law.[57] This suggests that *HTGAWM*'s status as a hybrid genre—where legal drama meets prime-time soap—actually undercuts its potential to spark reflection on contemporary injustice.

RQ 2. Do the live tweets posted by viewers of HTGAWM *reflect the research on gendered ethics, especially in terms of responses to so-called female antiheroes or "unlikable" characters?*

By analyzing how Annalise figures into small-scale critiques of the program, it becomes clear that some reactions to her characterization align with research on the reception of female antiheroes. For example, the dreaded buzzword *unlikable* was associated—although not as regularly as expected—with her character in viewer tweets. For example, on October 1, 2015, @laurentluvsfenty called Annalise "strangely unlikable" and, on October 17, 2015, T. J. Newton (@tnewton92) posed the question "Has there ever been such an UNLIKABLE lead on television before? Annalise is a truly horrible person."

Still others posted tweets critiquing Annalise alongside *Scandal*'s Olivia Pope, labeling them both as unlikable black female characters.

Moreover, Twitter data revealed that viewers were more willing to accept (and even embrace) Frank's unethical behavior than they were Annalise's, which is consistent with aforementioned scholarship concerning the double standards facing men and women. Most interesting was viewers' willingness to forgive Frank's extreme transgressions simply because they found him to be physically attractive. This also aligns with research concerning how characters with lighter skin are often perceived as being more attractive and friendly than characters with darker skin, suggesting that Frank's status as a white male factors heavily into his wrongdoings being so easily forgiven by fans.[58]

In comparison, Annalise faced a range of criticisms for her moral missteps —and not one of them was forgiven simply on the basis of her personal appearance or sex appeal. Although, unlike Frank, she had never committed murder, Annalise was more often called "terrible" or "evil." For example, on September 24, 2015, Nakia Morton (@NGMBeauty) called her "the devil." Meanwhile, users seem to have celebrated Frank's unethical actions. For example, on November 19, 2015, Marco Montalván (@desperategossip) tweeted: "Frank, you are the MVP." These data suggest that a large subset of the live-tweeting viewers are heterosexual women. They also indicate that the numerous harsh critiques targeted at Annalise are coming from female viewers.[59]

Contrary to what research concerning female antiheroes would expect, however, Annalise also prompted many supportive posts. Many tweets focused on the disloyalty of her law students and their lack of appreciation for all the extreme measures she went to to save them. For example, on October 15, 2015, B. Addison tweeted, "Like Annalise is giving her all to everybody trying to protect them all the while being called a killer." More telling, however, are the posts that praised her for her transgressions, specifically those that could be interpreted as caretaking attempts. That "motherly" acts are the primary motivators for forgiving her moral lapses is problematic but not surprising. In the present time line of *HTGAWM,* Annalise is not a biological mother. Season 2 did provide a backstory wherein she was pregnant and lost her child, a narrative inclusion that probably aims to help justify her later transgressions. Nevertheless, in the main narrative Annalise's motherly acts are those of a woman mentoring adult protégés, and viewer tweets often comment on this pseudo-parental role she plays for her students. For example, on October 29, 2015, Joan Bushur (@joanbushur) posted: "Asher's back in the fold. Let momma Annalise fix everything." The following week, on November 5, 2015, two other viewers similarly noted her protective, motherly role (@alisahelene referred to her as "Mama bear Annalise") and criticized the students for not respecting her as they should: "omg! They've all been talking back to Annalise this season. I never talk back to my mom" (@musicmonetradio).

The inclusion of this surrogate-mother plot device aligns with scholarship concerning how the stereotype of the mammy figure continues to linger in popular culture even into the twenty-first century.[60] It also raises the question: Would Annalise's acts be read as generously if they were done on behalf of her own biological children, or are they forgiven only because they are done in *service* for non-family members? What this underscores is that notions of nurturing are particularly troubling at the intersection of gender and race. While white women and women of color are received similarly when cast as antiheroes, race plays an additional role in how their moral slippage is framed.

The idea that viewers were more willing to accept illegal actions from female characters when they were viewed as "motherly" acts also aligns with research on gendered ethics.[61] Carol Gilligan has theorized the social construction of gendered morality, claiming that men operate according to "an ethics of rights," whereas women operate according to "an ethics of responsibility."[62] Gilligan's concept of female morality "emphasizes attachment and the urge to care" as being the driving forces underlying decisions about what is right and wrong, while her concept of male morality aligns more with traditional notions of justice (i.e., "commitment to rules, values, and principles").[63] Few characters on the show—male or female—could be read as operating successfully according to Gilligan's definition of masculine morality, but the fact that Annalise's behavior can be read as conforming to this feminized definition is significant. Since many—although not all—of her illegal acts are committed to protect her protégés, this contributes to her more positive reception among viewers who judge her actions as being justified. Reading Annalise's ethics through this gender lens also highlights the patriarchal aspects of the legal system—aspects that align with Gilligan's male-coded ethics of rights. Framed in this way, the show seems to suggest that the justice system often runs counter to female-centered ethics that focus on attachment and care.

Ultimately, the collected tweets imply that reactions to Annalise are quite idiosyncratic, and, even though she was the target of some harsh criticisms, many viewers embraced her actions regardless of whether they were seen as protective, caring acts. For example, a subset of viewers seemed to gain pleasure from her "bad" behavior. Her most frequently quoted lines of dialogue were almost always harsh—even shocking—comments directed at her legal team, and users seemed to celebrate these moments when she performed the role of "the bitch" or when, at times, she even embraced the title for herself. For example, in the episode "I Want You to Die," aired on November 5, 2015, Annalise told her adversary, the prosecutor Emily Sinclair, "You're messing with the wrong bitch."[64] In response, Twitter erupted with a series of tweets quoting this moment of dialogue. For example, @pentylu quoted the phrase, adding the exclamatory approval "yeeeeeessss" afterward.

Annalise's being embraced for being a self-described bitch is worth consideration. In some ways Annalise does not actually fulfill the typical role that the bitch often plays in fictional narratives. In her book *The Bitch Is Back: Wicked Women in Literature*, Sarah Appleton Aguiar argues that this figure is "formed by negative female archetypes that have been present . . . for centuries" and that her purpose is to serve as "the embodiment of female evil: the foil for literature's icons of morality and the scourge of the male hero."[65] First of all, Annalise really is not a foil for anyone—particularly any of the other female characters. Almost all the female characters could be classified as bitches in their own right, although perhaps to varying degrees. Further, the show is lacking any traditional heroes, male or female, to thwart. Quite simply, Annalise is not completely evil or virtuous, moral or immoral. Therefore, what this might suggest is that Rhimes has created a more complicated, nuanced portrayal of women who are forced to (or choose to) embody the paradoxical intersections of such arbitrary divisions.

There was, however, one particular story line that prompted mixed reactions concerning Annalise's so-called bad behavior, specifically her use of sexuality as a means to exert power. In the show's pilot Annalise sleeps with her boyfriend, Nate, a police officer, in order to win a case, which sets the precedent that she is willing to use sex as a means to an end. Throughout season 2, the pilot prompted tweets about her potential motivations whenever she has sex with someone. This history also influenced how some viewers reacted to her mentoring of Michaela Pratt (Aja Naomi King), whom she encourages to use her sex appeal to control clients. In the episode "Skanks Get Shanked," Annalise orders Michaela to keep their murder defendant, Caleb Hapstall (Kendrick Sampson), in line. When Michaela seems at a loss, Annalise asks: "What's the matter? Don't know how to use your boobs?"[66] Like most of her hard-cutting punch lines, this line of dialogue echoed across

Twitter as users quoted it in their own tweets. On October 15, 2015, Derek St. John (@Dieter117) even called it the "best line of the night." When Michaela falls short of Annalise's expectations and befriends Caleb rather than seducing him, she barks: "I told you to use your boobs, not your heart. Put them away."[67] Again, viewers voiced their appreciation of the line. On October 8, 2015, Joan Bushur (@joanbushur) quoted the line of dialogue, adding, "Love Mikaela and Annalise together." Though multiple viewers compared Annalise to a pimp, not all did so critically, as evidenced by this tweet posted by Paris Hodges (@brownxsuga) on October 15, 2015: "lmao annalise pimping Makayla." Even weeks after this episode, however, some were still expressing their outrage about this story line on Twitter. On November 12, 2015, @msmjfan14 posted, "Michaela is MORE than her boobs Annalise."

This last tweet aligns with criticisms concerning sexual or romantic story lines undermining female characters, particularly strong female characters like Annalise.[68] For example, E. Keating notes that a story line that involves a female protagonist using "her femininity and physical attractiveness to get what she wants" ultimately undermines the main character's "intellect and other characteristics that allow her to complete her mission."[69] Rhimes's other female powerhouse, Olivia Pope, has been subject to critiques of this nature. Many claim that the main romantic story arc, focused on Olivia's on-again-off-again romantic relationship with President Fitzgerald Grant, undercuts her status as a strong female character. Rising to her defense, however, Gallagher says: "While Olivia is by no means a role model for young women, she is much more nuanced, complex, and three dimensional than most black female characters that have risen to her level of popularity. *Scandal*'s success is a testament to the fact that female characters can be imperfect and still be popular. In fact, imperfect characters are much better vessels for representation. Audiences are ready for female characters that evoke contradictory emotions and encourage critical reflection."[70]

This same argument could easily apply to Annalise. The ways in which she is embraced by viewers suggests that audiences are hungry for more three-dimensional portrayals of women who do not fit easily into outdated, unrealistic gendered archetypes.

RQ 3. How useful is Twitter as a means of gauging cultural sentiments, particularly in regard to societal expectations for moral behavior?

This desire for multifaceted characters helps explain why there was very little criticism cast at *any* of the fictional characters in the show in regard to their deviant behavior. Although fans often noted the prevalence of lying, backstabbing, blackmail, and murder, most tweets simply seemed to acknowledge these acts rather than condemn them.

Further, the content of the tweets seemed, at times, to mirror the unethical morals of the characters onscreen. Concerning the show itself, one reviewer noted how casually the characters toss about words like *murder* and *kill*.[71] This sentiment surfaced in viewer tweets also. On October 1, 2015, @gingerbread615 tweeted: "Everybody in this law firm is way too casual about killing people." But apparently this did not bother all viewers. Some of the most often quoted lines of dialogue were, in fact, flippant remarks about murder, such as Annalise's threat, "You screw up again, you're gonna be the next dead body in this house," and Bonnie's order, "Either get on board or you're the next dead body out there."[72]

This casual treatment of murder was similarly witnessed on the Twitter feed when many users celebrated the deaths of certain characters and, perhaps more telling, advocated for the deaths of others. The character targeted most often in such tweets was Sinclair, but users were also quick to call for the deaths of even the central cast members if they were deemed to be too annoying. Concerning the plethora of death threats issued on the show, Kayla Kumari Upadhyaya asks, "Am I supposed to believe they're all just a merry ol' gang of psychopaths?"[73] Along the same line, we could then ask the same of the many viewers who were advocating acts of killing—are they all just a bunch of homicidal maniacs? Of course not. On the one hand, this example underscores the performative nature of Twitter and the difficulty of using Twitter as a means to gauge individual or cultural sentiments and moral beliefs. On the other, the data analyzed collectively *do* reveal some striking things about cultural practices, and, by extension, the cultural beliefs or anxieties they stem from. These tweets align with larger trends in Internet communication, such as the common practice of flaming or trolling. Since negative commentary online is often explicitly or implicitly focused on identity factors, such as gender or race, it stands to reason that individuals may be turning to platforms like Twitter as a means to channel their disenfranchised rage. The fact that so many of these tweets specifically celebrate murder also underscores the extent to which our culture is obsessed with murder and killing (see table 8.1). It also problematically reveals our desensitization to violence in an era that continues to see escalating crimes against women and people of color.

This particular example of viewer engagement on Twitter may be read as aligning with the research concerning the function that antihero narratives

Table 8.1. Tweets celebrating or calling for characters' deaths on *HTGAWM*.

Twitter User	**Time Stamp**	**Tweet**
pretentioususa	10/1/2015 9:05	When are they going to take Asher out? #HTGAWM #HowToGetAwayWithMurder
jaytweetze	10/22/2015 9:13	Might sound rude buuut. . . Someone kill Asher 😂😂😂 screw Asher man !! 🖕🖕🖕#HowToGetAwayWithMurder #HTGAWM
gvldgvenchy	10/1/2015 9:17	This Saint Clare bitch gotta go, she getting on my nerves #TGIT #HowToGetAwayWithMurder
gottdamm_jossi	10/1/2015 9:26	Someone kill this lawyer! #HowToGetAwayWithMurder
letragicmulatto	11/19/2015 9:28	Bravo Asher. . .BRAVO 👏👏👏. . . You killed Sinclair #HTGAWM #HowToGetAwayWithMurder #HowToGetAwayABC
3lwtv	10/1/2015 9:34	Someone needs to put this in prosecutor in a body bag. #HowToGetAwayWithMurder
feintennisfan93	10/1/2015 10:01	I'm so glad that woman dies in #HowToGetAwayWithMurder cuz she is hella annoying
ohemmtee	10/1/2015 10:01	Im glad that prosecutor getting whats coming to her. . .shes annoying #HowToGetAwayWithMurder

serve and why audiences—and live-tweeting audiences in particular—are drawn to such story lines to begin with. Perhaps posting tweets about antihero story lines allows audience members an extended sense of catharsis wherein they are not only living through the onscreen bad behavior of characters, but also *performing* similar bad behavior for an imagined community of fellow fans.[74] Further, such tweets seem to confirm Janicke and Raney's research about viewers' ability to "morally disengage" and violate their "own typical standards of morality" by enjoying and relating to the antihero. But these tweets celebrating bad behavior also indicate that viewers can use

Twitter to move beyond vicarious experiences by writing tweets that act as a form of individualized moral transgression.

While ample research has suggested that Twitter may be used to track cultural sentiment, these types of posts further highlight the performative nature of Twitter, and, therefore, problematize the notion that tweets can act as a societal mirror reflecting cultural values.[75] Of course, social performance does not always equate to falsehood; in fact, such performances often reveal our internal beliefs, attitudes, and values, or simply our most base instincts. In this regard, the more apt metaphor may be to consider Twitter as a magnifying glass or funhouse mirror that presents amplified, exaggerated, or slightly distorted views of culture and cultural beliefs.

The medium of communication also complicates our ability to claim that Twitter posts unequivocally reveal the poster's cultural anxieties. The types of writing that Twitter promotes make it challenging to read tweets as indicative of cultural values. Certain Twitter practices are privileged. For example, humorous and inflammatory posts tend to receive more attention in the form of retweeting or replying practices.[76] Therefore, savvy social media users may perform in ways that do not necessarily reflect their own moral beliefs—or that of society at large—in order to obtain visibility and popularity. But, of course, the fact that certain content—especially when it finds approval through crass or provocative posts—is privileged over others does shed light on cultural values on a larger scale.

RQ 4. In what ways do the live tweets posted by viewers of HTGAWM engage with Rhimes's social commentary or demonstrate that live-tweeting fictional television programs could be a form of digital activism?

As might be evident from the discussion so far, of the two classifications of critiques—small-scale criticisms focused specifically on the show and large-scale criticisms engaging with larger societal issues—the majority of the critiquing posts focused on rather trivial content. When particular moments within episodes pointedly drew attention to a societal issue, however, the latter type of critique became predominant. This was most often the case when Rhimes's social commentary took on the form of dialogue. In this instance, the most frequent tweeting practice was quoting: the poster simply would tweet the line of dialogue containing the social critique (either as a direct quote or a paraphrase). While this practice can logically be read as embracing or promoting the critique, the quoting of dialogue is, of course, ambiguous. Some posters provided additional commentary along with the quote that revealed their opinion of the dialogue or their purpose for citing it, but the majority simply tweeted the actual dialogue as a stand-alone post free of qualification or discussion. Though this lack of context could stem from the character limits imposed by the medium, it could also reveal our tendency to allow quotes to stand in place of making bold, potentially controversial statements. This practice is particularly prevalent on social media, where it is more acceptable to circulate a meme or quote from someone else concerning a controversial topic than to make a direct statement concerning one's own stance on the matter. Paradoxically, this allows posters to showcase how they feel about a topic while also employing a distancing technique that separates them from that very topic.

In terms of the quoting practices in this study, the comedic undertones of many circulated quotes further complicate their reading. Since some of these moments of dialogue were also delivered as punch lines, the tweets could be read as celebrating their humor *or* their cultural critique. The inability to determine authorial intent is yet another limitation of analyzing Twitter data, as is the difficulty in determining tone. For example, in a Twitter post on September 25, 2015, Dianne Carusell (@diannecarusell) wrote, "Another Black lawyer and a Black judge—I feel so empowered." This post could be read as a straightforward statement by a viewer—perhaps read as an African American viewer—celebrating the show's racially diverse casting practices. This post could also be read, however, as a sarcastic critique of such practices, perhaps indicating that the user feels they are overdone or not empowering enough on their own. Since Carusell's profile picture indicates—although not necessarily accurately—that she is a Caucasian woman, this could lead to further speculation concerning the intent of her tweet. Therefore, this one example alone shows the difficulty of determining meaning in these uncontextualized comments written within the constraints of a 140-character (now 280-character) limit. While this may make determining the purpose of an *individual* tweet difficult, analyzing trends within Twitter posts *collectively* seems to provide more reliable insight into cultural values and anxieties.

Still, analyzing the most frequent instances of this quoting practice does suggest that Rhimes's cultural commentary is not getting completely overshadowed by the melodramatic soap-operatic nature of *HTGAWM*. For example, the most frequently quoted moments of dialogue involved critiques about white privilege. One of the most often quoted lines of dialogue comes from the episode "It's Time to Move On": "White folks always bring up race when it suits them, never when it matters."[77] Another popularly tweeted line circulated weeks later during the episode "Meet Bonnie": "Add your whiteness on top of that, the police are trained to believe you."[78] These prompted supportive comments on Twitter. For example, on October 22, 2015, @refinedsmarts tweeted, "Preaching about white male privilege, yasss!" and @EDubb_41yfe tweeted: "White privilege is real y'all. I'm telling you."

Overall, often the highest volume of tweets during an episode's airing aligned with narrative moments that revealed Rhimes's social commentary. For example, her story lines related to sexuality garnered quite a bit of commentary online, although analysis of such posts does not indicate that these lessons are always well received. The episode airing on October 8, 2015, "It's Called the Octopus," involved the legal team representing the owner of a high-end sex club. Many tweets posted on this date celebrated Rhimes's decision to address sex shaming and nonnormative sexual practices. For example, @kpringer tweeted, "Hella sex shame-y episode tonight," Candace Nicole Werts (@candacenwerts) posted, "Sex fetish, yes!" and Monet Sutton (@MusicMonetRadio) wrote: "People shouldn't be ashamed of their sexuality. They shouldn't be ashamed of liking sex." Other posts, however, indicate resistance to the episode's message. For example, Micah Ouroboros (@micahouroboros) tweeted: "That's not sex positive. That's f-ing trashy and dirty. There's a difference"; and Inda Lauryn (@indascorner) wrote: "Sex parties tho? That's nasty." In other episodes, viewers also tweeted appreciation for the attention given to other important topics. For example, on October 22, 2015, @AverageCockram tweeted, "Viola Davis dropping some real talk on America's rape culture." On October 29, 2015, @EDubb_41yfe wrote, "Glad and surprised that Shonda inserted a transgender centered mini-storyline into the season." And on October 1, 2015, many praised a story line concerning sexual assault—including tweets that praised the public service announcement that followed season 2, episode 8. One such example was posted by @PretentiousUSA, who wrote: "Wow! What a great PSA/promo at the end of episode for sexual assault."

Connor and Oliver's same-sex relationship also generated numerous tweets. The story line about their romantic relationship was very well received, as almost any mention of their being together was positive, such as Ashley Graham (@Shleekins)'s September 24, 2015 post: "I ♥ Conner and Oliver so much!!!" The story line, however, related to Oliver's HIV diagnosis, and to Connor's decision to take PrEP (pre-exposure prophylaxis, a drug for people at high risk for being exposed to HIV) in order to continue with their sexual relationship, sparked diverse reactions (table 8.2). When one looks critically

Table 8.2. Tweets focused on the HIV/PrEP story line on *HTGAWM*.

Twitter User	**Time Stamp**	**Tweet**
itslouismcduff	9/24/2015 9:16	Wait HIV isn't a big deal? #HowToGetAwayWithMurder . . . Someone explain
chelsea_rana3	9/24/2015 9:16	Conner Awesome For Staying With Him Knowing He Has HIV. #BreakTheStigma #HTGAWM #HowToGetAwayWithMurder #TGIT 🙌
mandamari3	9/24/2015 9:16	Yes PrEP!!! #Awareness #HowToGetAwayWithMurder
Itsjaniez	9/24/2015 9:17	I love the way how Connor is dealing with this whole HIV situation. . . #HTGAWM #HowToGetAwayWithMurder #TGIT
sweetcorn4	9/24/2015 9:17	I'm sorry bae got AIDS ummm relationship over #HowToGetAwayWithMurder

at the lovefest that Connor and Oliver's relationship generates online, some noteworthy cultural values are revealed. For example, the many tweets praising Connor for staying with Oliver after his diagnosis conjure up the image of the white savior (as it is, importantly, the man of color who contracts HIV).

Although the "Coliver" story line prompted much Twitter activity, it actually paled in comparison to the season 2 reveal that Annalise once had a female lover. The scene that revealed Annalise's layered identity as a bisexual black woman prompted the most tweets of the entire data pool (table 8.3). During the six-minute scene recounting Annalise's history with a fellow attorney, Eve Rothlo (Famke Janssen), which includes a kiss—tweets under the #HowToGetAwayWithMurder hashtag skyrocketed, resulting in 1,206 tweets (which accounted for 20.78% of the tweets for the entire episode). These posts represent a range of reactions, from explicitly homophobic to implicitly homophobic to sex-positive to LGBTQA-inclusive. The tweets indicate that many embraced this new development in Annalise's backstory and applauded the show's inclusivity, but others reacted negatively to the plot

Table 8.3. Reactions to Annalise's bisexual story line on *HTGAWM*.

Twitter User	Time Stamp	Tweet
callingshots_	9/24/2015 9:48	HELL YEAH BI REPRESENTATION #HTGAWM #HowToGetAwayWithMurder
Shirlzrene	9/24/2015 9:50	Lesbian kiss!!! #HowToGetAwayWithMurder
jeremy_chino13	9/24/2015 9:50	Oh ok so Annalise is bi?? Cool #HowToGetAwayWithMurder
jamie132xo	9/24/2015 9:50	This is really awkward 💀💀 lmfao #HowToGetAwayWithMurder
Glamazonianash	9/24/2015 9:50	Why is everybody gay on all these shows? #HowToGetAwayWithMurder
Axto	9/24/2015 9:50	ANNALISE IS BISEXUAL WHAT THE FUCK THIS SHOW GETS BETTER AND BETTER #HowToGetAwayWithMurder ♡♡♡♡
britt_brat62	9/24/2015 9:50	Omg please don't let Annalise sleep with that woman! #HowToGetAwayWithMurder
Capricornboo	9/24/2015 9:51	How much money she gettin for kissin this woman?#howtogetawaywithmurder
_popdhattunechi	9/24/2015 9:51	Yes!!! Fluid sexuality! #HowToGetAwayWithMurder
a_kolquist	9/24/2015 9:51	I wanna be so dome with this show!! Shonda rimes just finds the most random, unnecessary ways to put in mess! #howtogetawaywithmurder wth

twist, immediately revealing that despite the good intentions of television writers, the social commentary they weave into their programs is not always well received.

Twitter provides a unique opportunity for those involved in the show, such as producers and actors, to interact directly with viewers, which allows them to be even more direct with their pedagogical lessons if they wish to be. Peter Nowalk, the show's creator, tweeted the following morning: "Thanks all for watching last night! And just a tip: *It's not a lesbian kiss, it's just a kiss.* Love you all" (emphasis added). Although Norwalk's tweet, upon first consideration, appears positive, it actually serves to erase the cultural significance of this narrative inclusion. Crafting this romantic relationship between these two female characters and revealing Annalise's bisexuality was an important decision made by the show's creators, but Norwalk's comment can be read as stripping away the significance of this kiss and the story line it crystalizes. His comment that it's "just a kiss" makes Eve's and Annalise's identities as lesbian and bisexual women, respectively, invisible. This seemingly supportive tweet then ultimately functions in a way similar to colorblind rhetoric that acts to erase racial difference in this supposed post-identity era. Norwalk's assertion that "it's not a *lesbian kiss*" is also telling on one other level: it is noteworthy that Annalise is portrayed as a bisexual woman and not a lesbian woman—the former, arguably, falling closer in line with heteronormativity. This decision, along with the one to make her former lover a white woman, may reveal the ways in which the show's creators were attempting to strategically use identity pairings to create the most palatable storyline.

The juxtaposition of tweets concerning Oliver and Connor's relationship and Annalise and Eve's relationship indicate that a variety of factors may be influencing why the former was better received. While both relationships feature interracial couples, the first features a white person and a light-skinned person of color. Further, the fact that the relationship between two gay men was more popular highlights our culture's patriarchal norms or the reality that representations of gay men are more prevalent in popular culture. The latter underscores the fact that LGBTQA politics are still largely white, gay male politics.

It is also worthy of note that of two main queer characters, it is the white male character's relationship that is embraced, as opposed to the black female character's. Bisexual women of color are a common TV plot device, and it is important to consider how these intersectional representations function on television. Analyzing queer female secondary characters on television, Michaela Meyer discusses how these characters are crafted so that their "'Otherness' is layered to produce a commodifiable image that is both economically profitable and exploitative through its erasure of difference, and by implication, identity."[79] She argues that compounding multiple "discourses of 'Otherness' in one character makes it easier to 'check all the boxes' of identity politics and appease the most number of identity constituents in a given audience."[80] Though Meyer's analysis focuses primarily on secondary characters, the implication for Annalise as the central protagonist is worth discussing. Davis has received much attention for being one of the few dark-skinned women of color starring in a prime-time drama. The queering of her character can be read as further marginalizing her and as detracting attention from high-profile racial politics by deflecting into queer politics.

And the Moral from Shondaland Is? Genre Matters When It Comes to Social Commentary

Obviously, Rhimes and those she works closely with want to "teach" audiences various lessons through narratives devoted to consciousness raising; her programs aim to reflect important aspects of the real world by representing identities and issues too often erased from pop culture imagery. Rhimes is completely upfront about this mission. For example, in 2015 Rhimes received an Ally for Equality award at the annual Human Rights Campaign Gala. In her acceptance speech she explained that her goals extend far beyond simply "diversifying television":

> I really hate the word "diversity," it suggests something . . . other. As if it is something . . . special. Or rare . . . as if there is something unusual about telling stories involving women and people of color and LGBTQ characters on TV. I have a different word: NORMALIZING. I'm normalizing TV. . . . Making TV look like the world looks. Women, people of color, LGBTQ people equal WAY more than 50% of the population. Which means it ain't out of the ordinary. I am making the world of television look NORMAL."[81]

Her quest to normalize television and address social inequalities, however, is complicated by the fact that this work is being done by means of melodramatic narratives. Her important lessons are often delivered through complicated plots featuring people behaving badly. This creates a type of narrative dissonance that masks any didactic role these story lines serve since viewers are expected to learn their moral lessons from arguably immoral characters. But does it work? While one dreaming of utopian uses of Twitter might hope to see more productive conversation unfolding on the streams about such topics, the prevalence of such dialogue does not indicate that many viewers are live-tweeting fictional programs—or at least this fictional program—in order to primarily engage with the social commentary they provide. The finding that live tweets for *HTGAWM* did not always align with the aims of the show's creators aligns with other research on the ways in which audiences often strategically diverge from the media text in which they engage through Twitter. Studying the live-tweeting practices of fans who role-play characters from *Glee,* Megan M. Wood and Linda Baughman determined that live tweets related to a television show have the potential to "alter the collective experience of the narrative from which they derive."[82] In the case of *HTGAWM,* this means that the live tweets could distract from the social commentary unfolding in the program.[83] In the end, though this study cannot necessarily claim this occurred, the number of tweets devoted to melodramatic commentary versus real-world social commentary suggests that Twitter users were more preoccupied by the fictional bad behavior of the characters onscreen than by the real-world bad behavior they were meant to draw attention to. This then suggests that live-tweeting fictional television programs may not constitute an easily recognizable form of digital activism.

At a glance, *How to Get Away with Murder* presents a typical post-identity wonderland of equality for all; after all, the main characters reflect a multicultural ensemble cast that includes various identifications with race, gender, and sexual orientation led by a powerful bisexual black female protagonist involved in interracial relationships. But as quickly as Rhimes sets up this ideal world, she forcefully shatters it. For example, she spins a fan-favorite story line about a gay couple productively coping with an HIV diagnosis, but then weaves in narrative moments that underscore the ignorance and bigotry that such couples still face in the real world (e.g., Asher's comment that *Philadelphia* is his favorite movie). In the midst of a slew of melodramatic plots, Rhimes carefully inserts narratives that highlight various abuses of power and other problematic societal practices. And, most pointedly, she punctuates her dialogue with hard-hitting comments about gender, race, sexuality, and social justice—moments wherein the characters potentially parrot Rhimes's own social critiques. The diverse reactions that stem from Rhimes's pointed social commentary in the program indicate that some viewers are particularly receptive to her messages and use Twitter as a space to further reinforce or comment on such messages (e.g., the practice of quoting dialogue). Other posts, however, show viewer resistance to such narrative lessons (e.g., the practice of ridiculing or challenging story lines and dialogue). Therefore, conflicting tweets ultimately show the warring sentiments (and different ideological camps) that still exist regarding various topics connected to identity politics, including women of color in lead roles, same-sex relationships, and interracial relationships.

9

Defending *The Bachelorette*

What Online Comments from Reality TV Fans Reveal about Contemporary Gender Expectations, and Live-Tweeting as a Form of Feminist Digital Activism

Paradoxically, reality television is both anything but real and all too real at the same time. Whereas infotainment and news programming reveal—and provide direct commentary on—cultural practices, and scripted television programs reflect them through their fictional plots, reality television sits somewhere in between, doing a bit of both. These programs capture "real" moments of social interaction that can shed light on social values and collective fears, but they also reinforce and cultivate those values and fears as those moments are edited into the end products that appear on our screens. In *Reality Bites: The Troubling Truth about Guilty Pleasure TV*, Jennifer Pozner argues this is part of the draw of the genre, that viewers watch these shows because they "frame their narratives in ways that both play to and reinforce deeply ingrained societal biases about women and men, love and beauty, race and class, consumption and happiness in America."[1] The reality television dating subgenre, for example, relies on heteronormative, sexist expectations concerning the ways in which men and women should interact in romantic relationships. The ways in which the contestants work toward, or fall short of, these cultural norms are captured on camera and then exploited "for the profits of networks, product placers, and media owners."[2]

Societal fears about gender equality are broadcast loud and clear in these dating shows, and women do not fare well. Pozner argues that humiliation is the primary "tactic by which reality TV spreads antifeminist backlash ideology. As a structural device, it is used to offer women an ugly, unstated, and all-too-clear message: 'This is where independence leads, ladies—to failure and misery.'"[3] Consider the common practice of the camera zooming "in on the tear-soaked face of some woman shattered by romantic rejection. Producers bank on such scenes to reinforce the notion that single women are simpering spinsters who can never be fulfilled without husbands."[4] The various stock characters female reality television contestants are molded into showcase the conflicting messages women are being sent in this "postfeminist" era: to be confident, but not too confident, sexy, but not too sexy, and so forth. Consider these familiar staples of the reality dating show: "The Weeper, whose self-doubt is played for laughs. The Antagonizer, whose confidence is framed as arrogance. The Slut, whose strategic use of sex appeal we're meant to condemn. Through their beauty-based bravado and anxiety, participants become vessels on whose bodies and from whose lips these shows can reinforce antifeminist backlash values."[5]

These gendered lessons influence not only the contestants on the shows, but also the viewers watching them. The online discussions among fans of these programs reveal the ways in which viewers resist or reinforce these televised messages.

For example, on June 22, 2015, the Twitterverse erupted when the star of ABC's *The Bachelorette* had sex with one of her male suitors before the show's pre-approved, pre-scripted time line. Far from being a PG-rated reality TV franchise, the long-running show is well known for broadcasting a slew of make-out sessions and an entire episode devoted to speculating on whether the bachelor or bachelorette will sleep with any or all of his or her final three contestants in the fantasy suite.[6] Yet when an episode aired revealing that Kaitlyn Bristowe, the season's bachelorette, and the repeat contestant Nick Viall had slept together at the close of their mid-season one-on-one date, Kaitlyn faced a wave of criticism from viewers through social media. Over 80,000 tweets with the hashtag #TheBachelorette appeared in the twenty-four hours during and after this episode, and a vast majority of them were negative posts consisting of judgmental quips and derogatory slurs focusing on Kaitlyn's sexual activity. These tweeters, the majority of whom were female, were quick to affix all the normal labels used to discuss so-called female promiscuity. Among the tamer tweets were chastising posts, such as "Kaitlyn needs to learn how to keep it classy & not so trashy" (@otrat_rowyso).

Amid the caustic remarks were also hundreds of tweets defending the star. For example, the comedian Amy Schumer (@amyschumer) posted: "Oh no someone slept with a guy they're dating and considering marrying! Showing love for @kaitlynbristowe." Tweets that challenged slut-shaming began to enter the feed, as did posts that specifically criticized ABC's producers for the ways in which the show participated in and encouraged such shaming. Support rang in from the blogosphere as well as critics analyzed fans' reactions to this episode and the way the network addressed it in the weeks that followed.

Media critics have long pointed out the problematic ways in which the *Bachelor* franchise portrays the sexual relationships between the contestants—simultaneously exploiting them and pretending as if they do not exist.[7] The show's distorted "puritanical value system" is perhaps best demonstrated by the inclusion of "the euphemistically named Fantasy Suite dates," which are offered only "to the final three remaining contestants vying for each season's single star's hand in marriage."[8] It is not surprising that Kaitlyn and Nick's sexual encounter, as a deviation from the show's protocols, sparked conversation among viewers. Their comments, however, reveal as much about society's norms concerning sexuality as they do about the show's.

The feminist media scholar Emma Gray spoke out against the mass judgment that the couple experienced: "To state what should be the obvious, sex is often an integral part of getting to know someone romantically—and falling in love. Prioritizing a physical connection and chemistry with another human being before agreeing to bind yourself legally to him or her just seems like common sense. Kaitlyn and Nick are in the unique position of having their relationship choices being broadcast to millions of viewers, opening themselves up to the judgment of the Internet. But if both parties feel good about a sexual situation, should much else really matter?"[9]

Gray continued to discuss how the backlash Kaitlyn received, largely by female viewers, shows the role that women play in "policing the bounds of 'acceptable' female sexuality."[10] In an interview with *People,* Kaitlyn pointed out the double standard women face when it comes to sexual activity. She stated frankly that she was criticized online "because [she's] a woman."[11]

Media critics drew attention to the ways in which the program itself plays into these double standards and encourages the policing of female sexuality. For example, toward the end of the season, during the "Men Tell All" episode, the program devoted a segment to the Internet abuse Kaitlyn received. The host, Chris Harrison, dramatically read aloud some of the most derogatory tweets targeting Kaitlyn under the pretense of drawing attention to the harassment people experience through social media.[12] As Jennifer Gerson Uffalussy points out, however, "The gluttonous tone of his reading seemed to suggest an ulterior motive. As Harrison rattled off each subsequent, increasingly violent and horrible accusation against Bristowe, he seemed to be doing more to remind viewers that Bristowe had done something perceived by [them] to be shameful."[13] Similarly, Emily Yahr criticized the producers for ignoring the ways that their portrayal of Kaitlyn prompted online hate speech. While the show may deserve "credit for addressing online abuse and shaming cyberbullies," as Yahr notes, "a quick segment wedged between the 'Men Tell All' blooper reel and other drama" is not quite sufficient.[14]

Even though some important conversations resulted from this sensationalized reality television episode, the initial social media response it provoked ultimately reveals how expectations for single women on the dating market today are entrenched in problematic sexual double standards that have remained unaltered for decades. Consider, for example, this tweet posted during the episode: "You can turn a housewife into a hoe. But you can't turn a hoe into a housewife" (@Heather Gossman). As the negative Twitter posts prove, many still believe that certain behaviors determine whether a woman is good girlfriend or wife material, and at the top of the list remains her sexual history.

This chapter analyzes the tweets pertaining to this *Bachelorette* "controversy," noting the pervasiveness of posts that reinforce problematic gender norms. It then turns to a subset of posts that seem to critique these norms and provide broader cultural commentary about societal expectations concerning female sexuality. These latter tweets—which combat gender stereotypes and provide cultural education—could be considered a form of digital activism. Thus, this study considers the ways in which Twitter's particular communication format might complicate or interfere with their societal critiques. Further, aligning with the conclusions of chapter 8, this study argues that different televisual genres prompt different viewing practices and fan behavior and that those practices affect the potential for viewers to critically engage with the show through second screening platforms such as Twitter.

An Analysis of Live-Tweeting Practices of a Dating Reality Television Program

Twitter data were collected weekly from May 18, 2015, through July 27, 2015, spanning the entire eleven-week season. Live tweets (posted between 8:00 P.M. EST and 10:00 P.M. EST during the original two-hour airing of the program) associated with the hashtag #TheBachelorette were scraped weekly using NodeXL. Focus was then narrowed to a three-week period that involved the public slut-shaming of the bachelorette contestant (tweets pertaining to the episodes that aired on June 15, June 22, and June 29). During the June 15 episode one contestant, Ian Thomson, criticized Kaitlin for making out with too many male contestants, prompting the first discussion of slut-shaming for the season; during the June 22 episode, as I discussed earlier, Kaitlin was recorded having sex with one contestant; and the June 29 episode focused on Kaitlin's confessing to her remaining suitors that she had had this early sexual encounter. The publicity for these episodes continually stressed Kaitlyn's sexual behavior (and anticipated reactions to it). The resulting data pool from these three episodes consisted of 56,764 total tweets.

The dataset was then coded to highlight "critiquing" tweets—tweets that expressed opinions or judgments about the show, its participants, or society. These tweets were further organized into two categories: (1) small-scale critiques directed at the contestants (including subcategories such as personal opinions, name calling, and jokes); and (2) large-scale cultural critiques directed at the producers or other Twitter users (including subcategories focused on media criticism—e.g., posts about editing or marketing choices—and cultural commentary). The following research questions guided the analysis of these data:

> RQ 1. Do the patterns of live-tweeting *The Bachelorette* align with the research concerning the reasons viewers watch reality television?
>
> RQ 2. What does this dataset reveal about cultural sentiments concerning societal expectations for gendered behavior?
>
> RQ 3. In what ways do the live tweets posted by viewers of *The Bachelorette* engage in a form of social commentary related to gendered expectations, and which particular Twitter practices assist or interfere with the effectiveness of this commentary?
>
> RQ 4. Does this dataset indicate that live-tweeting reality television programs could be a form of feminist digital activism?

Following the assumptions laid out in chapter 8, this study posits that viewer tweets may provide a glimpse into societal values and cultural anxieties. Therefore, attending to the emotional reasons that bring viewers to this particular televisual genre and considering how the genre itself may influence their online commentary seems valid.

RQ 1. Do the patterns of live-tweeting The Bachelorette align with the research concerning the reasons viewers watch reality television?

As chapter 2 discusses, the three theories that account for viewers' watching reality television include schadenfreude (they watch to rejoice in the misery of others or to feel superior to them), voyeurism (they watch to see that which they would normally not see), and vicarious affect (they watch to live vicariously through the experiences of the onscreen contestants). Since research on live-tweeting television indicates that the most common purpose for live-tweeting is to state opinions, followed by aiming to bring attention to oneself, it was predicted—on the basis of the content of the program—that the vast majority of the tweets would critique the individual contestants (the bachelorette and her suitors), thereby aligning with the schadenfreude viewing theory and the research on live-tweeting practices.[15] Analysis of the data confirmed this hypothesis: the majority of the posts were carping or humorous critiques stating the viewers' opinions of the reality TV participants. A few posts, however, rooting for particular suitors—most often Shaun—aligned with the vicarious affect theory for why viewers tune into reality TV programs. For example, tweets like "Ugh Shaun makes me melt when he walks in the room. And that's sad, it's only via television. #TheBachelorette" (@hegartykaty).[16] A few posts also aligned with the voyeurism theory for the reasons people watch reality TV, as tweets referred to watching or hearing things they should not be seeing or hearing. For example: "This feels a lot like an invasion of privacy but I can't not watch it #TheBachelorette" (@feeeeeney) or "Anyone else feel like a perv eavesdropping outside the bedroom door? #TheBachelorette" (@Heidi_00). The overall tendency toward schadenfreude-ridden and attention-seeking posts (most of which took on attempts at humor), however, complicated the findings concerning the second research question.

RQ 2. What does this dataset reveal about cultural sentiments concerning societal expectations for gendered behavior?

As chapter 8 reveals, though there can be challenges in viewing Twitter as an accurate indicator of cultural values, this dataset does document prevalent sexism. The most common sexist tweets involved slut-shaming (see table 9.1), reinforcing double standards concerning sexual behavior, and accepting (or at least not criticizing) vulgar and violent language directed at women.[17] All these could be viewed as products of the continued postfeminist backlash.

The pure quantity of tweets produced indicates that commenting on a woman's sexual behavior is an acceptable cultural practice. (The June 22 episode nearly doubled the average weekly tweet total for this hashtag.) The controversial scene between Kaitlyn and Nick aired over eight minutes, between

Table 9.1. Twitter posts slut-shaming contestants on *The Bachelorette.*

Twitter User	Time Stamp	Tweet
niiecy_babii	6/22/2015 9:09	I feel so bad for the original men in the house. Kaitlyn really is doing them dirty, she has no respect😐. #TheBachelorette
Scarlettmerk	6/22/2015 9:12	You're having sex on national television #classy #TheBachelorette
HollyDurst	6/22/2015 9:12	I bet her parents like this episode. #TheBachelorette
CocoNutsNYC	6/22/2015 9:16	They deserve each other. She's as deep as bucket of water in the desert and he's just gross. NOT A GENTLEMAN! NOT A LADY! #TheBachelorette
AbsolutelyAnna	6/22/2015 9:16	COMMENCE WALK OF SHAME. #thebachelorette
RoxieKat	6/22/2015 9:20	Fix it. . .? How about keeping your v-jayjay in your pants?
Melanie_G123	6/22/2015 9:22	"I wouldn't want my son dating her"-mom #TheBachelorette @PrincessProbz

9:08 and 9:16. This scene began with a series of make-out sessions (juxtaposed with clips of the other men expressing their feelings for her). Next came six minutes of footage recording their sexual encounter. While the actual interaction occurred behind closed doors, it was captured on audio, and the producers decided to air it with subtitles added (and to edit in shots of birds and bees and erupting water fountains as a form of crass symbolism). The scene ended with Nick's leaving Kaitlyn's hotel room in the morning, providing further clarity about what had occurred. Throughout this eight-minute scene, 7,312 total tweets (original tweets plus replies and retweets) were posted under this hashtag (at a rate of 914 tweets per minute).

Unsurprisingly, the authors of these posts were predominantly female.[18] This aligns with previous research concerning how women are as likely, if not more, as men to critique another woman's sexual activity on Twitter.[19] The fact that more women than men participated in this slut-shaming also is probably due to the fact that viewership of the program is composed largely of women. Beyond the general criticism directed at Kaitlyn, the casual use of derogatory terms is also noteworthy (see table 9.2). A secondary dataset

Table 9.2. Derogatory name-calling tweets on *The Bachelorette.*

Twitter User	Time Stamp	Tweet
afterfivenow	6/22/2015 9:10	Ho dee Ho Ho Ho #TheBachelorette
kellieewalton	6/22/2015 9:10	My mom said "she's a scuz-bucket" #nuffsaid #TheBachelorette
sabymarie7	6/22/2015 9:10	TRAMP #TheBachelorette
Californiaashes	6/22/2015 9:12	All aboard the slut train. ALL ABOARD!!!! #TheBachelorette
aiken4jr	6/22/2015 9:12	Uh oh this is turning into 50 shades of slutty!!!#TheBachelorette
liv_cappucci	6/22/2015 9:12	kaitlin is a whoreeeee #TheBachelorette
courtyvonne	6/22/2015 9:16	So, Kaitlyn BristHOE? #TheBachelorette
miranda0678	6/22/2015 9:17	If you didn't want it to be an issue, you should have kept your legs closed! Bloody whore! #TheBachelorette
marlin_hargrove	6/22/2015 9:23	#TheBachelorette. Kaitlyn is trashy.

obtained by using keyword searches on Topsy, an online social media search engine, determined that in the days surrounding the June 22 episode, 293 tweets under the hashtag #The Bachelorette included the word *slut* (although this number is slightly misleading since a portion of these included critiques of slut-shaming); 151 tweets included the adjective *dirty;* 112 tweets included the word *classy* (used in a sarcastic fashion); 102 included the term *hoe*; 85 included the slur *whore*; 43 included the insult *trashy*; 38 included the label *skank*; 32 included the expression *tramp*; and 25 included the descriptor *tacky*. Context, of course, cannot always be gleamed from simple word-count analyses, and what the data suggest is that these numbers actually underrepresent the amount of times vulgar terms were directed at the star since often such insults are purposely misspelled to add emphasis or humor. Take, for example, the poster (@courtyvonne) who integrated the word *hoe* into the spelling of Bristowe's name (see table 9.2).

RQ 3. In what ways do the live tweets posted by viewers of The Bachelorette engage in a form of social commentary related to gendered expectations, and which particular Twitter practices assist or interfere with the effectiveness of this commentary?

As chapter 8 discusses, ample research has suggested that Twitter may be used to track cultural sentiment, but the type of writing Twitter promotes contributes to its performative nature and, therefore, problematizes the notion that tweets can act as a societal mirror reflecting cultural values.[20] For example, as the previous chapter noted, humorous and inflammatory posts tend to receive more attention in the form of retweeting and replying.[21] This could result in social media users who perform in ways that do not necessarily reflect their own beliefs in order to obtain visibility and popularity. The collective data, however, still have the potential to reveal cultural practices, and, by extension, the cultural beliefs they are grounded in.

Negative or comedic tweets from this dataset were more likely to be retweeted, a fact which aligns with the research. And while the content of these tweets may not necessarily perfectly reflect societal beliefs, they do at least reveal common practices for live-tweeting televised content. The comedic tweets indicated an expectation for synchronous communication—posts intended for an imagined audience of fellow viewers watching the program *during* the live broadcast.[22] Unsurprisingly, the sexual encounter prompted a slew of jokes referring to the sounds and actions editors allowed viewers access to during the eight-minute scene (see table 9.3). The specificity of these tweets highlights the ephemeral nature of tweets, in general, but also how their humor often depends on when the tweet is received. Consider, for example, this joke that alluded to a commercial campaign running concurrently with the season: "I think we ALL know what never-before-seen #BleachableMoment we want Clorox to unlock tonight" (@KristenGBaldwin).

Another example is the increased number of STD jokes posted during a bizarre group date that followed Kaitlyn and Nick's sex scene. This date—held at a funeral parlor—found Kaitlyn posing as a corpse in a coffin while her suitors recited eulogies. Quite often these comedic tweets make sense only to someone watching the show live (e.g., "Oh, dear. This is going to bad places. Don't do it, Kaitlyn! You will get chlamydia. And die"; "Nick's coming back with something alright, and it rhymes with 'schmerpes'"; "Kaitlyn is dead. Nick gave her a toxic case of the clap"; "I figured @viallnicholas28 had megaherpes, I just didn't think it would kill @kaitlynbristowe this fast").

Some program-specific complications arose that made it more difficult to determine whether larger cultural sentiments could be gleaned from this dataset. Some of the critical posts directed at Kaitlyn's sexual activity were influenced by viewers' preexisting feelings for Nick, a contestant on the previous season. For example, one viewer tweeted: "Not shaming her for what

Table 9.3. Joking tweets on *The Bachelorette.*

Twitter User	Time Stamp	Tweet
Jenniferweiner	6/22/2015 9:03	"The chemistry's there. The emotions are there. Everything I'm looking for is there." Hoping the birth control is there. . .
Eonline	6/22/2015 9:11	Something tells us they aren't just playing Scrabble in there. . . #TheBachelorette
chamie713	6/22/2015 9:12	Can you imagine the looks the camera guys are giving each other during this scene 😂 #TheBachelorette
Jasonpinter	6/22/2015 9:12	I think I'd rather fill my ears with pregnant scorpions than listen to more of Nick's bedroom talk. #TheBachelorette
jenniferweiner	6/22/2015 9:12	Sighs. Coos. Kisses. Soprano groans. Either they're having sex or eating a really delicious sundae. Mmm. Sundae. #thebachelorette
LaurenDenhamXo	6/22/2015 9:13	And suddenly, watching #TheBachelorette with my mom seems like a not so good idea
Jamienotis	6/22/2015 9:18	Watching #TheBachelorette is like listening to the audio book of a harlequin romance novel. #Bachelornation
butterflyblob	6/22/2015 9:18	"Off-camera time" is my new favorite euphemism for sex. #TheBachelorette
AnonBachelorFan	6/22/2015 9:22	Which producer drew the short stick and had to film the door while they did it? #TheBachelorette

she is doing. . . . My issue is who she is doing it with. Huge difference" (@ellabella1792). Such critiques are further complicated by the reason many viewers disliked Nick.[23] Ironically, he himself had engaged in a form of televised slut-shaming. During an "After the Final Rose" episode, he criticized Andi Dorkman, the previous bachelorette, for sleeping with him when she had not intended to marry him. So, oddly enough, Kaitlyn was shamed more for *her* sexual acts because she was with a partner who had previously (inadvertently or not) shamed another woman for hers.[24] Viewers' history with the program influenced other critiques as well. For example, many saw the interaction between Kaitlyn and Nick as deviating from the normal program arc, and her sexual activity was interpreted as violating the so-called rules of the show (e.g., the expectation that the star will wait until the fantasy suite to have sex).

While the majority of the critiquing posts focused on the specific behavior of the contestants rather than on societal issues, there was a subset that countered the normative messages found in the larger thread. Multiple viewers used Twitter to combat the sexist commentary present in the program or the fan tweets.[25] Some users pointed out the misogyny of fellow viewers, some called for more positive discussions of sex, and some simply celebrated Kaitlyn's choice without qualification (see table 9.4).[26] The practice of specifically labeling the sexism and misogyny present in the feed aligns with one of the more common feminist activist practices online: educating about feminism and feminist issues.[27] Still others used Twitter to criticize the network, arguing that ABC had finally crossed a line with its treatment of Kaitlyn (see table 9.5).

Table 9.4. Anti-slut-shaming/contestant-support tweets on *The Bachelorette.*

Twitter User	Time Stamp	Tweet
jenniferweiner	6/22/2015 8:23	Kaitlyn will not apologizing for kissing guys. Because intimacy is important. Also, she's thirty years old and not Amish. #thebachelorette
UnSlutProject	6/22/2015 9:07	Everyone "slut"-shaming #TheBachelorette needs to knock it the hell off. @kaitlynbristowe we've got your back! #unslut
AshleySpivey	6/22/2015 9:08	All these girls on Twitter acting like they haven't hooked up with a dude on the first date. Come on. #TheBachelorette
KarisaHolden	6/22/2015 9:09	OMG! A woman in 2015 wants to have sex with a guy she's attracted to! It's like Sodom & Gomorrah up in there. #TheBachelorette
Shilohbarkley	6/22/2015 9:10	Get your orgasm on, girlfriend! #TheBachelorette
EmilyLFoley	6/22/2015 9:11	The only things Kaitlyn should be embarrassed about it not turning off her mic pack. #TheBachelorette

BluntAssJenny	6/22/2015 9:16	Here comes sexism/misgynoticism in 3. . .2. . .1. . . #TheBachelorette 😒😒😒
jcapejcape	6/22/2015 9:17	GIRL CAN HAVE SEX IF SHE WANTS EVERYONE props to @kaitlynbristowe for bein real about her desires everyone else shhhh #TheBachelorette
CelebrityFind	6/22/2015 9:17	Hey! Don't say that! #Nymphomaniacs have rights, too! #DontJudge #Each2HisOwn #havingfun #TheBachelorette #NiceGirl ;D
guyisonahorse	6/22/2015 9:17	So much embarrassing slut shaming happening on #TheBachelorette tags. Yall are at best, hypocrites. At worst, poopy faced scum bags.
bachrants	6/22/2015 9:17	And so begins the "Slutshaming Special" episode of #TheBachelorette
HegartyKatie	6/22/2015 9:18	Kaitlyn says she doesn't feel guilt for "the act." Very glad to hear that because the show will FIGHT to take that from her #TheBachelorette
AshleySpivey	6/22/2015 9:23	I think we all need to have a big discussion about how sex can actually make you feel powerful, ladies. #TheBachelorette

Expanding the Twitter collection beyond the live-tweeting window reveals that tweets of this nature were more likely to occur outside the live broadcast time. Those criticizing the practice of slut-shaming under this hashtag were often joining the conversation after the fact, which indicates that this sort of digital activism—although engaging with viewers of *The Bachelorette*—may not be coming from those who watch the show live (if at all). Interestingly, unlike the comedic tweets, these often seem crafted for asynchronous communication (see table 9.6).

RQ 4. Does this dataset indicate that live-tweeting reality television programs could be a form of feminist digital activism?

There were, however, still a number of live tweets that engaged in cultural commentary while the episode aired. Unfortunately, they suggest some challenges of using Twitter to provide such critiques—or at least such critiques inspired by a long-standing reality television program. Although some have argued that Twitter's minimalism can be viewed as an affordance, persuasive

Table 9.5. Critical tweets directed at the producers of *The Bachelorette*.

Twitter User	Time Stamp	Tweet
Eonline	6/22/2015 9:10	The heavy breathing? The sound effects? STOP. THIS. #TheBachelorette
TayMartin13	6/22/2015 9:11	You've went too far, ABC. Too far. #TheBachelorette
Possessionista	6/22/2015 9:11	Hey ABC we all know what's happening. We could do without the sound effects. #TheBachelorette
NMariRogers	6/22/2015 9:11	Ew. Slurping and subtitles?! Too much. It's too much. #TheBachelorette
Possessionista	6/22/2015 9:12	Oh sure, the bleep out the word "erection," but Kaitlyn moaning is a-ok? #TheBachelorette
GitrDUNNashton	6/22/2015 9:13	I'm really disappointed in the way @ABCNetwork @BacheloretteABC is showing this. Very poor taste. #TheBachelorette
Colindonnell	6/22/2015 9:13	Gotta hand it to #TheBachelorette editors. The fountain at the end of that whole thing was genius
Leonicka	6/22/2015 9:16	LOL at the birds and bees footage. I SEE WHAT YOU DID THERE @BacheloretteABC #TheBachelorette

social commentary is arguably difficult to achieve in 140 (or 280) characters.[28] The length restrictions, coupled with the text-based messaging, often leads to ambiguous posts.[29] For example, consider the first four posts in table 9.7. The first tweet, "So I guess self-slut-shaming is possible," could be interpreted as criticizing slut-shaming or as saying that finally a contestant has crossed a line and deserves to be the target of such-shaming. The words in the second tweet, "this girl is dirty," seems like a criticism—but then the post includes two contradictory emoticons that could be viewed as criticizing or celebrating her actions. The third tweet, "Let the slut shaming commence," could be read as predicting, criticizing, or encouraging the series of slut-shaming tweets that would follow. And the fourth tweet, "I'm embarrassed for this girl," could be viewed as empathetic or judgmental.

Table 9.6. Anti-slut-shaming Tweets, June 22–June 30, 2015 (during and between episodes of *The Bachelorette*).

Twitter User	Time Stamp	Tweet
brosandprose	6/22/2015 1:37pm	fuck it, I'm spending this weekend writing about #TheBachelorette, social media harassment and slut-shaming. A Bachelorella manifesto.
BachBlackBox	6/22/2015 2:12pm	Let's all make a promise that tonight we will not slut-shame @kaitlynbristowe Support women's decisions, dont be degrading #TheBachelorette
jennyrocks	6/22/2015 5:31pm	also, we've got what will surely be the most slut-shamingest #thebachelorette of the season tonight, so yay feminism
Fortitude1913	6/22/2015 6:36pm	Watching #TheBachelorette tonight just to scc if @ABCNetwork will remain true to form & let Caitlyn get slut-shamed on national TV. . .
Cckessler	6/23/2015 8:05am	All these people slut-shaming Kaitlyn and yet very little about Nick who has now slept two Bachelorettes on national TV. #TheBachelorette
LindsWilliams_	6/23/2015 8:43pm	Catching up on last nights episode of #theBachelorette &BOY OH BOY. I'd never slut-shame you, @kaitlynbristowe -but who edited it did girl.
CalgarySarah	6/24/2015 5:51pm	To #TheBachelorette viewers: Slut-shaming is never okay. Never slut-shame yourself or others.
YahooStyle	6/25/2015 5:19pm	Feminism in retrograde: Why we NEED to stop slut-shaming #theBachelorette @kaitlynbristowe. http://yhoo.it/1HjHhWQ
LaDiavolina	6/25/2015 11:42pm	It makes me irrationally angry that the majority of those slut-shaming Kaitlyn Bristowe are women. Judgmental prudes. #TheBachelorette
bachelorbenhair	6/30/2015 8:54pm	UGH, Kaitlyn take your power back. You're #TheBachelorette and you apologize for nothing!

Table 9.7. Mixed messages and ambiguous posts on *The Bachelorette*.

Twitter User	Time Stamp	Tweet
VaughnFry	6/22/2015 9:09	#TheBachelorette So I guess self-slut-shaming is possible.
_MissNessaJ	6/22/2015 9:10	😟 this girl is dirty 😂 #TheBachelorette
devonrgoss	6/22/2015 9:10	#Let the slut shaming commence #TheBachelorette
msemilymosley	6/22/2015 9:12	I'm embarrassed for this girl! #TheBachelorette
youngmathgenius	6/22/2015 9:13	I won't condemn Kaitlyn for what she did even though it's inappropriate, but why Nick? #TheBachelorette
AbbeWright	6/22/2015 9:14	I would DIE if my moans were on national TV. #ReasonsWhyICouldntBeTheBachelorette But go on and get it girl! #TheBachelorette
ellabella1792	6/22/2015 9:14	Not shaming her for what she is doing. . . My issue is who she is doing it with. Huge difference #TheBachelorette
click4Amanda	6/22/2015 9:14	#TheBachelorette Kaitlyn's not gross for boning a guy; she's gross for boning a guy 3 feet from an entire production crew
charleen383	6/22/2015 9:15	Dumbbell! Everyone gets one dumbbell moment, don't they? #TheBachelorette
bluntassjenny	6/22/2015 9:16	Should have just held out until the fantasy suites where it's perfectly acceptable to bone on national TV #TheBachelorette

Ultimately this study suggests that live-tweeting reality television programs—or at least this particular reality television program—may not be an effective form of digital activism. Overall, the social activist posts were greatly outnumbered by misogynistic posts that decreased the visibility of the activist posts within the feed. The posts containing social commentary were also less likely to be retweeted than those that provided gendered insults, slurs, or jokes. Further, even the tweets critiquing the sexist, heteronormative, and patriarchal tropes of the show were influenced by viewers' expectations for the television genre, the program's particular structure, and the communication platform with which they were engaging.

Successful feminist digital activism engages like-minded individuals online, who voice concerns and share information with the intent to raise awareness about feminist issues among the general public.[30] Hashtag feminists —those employing hashtags to draw attention to specific feminist issues— have successfully intervened in "oppressive discourse produced by commercial, news, and entertainment media."[31] The live-tweeted critiques of *The Bachelorette* can be viewed as attempts at hashtag feminism, but they falter largely because the tweets were made under the #TheBachelorette hashtag, which has a limited reach. Very few posts included targeted feminist hashtags that could link their critiques to those of others; this practice would give visibility to these counter-messages, entering them into broader conversations about feminist issues beyond the context of the program. If done effectively, appending a social justice–orientated hashtag to that of a major broadcast *can* allow users to co-opt the conversation concerning television programming. Consider, for example, the Representation Project's launch of the #NotBuyingIt hashtag and iPhone app six days before the 2014 Super Bowl. The campaign encouraged users to combat gender misrepresentation, prompting over fifteen thousand tweets—reaching more than 2.4 million people—during the nationally televised game.[32] Hashtag activism works best when individual posts—often those involving personal stories—coalesce into a unified protest, and this did not occur in this particular dataset.[33] This study suggests that live-tweeting television shows as a form of cultural commentary will be effective only if the individual tweets pointing out social injustice reach a high level of visibility and interconnectivity.

The failures of this example of digital activism, however, may actually reflect the pitfalls of hashtag feminism in general. Many critics have argued that feminist digital activism is ineffective at best, and superficial and divisive at worst. In an article for *Feminist Current,* Meghan Murphy writes: "Twitter feminism is all about hashtags and mantras. We all compete to make the most meaningful, (seemingly) hard-hitting statement in order to gain followers and accolades. Invent the right hashtag and you can become a feminist celebrity. While I'm not excluding myself completely from this phenomenon, as I do participate from time to time, I find it all a bit empty."[34]

Since Twitter's design in a sense encourages popularity contests among users, feminist messaging often gets lost in the quest to craft a post that will cut through the volume of online noise and actually have an effect. Worse, this space also prompts competition among feminists, which leads many to label this fourth-wave, digital form of feminism as toxic.[35] One of the largest criticisms that Twitter feminism receives is that it works against intersectional feminism, further silencing the voices that already have less representation in offline spaces.[36] For example, Jessie Daniels argues that the digital era just perpetuates "the dominance of white women as architects and defenders of a framework of white feminism."[37] Further, Twitter gives off the illusion of being a microcosm of society at large, but that is not necessarily the case. Murphy argues vehemently that "Twitter is not representative. But we seem to believe it is. Twitter tends to amplify certain perspectives and voices and erase others—either because they aren't there or because they're too scared to speak up, lest they become the next target. Thinking about *who* is on Twitter and whose voices are loudest on Twitter is worthwhile. Are poor women on Twitter? Are people who are busy working on Twitter? Are people who are sick of being harassed and bullied and attacked on Twitter participating in conversations? Who's there? Who feels safe to speak there?"[38]

On top of all this, the odds are stacked against those who wish to disseminate feminist critiques on Twitter because the space is inundated with "anti-feminist and sexist messages."[39] Since online debates about gender are "increasingly infiltrated by these positions," counter-messages often get eclipsed by hate speech and trolling.[40]

Bachelor/Bachelorette Fans Police Gender Norms through Twitter

While live-tweeting a reality television program may not be the most effective form of digital activism, if such a thing exists, it does reveal the types of anxieties concerning gender relations that have been discussed throughout this book. The policing of normative gender behavior is a common societal practice, and therefore its consistent presence across seasons of *The Bachelor/Bachelorette* is not surprising. Studying almost any season from this franchise would have probably produced the same conclusions. For example, months after Kaitlyn's season ended, one of her former suitors, Ben Higgins, starred as *The Bachelor* in his very own season and his, too, was surrounded by much-hyped controversy.[41]

When his season of *The Bachelor* drew to a close in March 2016, the double standards that exist for women and men on the dating scene—onscreen and off—were, once again, broadcast loud and clear. Ben followed protocol and proposed to one of the contestants, Lauren Bushnell, in the season finale. Two weeks earlier, however, he had committed a big show no-no: he said he loved her on camera—right before he said he loved another contestant, JoJo

Fletcher. Higgins was not the first bachelor in history to say he was falling *in love* with two contestants, but he was the first to say it directly to the women (while caught on camera at least). Even though the trope of the bachelor torn between his affections for two women has become a staple of the program, Higgins's proclamations infuriated fans. One viewer (@karachristine16) tweeted: "Why on earth would Ben say I love you to two different girls. Whoever gets sent home is going to be crushed." Another viewer (@Jacquelyne-Ander) posted: "I really can't stand Ben. He doesn't understand the meaning of 'I love you,' if he says it to two women." While many of the tweeters were concerned with the ethics behind his multiple confessions of love, others were simply angry that he broke the show's so-called rules: "Ben's already broken two rules. Never say 'I love you' and never ever say 'I love you' multiple times. Someone's in the dog house" (@MrsEllis4Eva). Higgins defended his actions in an interview with *E!News:* "I don't know of a rule book, maybe there is one, maybe [one] fans out there are hiding. . . . I keep hearing he broke all the rules. I didn't know there were rules to this."[42]

A few things surface when looking at these back-to-back seasons together. First, Bristowe's character was torn apart in social media—and she even received death threats[43]—because she was physically intimate with a man, whereas Higgins was criticized—albeit to a lesser degree—not for his three fantasy suite encounters with women (which also probably involved sex), but for his verbal intimacy. Perhaps these reality television tweet-inspiring events received such attention because they flipped the societal gender script. After all, traditional gender stereotypes would have us believe that it is the girl who is supposed to be overly emotional and the guy who is supposed to be overly sexual. Since the dating reality television programs are founded on outdated gender norms such as these, it is unsurprising that viewers reinforce them when recording their reactions to the show on Twitter. Sadly, live-tweeting reality dating programs simply seems to be a new way to police, rather than critique, gender norms. #SexismPrevails

Afterthought: A Glimmer of Hope (Connected to Fan Activism?)

While the antisex shaming tweets analyzed here showed no evidence of having a direct effect on other viewers' discussions of gender and sexuality, they—along with mainstream cultural criticism—may have had an influence on the producers' future choices. Kaitlyn was not the last Bachelorette to be critiqued for her so-called sexual promiscuity; however, later seasons dealt with it quite differently. The 2019 season featured a multiweek promotional clip of the star, Hannah Brown, responding to a question about her sexual activity from one of the final suitors, Luke P. The two had bonded over their shared faith throughout the season, and he then attempted to use religion to justify his inquiry about whether she had slept with any of the other men in the fantasy suite. He said, "I am very confident that we're on the same page with our morals," but then added that if she *had* had sex, he'd "be wanting to go home. 100 percent."[44] In the back-and-forth that ensued, Hannah responded: "You're questioning me, you're judging me and feel like you have the right to when you don't at this point." Eventually she sent Luke home, but not before making the statement that would become the promotional punch line for the network (and a tagline for the season): "I have had sex . . . and Jesus still loves me."[45]

Now, admittedly the producers didn't script this "rare moment of sex-positivity," but they did make the decision to highlight and exploit it.[46] Scholarship on fandom has long talked about the influence that consumers have on the entertainment industry in the age of digital communication. Perhaps this is one example of how fans can affect the cultural commentary that makes its way onto our screens. Or, more cynically, it could simply serve as an example of how producers will capitalize on social commentary if it yields a spike in viewership. In either case, these viral moments have the potential to influence cultural sentiments.

10

"I'm (Not) with Her"

How the Political Commentary Surrounding the 2016 U.S. Presidential Election Reflects Anxieties Concerning Gender Equality

There is perhaps no better site of study to end this book on than the 2016 presidential election, which, arguably, evolved as it did in part because of a combination of the cultural fears discussed throughout the previous chapters. For example, the presidential campaign run by Donald Trump played on post-9/11 insecurities about homeland security and employed fear-based, divisive rhetoric about race, gender, class, and sexuality. In contrast, the presidential campaign of his opponent, Hillary Clinton, as she had in her first campaign, cast a spotlight on the continued backlash that women face as they inch closer toward gender equality.

All these amplified anxieties were broadcast 24/7 across our television screens, computers, and smartphones, creating unprecedented tension about the pending election in the weeks and months leading up to it. Although presidential elections for over half a century have been influenced by the medium of television, no election before this one seemed to be "made for TV" in the way that this one was.[1] First of all, it quickly spun into a media spectacle featuring a man who was literally a former reality television star and a woman who had spent three decades of her professional life as the target of ceaseless scandals and smear campaigns captured (and amplified) by the media. It certainly made for good ratings, although not good citizen morale.[2] Though entertainment genres often are affected by peak political moments, this particular election found the entertainment industry playing an active role in attempting to shape the outcome of the race. As in years past, the various infotainment and satire genres (discussed in chapter 3) played a role in the election, offering scathing critiques of Trump (e.g., *The Daily*

Show with Trevor Noah, This Week Tonight with Jon Oliver, Full Frontal with Samantha Bee). *Saturday Night Live,* for example, amassed a huge viewing audience—through television and the Internet—when it featured Alec Baldwin as Donald Trump. The fact that the parody shows would include commentary on the election is not surprising, but the role that fictional television played was more unusual in this particular election. Shonda Rhimes's determination to use television as a social justice tool (as chapter 8 discusses) was evident when she ran a political advertisement for Hillary Clinton featuring the female stars of her three blockbuster shows: *Scandal* (Kerry Washington), *Grey's Anatomy* (Ellen Pompeo), and *How to Get Away with Murder* (Viola Davis). Perhaps more surprising was the revival of the hit sitcom *Will and Grace,* which returned to the screen after ten years to release a faux online episode focused on the election, and then later a reboot. In this nine-minute video, Will (Eric McCormack) and Grace (Debra Messing) discuss the dangers of a Trump presidency and ultimately persuade Jack (Sean Hayes) to vote for Clinton.[3]

While these moments of politics merging with entertainment are interesting and worthy of study in and of themselves, this chapter ends this book's coverage of various televisual genres by turning to the nonfiction coverage of the 2016 election. It focuses specifically on the first presidential debate and the ways in which it stimulated conversation among viewers during the live broadcast as well as ongoing dialogue and activism beyond it. The importance and potential effect of major live television events has been well documented by scholars.[4] The TV-Internet tag team, as we will see shortly, allows these "live" televisual moments to have an afterlife that they did not have in decades past. In the case of the presidential debates, for example, the ability to rewatch key moments (in the form of YouTube clips, gifs, or memes), to have access to annotated transcripts from the broadcasts, or to read countless online critiques of the debate performances (by laypersons and experts alike) expands our ability to share in this "live" television moment.[5] It also allows for a new type of "water-cooler conversation" wherein participants need not have necessarily watched the event live in order to enter into dialogue with friends, family, or colleagues the next day about it.[6]

This chapter, like others in part III, examines live tweets from viewers watching the first presidential debate; but it then, unlike the previous chapters, expands its scope to other online platforms (e.g., Facebook, memes, online merchandising) to discuss the subsequent debates and election fallout.[7] Many cultural anxieties could have been the focus of this study, but this chapter continues chapter 9's focus on sentiments related to feminism and gender equality. It starts by attending to the role that sexism plays in politics, focusing specifically on Clinton's two presidential campaigns. It then turns to the ways in which the 2016 election cycle highlighted the misogynistic behavior of Trump (and some of his supporters). Both these phenomena reflect continued resistance and roadblocks to gender equality. This discussion then moves on to showcase the ways in which people are turning to digital activism to address and combat these.

Gender Stereotypes and Political Outcomes: Where Reality and Research Diverge

There has been plenty of research detailing the gender gap in politics, and scholars have offered multiple reasons for men continuing to outnumber women in the highest governmental offices. These range from hypotheses that the issues most important to women motivate them to hold offices at more local levels, that family obligations prevent them from running for political office, and that the economic system is still rigged so that men have more financial means to launch such campaigns.[8] Many, however, have detailed the ways in which one additional, and not surprising, factor—sexism—plays a role in preventing women from gaining these positions. As Deborah Carr explains, it is not necessarily that people consciously decide that they will not vote for a woman, but rather that "voters may hold stereotypes about what women can and should be, and being assertive, self-assured, and focused on global politics may violate idealized notions of what a woman 'should be.' At the same time, even the most assertive candidate may be viewed as 'too soft' to take a hard line with terrorists."[9]

Studies on whether sexism influences a female candidate's chances of winning an election have produced mixed results. For example, a 2010 study focused on women candidates running against men during the U.S. House elections determined that there is "no evidence of any *direct,* consistent, or substantial impact for gender stereotypes on evaluations of, or voting for, women candidates."[10] Additional research found that gender stereotypes may have a greater effect on voters depending on their party affiliation. For example, Kira Sanbonmatsu and Kathleen Dolan determined that "Democrats are more likely to hold gender stereotypes that benefit women in politics."[11] This may be due in part to the fact that gender stereotypes tend to lead voters to infer that female candidates are more liberal than they actually are.[12]

Other myths that academic research has debunked is that women campaign differently from men. For example, a comprehensive analysis of the campaign advertisements for the 2000 and 2002 U.S. House elections determined that the television advertisements for male and female candidates were quite similar.[13] Ads for female candidates, however, were more likely "to present them with the characteristic of toughness or strength," traits more stereotypically associated with males, perhaps as a way to counter the stereotype that women struggle with leadership responsibilities.[14] Another misperception is that female voters are more likely to vote for female candidates (or, to use the crass wording of the 2016 election, that they will "vote with their vaginas").[15] Studies have indicated that while women voters often "do feel positively toward female candidates," they still evaluate those "candidates through the lens of political party."[16] This means that a steadfast Democrat may have some gender affinity to a female Democratic candidate, but those feelings do not extend across the aisle to female Republican candidates.[17] What research has confirmed is that gender does play a role to some extent in the outcome of elections when women's issues are a large part of the campaign discourse. When this is the case, women are "more likely to vote for Democratic candidates. On the other hand, the voting decisions of men [are] not influenced by the prevalence of women's issues on the campaign agenda."[18]

Campaigning against Madam(e) President: The Case of Hillary Clinton

While scholars have found it difficult to prove that gender stereotypes have an influence on election results, most agree that female politicians navigate a patriarchal system and often face extreme sexism throughout their careers. Hillary Rodham Clinton is, undoubtedly, the best example of this. As a first lady she faced scrutiny for maintaining her law profession, being involved in governmental decisions, and not upholding the traditional domestic roles of the post.[19] When, after having served as a New York senator for six years, Clinton decided to run for the presidency in 2008, the sexism directed at her was put on display at the national level.[20] Though the 2008 election—which for the first time included women as contenders for the presidency and vice presidency—should have been a reason for celebration, "any excitement generated by these historic candidacies was tempered by discussions of whether Clinton was too abrasive and not sufficiently warm to be president and whether [Sarah] Palin was smart enough, too pretty, or too encumbered by motherhood to be one heartbeat away" from the Oval Office.[21] Writing on the 2008 election, Emily Douglas observes that it delivered "an ugly, raw misogyny that hadn't emerged into plain sight for years."[22]

Mainstream journalists and scholars took the opportunity during the 2008 election cycle to document the ways in which sexism affected these women's campaigns. For example, Joseph Uscinski and Lilly Goren analyzed the ways in which news broadcasters discussed the candidates, determining that Clinton was addressed "more informally than her male competitors."[23] As the researchers note, "Given her prior experience and successes during the campaign, the media should have treated [Hillary Clinton] equivalent to her male competitors," but instead she "was named by first name four times more than her main male rival," Barack Obama.[24] And this, of course, was the implicit sexism. More overt instances of sexism occurred when Clinton was portrayed as an emotional woman after tearing up on the campaign trail, or when the media simply could not help referencing her "menstrual cycle, pantsuits, laugh, and her husband's infidelity."[25] Even graver instances took the form of attacks on her body (discussions about the thickness of her ankles or nicknames that included "Her Royal Thighness") and her voice (being referred to as "Shrillery"), as she became fodder for crass political cartoons, ads, and campaign paraphernalia for her opponent's followers.[26] But in the end, did all this actually affect the outcome of the election? Media pundits and scholars would debate for years whether Clinton's failure in the 2008 presidential run was due to sexism or whether she was simply outshone by the charismatic Obama.

Eight years later, when Clinton was the presumptive Democratic candidate from the onset, people were primed to watch for the ways in which her gender would be held against her. In a hard-fought primary season against Senator Bernie Sanders, this became an issue, as Clinton supporters accused Sanders supporters—specifically his "Bernie Bros," a large following of white male Democrats—of being sexist. As the 2016 primary elections drew to a close, articles proliferated with titles such as "Bernie Bros Made Me Finally Recognize Misogyny in America" and "I Felt the Bern but the Bros Are Extinguishing the Flames," written by former Sanders supporters who were changing camps.[27] (It should be noted that four years later, sexism was again credited with shaping the outcome of the 2020 Democratic primaries after Senator Elizabeth Warren, who at one point had been considered the frontrunner for the presidential nomination, struggled to gain delegates and dropped out, which resulted in a two-*man* race between Bernie Sanders and former Vice President Joe Biden.)[28]

As had occurred during the 2008 election, scholars stepped in to determine whether data would support the accusations that Clinton was hit by sexism on both sides of the aisle during the 2016 election.

In one particular study, Rebekah Tromble and Dirk Hovy analyzed tweets from the New Hampshire primary, determining that words associated with @HillaryClinton were, indeed, far more negative than those associated with @BernieSanders: "Only nine words associated with Sanders are negative in tone, and 40 are positive. Just eight words associated with Clinton are positive, and 53 are negative."[29] When these words were further analyzed for gendered implications, they determined that only twelve words associated with Sanders carried any gendered meaning, and none of these were negative.[30] On the other hand, "among the 29 gendered words associated with Clinton, 13 carry a negative connotation, including several related to her husband. Indeed, the vast majority of the tweets mentioning Bill Clinton either blame Hillary Clinton for, or suggest her complicity in, her husband's sexual misdeeds."[31] The researchers then analyzed the data, specifically looking for instances wherein gendered slurs (e.g., "bimbo," "whore") were directed at Clinton. Of the 52,181 tweets mentioning Clinton, 606, or 1.16 percent, contained these insults.[32] They then coded this subset to determine whether the slurs originated from an account associated with a Trump or Sanders supporter. They determined that "the vast majority of the slurs were associated with Twitter users on the right—particularly self-identified Trump supporters. But 14.7 percent came from those backing Sanders. Among Sanders supporters, 60.6 percent tweeting gendered slurs were men, 29.2 percent women, and 10.1 percent unknown."[33] Their study is interesting in that it clearly documents the sexist slurs directed at Clinton, but also the ways in which the attention given those instances might lead to misperceptions about their frequency or origins.

Trumped-Up Sexism: When Misogyny Takes on the Form of a Political Candidate

With all the attention on the ways in which gender stereotypes have plagued Clinton's political career in mind, this project was designed to pull tweets from the first presidential debate in order to track the ways in which sexism directed at Clinton would manifest itself in live tweets and the ways in which her supporters would take to the communication platform to try to combat it. The presidential election being an unwieldy, moving cultural micro-organism, however, the conversation quickly pivoted away from Clinton's gender (and the discrimination she faced because of it) and began to focus to more on Trump's misogynistic behavior.[34] Toward the end of the first debate, Clinton sparked the conversation regarding Trump's long history of sexist behavior when she broached the subject of Alicia Machado, the former Miss Universe contestant whom Trump had fat-shamed after she gained weight following her crowning. The tweets analyzed in this study represent the first moments of attention to Trump's sexual abuse that would factor heavily into the media coverage preceding and following the election.

Research Questions and Methodology for Twitter Analysis

To study live tweets from the first presidential debate, attending to the ways in which they reflect cultural anxieties regarding gender equality, I focused my analysis on tweets that reinforce or counter sexist views in order to answer the following research questions:

> RQ 1. How do cultural sentiments concerning gender (particularly sexism and animosity toward feminism) appear in the live tweets from the presidential debate?
>
> RQ 2. What strategies were used to combat sexist rhetoric (present in either the live broadcast or the Twitter feed) by live-tweeting viewers?
>
> RQ 3. What role do major television events play in shaping or shifting cultural beliefs and anxieties?

Twitter data were collected on September 26 from 9:00 P.M. to 10:45 P.M. EST during the first presidential debate between Clinton and Trump—the debate that broke records as the most-watched in U.S. history: over 80 million viewers tuned in.[35] Live tweets associated with the hashtag #debatenight were scraped (i.e., collected) using NodeXL—a program that gathers all tweets associated with a specific hashtag. Because of the quantity of live tweets produced during the debate, and limits placed on the number of tweets that could be collected, data were collected six times (every ten to fifteen minutes) during the debate. The data pool includes original posts, retweets, and replies in order to include posts that were made throughout the debate and not just at these six intervals. This primary data pool consisted of 13,231 tweets.[36] To gain a more comprehensive overview of the tweets associated with this debate, and to see the ways in which the conversation grew in the hours surrounding it, additional tweets were gathered through keyword searches under this hashtag through Twitter's Advanced Search option. This secondary data pool consisted of 675 tweets.

Discussion of Findings from the Original Twitter Collection

Trump dominated the discussion on Twitter on this specific night, which is consistent with other research on social media for this campaign. Of the 13,000-plus tweets, direct references to Trump appeared 8,362 times (63.2 percent), whereas direct references to Clinton appeared only 6,236 times (47.1 percent).[37] This dominance extended to the subset of tweets focused on here: tweets that reinforced or rejected sexism.

RQ 1. How do cultural sentiments concerning gender (particularly sexism and animosity toward feminism) appear within the live tweets from the presidential debate?

To locate the types of sexist rhetoric that was commonly directed at Hillary Clinton, two broad categories of tweets were attended to: those that discussed her personality and those that commented on her physical appearance. Concerning the former, the majority of the negative tweets associated with Clinton expectedly portrayed her as being overly poised ("fake," "scripted"), emotionally distant ("robotic"), unlikable ("shrill," "bore"), elitist ("smug," "holier than thou"), and ambitious (having a "thirst for power").[38] These descriptions align with the research discussed in chapter 8 concerning the adjectives often used to describe strong female women (real and fictional alike). Surprisingly, even compliments directed at Clinton often had connections to this rhetoric. While obviously meant as praise, the phrase "chill as hell" inadvertently aligns with the ice queen persona assigned to powerful women. Likewise, one tweet, assumedly intended as a joke, offered up a new conspiracy about Hillary Clinton, that "she's not human because she is showing an inhuman amount of self-control and poise." Both critiques conform to the discourse surrounding her "robotic" nature, although the latter may intend to critique such rhetoric. Further, posts celebrating the fact that she "emasculated" Trump onstage also are problematic in that they play into the script for the power-hungry female and the so-called crisis of masculinity plaguing American (see table 10.1).

Along with critiques of her personality were those focused on her appearance. The most frequent among these, sixty-two in total, commented on her attire, a pantsuit, an outfit most often associated with professional, perhaps

Table 10.1. Tweets critiquing Hillary Clinton's personality during the first presidential debate, 2016.

Twitter User	Time Stamp	Tweet
Asamjulian	9/26/2016 9:08	Hillary comes so off fake and scripted. #Debates2016 #DebateNight
KyleKulinski	9/26/2016 9:09	Hillary sounds aloof and robotic like a standard politician, Trump doesn't. Bad start. #debatenight #Debates2016
Altrightcelt	9/26/2016 9:12	#DebateNight Hillary can't help but sound shrill and smug.
Elliottrhams	9/26/2016 9:12	Now Clinton is bringing out the claws already. Bad move. #debatenight
BuckSexton	9/26/2016 9:32	Hillary Clinton's plan is to bore and scold America into abject submission as POTUS. Just make it stop. #debatenight
freerangewrite	9/26/2016 9:33	#debatenight Oh the eye rolling. She reminds me of my mother. Killer. #Debates2016
anash_89	9/26/2016 9:36	Here comes the Hillary rehearsed response 😴#debatenight
lauritatellado	9/26/2016 9:36	Damn. Hillary is chill as hell. I'll have what she's having, por favor. #Debates2016 #debatenight
Juscohen	9/26/2016 9:36	She just emasculated him on stage and it was beautiful #debatenight
SOcean5	9/26/2016 10:08	#debates "Holier than thou" there's been no truer line explaining Hillary #debatenight
TomiLahren	9/26/2016 10:37	Hillary will come back from the dead just to attain power. That is all she has in life is a thirst for power. #debatenight
Tay_76	9/26/2016 10:38	New conspiracy about Hillary Clinton: she's not human because she is showing an inhuman amount of self control and poise #debatenight

feminist, women. While not all these were negative (e.g., "Just ironed my Official DNC @HillaryClinton pantsuit to wear as I cheer her on during #debatenight," gigglechick, 3:04 P.M.); "Hilz in her power pant suit. #debatenight #ImWithHer #powerpose #iseered," Olivia_says, 9:12 P.M.), many were. The negative jibes ranged from catch phrases (e.g., "liar liar PANTSUIT on fire #NeverHillary #debatenight," PannebakerFore4, 10:42 P.M.; to jokes (e.g., "Hillary's clearly a monster, she's wearing a pantsuit made out of Elmo's skin #debatenight," MalcolmWHW, 9:13 P.M.); to references to her economic privilege (e.g., "I wonder how much @HillaryClinton's designer pantsuit costs, since she's talking about the 1% and all," CamCastr014, 9:09 P.M.). The fact that people were musing about the color of Clinton's pantsuit hours before the debate (e.g., "Inquiring minds want to know: What color of pantsuit will @HillaryClinton be wearing tonight?!! #debatenight," HenryCoGOPer, 6:07 P.M.) reveals just one of the many ways in which she faced gendered scrutiny that her opponent did not. Along with these posts focusing on her clothing were tweets devoted to her makeup, her eyebrows, her smile, her accessories (or lack thereof), and her overall perceived energy level (table 10.2).

Of course, televised debates lend themselves to observations of the candidate's appearance, speech, and body language, so such comments are not unexpected. The ways in which they fold in gender stereotypes, however, are noteworthy. To be fair, Trump received his fair share of tweets critiquing his own appearance. But while these were often as mean-spirited as those targeting Clinton, they did differ in that the quips about his appearance were not grounded in any stereotypes concerning how a man should present himself (table 10.3).

Accompanying implicit sexist comments concerning Clinton's appearance and personality were more explicit sexist remarks. For example, one recurrent theme throughout the night was her husband's infidelity (e.g., "The Clintons were just introduced—the only family with more drama than the Kardashians" 9:03 P.M.; "'Trump loves hanging around beauty pageants.' So does YOUR husband Hillary" 10:36 P.M.; "Was Trump about to pull the Lewinsky card?" 10:38 P.M.; "Ur a liar @HillaryClinton u stood against women ur husband raped" 10:38 P.M.; "Hillary Clinton called Bill's many women bimbos and trailer trash" 10:38 P.M.). While the tweets did not always mention Hillary Clinton specifically, they joined the broader rhetoric that she herself was (at least partially) to blame for Bill Clinton's past sexual indiscretions. Her opponent amplified this discourse in the early months of the campaign when he retweeted the post "If Hillary Clinton can't satisfy her husband,

Table 10.2. Tweets critiquing Hillary Clinton's appearance during the first presidential debate, 2016.

Twitter User	Time Stamp	Tweet
TimRunsHisMouth	9/26/2016 9:06	I see Hillary went with a Mrs. Claus look instead of Chairman Mao tonight to seem more approachable. #debatenight #TheGreatDebateFox5
PresTheodore	9/26/2016 9:07	Hillary Clinton is definitely wearing Kim Jong-un's Christmas suit #debatenight
codyausanders	9/26/2016 9:12	Where is your American flag pin @HillaryClinton?!? Are you not a patriot?!?! #debatenight
Lindseyleveck	9/26/2016 9:12	Hilary's makeup artist should have given her more contour & blush. She looks pale. . .really pale.#ghost #debatenight #contouring #fail
Rafedean	9/26/2016 9:12	Hilary's onesie is made of 3000 power ties! #debatenight
lisa_henneman	9/26/2016 9:12	Hillary's eyebrows are higher tonight #debatenight
amtucker444	9/26/2016 9:12	I wish Hillary would get some sort of eyebrow relaxant so her face is less like her face. #DebateNight
Adlerdavison	9/26/2016 9:19	hey @HillaryClinton can I please have your pantsuit so I can go bullfighting #debatenight
Fcorpaci	9/26/2016 9:36	Hillary looks tired. Maybe she needs to take a nap. #SickHillary #debatenight
markramseysrec7	9/26/2016 9:36	Hillarys meds are wearing off. She looks and sounds terrible. #debatenight
USAforTrump2016	9/26/2016 10:03	Hillary wipe that smug smile off your face. . .you murderer #debates #debatenight
mike92882	9/26/2016 10:13	Is it just me, or does it seem Hillary's batteries are running down? #Debate #debatenight
Sleepygramy	9/26/2016 10:13	She's like a limp noodle! #debatenight

Table 10.3. Tweets critiquing Trump's appearance during the first presidential debate, 2016.

Twitter User	Time Stamp	Tweet
JessicaValenti	9/26/2016 9:08	Someone told Trump to stay still and he's having a hard time with it #debatenight
robyns323	9/26/2016 9:12	#Trump has his 'bring it biotch' game face on. #debatenight
ch00chelo	9/26/2016 9:12	Is it me or does Trump looks less orange than usual tonight? #debatenight
joshua_ariza	9/26/2016 9:12	Donald Trump's hair is like a bootleg version of Hillary's hair. #debatenight
stedd1177	9/26/2016 9:36	YES the Trump faces have returned!! #DebateNight
heidibrander	9/26/2016 9:36	Kudos to Hillary Clinton for shaking Trump's hand even though he's got DOUBLE PINKEYE! #debatenight
h6yd6n6	9/26/2016 9:36	Orange is the new Hitler #DebateNight
emily_gerds	9/26/2016 9:36	Trump's hair looks like the aftermath of a 7 yr old "brushing" through a tangled American Girl doll's hair #debatenight

what makes her think she can satisfy America?"[39] Comments like these that allude to Clinton's supposed lack of sex appeal underscore the ways in which ageism and sexism combine to undermine women. And though we might at least take some comfort from the fact that Clinton was not often sexualized in Twitter posts—another strategy used to undercut a woman's power—there was the rogue comment here or there that reveals that *any* woman is subject to random sexual commentary (e.g., "I wonder if Hillary sexts #debatenight," barstoolnate, 10:13 P.M.).

In terms of blatantly gendered slurs of the nature Tromble and Hovy studied during the primaries, there were fewer than expected in the debate's live-tweeting stream. More mild instances characterized her as a witch (e.g., "Hillary is just missing her witch's broom tonight. She's a wolf in sheep's clothing. Watch out. Make America great again! #debatenight," hannysan_xo, 10:38 P.M.), but others involved more vulgar language (e.g., "Release your emails, bitch. #debatenight," @mikemikedc777, 9:36 P.M.; "#debatenight Bitch!! You armed ISIL! Is she insane?" teslintobe, 10:13 P.M.; "The Whore of The Wall Street is mocking the Wall Street? #debatenight #debates #Debates2016," America_1st_, 9:18 P.M.).[40] Of course, instances of such slurs are not surprising because, as previous chapters discussed, it has been well documented that Internet communication makes such inflammatory sexist language more prevalent.

While many users' stances on feminism might be deduced from their language concerning Clinton, some pointedly critiqued the movement (or Clinton's role as its current figurehead). Thus, tweets specifically mentioning feminism, misogyny, and sexism were not always doing so in a pro-Clinton fashion. A subset of these were critical of the ways in which her campaign used the so-called woman card.[41] Some parroted the oft-made argument that voting for a woman simply because she was a woman was not feminism. And others brought up the fact that Trump was the first presidential candidate to hire a woman to be his campaign manager as evidence of progress in the women's movement (and perhaps as an implied argument that this choice should then prevent him from being labeled as sexist) (see table 10.4). Others outrageously suggested that Trump's treatment of Clinton was evidence of feminism's success: "Surely it's a win for feminism that Trump feels able to attack his opponent, without chivalry, as if her gender was irrelevant? #debatenight" (timothy_stanley, 10:34 P.M.). The reframing of Trump's misogynistic behavior as a positive move away from an outdated model of "chivalry" is representative of postfeminist sentiments that work to solidify the problematic notion that feminism itself is antiquated. And, of course, there were posts that expressed flat out their disregard for the women's movement in less tactful ways (see the hashtag #feminismiscancer in table 10.4).

Despite this subset of tweets that rejected any positive association with Clinton as a champion or representative of feminism, the vast majority of the tweets including the words feminism, sexism, misogyny, patriarchy, or double standards seemed to be using this labeling strategy as a means to engage in a form of feminist digital activism or feminist social education. These posts (table 10.5) discussed feminism more broadly, or in relation the election, and tagged specific moments in the debate as instances of misogyny. In terms of frequency of such posts, fifty-four tweets specifically mentioned sexism, forty-seven used the term *sexist,* forty-one included the term *feminism,* fifty-four included the word *misogyny,* and twenty-eight referred to patriarchy. Some of these took the form of direct addresses. For example, many posts specifically integrated Hillary Clinton's Twitter handle to comment on the ways in which she personally was experiencing or combating sexism (e.g., "As

Table 10.4. Tweets critiquing aspects of feminism during the first presidential debate, 2016.

Twitter User	Time Stamp	Tweet
Samantha_uren23	9/26/2016 7:35	A woman president would be amazing. But to vote 4 her becuz she's a woman isn't #feminism. . . know the facts and get educated. #debatenight
Yvonne2016MAGA	9/26/2016 9:01	Wow the 1st rigged primary elected female candidate for president #debatenight about to begin yay! for feminism?
TomiLahren	9/26/2016 10:35	Oh Hillary don't you even go there with the woman card. Don't even crack that can of worms. #debatenight
DLoesch	9/26/2016 10:36	Clinton playing that #Vagina2016 card. #debatenight
LilithLovett	9/26/2016 10:36	Oops, Hillary pulling the "Sexist, misogynist" card, time to take another shot.
Michael_Voris	9/26/2016 10:36	Trump is the first presidential candidate to have a woman as his campaign manager. #Feminism #debatenight
muhfeelz	9/26/2016 10:36	Hillary thinks women should get equal pay, but not have to do equal work? #debates #debatenight #feminismiscancer
alli_dance1999	9/26/2016 10:38	Of course they would bring up the sexism card. . . #debatenight #Debates2016

a woman who's endured 50 years of sexism and misogyny, I want to thank @HillaryClinton for standing up for all of us. #DebateNight," bluebelletrist, September 27, 12:13 A.M.). But more common were relational posts wherein viewers of the debate referenced the ways in which the sexism directed at Clinton mirrored their own experiences. Arguably, the popularity of the feminist cultural critic Jessica Valenti's post encapsulating this issue—the post received 4,533 likes and 2,917 retweets—proves how much Clinton's

Table 10.5. Tweets discussing feminism, patriarchy, misogyny, and double standards during the first presidential debate, 2016.

Twitter User	Time Stamp	Tweet
SikhProf	9/26/2016, 7:49	My #DebateNight prediction: Man will speak nonsense. We will excuse him. Woman will slip up slightly. We will skewer her. (See: sexism)
Johnbrougher	9/26/2016, 8:34	no matter what happens tonight, it looks like the real winner will (of course) be sexism and patriarchy. #debatenight
emmaladyrose	9/26/2016 9:04	"First time there's been a woman on this debate stage. . ." Let that sink in. #debatenight
somethingmonica	9/26/2016 9:07	That Hillary's legitimacy has to be juxtaposed to Trump is a real freaking tragedy for feminism #debatenight
AAUWTX	9/26/2016 9:08	Equal pay and family paid leave mentioned in the first few moments of the debate. #debatenight #feminism
edutinker	9/26/2016 9:12	She's calling him "Donald" to un-sexist her getting called "Hillary", right? #Debates2016 #debatenight
girlactor	9/26/2016 9:27	I love watching a strong woman smile and stay calm while a man screams nonsense over her. #debatenight
minaradman	9/26/2016 9:28	Donald yelling over Hillary is a metaphor for the patriarchy and how men have treated women for decades #debatenight
TamaraLChambers	9/26/2016 9:29	Girl: I have a feeling I'll be blamed for everything by the end of the night. Guy: WHY NOT 😕🤮😰#debatenight #feminism
crissteding	9/26/2016 9:29	All women recognize Hilary's please-stop-talking-over-me-asshole smile. #debatenight
TBombin	9/26/2016 9:30	Donald Trump is literally the patriarchy personified into one horrible person #debatenight

(continued)

Table 10.5. (continued)

realtrueheather	9/26/2016 9:35	In case u don't live in the oppressive structures of sexism and misogyny now u get to watch it live on tv #debatenight
Aidan	9/26/2016 9:36	a rude white man not letting a women speak, what's new #debatenight
piacreyes	9/26/2016 9:36	New drinking game: every time Trump interrupts Clinton everyone takes a shot #debatenight
sammitche	9/26/2016 9:59	A white female in a position of power standing up for male poc is feminism. #debatenight
everywhereist	9/26/2016 10:01	As a woman, this feels so personal b/c I've felt this sort condescension from men before.
EmilyLindin	9/26/2016 10:11	This debate should go down in history as the moment everyone realized that we need more women in leadership #debatenight
VictoriaAveyard	9/26/2016 10:11	Trump has never been forced to listen to or allow a woman to speak this long in his entire life. #debatenight
juliarosen	9/26/2016 10:13	Lull right now. Guess I got used to Trump shouting over Hillary. #debatenight #normalizingsexism
raymita	9/26/2016 10:13	Secretary Clinton made women's rights an international issue: fighting sex trafficking, child marriage, and sexual violence. #DebateNight
Romper	9/26/2016 10:25	Pouring one out for every woman who has been criticized for her "temperament" by a screaming man.
wtflanksteak	9/26/2016 10:35	"Until he [LISTS RESUME], he can talk to me about stamina." EVERY FUCKING WOMAN JUST FELT HER HEART GROW.#debatenight
brosandprose	9/26/2016 10:35	When a woman is more qualified, it's deemed "bad experience." I see you, Donald. I see you. #debatenight #sheslays
DylanRatigan	9/26/2016 10:36	His misogyny. This is where she correctly kills him. #debatenight

TeaPartyCat	9/26/2016 10:36	Trump: "I never said all these demeaning things about dumb ugly bitches that Hillary claims I did."
mess_ofme	9/26/2016 10:36	"It's okay that I said rude and sexist things against Rosie O'Donnell because she was mean to me." #temperament #debate2016 #debatenight
Jackie_Emerson	9/26/2016 10:36	YES @HillaryClinton calling out @realDonaldTrump's BLATANT SEXISM. #debatenight
realsesmith	9/26/2016 10:36	Secretary Clinton brings up Trump's sexism while Trump tries to mansplain her. Thanks for proving the point! #debatenight
deweysnotdead	9/26/2016 10:36	@HillaryClinton tearing down the patriarchy, y'all #debatenight
wtflanksteak	9/26/2016 10:37	Every woman is relating to this debate in a painful and emotional way right now.
msrita68	9/26/2016 10:38	So he is doubling down on his sexism. . .this is unreal #debatenight https://t.co/bC3NDWe3SI
bo0tlegfendi	9/26/2016 10:38	trump is such a sexist pig its disgusting #debatenight
cottagedogs	9/26/2016 10:38	Agreed. We've come too far as a nation to elect a #racist #misogynist. #americaisalreadygreat #debatenight
justplainjess1	9/26/2016 10:38	Trump: I was going to say something VERY AWFUL about Hillary but I didn't. HALLELUJAH SEXISM IS OVER!! #DebateNight
chicagojewlz	9/26/2016 10:38	Donald Trump said Hillary Clinton doesn't have the penis, i mean look, to be president. Which is apparently orange. #debatenight #Debates2016
allistewart	9/26/2016 10:38	Would Hillary be expected to be nice if she were a man? #debates #debatenight #sexism #unconsciousbias #consciousbias
LiberalMmama	9/26/2016 10:57	Hillary calmly explains Trump's misogyny. Trump interrupts 2x&then randomly attacks Rosie O'Donnell. #debatenight #TrumpHatesWomen

experiences on the stage resonated with female viewers watching at home: "A lot of women watching are going to recognize the way that he's interrupting her & yelling #debatenight," 9:26 P.M.).

RQ 2. What strategies were used to combat sexist rhetoric (present in either the live broadcast or the Twitter feed) by live-tweeting viewers?

Labeling was simply one strategy used by Twitter users to draw attention to and resist sexist rhetoric. As chapters 8 and 9 discuss, since Twitter privileges humorous tweets (in that they circulate more frequently), many of the successful strategies—in terms of bringing visibility to the critique at hand—used to address sexism took on the form of jokes. One popular strategy was subversive tweets that co-opted common sexist commentary in order to amplify and counter the stereotypes contained within them. The most prevalent collection of these tweets reframed or redirected the misogynistic advice that women should be outwardly friendly. As table 10.6 shows, many users sarcastically posted direct addresses to Donald Trump, encouraging him to "smile more." Many of these posts critiqued multiple instances of sexism at the same time by also addressing expectations that women should serve in domestic roles (e.g., "make us some sandwiches"), avoid "shrieking" or nagging, not be "emotional," and, of course, be pretty.

In total, seventy-five tweets focused on the smiles of the candidates or the moderators in carrying out their social critique.

Another instance of repurposing sexist rhetoric took on the form of tweets wherein Clinton's status as a grandmother was highlighted. As mentioned earlier, Clinton faced ageist queries concerning whether an older woman could serve as commander in chief; people posed questions about whether her status as a grandmother or postmenopausal woman would impede her abilities to lead.[42] Concerning this, *Time* magazine "dealt Clinton the supreme backhanded compliment of declaring her 'The Perfect Age to be President,' before going into great detail about the 'hormonal ebbing' she might be experiencing" at this stage in her life.[43] With rhetoric such as this circulating in the media, tweets that negatively attended to Clinton's age or labeled her as a grandmother as a form of insult were expected. Surprisingly, there were relatively few of these (e.g., "Grandma looks portly in red #debatenight," JammieWF, 9:06 P.M.; "Can't wait to watch Americas most annoying grandma face off against a giant angry orange," _GreenEggnSam, 7:35 P.M.). The majority of the tweets that contained variations on the term *grandmother* did so as a means of praise, or as the form of a benign joke

Table 10.6. Subversive tweets commenting on the gendered directive to smile during the first presidential debate, 2016.

Twitter User	Time Stamp	Tweet
OhNoSheTwitnt	9/26/2016 8:38	Hillary should smile more and not raise her voice. Maybe bring us coffee. Also would it kill her to make us some sandwiches? #debatenight
MileyMalfoy	9/26/2016 9:09	@realDonaldTrump You should smile more. You'd be prettier if you smiled. #yesallwomen #ImWithHer #debatenight
RaquelEvita	9/26/2016 9:09	Donald, why do you look so tired? Why don't you smile? #debatenight
Jeremyscheuch	9/26/2016 9:10	What's up with @realDonaldTrump's outfit and naggy voice? He should smile more. #debatenight
frdmfightr	9/26/2016 9:12	He would be friendlier if he smiled. #debatenight
dianelyssa	9/26/2016 9:27	Why are you so angry, @realDonaldTrump? You should stop shrieking. Smile more. #debatenight
ClinicEscort	9/26/2016 9:29	Men get so EMOTIONAL. Possibly, @realdonaldtrump should smile more. #debatenight
erinlooney11b	9/26/2016 10:03	My brother: "Listen, #Hillary. Next time, don't smile so big when he's making an ass out of himself." #debatenight
ElayneBoosler	9/26/2016 10:07	How come no one told HIM to "smile more"? #knowyoursexism #debatenight
JessicaValenti	9/26/2016 10:25	Donald really should smile more. #debatenight
rickporter	9/26/2016 10:27	Don, smile more. Don't shout so much. Show us that "winning" temperament. #debatenight And maybe don't grip the podium so hard.
IanGonzales	9/26/2016 10:37	Wow @realDonaldTrump, you're sounding pretty shrill there. Maybe you should smile more. #Debates2016 #debatenight

Table 10.7. Subversive grandma tweets during the first presidential debate, 2016.

Twitter User	Time Stamp	Tweet
Tyler2ONeil	9/26/2016 9:12	"I call it Trump-ed up trickle down." Hillary, you're a grandma. No telling dad jokes. #debatenight
AnnieScott	9/26/2016 9:26	Things this #debatenight is like: watching your sassy grandma argue with Comcast
BabeParker	9/26/2016 9:31	We know Hillary is a good grandma bc she's unfazed by non sequiturs and tantrums #debatenight
smartashsahm	9/26/2016 9:36	That was a KO from a granny in a pant suit @realDonaldTrump & damn we all loved it! #DebateNight
mrdavechild	9/26/2016 10:04	I'm in awe of cool grandma #debatenight
JinxAdam	9/26/2016 10:14	Hillary Clinton kinda looks like a grandma who tries to be hip so she buys you cigarettes when you're 15 #debatenight
Kpfallon	9/26/2016 10:23	Love when Hillary goes nerdy grandma. "Woo! Ok!" *shimmy shimmy* #debatenight
AdamSmith_usa	9/26/2016 10:36	". . .he can come talk to me about stamina." YASSSSS GRANDMA-IN-CHEIF #debatenight

(see table 10.7). By reframing Clinton as a "sassy grandma" and enthusiastically tagging her as a "grandma-in-chief" on Twitter, this ageist rhetoric finds its power defused ever so slightly.

These strategies, as well as many others, were highlighted at particular moments during the presidential debate. One of these was when the debate moderator, Lester Holt, gave Trump the opportunity to explain (and potentially retract) his previous comment that Clinton did not have a "presidential look." Instead of apologizing for the statement, Trump attempted to explain that he simply meant she did not have the "stamina" to be president—a comment that was probably intended to draw attention to Clinton's recent bout of pneumonia (which she worked through, against medical advice). Twitter erupted at this moment, as users countered with their own critiques of Trump's perceived levels of energy and health, commenting on how much he sniffled, how many glasses of water he drank, and how pale he was (see table 10.8). Others posted jokes to show how invalid they found Trump's claims (e.g., the tweet that imagines Clinton completing backflips across the stage while Trump disintegrates, 10:36 P.M.). Still others simply pointed out the long misogynistic history of implying that women were weaker than men (e.g., "Accusing women of ill health has long, anti-feminist history. #debatenight," womeninhighered, 10:38 P.M.). And others turned to information sharing to defend Clinton's stamina (e.g., "Hillary Clinton went to 112 countries, more than any other Secretary of State before her. That's stamina. #debatenight," FemMajority, 10:34 P.M.; "Hillary Clinton traveled 956,733 miles as Secretary of State. Trump repeatedly dodged Vietnam for "bone spurs." STAMINA, lol. #debatenight," goldengateblond, 10:36 P.M.).

One of the most common strategies used was quoting, in this instance the retweeting of Clinton's own response, tweeted from her account almost immediately as she said it onstage: "When Donald Trump spends 11 hours testifying in front of a congressional committee, he can talk to me about stamina." This comment received 44,907 likes and was retweeted 20,393 times. Although, as chapters 8 and 9 discuss, the use of quoting as a form of social commentary can lead to ambiguity, in this case one can only assume the user is quoting because she agrees with the statement.[44]

Another key moment in the debate that led to a large number of quotes, commentary, and fact-checking was late in the evening when Clinton highlighted Trump's history of misogynistic behavior by discussing how he publicly shamed a former Miss Universe for weight gain. Two of her comments, "This is a man that has called women pigs, slobs, and dogs" and "The woman Trump called 'Miss Piggy' has a name: Alicia Machado," became two of the most-tweeted lines of the debate (the latter receiving 38,241 likes and 23,817 retweets from Clinton's Twitter account, in addition to quotes and paraphrases). Trump's response included a reference to a former Twitter war he had engaged in with the celebrity Rosie O'Donnell, whose appearance he had also criticized. Rather than apologizing for his past comments, Trump doubled down, arguing that they were justified. Immediately tweets began responding to his answer (e.g., "I'm sorry, she DESERVED it?! Our girls deserve so much better than this clown. #ImWithHer #debatenight," amytondreau, 10:38 P.M.; "The way you fucking treat females isn't nice, my mf dude. #debatenight," babocheoreoms, 10:38 P.M.) and pointing out the victim-blaming in this type of rhetoric (e.g., "Trump just literally victim blamed people he's verbally harassed on national television. #DebateNight," rj4gui4r, 10:38 P.M.). Information-sharing and fact-checking posts also started appearing that

Table 10.8. Tweets critiquing Trump's comment on Clinton's stamina and presidential look during the first presidential debate, 2016.

Twitter User	Time Stamp	Tweet
thegeorgethomas	9/26/2016 9:12	@realDonaldTrump is lookin pale. Are you ok? Sick? Unwell? #debatenight
inkandfolly	9/26/2016 10:03	Hey guys, Donnie is sniffling quite a bit. IS HE DYING? #debatenight
atomic_13	9/26/2016 10:03	@HillaryClinton is that sniffle from @realDonaldTrump bothering you? Is he feeling okay? It's bothering me #debatenight
jilliscol	9/26/2016 10:33	Glad that @LesterHoltNBC is calling Trump out on his sexist comments about Hillary's Presidential "look" #ImWithHer #debatenight
slouisehenry	9/26/2016 10:33	She doesn't have the presidential look. But you've needed six glasses of water to get through this. #debatenight
Meladoodle	9/26/2016 10:34	"She doesn't have the look" says the talking hairy pumpkin man #debatenight
Alicegoldfuss	9/26/2016 10:34	Breathless man leans on podium, says woman doesn't have stamina #debatenight
PiaGlenn	9/26/2016 10:34	this wild gendered use of "stamina" tho #debatenight
catie_warren	9/26/2016 10:34	I physically flinch whenever I hear the "she doesn't have a presidential look" quote. It's 2016. She's a woman. Get over it. #debatenight
asmamk	9/26/2016 10:35	Trump just lectured the moderator about the first woman nominated for pres from a major party lacking "stamina" #debatenight
angeli_bean	9/26/2016 10:35	Hillary has a whole career's worth of stamina standing up to men like Trump #debatenight
SamDoesPolitics	9/26/2016 10:35	"I just don't think she has a Presidential look" says a spray-tanned cheese-puff with a poodle on his head #debatenight
DalDeta	9/26/2016 10:36	Trump: "She doesn't have the stamina." *Hillary walks center stage and backflips* *Trump disintegrates* #debatenight
Mariashriver	9/26/2016 10:36	She's showing stamina in this debate. She looks damn presidential to me. Smart. Calm. Classy. #debatenight

provided links to articles that documented Trump's previous instances of misogynistic remarks. For example, the publication *Wired* posted "Fact Check: True. Donald Trump did say all those terrible things about women" (10:36 P.M.) and included a link where readers could learn more about them.

RQ 3. What role do major television events play in shaping or shifting cultural beliefs and anxieties?

After each of the presidential debates, which all contained moments of gendered microaggressions or blatant sexism perpetrated by Trump, polling data showed Clinton's lead over Trump increasing. This causal relation suggests, as this book as a whole does, that material presented on television does influence cultural mind-sets and moods. Since major live-broadcast events tend to get more national attention and viewership, it stands to reason that they have the potential to have an even greater effect. Data from live tweets seem to support this claim. The most high-frequency topics tweeted about during the debate often dominated the blogosphere and the mainstream media in the days that followed. One of the dominant news stories was, of course, Trump's past derogatory remarks aimed at Machado and O'Donnell.[45] In general, the first debate redirected the national attention on the way that gender was affecting this election. As Emily Crockett and Sarah Frostenson note: "Gender dynamics were always going to be a big deal at Monday's debate. It wasn't just America's first major party presidential debate between a man and a woman; it was this *particular* man and woman—Donald Trump, who typically uses bullying, hypermasculine dominance as a weapon, and Hillary Clinton, who has spent decades weathering sexist attacks in the public eye."[46]

A wave of articles appeared that continued the conversations begun on Twitter during the debate. These ranged from scholarly analyses to satire to listicles; they documented the toxic masculinity and gendered microaggressions that were present during the debate.[47] In a piece titled "The First US Presidential Debate Will Be Shown in Gender Studies Classes for Years to Come," Annalisa Merelli—like many on Twitter hours before—focused on the ways in which Trump's constant interrupting of Clinton was emblematic of common experiences women face: "There is a[n] unwritten rule in presidential debates—and general conversation—that people should not interrupt each other. All too often in professional situations, men interrupt women. The first US presidential debate in history to feature a woman candidate has proven to be a textbook example of this practice. In 90 minutes Donald Trump interrupted Hillary Clinton 51 times, often talking over her for several seconds. Trump's conduct during the debate exemplifies the type of microaggression that belittles women publicly as a way to assert power, and to dismiss women."[48]

Besides countless pieces focused on Trump's interruptions were pieces addressing the notion of mansplaining, which he helped illustrate quite well. (Alexandra Petri posted a satirical transcript of the debate subtitled "The Mansplaining Olympics.")[49]

In an article for the *Huffington Post,* Emma Gray labeled Donald Trump "the ultimate 'manterrupter'" and went on to explain the term and the effect it has on gender inequality. Using Jessica Bennett's definition from *Feminist Fight Club,* Gray explained that *manterrupting* is any "unnecessary interruption of a woman by a man" and supplied statistics to document the frequency of this practice. Coupled with the problem of women becoming voiceless when men take away their opportunities to speak, research also shows that when women do get the opportunity to talk, "their words are given less weight and treated as less valid than men's."[50] Gray argues the result of this phenomenon—especially in fields like politics—is extremely problematic because it generates fields dominated by male perspectives.

It's Complicated: Why These Particular Political Opponents May Skew the Data

Studying the first presidential debate of 2016 and the dialogue regarding it certainly reveals problems concerning gender equality, but it is hard to make broader conclusions on the basis of the Twitter data alone (which is often the case when studying tweets) or the commentary that followed. The candidates themselves make it hard to draw these conclusions because of the complicated relationships citizens have with them. For example, people debated constantly whether the negative opinions of Clinton stemmed from personal dislike for her (or her policies) or distrust of powerful women more generally. The contradictory criticisms she faced also make it hard to draw conclusive lessons about cultural mind-sets concerning gender roles. As we saw earlier (see table 10.1), she was often harshly critiqued for not aligning with traditional female stereotypes (i.e., not being seen as friendly or likable but, rather, as power hungry and aggressive). Negative remarks targeted at Clinton, however, also conjured up opposite criticisms, linking her to traditional stereotypes associated with femininity (e.g., weak, nurturing). Take, for example, this tweet: "Hillary Clinton will destroy ISIS by coddling and hugging them to death. #debatenight" (M1nd0fAMadman, 10:33 P.M.).

The defenses of Trump were also surprising in terms of gender norms. The problematic binary associating men with rationality and women with emotionality has endured for centuries. In modern times, men are still often policed if they are viewed as too emotional. During this campaign, Trump and Clinton existed as an inversion of this long-standing binary. While Clinton was criticized for deviating from expectations because viewers saw her as lacking in emotion, Trump did not receive the same amount of criticism from veering from cultural expectations. In fact, he was often praised by his supporters for his emotional tendencies (e.g., "Trump gets heated during the debates because he CARES and because people twist his words from past and present #debatenight," jesshedrick, 10:03 P.M.; "I kind of like that trump shows his emotions on his face. Rather see that than Hilary's fake smirk and laugh. Makes me cringe. #debatenight," ktcook016, 10:13 P.M.). But that is not to say that he never received criticism from his opponents for his emotional behavior (e.g., "trump—'lesterrrrrrr, hillary's being not being nice to meeeeee' DONALD YOU ARE A GROWN ASS MAN STOP WHINING #debatenight," amfliflier, 10:38 P.M.).

In comparing the conversations concerning the two candidates, it does appear that Trump was afforded more leeway when it came to supposed gender transgressions. One moment in the debate—which would go on to inspire the most popular GIFs—further shows that Clinton was rewarded when she conformed to gender expectations. After Trump boldly claimed that he, rather than Clinton, had the better temperament for holding the office of the presidency, Clinton, apparently not able to contain her amusement at this claim, broke her steely reserve, smiled widely, did a little shoulder shimmy, and then started her response with an amused exclamation, "Whew, okay." The moment won her laughter from the audience and, according to some, the debate win as well.[51] While the moment is worth applauding—a professional woman was able to drop her guard and joyfully combat an ignorant claim made by her opponent—it is problematic that Clinton was rewarded more for this moment of *emotional* reaction, for her (one could argue) feminine body movement, than for the other eighty-nine minutes of her well-prepared, intellectual (and more emotionally constrained) performance.

Election-Related Digital Activism and Social Commentary beyond Twitter

Attention to gender issues did not fall away after the first debate; in fact, it was amplified when—just before the second debate—previously unaired footage from an appearance of Donald Trump on the television program *Access Hollywood* was leaked to the press. In this video clip viewers could hear Donald Trump admitting to sexual assault. Speaking to Billy Bush, the host of the show, Trump was caught on a hot microphone speaking about sexual advances on women (grabbing them "by the pussy"), stating, "When you're a star, they let you do it."[52] While not a live television event in the traditional sense—since it was footage that had never aired and was recorded eleven years earlier—this televisual moment (which most then experienced through their smartphones and computers) functions like those "water-cooler" live TV moments in that the majority of the population shared in it—watching the video, reading about it, or hearing about it secondhand around the same time. Just as it is hard to escape knowing the victor of the Super Bowl even if one chooses not to watch the annual event, it was impossible not to learn of Trump's sexually lewd comments even if one did not purposefully attempt to seek out the video or the transcript of it. Quite evidently, online platforms increase television's influence and its ability to shape cultural sentiments and conversation.

The second debate, which began by addressing the *Access Hollywood* footage and led Trump to attempt to redirect the conversation toward Bill Clinton's sexual past, gave viewers a slew of issues relating to sexism to comment on while it aired. For example, as I discussed above, while commenting on the many "manterruptions" was a predominant theme during the first debate, the second debate found people tweeting their discomfort in the ways in which Trump stalked Clinton around the stage during the Town Hall forum. He often crossed the stage and loomed behind her with a menacing expression on his face while she answered questions. If Clinton's shimmy was the most GIF-worthy moment of the first debate, Trump's predatory stances onstage won that category for the second debate.

These conversations extended beyond the ninety minutes of live coverage: people debated within their own social networks about the issues brought up in the debate. Originally, I intended to study this dialogue on Twitter alone, but then I watched as my own Facebook feed filled up with conversations that I read as attempts at pseudo–social education among "friends." For example, in the days following the debate, I saw people discussing the validity of the many sexual allegations launched against Trump and the related practice of victim blaming. For example, one well-circulated meme sparked an intense conversation that unfolded on my friend's Facebook page. The meme questioned (and minimized) the outrage women were expressing over Trump's comments by implying that their anger was incongruent with the recent popularity of E. L. James's erotic romance novel: "If American women are so outraged by the way Donald Trump talked . . . , who in the hell bought 50 million copies of *Fifty Shades of Grey?*" I watched as friends (many feminist academics) respectfully criticized the meme, pointing out its logical fallacies and providing education on a crucial aspect of S&M practices (consent) that makes it very different from the sexual assaults Trump was apparently admitting to. Eventually the person who had posted it on Facebook removed it.

I watched two other moments of cultural education within personal Facebook networks unfold in the weeks surrounding the second debate as well. One colleague of mine responded to a sudden wave of people posting photos of women adorned in pro-Trump T-shirts (wearing them even after the recent revelations about his sexual comments were made public) along with comments that attacked their character and judgment. This consciousness-raising post asked those engaging in this practice to stop and rethink the culture of abuse against women that they were participating in:

> I'd like to suggest that there is a better way to think of their devotion to T'Rump. May we never forget that these women may very well be victims of gendered violence, too, and have internalized the CONSTANT and WELL-FUNDED messaging that it is all their own faults and not their victimizers'. These women deserve our compassion just the same as the brave women who are posting their personal stories of sexual impropriety. Chani Nicholas writes, "We have been taught to mistrust women. Taught to mistrust ourselves. Taught to mistrust the feminine within ourselves no matter our gender orientation." We have all been taught to distrust the feminine and, by not-quite-logical extension, women. Some of us have been privileged enough and/or fortunate enough to unlearn this lesson through our relationships, our educations, our inherent suspicion of easy answers. Let us not revile those who have not been so fortunate.[53]

A feminist blogger I follow on Facebook also picked up on this issue of how our culture has trained us not to trust women, focusing specifically on how people were doubting the increasing number of women who were coming forward to share stories about unwanted sexual advances they received from Trump.

> I keep seeing the argument that if Trump's accusers were credible they would have come forward immediately. Let's talk about this

> a minute. We already know that women who are raped are not believed. We live in a country where you can be caught sexually assaulting an unconscious woman behind a dumpster and get a slap on the wrist. FOR RAPE. So why in the world would women who have been "just" groped or kissed without permission come forward? This is something that happens to us on a regular basis—on subways, in bars, at schools and on the street. How do you report the everyday? If women reported every unwanted touch throughout our lives we wouldn't have time to do anything else. And if the criminal justice system treats rape victims terribly, how do you think they'd react to a woman wanting to report a man who grabbed her ass or breasts? We'd get laughed out of the station because being touched without permission—putting up with a never-ending stream of unwanted attention—is considered the cost of doing business while female. So give me a fucking break with all of this.[54]

These examples showcase how people used a range of social media to engage in feminist activism and informal cultural education within more closed circles.

These online engagements continued throughout the election cycle. One other area of Internet activity found a way to highlight (and profit from) election-inspired feminist activism: online merchandising. The third debate, in particular, ended up sparking a lucrative line of election-related products. This is ironic on some level because the third meeting between the two candidates presented fewer opportunities for those watching live to point out gendered microaggressions; overall, Trump decreased his number of interruptions and was firmly placed behind a podium instead of his opponent's back. Any restraint Trump had mastered in the early part of the debate, however, was undone toward its end when he could not help interrupting Clinton while she was answering a question on social security with an insult that then went viral. He looked out into the audience and called Clinton "such a nasty woman." At that moment hundreds of online retailers rejoiced, knowing that a tagline fit for a range of merchandise had been born. And so it had been. Within hours his insult sparked the Nasty Woman Economy, a line of T-shirts, coffee mugs, and even embroidered pillows boasting this phrase.[55] Some companies sweetened the pot by donating portions of their proceeds to Planned Parenthood, an organization anyone tempted to purchase a Nasty Woman product would probably support.[56] And all these efforts were successful as

Image 10.9. Nasty Woman T-shirt; proceeds from sales were donated to Planned Parenthood. (Photo by the author.)

women enthusiastically purchased the items and wore them as a form commercial protest against Trump—myself included (image 10.9).

The onslaught of sales of Nasty Woman products shows the ways in which commercialism met politics during this election cycle and how some people found purchasing and wearing such items to be a form of mild political protest against a candidate they disagreed with—or a badge of solidarity with the candidate they backed.

The Trump Effect: The Consequences of Televised Misogyny

Just as Clinton's camp inspired attire like the Nasty Women clothing line, Trump's followers were often adorned in products touting popular election phrases (most notably the red "Make American Great Again" hats that populated his rallies). Trump supporters, however, were also photographed wearing blatantly sexist anti-Clinton attire—whether commercially produced or self-made. Buttons ran with slogans such as "Life's a Bitch, Don't Vote for One" and "KFC Hillary Special: 2 Fat Thighs 2 Small Breasts . . . Left Wing"; shirts sported the statements "Hillary Sucks, But Not Like Monica"; "Donald Trump: Finally Someone with Balls"; "She's a Cunt, Vote for Trump"; and "I Wish Hillary Had Married OJ"; people carried signs that read, "Trump vs. Tramp"; "Don't Be a Pussy, Vote for Trump"; and "Better to Grab a Pussy Than Be One." And, of course, the popular rally chant "Trump That Bitch" popped up on all types of merchandise.[57] What these items reveal is that while the election undoubtedly highlighted Trump's own misogynistic attitudes and actions, it appears to have made it more socially acceptable for others to embrace sexism as well. The behavior embraced at Trump's rallies perhaps should have prepared the country for the rise in hate crimes that spiked after his election, but since his election in and of itself was not predicted by news outlets, many were unprepared for the violence that would soon quickly surface.[58]

But, of course, these beliefs and behaviors do not simply stem from Trump's rise to power. The presidential election merely revealed cultural biases that were well woven into our cultural fabric, just as 9/11 had renewed antifeminist backlash (as chapter 1 discusses). What ended up surprising people was who held these biases. In the weeks leading up to the election, graphics circulated online that detailed projected vote outcomes by various demographics. One set of data that received a great deal of attention was FiveThirtyEight's projections on how the election would look depending on gender—if only men or women were to cast their ballots on November 8, 2016. For the first scenario (only men voting), the electoral map was predominantly red and the electoral votes were listed as 188 for Clinton and 350 for Trump (well beyond the 270 needed to win). Its sister map, representing the projected election results if only women voted, was predominantly blue, and the electoral votes were listed as a staggering 458 for Clinton against 80 for Trump.[59] In the end these charts did not accurately predict the final results of the election because, despite winning the popular vote, Clinton did not win the presidency (as pollsters had predicted), and the blame for that did not rest solely on male voters (as projections would have suggested).

The Problem with Feminism: Post-Election Liberal Soul-Searching

The most unexpected voter statistic in the 2016 presidential election pertained to women. Polls leading up to the election indicated that Clinton had a decided advantage over Trump when it came to female voters, but, in reality, she ended up having only a moderate advantage over him. According to CNN, 54 percent of women voted for Clinton and 41 percent of women voted for Trump.[60] And while Clinton did win the majority of women of color by large margins (94 percent of the black female vote and 69 percent of the Latina vote), she did not win among white females (earning only 43 percent of their votes).

Much of the post-election commentary focused on how the results of the election ultimately stemmed from issues relating to class and culture divides; "identity politics" landed much of the blame.[61] Gender and sexism were not high on the list for many analyzing the election results, although some did return to the argument that ultimately Clinton lost the election because she was a woman. (In an amusing essay, Max Weiss ranked the things he blamed for Clinton's loss, ranking misogyny as reasons 1 through 199.)[62] But within the subset of conversations that did suggest that gender and sexism were (at least partially) at fault, again the spotlight was directed at the problems within so-called white feminism and the "quiet racism" that allowed white women to cast their votes for Trump.[63]

Conclusion: Archiving Affect from the 2016 Election

Even before the election results rolled in, reports were surfacing that the 2016 election had produced more cultural and personal anxiety than any election to date. Scholars discussed how the fear that dominated the cultural landscape—coalescing into a structure of feeling or national mood—affected people's daily life during these months.

> The turbulence of this time of national transition can cause anxiety that makes day-to-day life more alarming, but people's existing fears can also be inflamed by what they see happening in the election. This creates a sort of feedback loop between personal and national anxiety. Social media and a 24-hour news cycle [have] made it difficult to avoid talk of the election, and Donald Trump's candidacy in particular has given people many reasons to be anxious. Name-calling has devolved into physical violence at multiple Trump rallies, with Trump often egging the perpetrators. . . . "Hope" was the keyword that carried many voters through the 2008 and 2012 elections, and "fear" has replaced it in 2016: The GOP nominee has inspired fear in minorities and women almost since he came onto the national stage, suggesting that Mexico is sending rapists across the border; that Muslims should be banned from entering the country; that women are available for men to do with whatever they want.[64]

The media—television and social media like—were indeed a "feedback loop" that modulated our personal and cultural affect during and after this election cycle. They likewise now serve as a storage house of this affect, recording traces of those feelings and the actions they sparked.

What this section, and book as a whole, has aimed to prove is that cultural anxieties play out across televisual genres, influencing viewers and the larger cultural conversations that continue in various media about these issues. In the concluding chapter we turn to the ways in which this tag team of Internet and television can be empowering and problematic in this period when we immerse ourselves in niche programming and live out our social media lives in an echo chamber that reinforces those cultural anxieties and ideologies.

Conclusion

Screening Emotion, Archiving Affect, Circulating Feelings: Final Thoughts and Even More Questions

Screening Emotion

As it always has, television programming will continue to draw on current events and reflect and reinforce cultural anxieties. Consider just these few examples that occurred during the final stages of revising this book manuscript. Following the 2017 National Football League's #TakeAKnee protest (fueled by Donald Trump's criticism of players opting not to stand during the national anthem as a statement against racial inequality), ABC's *Black-ish* (2014–present) filmed an episode, "Please, Baby, Please," that touched on issues of police brutality and the activism responding to it. The episode was shelved and never aired because of "creative differences" among producers.[1] The fourteenth season of Shonda Rhimes's *Grey's Anatomy* (2005–present) touched on two emotionally charged current events. During the second half of the season multiple episodes alluded to the 2018 #MeToo movement with a story line revealing that Harper Avery—the namesake of the much sought-after medical innovation award and the man responsible for the foundation that runs the Grey-Sloan Memorial Hospital (the main setting for the show)—had sexually victimized many subordinates during his years in executive power. The show also provided commentary on the debate surrounding the Deferred Action for Childhood Arrivals (DACA) immigration legislation. In the episode "Beautiful Dreamer," viewers learn that one of the star interns is an undocumented immigrant and a DACA recipient facing deportation.[2] Preceding and following the #MarchForOurLives activism for gun control (launched by the survivors of the Stoneman Douglas High School shooting), the first two seasons of Netflix's *13 Reasons Why* (2017–present)—with story lines packed full of adolescent bullying and school violence—aired alongside real-life news coverage of continuous cyber–hate crimes and mass shootings occurring across the country.[3] The 2019–20 season of *Madam Secretary* provided a moment of wish fulfillment featuring Elizabeth McCord (Téa Leoni) as the first female president. It then, however, introduced a story line wherein the legitimacy of her presidency was called into question after evidence surfaced that a foreign country (in this fictional context Iran replaced Russia) had interfered in the election.

Perhaps the most notable, and ironic, example of the ways in which fictional television in particular is often aligned with the contemporary cultural environment would be the reboot and, soon following, cancellation of ABC's hit sitcom *Roseanne* (1988–1997, 2018). In a much publicized relaunch, in March 2018—twenty-one years after the series first went off the air—the show returned to prime-time television. The show's creators made a conscious effort to rework the program to speak to the current political environment. The main characters, Roseanne (Roseanne Barr) and Dan Conner (John Goodman), had always been part of a working-class family, but in this reiteration they were working-class citizens who had bought into Trump's promise to "make American great again." On the other side of the political spectrum, Roseanne's sister, Jackie (Laurie Metcalf), returned to the screen wearing a pink pussy hat, greeting her sister and brother-in-law with a catch phrase from the 2016 presidential election cycle: "Hey, Deplorables."[4] Throughout the nine episodes of the series' final run, the show touched on many cultural anxieties related to affordable health care, Islamophobia, illegal immigrants, gender identity, and so forth. The reboot gained a wide viewing audience and sparked a wave of media commentary. Debates surely would have continued concerning whether the show was progressive in its social commentary or whether the laughter engendered by its integration of current events would spark critical thinking, reinforce existing stereotypes, or defuse anger or activist impulses, but it was canceled shortly after its renewal for the 2019 season was announced.[5] ABC made the decision to drop the show after Barr posted a political racist tweet on Twitter. Part III of this book has detailed the ways in which television and the Internet are intertwined, and this is but one more example. In this instance it is clear that a celebrity's remarks on social media—and the emotional reactions they trigger—can affect any entertainment outlet she is associated with.

These examples clearly show that the societal fears traced throughout this book are alive and well and being aired in contemporary television programs. For example, the debates concerning compulsive patriotism discussed in chapter 1 can be seen in *Black-ish*'s attempt to discuss the #TakeAKnee movement. The recurring theme of the fear of the "other," showcased in several chapters, appears here again in *Grey's Anatomy* and *Roseanne*. And the list could go on and on. But why is this important? What is at stake when our television programming reflects and reinforces cultural anxieties ad nauseam?

This book has argued that the U.S. televisual landscape sheds light on the general fear culture of the twenty-first century experienced by all, but in practice the programs we are exposed to probably show only a subset of those cultural anxieties. In the made-for-me moment of personalized entertainment, viewers have almost complete control of how and when they consume their preferred popular culture texts. In terms of TV, long gone are the days of viewers sitting down on the couch to watch a set programming lineup established by a network. Now viewers pick and choose their programs across networks and platforms, watch on delay and zip through commercials with the help of DVRs; they curate their own television experiences by viewing whole television programs on DVD or binge-watching entire seasons within twenty-four hours of their drop date.[6] The plethora of programs, coupled with the agency afforded to viewers in the post-network era, means that we are seeing what we want to see. If television is "screening" emotions, as in broadcasting them, then it is also "screening" them in the other sense. Through our self-selection we filter out the content we do not want to see; therefore, we are then consuming only the emotions (or emotion-trigger material) we want to consume.

While research is on the rise concerning the ways in which we exist within ideological echo chambers online, this is true of television programming as well.[7] Online, the pages and posts we like and "favorite," the friends and celebrities we follow, all play a role in confirmation bias. This is true of the television shows and channels we tune in to. As chapter 3 discussed, we flock toward texts with messages that are in line with our own beliefs. Therefore, we consume texts engaging with cultural anxieties we are probably already concerned with. Consider the social commentary provided by Shonda Rhimes in *Grey's Anatomy*, *How to Get Away with Murder*, or *Scandal*. The viewers watching her programs can expect to encounter—and probably are receptive to—her social justice–oriented plots. Likewise, viewers tuning into Fox News can expect to encounter commentary related to fears troubling the conservative base that it is likely they are a part of. Different anxieties, different programming for different viewing populations. We very well may exist in an emotional echo chamber as well as an ideological one. Or perhaps they are one and the same.

Archiving Affect

If it is true that our entertainment products and social media outlets inform and project our social anxieties, then what does it mean that we now have a permanent record of these anxieties? The digital records of television programming and social media communication can now serve as an archive of sorts, storing these emotions forever—for better or worse. What is the consequence of TV and other media acting as a record of personal and collective emotion? How does and will this affect cultural memory and history?

It is easy to theorize television as a storage house for affect on different levels.[8] Most obvious would be that television programs store the emotions of actors in fictional programming and the usually unscripted (although probably performative) emotions of non-actors in nonfiction programming. These stored programs can then act as an archive of affect in terms of the affect they created in their viewers at that time. Analyzing television programs from the same period allows one to see trends in collective affect at that time. What makes this notion of television as keeper of affect so relevant, however, is that it gives a technological apparatus a power usually associated with humans alone. In terms of cultural anxieties, consider the emotions television has captured in regard to twenty-first-century tragedies: live footage of people at Ground Zero on September 11, family members mourning outside the Sandy Hook Elementary School, displaced persons returning to their destroyed homes in the wake of Hurricane Katrina, the last moments of victims of police brutality (captured on smartphones and then broadcast on television screens), the crowds of protesters participating in the various Women's Marches the day after Trump's inauguration, and so forth. This footage quite obviously shows the actual emotions of the people caught on camera, but it also reveals the collective affect—the cultural climate—that surrounded them. Television arguably always had this capacity, but what does it mean that we can now review such footage and relive such events and emotions at will through the help of the Internet? What might it mean to remediate emotions? How does our ever-expanding digital archive of filmed events and online communication capture and create national affect states? What is at stake when we have access to all this? Discussing archives of feelings, Jennifer Pybus argues that they are "an important space of interpretation and contestation that has the power to make meaning through its ability to privilege certain discourses over others. Who and what gets remembered, and who gets to make these existential decisions, are issues with important social, political, and economic ramifications."[9]

Moreover, it stands to reason that *how*—emotionally speaking—people and events get remembered also has major ramifications.

Circulating Feelings

If television stores affect, it also—as I have argued throughout this text—circulates it. As of late scholarly attention has turned to the ways in which affect is experienced and spread in online spaces. Susanna Paasonen, for example, has discussed how social media trigger, intensify, and circulate affect.[10] In the broadest sense we can easily say that *all* our screens do this. So how will we be influenced emotionally by our constant exposure to endless screens and the heightened emotions we engage with through them?

And to complicate this further, scholars interested in studying the affective dialogues unfolding online about television programs may have to consider the ways in which nonhuman actors are circulating such emotions. While the manipulation of social media for political means is well known, less well known is how this practice extends to online conversations about popular culture. For example, a study of tweets featuring the highly publicized fan dispute over *Star Wars Episode VII: The Last Jedi* revealed that many of the tweets that critiqued the film for having a liberal agenda, or attacked its director for being a so-called social justice warrior, were simply using the debate "to propagate political messages supporting extreme right-wing causes and the discrimination of gender, race or sexuality."[11]

Returning to the assumption concerning affect-object reciprocity laid out at the beginning of this book: regardless of where these emotions originate, how might we break the affective feedback loops our screens place us in? Is self-awareness enough? Is a more expansive media diet the key? Could media literacy education help solve the problem? Grappling with these questions will continue to be important as we continue into the twenty-first-century era of amplified affect and screen saturation.

Acknowledgments

This project was a long time in the making, evolving with my scholarly interests and the social climate of the early twenty-first century. As such, it has ties that stretch all the way back to my doctoral studies at Wayne State University and the mentorship I received there. Special thanks extend to Richard Grusin and Steven Shaviro, whose expertise in affect theory and media studies forever shaped my research interests. I am extremely excited for this book to be published by the University Press of Kentucky and would like to thank Anne Dotson, who enthusiastically championed this manuscript from the start, as well as the entire editorial team who saw it through to publication. I would like to thank those involved in the creative and important work being done today in the television industry; without such a rich televisual landscape, this investigation into contemporary culture would not have been possible. And, of course, I would like to thank my friends, family, and colleagues for their ongoing support.

Among these, I would like to thank Eastern Illinois University, and the English Department specifically. I work alongside incredible, talented, thoughtful colleagues and for a terrific supervisor, our department chair, Angela Vietto, who encourages our efforts to be both engaged scholars and teachers. Particular thanks go to the supportive colleagues whom I have gained from my years at EIU: from the daily camaraderie provided by my Coleman Hall corridor companions (Randy Beebe, Donna Binns, Tim Engels) to the friendships fostered over long commutes, conference travel, writing groups, book clubs, professional collaborations, and social outings (among them Melissa Caldwell, Linda Coleman, Terri Fredrick, Jeannie Ludlow, Kristi McDuffie, and Marjorie Worthington). Special thanks also extend to Sarah Burcon and Letitia Moffitt, who provided some of the earliest and final feedback on this completed manuscript.

I am grateful to have worked with some terrific students and talented graduate research assistants over the past decade as well. Evee Cunico,

Dymine Dorsey, and Maxie Phillips, students from ENG 4765 (Professional Editing), completed an early round of copy editing on this manuscript for a class project. Thanks go to TJ Martinson for coding data related to post-9/11 programming (chapter 1) and gathering research on television viewing practices on Twitter (chapters 8–10), Jessica Glade for her work charting reality television trends (chapter 2), as well as Nathan Crews, Ann Hart, and Tamara Norris, whose work on affect and live-tweeting informed projects inspired by this one. I would also like to thank my undergraduate students from ENG 4742: Studies in Genre (Vampire & Zombie Narratives) and graduate students from ENG 5010: American Literature & Culture (Remediating 9/11), who provided me with the opportunity to continue grappling with so many of the issues presented in this text. My own work was influenced by Hannah Green's seminar project on fictionalized zombies (chapter 5) and Sara Amato's thesis on female antiheroes (chapter 8). This project also benefited from the generous internal grants and research-release time provided by EIU.

Next I would like to thank my many friends outside work. My many close girlfriends received shout-outs in my last book (with Sarah Burcon) on portrayals of girls and women in popular culture (*How Pop Culture Shapes the Stages of a Woman's Life: From Toddlers-in-Tiaras to Cougars-on-the-Prowl*). So it is only fair that I take space in this book to thank the men in my life who have influenced this project. Thanks go to Tamer Ahmed, Eric Donohue, Jason Emrick, and Mark Palise for watching so many of these shows with me (from physically viewing season debuts or series finales beside me to talking or texting about them across state lines), for introducing me to these programs that would captivate me throughout the years (or for watching them because of my recommendations), or for simply humoring me over the years as I talked about them and my research on so many occasions. I hope you hear the echoes of our conversations embedded within these pages.

And I would like to thank my parents, Dianne Fromm and Ken Wood, and my sister, Krystal Cline, who might have been able to predict my future career as a television scholar all the way back during my days of highlighting the television guide, programming the VCR to record soap operas, sending off fan letters, and logging countless hours on our family room couch watching TV (and eating Doritos). To my nieces and nephews (both by blood and through the good fortune of having fostered so many extended family relationships throughout the years): I hope that the work we media critics do can help make the world a slightly better place for you to grow up in. To my own daughters, McKinley and Madison: I completely see the irony that I'm a media scholar who constantly cautions you on the dangers of screen addiction. May you love getting lost in and, more important, *seeing through* popular culture for the rest of your lives.

I am grateful for the permissions granted to republish my earlier work in this book. Portions of chapter 1 were published in "How to Save . . . a Nation? Televisual Fiction Post-9/11," in *Manufacturing Phobias: The Political Production of Fear in Theory and Practice,* edited by Hisham Ramadan and Jeff Shantz (University of Toronto Press, 2016), 116–42. A previous version of chapter 4 was published as "Where Have All the Good Men Gone? A Psychoanalytic Reading of the Absent Fathers and Bad Dads in ABC's *Lost,*" *Journal of Popular Culture* 47, no. 3 (2014; John Wiley and Sons): 430–50. Portions of chapter 8 appeared in "Media Criticism and Morality Policing on Twitter," in *Adventures in Shondaland: Identity Politics and the Power of Representation,* edited by Rachel Alicia Griffin and Michaela Meyer (Rutgers University Press, 2018), 214–34. A previous version of chapter 9 was published as "From Slut Shaming to Cultural Commentary: What Live Tweeting Practices of Viewers of ABC's *The Bachelorette* Reveal about Gender Policing and Digital Activism on Twitter," *Computers & Writing Proceedings* 1 (2016–17): 122–31.

Notes

Introduction

1. For more on television's role in shaping history and popular memory, see Steve Anderson, "History, TV, and Popular Memory," in *Television Histories: Shaping Collective Memory in the Media Age,* ed. Gary R. Edgerton and Peter C. Rollins (Lexington: University Press of Kentucky, 2001), 19–36.

2. While this text focuses solely on U. S. programming and cultural events, Marusya Bociurkiw, *Feeling Canadian: Television, Nationalism, and Affect* (Waterloo, Ont.: Wilfrid Laurier University Press, 2011), studies nationalist themes in television programming through the lens of affect theory.

3. On the ways in which "phobias provide the means for expression of collective insecurity," see Hisham Ramadan and Jeff Shantz, eds., *Manufacturing Phobias: The Political Production of Fear in Theory and Practice* (Toronto: University of Toronto Press, 2016), 4. Some useful studies on the post-network era of television include Lynn Spigel and Jan Olsson, eds., *Television after TV: Essays on a Medium in Transition* (Durham, N.C.: Duke University Press, 2004); Amanda Lotz, *The Television Will Be Revolutionized* (New York: New York University Press, 2007); Janet McCabe and Kim Akass, eds., *Quality TV: Contemporary American Television and Beyond* (London: I. B. Tauris, 2007); and Todd M. Sodono, "Television's Paradigm (Time)shift: Production and Consumption Practices in the Post-Network Era," in *Time in Television Narrative: Exploring Temporality in Twenty-First-Century Programming,* ed. Melissa Ames (Jackson: University Press of Mississippi, 2012), 27–42.

4. On September 11th, 2001, al-Qaeda, a militant Islamic group led at the time by Osama bin Laden, executed a series of four terrorist attacks that killed approximately three thousand persons.

5. Richard Grusin, *Premediation: Affect and Mediality after 9/11* (New York: Palgrave Macmillan, 2010), 28.

6. Walter Kalaidjian, "Incoming: Globalisation, Disaster, Poetics," *South Atlantic Quarterly* 106, no. 4 (2007): 829. On 9/11's role as a temporal pivot point, see Art Spiegelman, *In the Shadow of No Towers* (New York: Viking, 2004), and

Bill Brown, "The Dark Wood of Postmodernity (Space, Faith, Allegory)," *PMLA* 3 (2005): 734–50.

7. "Interview with Brian Massumi," International Assembly, http://www.assembly-international.net/Interviews/html/brian%20massumi.html.

8. Brian Massumi, "Fear (The Spectrum Said)," *Positions: East Asia Cultures Critique* 13, no. 1 (2005): 31–48.

9. R. Michael Fisher, *The World's Fearlessness Teachings: A Critical Integral Approach to Fear Management/Education for the 21st Century* (Lanham, Md.: University Press of America, 2010), xxxiii.

10. For a collection of essays reflecting on the twenty-first century as a century of fear, see Ramadan and Shantz, *Manufacturing Phobias.*

11. Brian Massumi, *The Politics of Everyday Fear* (Minneapolis: University of Minnesota Press, 1993), viii–x.

12. Ramadan and Shantz, *Manufacturing Phobias,* 295.

13. See Liu yi Lin, Jaime Sidani, Ariel Shensa, Ana Radovic, Elizabeth Miller, Jason Colditz, Beth Hoffman, Leila Giles, and Brian Primack, "Association between Social Media Use and Depression among U. S. Young Adults," *Depression & Anxiety* 33, no. 4 (2016): 323–31; Holly Shakya and Nicholas Christakis, "Association of Facebook Use with Compromised Well-Being: A Longitudinal Study," *American Journal of Epidemiology* 185, no. 3 (2017): 203–11; and "Unsocial Media: Jealousy of Online Friends Leaves People Feeling Down," *Kaspersky Lab,* January 5, 2017, https://usa.kaspersky.com/about/press-releases/2017_unsocial-media-jealousy-of-online-friends-leaves-people-feeling-down-kaspersky-lab-study-reveals.

14. Grusin, *Premediation,* 126.

15. Ibid., 127.

16. Zygmunt Bauman, *Liquid Fear* (Cambridge, U.K.: Polity Press, 2006), 18.

17. See Aniko Bordroghkozy, *Groove Tube: Sixties Television & the Youth Rebellion* (Durham, N.C.: Duke University Press, 2001), and Jane Feuer, *Seeing through the Eighties: Television and Reaganism* (Durham, N.C.: Duke University Press, 1995).

18. Patricia Ticineto Clough with Jean Halley, eds., *The Affective Turn: Theorizing the Social* (Durham, N.C.: Duke University Press, 2007), 1–3.

19. Alexia Smit, "Media Audiences: Television, Meaning and Emotion; Reality Television, Affect and Intimacy: Reality Matters (Book Reviews)," *Screen* 15, no. 1 (2010): 92–95.

20. For affect and film viewership, see Murray Smith, *Engaging Characters: Fiction, Emotion, and the Cinema* (Oxford: Clarendon Press, 1995); Torben Grodal, *Embodied Visions: Evolution, Emotion, Culture, and Film* (Oxford: Oxford University Press, 2009); Carl Plantinga, *Moving Viewers: American Film and the Spectator's Experience* (Berkeley: University of California Press, 2009). Also see

Linda Williams, "Film Bodies: Gender, Genre, and Excess," *Film Quarterly* 44 (1991): 2–13, on body genres—horror, melodrama, and pornography—that prompt emotional reactions registered on the body.

21. A sampling of such soap opera scholarship includes Tania Modleski, *Loving with a Vengeance: Mass-Produced Fantasies for Women* (Hamden, Conn.: Archon Books, 1982); Ien Ang, *Watching "Dallas": Soap Opera and the Melodramatic Imagination,* trans. Della Couling (New York: Methuen, 1985); Carol Traynor Williams, *"It's Time for My Story": Soap Opera Sources, Structure, and Response* (London: Praeger, 1992); Mary Ellen Brown, *Soap Opera and Women's Talk: The Pleasure of Resistance* (London: Sage, 1994); C. Lee Harrington and Denise D. Bielby, *Soap Fans: Pursuing Pleasure and Making Meaning in Everyday Life* (Philadelphia: Temple University Press, 1995); Laura Stempel Mumford, *Love and Ideology in the Afternoon: Soap Opera, Women, and Television Genre* (Bloomington: Indiana University Press, 1995); and Louise Spence, *Watching Daytime Soap Operas: The Power of Pleasure* (Middletown, Conn.: Wesleyan University Press, 2005). Some examples of audience/fan studies include Ien Ang, ed., *Living Room Wars: Rethinking Media Audiences for a Postmodern World* (New York: Routledge, 1996); Jennifer Hayward, *Consuming Pleasures: Active Audiences and Serial Fictions from Dickens to Soap Opera* (Lexington: University Press of Kentucky, 1997); Henry Jenkins, Tara McPherson, and Jane Shattuc, eds., *Hop on Pop: The Politics and Pleasures of Popular Culture* (Durham, N.C.: Duke University Press, 2002); and Lynne Joyrich, *Re-Viewing Reception: Television, Gender, and Postmodern Culture* (Bloomington: Indiana University Press, 1996).

22. Henry Jenkins, *The Wow Climax: Tracing the Emotional Impact of Popular Culture* (New York University Press, 2007), 3. For a more scientific explanation of this process, see Grodal, *Embodied Visions,* 148–49, where he uses his PECMA (perception, emotion, cognition, and motor action) flow model to explain how different audiovisual genres work on our bodies.

23. Scholars have in the past argued that television and film need to be analyzed and theorized differently. For example, Smith, *Engaging Characters,* 11–12, discusses the ways in which film was originally conceptualized as for public consumption and television for private consumption (11–12). Sandy Flitterman-Lewis, "Psychoanalysis, Film, and Television," in *Channels of Discourse, Reassembled: Television and Contemporary Criticism,* ed. Robert C. Allen (Chapel Hill: University of North Carolina Press, 1992), 217–18, argues for the different ways in which the media are watched, arguing that if the gaze theory applies to film, a glance theory might more readily apply to television. Because of the changes to the ways in which both media are produced and consumed, however, such differences are markedly reduced.

24. Plantinga, *Moving Viewers,* 2, 5, 6.

25. Lauren Zalaznick, "The Conscience of Television," TED, 2010, https://www.ted.com/talks/lauren_zalaznick?language=en.

26. See, for example, Mary Ann Doane, "Information, Crisis, Catastrophe," in *Logics of Television,* ed. Patricia Mellencamp (Bloomington: Indiana University Press, 1990), 222–39, and Patricia Mellencamp, "TV Time and Catastrophe, or *Beyond the Pleasure Principle* of Television," in Mellencamp, *Logics of Television,* 240–66.

27. Doane, "Information, Crisis, Catastrophe," 222; emphasis in original. See also Roland Barthes, *Camera Lucida: Reflections on Photography,* trans. Richard Howard (New York: Hill and Wang, 1981).

28. Jay David Bolter and Richard Grusin, *Remediation: Understanding New Media* (Cambridge: MIT Press, 2000), 70.

29. Mellencamp, "TV Time and Catastrophe," 243; emphasis added.

30. Ibid., 254.

31. Doane, "Information, Crisis, Catastrophe," 228.

32. Mellencamp, "TV Time and Catastrophe," 249; Doane, "Information, Crisis, Catastrophe," 229.

33. Doane, "Information, Crisis, Catastrophe," 231.

34. Grusin, *Premediation,* 1–2.

35. Ibid., 2.

36. Ibid., 4.

37. Elly Konijn, "Affects and Media Exposure," 2008, https://home.fsw.vu.nl/ea.konijn/files/Konijn_2008_Affects_Media_chapter_32_Encyclopedie_Communication.pdf, 2.

38. Ibid.

39. Jonathan Flatley, *Affective Mapping: Melancholia and the Politics of Modernism* (Cambridge: Harvard University Press, 2008), provides a useful glossary of affect terminology.

40. Eve Kosofsky Sedgwick and Adam Frank, eds., *Shame and Its Sisters: A Silvan Tomkins Reader* (Durham, N.C.: Duke University Press, 1995), 45.

41. Ibid., 74.

42. Massumi, *Politics of Everyday Fear,* 31.

43. Ibid., 25.

44. Ibid., 24.

45. Ibid., 31; emphasis in original.

46. On affect as an umbrella concept, see also Susan McLeod, *Notes on the Heart: Affective Issues in the Writing Classroom* (Carbondale: Southern Illinois University Press), 8, and Alice Brand, "Defining Our Emotional Life: The Valuative System—A Continuum Theory," in *Presence of Mind: Writing and the Domain beyond the Cognitive,* ed. Alice Brand and Richard Graves (Portsmouth, N.H.: Boynton/Cook, 1994), 160–61.

47. William James and Carl Georg Lange, *The Emotions* (Baltimore: Williams & Wilkins, 1922), 13.

48. Raymond Williams, *Marxism and Literature* (Oxford: Oxford University Press, 1977).

49. Flatley, *Affective Mapping,* 21–22.

50. Ibid., 26.

51. Ibid.

52. In discussing affect in particular—although not necessarily emotion—Gilles Deleuze and Felix Guattari, *A Thousand Plateaus: Capitalism and Schizophrenia,* trans. Brian Massumi (Minneapolis: Minnesota University Press, 1991), argue against the idea that it is not personal and is independent of intellectual interpretation.

53. Aristotle, "Rhetoric," in *The Basic Works of Aristotle,* trans. W. Rhys Roberts, ed. Richard McKeon (New York: Modern Library, 2001), 20.

54. Sedgwick and Frank, *Shame and Its Sisters,* 37. Studies have determined this does not extend only to human beings. In a study of social emotions in primates, Robert Hinde concluded that a monkey's seemingly innate fear of snakes actually requires both an exposure to said snake and the obviously fear-related reaction of his mother to that snake. See Antonio Damasio, *Looking for Spinoza: Joy, Sorrow, and the Feeling Brain* (Orlando: Harcourt, 2003), 47.

55. See Thomas Patternson, "News Coverage of the 2016 General Election: How the Press Failed the Voters," Shorenstein Center, December 7, 2016, https://shorensteincenter.org/news-coverage-2016-general-election/, and Allan Smith, "Stunning Chart Shows How Donald Trump Has Dominated Media Coverage of the 2016 Race," *Business Insider,* March 15, 2016, https://www.businessinsider.com/donald-trump-media-coverage-chart-2016–3.

56. Robyn Warhol discusses the mood management model of audience response to popular texts, explaining that viewers "ought to be able to perpetuate a good mood, or get out of a bad one, by choosing entertainment that will cheer them up or calm them down." She also addresses the question of why anyone would "choose to read a novel or see a film that might lead to crying." See Warhol, *Having a Good Cry: Effeminate Feelings and Pop-Culture Forms* (Columbus: Ohio State University Press, 2003), 30, 31.

57. Joseph LeDoux makes the distinction between people being able to create situations wherein certain emotions are likely and their being able to conjure up such emotions independently of outside stimuli. He argues that we "have little direct control over our emotional reactions." See LeDoux, *The Emotional Brain: The Mysterious Underpinnings of Emotional Life* (New York: Simon & Schuster, 1996), 19.

58. Beverley Skeggs, "The Value of Relationships: Affective Scenes and Emotional Performances," *Feminist Legal Studies* 18, no. 1 (2010): 40.

59. For a useful overview of this debate in regard to the Internet, see Nicholas Carr, *The Shallows: What the Internet Is Doing to Our Brains* (New York: W. W. Norton, 2010), 46–47.

60. See, for example, Susan Greenfield, *Mind Changes: How Digital Technologies Are Leaving Their Mark on Our Brains* (New York: Random House, 2015); Richard Restak, *The New Brain: How the Modern Age Is Rewiring Your Mind* (Emmaus, Pa.: Rodale Books, 2003); Adam Gazzley, *The Distracted Mind: Ancient Brains in a High-Tech World* (Cambridge: MIT Press, 2017); and Mari Swingle, *i-Minds: How Cell Phones, Computers, Gaming, and Social Media Are Changing Our Brains, Our Behavior, and the Evolution of Our Species* (Gabriola Island, B.C.: New Society Publishers, 2016).

61. Walter Benjamin, *Illuminations*, ed. Hannah Arendt, trans. Harry Zohn (1968; repr., New York: Schocken Books, 1988), 175.

62. Joyrich, *Re-Viewing Reception,* 22. N. Katherine Hayles makes a similar claim, arguing that our "rapidly developing mediascape" is transforming how we think. See Hayles, "Hyper and Deep Attention: The Generational Divide in Cognitive Modes," *Profession* (2007): 187.

63. Grusin, *Premediation,* 96. See also the concept of "technogenesis" in Mark B. N. Hansen, *New Philosophy for New Media* (Cambridge: MIT Press, 2004).

64. Jason Mittell, *Complex TV: The Poetics of Contemporary Television Storytelling* (New York: New York University Press, 2015). Also see Steven Johnson, *Everything Bad Is Good for You: How Today's Popular Culture Is Actually Making Us Smarter* (New York: Riverhead, 2005), which argues that entertainment media of the last three decades have been increasing in complexity and have resulted in the smartening, rather than the "dumbing down," of American consumers. Two other noteworthy studies, focused more specifically on televisual trends, include Robert Thompson, *Television's Second Golden Age: From* Hill Street Blues *to* ER (Syracuse: Syracuse University Press, 1996), and M. Keith Booker, *Strange TV: Innovative Television Series from* The Twilight Zone *to* The X-Files (Westport, Conn.: Greenwood Press, 2002).

65. Ramadan and Shantz, *Manufacturing Phobias,* 4.

1. Screening Terror

1. Lynn Spigel, "Entertainment Wars: Television Culture after 9/11," *American Quarterly* 56, no. 2 (2004): 235.

2. Ibid., 236.

3. Ibid.

4. Ibid., 238. Note that at least partly because of the slow pace of academic publishing, it was over a decade after the attacks before publications focused on their effects on television programming were available. See, for example, Stacy

Takacs, *Terrorism TV: Popular Entertainment in Post-9/11 America* (Lawrence: University Press of Kansas, 2012).

5. Spigel, "Entertainment Wars," 238.

6. Ibid.

7. Louis Chunovic, "Will TV News—or Its Audience—Finally Grow Up?" *Television Week*, September 24, 2001, 15.

8. Spigel, "Entertainment Wars," 241.

9. Slavoj Žižek, *Welcome to the Desert of the Real! Five Essays on September 11 and Related Dates* (New York: Verso, 2002), 11.

10. Marc Redfield, "Virtual Trauma: The Idiom of 9/11," *Diacritics* 37 no. 1 (2007): 68.

11. Susan Sontag, *Regarding the Pain of Others* (New York: Picador, 2003), 22.

12. Redfield, "Virtual Trauma," 69; emphasis in original.

13. Ibid., 56.

14. Ibid.

15. Ibid.

16. Susan J. Douglas, "The Turn Within: The Irony of Technology in a Globalized World," *American Quarterly* 58, no. 3 (2006): 635.

17. Louise Spence, "Teaching 9/11 and Why I'm Not Doing It Anymore," *Cinema Journal* 43, no. 2 (2004): 100.

18. Dennis Broe, "Fox and Its Friends: Global Commodification and the New Cold War," *Cinema Journal* 43, no. 4 (2004): 98.

19. Spigel, "Entertainment Wars," 255.

20. Ibid.

21. Cinnamon Stillwell, "'24': Television for a Post-9/11 World," *SFGate*. January 31, 2007, https://www.sfgate.com/politics/article/24-Television-for-a-Post-9-11-World-2652979.php.

22. Broe, "Fox and Its Friends," 100.

23. Ibid., 101.

24. Stillwell, "'24': Television for a Post-9/11 World," 3.

25. Redfield, "Virtual Trauma," 73.

26. Michael J. Bader, "The Psychology of Patriotism," *Phi Delta Kappan* 87, no. 8 (2006): 584.

27. Ibid.

28. Spence, "Teaching 9/11 and Why I'm Not Doing It Anymore," 102–3. Reactions from students in a similar 9/11-focused course offered in 2012—almost a decade after Spence's course—showed slightly more nuanced reactions to the attack. See Melissa Ames, "Exploding Rhetorics of 9/11: An Approach for Studying the Role That Affect and Emotion Play in Constructing Historical Events," *Pedagogy* 17, no. 2 (2017): 177–202.

29. Spence, "Teaching 9/11 and Why I'm Not Doing It Anymore," 104.

30. Lynnette Porter, David Lavery, and Hillary Robson, *Saving the World: A Guide to* Heroes (Toronto: ECW Press, 2007), 6.

31. Ibid., 33.

32. *Heroes,* episode 1.23, "How to Stop an Exploding Man," NBC, aired May 21, 2007.

33. Porter, Lavery, and Robson, *Saving the World,* 59.

34. *Heroes,* episode 1.2, "Don't Look Back," NBC, aired October 2, 2006.

35. Porter, Lavery, and Robson, *Saving the World,* 149.

36. Ibid.

37. Numerous scholars have noted the increased prevalence of temporal play on television narratives after 9/11. See Melissa Ames, *Time in Television Narrative: Exploring Temporality in Twenty-First-Century Programming* (Jackson: University Press of Mississippi, 2012).

38. Porter, Lavery, and Robson, *Saving the World,* 162–63.

39. Redfield, "Virtual Trauma," 63.

40. Ibid., 62.

41. Ibid.

42. Ibid., 63; emphasis in original.

43. *Heroes,* episode 1.19, ".07%," NBC, aired April 23, 2007.

44. Ibid.

45. *Heroes,* episode 1.20, "Five Years Gone," CBS, aired April 30, 2007.

46. Ibid.

47. *Fringe,* episode 1.20, "There's More Than One of Everything," Fox, aired May 12, 2009.

48. Evelyn Alsultany quoted in David Zurawik, "Muslims on TV Seen through Terror Prism," *Baltimore Sun,* December 11, 2015, https://www.baltimoresun.com/opinion/columnists/zurawik/bs-ae-zontv-muslim-20151211-story.html.

49. Alsultany quoted ibid. See also Cynthia P. Schneider, "Islamophobia, ISIS, and Authentic Muslim Narratives: Television's Potential Role," *Huffington Post,* February 22, 2016, https://www.huffpost.com/entry/hollywood-needs-to-end-islamophobic-portrayals-of-muslims_b_9292004.

50. *Madam Secretary,* episode 2.6, "Catch and Release," CBS, aired November 8, 2015.

51. Graeme Wood, "What ISIS Really Wants," *Atlantic,* March 2015, https://www.theatlantic.com/magazine/archive/2015/03/what-isis-really-wants/384980/.

52. Ibid.

53. James Hibberd, "'Homeland' Producer on Show's Tragically Relevant ISIS Storyline," *Entertainment Weekly,* December 11, 2015, https://ew.com/article/2015/12/11/homeland-isis-interview/.

54. *Homeland,* episode 5.1, "Separation Anxiety," Showtime, aired October 4, 2015.

55. Ibid.

56. Ibid.

2. Escaping Reality by Watching Reality TV?

1. Susan J. Douglas, "The Turn Within: The Irony of Technology in a Globalized World," *American Quarterly* 58, no. 3 (2006): 619.

2. Ibid., 620.

3. Ibid., 621.

4. William Hudson, *American Democracy in Peril: Eight Challenges,* 8th ed. (Los Angeles: CQ Press, 2016), 130.

5. "10 Years of Primetime: The Rise of Reality and Sports Programming," Nielsen, September 21, 2011, https://www.nielsen.com/us/en/insights/article/2011/10-years-of-primetime-the-rise-of-reality-and-sports-programming/.

6. The rise in unscripted programming in general (which includes programs such as talk shows as well) is worth noting. A study by the National Geographic Channel reports that in 2016 alone there were 750 unscripted series on the air. See Andy Dehnart, "The Number of Reality Shows on Cable TV Last Year," Reality Blurred, January 7, 2016, https://www.realityblurred.com/realitytv/2016/01/total-reality-show-unscripted-tv-2015/, and Bill Carter, "Tired of Reality TV, but Still Tuning," New York Times, September 13, 2010, https://www.nytimes.com/2010/09/13/business/media/13reality.html.

7. A study conducted by the University of Missouri School of Journalism found that viewers and nonviewers alike reported an elevated mood after watching segments of reality television. See Cynthia Frisby, "Getting Real with Reality TV," *USA Today Magazine,* September 2004, 54.

8. Mark Andrejevic, *Reality TV: The Work of Being Watched* (Lanham, Md.: Rowman & Littlefield, 2004), 66.

9. Ibid., 71.

10. Ibid.

11. Jennifer L. Pozner, *Reality Bites Back: The Troubling Truth about Guilty Pleasure TV* (Berkeley, Calif.: Seal Press, 2010), 14. As Pozner goes on to observe, reality television shows often cost half of what a scripted program does, and at times the cost difference is even greater. For example, she notes, "In 2001, NBC paid $9 million per hour for *The West,* while the *Weakest Link* clocked in at $5,000 per episode."

12. David Grazian, "Neoliberalism and the Realities of Reality Television," *Contexts* 9 no. 2 (2010): 69. This was not an isolated incident. As Grazian explains, the first-generation reality television programs like *Cops* and *America's Most Wanted* were introduced, in part, as a response to the 1988 Writers Guild of America Strike.

13. Jérôme Bourdon points out that the criticism of reality television—that viewers are "manipulated by something that 'looks real' but is, in fact, fiction"—is one that has been made about documentaries and talk shows as well throughout recent years; see Grazian, "Neoliberalism and the Realities of Reality Television," 69.

14. Andrejevic, *Reality TV*, 4.

15. Ibid., 3.

16. Linda Grindstaff, *The Money Shot: Trash, Class, and the Making of TV Talk Shows* (Chicago: University of Chicago Press, 2002), 25.

17. Ibid., 26.

18. Michael Hirschorn, "The Case for Reality TV," *Atlantic*, May 2007, https://www.theatlantic.com/magazine/archive/2007/05/the-case-for-reality-tv/305791/; emphasis added.

19. For other research on the role emotion and affect play in reality television, see Grindstaff, *The Money Shot;* J. Z. Bratich, "'Nothing Is Left Alone for Too Long': Reality Programming and Control Society Subjects," *Journal of Communication Inquiry* 30, no. 1 (2006): 65–83; Joseph Harry, "*Cheaters:* 'Real' Reality TV as Melodramatic Parody," *Journal of Communication Inquiry* 32, no. 3 (2008): 230–48; Misha Kavka, *Reality Television, Affect and Intimacy: Reality Matters* (New York: Palgrave Macmillan, 2008); Lemi Baruh, "Publicized Intimacies on Reality Television: An Analysis of Voyeuristic Content and Its Contribution to the Appeal of Reality Programming," *Journal of Broadcasting & Electronic Media* 53 (2009): 190–210; and Atte Oksanen, "Affect and Addiction in the *Celebrity Rehab* Reality Television Show," *Addiction Research and Theory* 22, no. 2 (2014): 137–46.

20. The term *schadenfreude* actually has no direct English equivalent. Borrowed from the German language, the word means quite literally pleasure taken from someone else's misfortune. The closest English equivalent to the word would be epicaricacy, derived from the Greek word *epichaerecacia,* which is a solid translation of the phrase *Roman holiday,* meaning pleasure derived from watching someone else's suffering à la the gladiatorial spectators in the Colosseum.

21. Oksanen, "Affect and Addiction in the *Celebrity Rehab* Reality Television Show," 140.

22. Ibid., 143.

23. John Ellis, "The Performance on Television of Sincerely Felt Emotion," *Annals of the American Academy of Political and Social Science* 625, no. 1 (2009): 110.

24. Ibid.

25. Zygmunt Bauman, *Liquid Fear* (Cambridge, U.K.: Polity Press, 2006); Ellis, "Performance on Television," 110.

26. Ellis, "Performance on Television," 110.

27. Annette Hill, *Reality TV: Audiences and Popular Factual Television* (New York: Routledge, 2005), 133.

28. Catherine Orenstein, "Housewife Wars: The Cultural Conversation behind the Hedges of Wisteria Lane," *Ms.*, Spring 2005.

29. Ibid.

30. Ibid.

31. Susan Gilbert, "Those Televised Supernannies May Be Just a Bit Too Super," *New York Times*, August 2, 2005, https://www.nytimes.com/2005/08/02/science/those-televised-supernannies-may-be-just-a-bit-too-super.html.

32. Ibid. The programs have also been criticized for not broadcasting the diversity of families that exist in the United States, as "these shows focus mostly on middle-class, white, heteronormative families"; see Avital Norman Nathman, "Mom & Pop Culture: The Reality of Reality TV Parenting," Bitch Media, December 15, 2011, https://www.bitchmedia.org/post/mom-pop-culture-the-reality-of-reality-tv-parenting-feminism.

33. Nathman, "Mom & Pop Culture."

34. Hirschorn, "The Case for Reality TV."

35. Benyamin Cohen, "Why Do We Enjoy Watching Reality TV? It's Not What You Think," *Grapevine*, September 14, 2016, https://www.fromthegrapevine.com/arts/enjoy-watching-reality-tv-humiliation-jonathan-cohen-michal-hershman-shitrit.

36. Ibid.

37. Ibid.

38. Randall Rose and Stacy Wood, "Paradox and the Consumption of Authenticity through Reality Television," *Journal of Consumer Research* 32, no. 2 (2005): 284.

39. Steven Shaviro explains how this works with celebrities rather than everyday people—the "investment (in both the economic and the affective senses) of the personality or aura" that drives mass media. Media consumers experience their "feelings vicariously, through the triumph and tribulations of others, in a process of continual exchange. The experiences of celebrities [are] every bit as real" to them as their own. Arguably, in the post–reality TV, post–social media era the cult of the celebrity is now interchangeable with the cult of the quasi celebrity, the everyday person-turned-star whom we turn to for vicarious experience and emotions. See Shaviro, "The Life, after Death, of Postmodern Emotions," *Criticism* 46, no. 1 (2004): 136.

40. John Timpane, "After 9/11 in the Arts: More Reality, but Also More Fantasy," *Philadelphia Inquirer*, September 4, 2011, http://www.source.ly/10I5e#.XX_Aki5KjIU.

41. Hirschorn, "The Case for Reality TV."

42. Grazian, "Neoliberalism and the Realities of Reality Television," 68.

43. Hirschorn, "The Case for Reality TV."

44. Rose and Wood, "Paradox and the Consumption of Authenticity," 284. A study conducted by the University of Missouri School of Journalism found that that viewers and nonviewers alike compare themselves to the star of the program when viewing reality television; see Frisby, "Getting Real with Reality TV," 54.

45. See Lemi Baruh, "Mediated Voyeurism and the Guilty Pleasure of Consuming Reality Television," *Media Psychology* 13 (2010): 201–21. This applies to those with trait voyeurism (whereby they enjoy getting a chance to see "what they cannot otherwise see") more than to those with pathological voyeurism (whereby that which they cannot otherwise see is sexually directed). Those with both voyeuristic tendencies were the most likely to watch reality TV; see Susan Krauss Whitbourne, "Who Watches Reality Shows, and Why?" *Psychology Today,* May 21, 2013, https://www.psychologytoday.com/us/blog/fulfillment-any-age/201305/who-watches-reality-shows-and-why.

46. Arthur Cassidy, "Celebrities, Obsession and Reality Television," *Bluefire Media,* 2017, http://blufiremedia.com/dr/celebrities-obsession-and-reality-television/.

47. Some research supports the idea that for people with low self-esteem, even writing about their favorite celebrity can actually increase their own sense of worth, at least temporarily; see Michael S. Levy, *Celebrity and Entertainment Obsession: Understanding Our Addiction* (Lanham, Md.: Rowman & Littlefield, 2015), 167.

48. Antonio Lopez, *Mediacology: A Multicultural Approach to Media Literacy in the 21st Century* (New York: Peter Lang, 2008), 68.

49. Ibid.

50. Ibid.

51. Ibid.

52. Andrejevic, *Reality TV,* 44.

53. Kelly Field, "What Reality TV Taught Trump, According to Professors Who Study It," *Chronicle of Higher Education,* February 15, 2017, https://www.chronicle.com/article/What-Reality-TV-Taught-Trump/239200.

54. Ibid.

55. Ibid.

56. Ibid.

57. Ibid.

58. Ibid.

59. Kelsey Sutton, "Harvard Study: General Election Media Coverage 'Overwhelmingly Negative' in Tone," *Politico,* December 7, 2016, https://www.politico.com/blogs/on-media/2016/12/report-general-election-coverage-overwhelmingly-negative-in-tone-232307.

60. Field, "What Reality TV Taught Trump."
61. Ibid.
62. Danielle Lindemann is quoted ibid.
63. Ibid.

3. Performing and Experiencing Anger (through Humor)

1. Amber Day, *Satire and Dissent: Interventions in Contemporary Political Debate* (Bloomington: Indiana University Press, 2011), 30.
2. Barbara Matusow, *The Evening Stars: The Making of the Network News Anchor* (Boston: Houghton Mifflin, 1983), 83.
3. Ibid.
4. Daya Kishan Thussu, *News as Entertainment: The Rise of Global Infotainment* (London: Sage, 2007), 7.
5. Bonnie Anderson, *News Flash: Journalism, Infotainment, and the Bottom-Line Business of Broadcast News* (San Francisco: Jossey-Bass, 2004), x–xi.
6. Jeffrey P. Jones, *Entertaining Politics: Satiric Television and Political Engagement,* 2nd ed. (Lanham, Md.: Rowman & Littlefield, 2010), 6.
7. Neil Postman and Steve Powers, *How to Watch TV News,* rev. ed. (New York: Penguin Books, 2008), 20.
8. Ibid.
9. W. Lance Bennett, *News: The Politics of Illusion,* 5th ed. (New York: Longman, 2003), 3.
10. Aparna Kumar, "Is the FCC Quelling Free Speech?" *Wired,* April 18, 2001, https://www.wired.com/2001/04/is-the-fcc-quelling-free-speech/.
11. Ibid.
12. Thussu, *News as Entertainment,* 61.
13. "The Great Divide: How Westerners and Muslims View Each Other," Pew Research for the People and the Press, 2006, https://www.pewresearch.org/global/2006/06/22/the-great-divide-how-westerners-and-muslims-view-each-other/. More recent studies have complicated earlier findings to some extent. Though a 2013 Pew Research study indicates that Fox News still has the most dedicated viewing audience in terms of ideological affiliation (24 percent of American adults report that they watch only Fox News), reports have found that one-quarter of the Fox News viewing population at large also are tuning in to the more liberal MSNBC. See Mark Jurkowitz, Amy Mitchell, Jodi Enda, and Kenneth Olmstead, "How Americans Get TV News at Home: Methodology," Pew Research Center—Journalism & Media, October 11, 2013.
14. Anderson, *News Flash,* 190.
15. Postman and Powers, *How to Watch TV News,* 14.
16. Anderson, *News Flash,* 30.

17. "The Reason Your Feed Became an Echo Chamber—And What to Do about It," NPR, July 24, 2016, https://www.npr.org/sections/alltechconsidered/2016/07/24/486941582/the-reason-your-feed-became-an-echo-chamber-and-what-to-do-about-it.

18. Thussu, *News as Entertainment,* 3.

19. See Project for Excellence in Journalism, *The State of the News Media: An Annual Report on American Journalism* (Washington, D.C.: Project for Excellence in Journalism, 2006); and David Mindich, *Tuned Out: Why Americans under 40 Don't Follow the News* (New York: Oxford University Press, 2005).

20. Pew Research Center, "Key Indicators in Media & News," March 19, 2014, https://www.journalism.org/2014/03/26/state-of-the-news-media-2014-key-indicators-in-media-and-news/key-indicators-in-media-and-news-2014/.

21. Thussu, *News as Entertainment,* 3.

22. The quantity of news coverage began to trouble critics as early as the 1990s. The investigative journalist Carl Bernstein "lamented that the speed and quantity of news was undermining its quality, accuracy, and context and normalizing" a "sleazoid infotainment culture"; see Thussu, *News as Entertainment,* 4; Carl Bernstein, "The Idiot Culture," *New Republic,* June 8, 1992, 24–25.

23. Postman and Powers, *How to Watch TV News,* 4.

24. Ibid. The blossoming genre of reality television, which expanded in the 1990s and dominated the televisual landscape during much of the 2000s, might have further influenced broadcast journalism; see Thussu, *News as Entertainment,* 82. For more on the global expansion of reality television—and its strategic blending of nonfiction and entertainment—see Marc Andrejevic, *Reality TV: The Work of Being Watched* (Lanham, Md.: Rowman & Littlefield, 2004); Annette Hill, *Reality TV: Audiences and Popular Factual Television* (New York: Routledge, 2005); Richard Kilborn, *Staging the Real: Factual TV Programming in the Age of Big Brother* (Manchester, U.K.: Manchester University Press, 2003).

25. Thussu, *News as Entertainment,* 2.

26. Ibid., 3.

27. For more on this see Leonard Downie Jr. and Robert G. Kaiser, *The News about the News: American Journalism in Peril* (New York: Knopf, 2002); Todd Gitlin, *Media Unlimited: How the Torrent of Images and Sounds Overwhelms Our Lives* (New York: Metropolitan Books, 2001).

28. Anderson, *News Flash,* 2; Postman and Powers, *How to Watch TV News,* 91.

29. Anderson, *News Flash,* 17.

30. Ancier quoted ibid., x; emphasis added.

31. Jones, *Entertaining Politics,* 49.

32. Ibid., 48.

33. Anderson, *News Flash,* 16; Jones, *Entertaining Politics,* 6; Thussu, *News as Entertainment,* 28.

34. Jones, *Entertaining Politics,* 6.

35. Ibid., 61.

36. Anderson, *News Flash,* xiii.

37. Thussu, *News as Entertainment,* 30.

38. Jones, *Entertaining Politics,* 5.

39. Joy Lanzendorfer, "How Reality TV Made Donald Trump President," Vice, November 18, 2016, https://www.vice.com/en_us/article/avak5a/how-reality-tv-made-donald-trump-president.

40. Stephen Collinson, "How Donald Trump Changed the Presidency in 7 Days," CNN, January 27, 2017, https://www.cnn.com/2017/01/27/politics/donald-trump-first-week/index.html.

41. Anderson, *News Flash,* xi.

42. Schonfeld quoted ibid., 6.

43. John Simpson, *News from No Man's Land: Reporting the World* (London: Macmillan, 2002), 288.

44. Neil Postman, *Amusing Ourselves to Death: Public Discourse in the Age of Show Business* (New York: Viking, 1985), 106.

45. Andrew Marr, *My Trade: A Short History of British Journalism* (London: Macmillan, 2004), 381.

46. Thussu, *News as Entertainment,* 5. An example of this was the 2011 coverage of England's royal wedding of Prince William and Kate Middleton, which received massive amounts of airtime in the United States before, during, and after the festivities. The coverage probably would have remained the top "news" story for much longer had not the vicarious celebration been interrupted by the announcement that Osama bin Laden had been killed.

47. Project for Excellence in Journalism, "State of the News Media Report 2004," Pew Research, May 13, 2017, http://assets.pewresearch.org/wp-content/uploads/sites/13/2017/05/24141554/State-of-the-News-Media-Report-2004-FINAL.pdf, 44.

48. Jones, *Entertaining Politics,* 5.

49. Ibid., 5–6.

50. Day, *Satire and Dissent,* 1.

51. Ibid.

52. Kevin Barnhurst, "Politics in the Fine Meshes: Young Citizens, Power and Media," *Media Culture & Society* 20 (1998): 201–18; Mindich, *Tuned Out,* 19.

53. Thussu, *News as Entertainment,* 163; for more on this see Matthew Baum, "Talking the Vote: Why Presidential Candidates Hit the Talk Show Circuit," *American Journal of Political Science* 49, no. 2 (2005): 213–34.

54. Jody Baumgartner and Jonathan S. Morris, "*The Daily Show* Effect: Candidate Evaluations, Efficacy, and American Youth," *American Politics Research* 34, no. 3 (2006): 341–67.

55. Cass Sunstein, *Republic.com 2.0,* 2nd ed. (Princeton: Princeton University Press, 2007).

56. Jones, *Entertaining Politics,* 21.

57. Ibid., 14.

58. Ibid.

59. Ibid.

60. Ibid.

61. Thussu, *News as Entertainment,* 15.

62. Ibid.

63. In the context of this chapter, *fake news* is considered faux news programming that is recognized by the viewer as fictional or exaggerated. More recently this phrase has been used by the Trump administration to criticize particular news outlets for airing news that unfavorably portrays the president or reporting positions or facts that conflict with his platform.

64. Rachel Sotos, "The Fake News as the Fifth Estate," in *The Daily Show and Philosophy: Moments of Zen in the Art of Fake News,* ed. Jason Holt (Malden, Mass.: Blackwell, 2007), 32.

65. Ibid.

66. Day, *Satire and Dissent,* 6. This trend is not restricted to English-speaking countries, either. An Iraqi fake news show, *Hurry Up, He's Dead,* for example, launched in 2006. And the most notable example of political satire in the Middle East has to be *Al Bernameg* (The Program), hosted by the Egyptian satirist Bassem Youssef, which drew an average of more than 30 million viewers during its 2011–14 run. See Patrick Kingsley, "Egypt's Jon Stewart? Al Bernameg Is a Political Satire to Rival The Daily Show," *Guardian,* March 6, 2013, https://www.theguardian.com/world/2013/mar/06/egypt-jon-stewart-al-bernameg.

67. *SNL*'s political portraits have traditionally not been very influential in the public sphere. For example, the comedic portrayals of Bill Clinton as a womanizer or George W. Bush as a "dim-witted frat boy" did little to change public perception of either politician. The program is credited, however, with influencing the public's reaction to Alaska governor and vice presidential candidate Sarah Palin during the 2008 election through Tina Fey's multiple (and often spot-on) comedic portrayals. More recently, Alec Baldwin's performance as Donald Trump has been among the most-watched sketch comedy, prompting multiple tweets from the president, who criticized the actor and program. See Day, *Satire and Dissent,* 51–52.

68. Ibid., 1.

69. Ibid., 11.

70. Sigmund Freud once argued that "even if the satirist's intent is radical, she translates her anger and resentment into a satirical attack, purging both herself and her audience of the need for direct action"; see ibid.

71. Ibid., 28. See also Linda Hutcheon, *Irony's Edge: The Theory and Politics of Irony* (New York: Routledge, 1995), 30.

72. Day, *Satire and Dissent,* 2.

73. Jones, *Entertaining Politics,* 109.

74. Warren St. John, "The Week That Wasn't," *New York Times,* October 3, 2004, https://www.nytimes.com/2004/10/03/fashion/the-week-that-wasnt.html.

75. Day, *Satire and Dissent,* 4.

76. Ibid.

77. Jones, *Entertaining Politics,* 8; Michael Schudson, "What's Unusual about Covering Politics as Usual," in *Journalism after September 11,* ed. Barbie Zelizer and Stuart Allan (New York: Routledge, 2002), 43.

78. James W. Carey, "American Journalism, on, before, and after September 11," in Zelizer and Allan, *Journalism after September 11,* 74.

79. Aaron McKain, "Not Necessarily Not the News: Gatekeeping, Remediation, and the Daily Show," *Journal of American Culture* 38, no. 4 (2005): 415–30.

80. Jonathan E. Barbur and Trischa Goodnow, "The *Arete* of Amusement: An Aristotelian Perspective on the Ethos of *The Daily Show,*" in The Daily Show *and Rhetoric: Arguments, Issues, and Strategies,* ed. Trischa Goodnow (Lanham, Md.: Lexington Books, 2011), 4.

81. Jones, *Entertaining Politics,* 74.

82. Ibid.

83. R. Lance Holbert, Jennifer L. Lambe, Anthony D. Dudo, and Kristin A. Carlton, "Primacy Effects of *The Daily Show* and National TV News Viewing: Young Viewers, Political Gratifications, and Internal Political Self-Efficacy," *Journal of Broadcasting & Electronic Media* 51 no. 1 (2007): 20–38.

84. Day *Satire and Dissent,* 56; Jones *Entertaining Politics,* 8.

85. Day, *Satire and Dissent,* 56.

86. Ibid., 26.

87. Judith Barad, "Stewart and Socrates: Speaking Truth to Power," in Holt, *The Daily Show and Philosophy,* 73.

88. McKain, "Not Necessarily Not the News," 418.

89. "Bill Moyers Interviews Jon Stewart," *NOW with Bill Moyers,* PBS, aired July 11, 2003; Day, *Satire and Dissent,* 78.

90. Aaron Hess, "Purifying Laughter: Carnivalesque Self-Parody as Argument Scheme in *The Daily Show with Jon Stewart,*" in Goodnow, The Daily Show *and Rhetoric,* 102. See also Geoffrey Baym, "*The Daily Show:* Discursive Integration and the Reinvention of Political Journalism," *Political Communication* 22 (2005): 259–76; Geoffrey Baym, "Crafting New Communicative Models in the Television Sphere: Political Interviews on *The Daily Show,*" *Communication Review* 10 (2007): 93–115; Robert Hariman, "Political Parody and Public Culture," *Quarterly Journal of Speech* 94, no. 3 (2008): 247–72; Don J. Waisanen, "A

Citizen's Guides to Democracy Inaction: Jon Stewart and Stephen Colbert's Comic Rhetorical Criticism," *Southern Communication Journal* 74, no. 2 (2009): 119–40.

91. Marc Peyser, "Who's Next 2004: Red, White and Funny," *Newsweek*, December 29, 2003, 71.

92. Stephen Hedgpeth, "*The Daily Show's* Satiric Eye," *Cleveland Plain Dealer*, July 30, 2000, 61.

93. Gerald J. Erion, "Amusing Ourselves to Death with Television News: Jon Stewart, Neil Postman, and the Huxleyan Warning," in Holt, *The Daily Show and Philosophy*, 5; Jones, *Entertaining Politics*, 76; Day, *Satire and Dissent*, 78.

94. Day, *Satire and Dissent*, 78.

95. Ibid., 77; Steven Michels and Michael Ventimiglia, "Can *The Daily Show* Save Democracy? Jon Stewart as the Gadfly of Gotham," in Holt, *The Daily Show and Philosophy*, 88. Many academics have studied the content of *The Daily Show* against traditional news coverage. For example, a study by Julia Fox, Glory Koloen, and Vokan Sahin analyzed the contents of *The Daily Show*'s coverage and compared it to that of mainstream broadcast journalism during the lead-up to the 2004 presidential campaign and found that *The Daily Show* incorporated roughly the same about of "substance" as the news shows it drew on, and the show often devoted more time to the stories covered than the regular networks did; see Barbur and Goodnow, "The *Arete* of Amusement," 9.

96. Michele Greppi, "10 Most Powerful People in TV News," *Television Week* 25, no. 17 (2006): 59.

97. Steve Young, "The 1974 Cronkite," *Los Angeles Daily News*, September 20, 2004, N11.

98. Stephen M. Silverman, "Jon Stewart Named Most Influential Man of 2010," *People*, October 27, 2010, https://people.com/celebrity/jon-stewart-named-most-influential-man-of-2010/.

99. Terrance MacMullan, "Jon Stewart and the New Public Intellectual," in Holt, *The Daily Show and Philosophy*, 62; *The Daily Show*'s Emmy nomination streak ended with Stewart's departure from the show.

100. Jones, *Entertaining Politics*, 75.

101. Barad, "Stewart and Socrates," 71.

102. Ibid.

103. Ibid.

104. Ibid.

105. Barbur and Goodnow, "The *Arete* of Amusement," 16.

106. Baumgartner and Morris, "*The Daily Show* Effect," 361.

107. Michels and Ventimiglia, "Can *The Daily Show* Save Democracy?" 90. Amber Day also critiques Baumgartner and Morris's study, citing specific problems with their methodology; see Day, *Satire and Dissent*.

108. Michels and Ventimiglia, "Can *The Daily Show* Save Democracy?" 90.

109. Robert N. Spicer, "Before and after *The Daily Show:* Freedom and Consequences in Political Satire," in Goodnow, The Daily Show *and Rhetoric,* 20.

110. Ibid., 34.

111. Olivia Barker, "Look Out, Jon Stewart," *USA Today,* November 2, 2004, 1D.

112. Baym, "*The Daily Show,*" 273; James Trier, "*The Daily Show with Jon Stewart:* Part I," *Journal of Adolescent and Adult Literacy* 51, no. 5 (2008): 424.

113. John Ellis, "Television as Working Through," in *Television and Common Knowledge,* ed. Jostein Gripsrud (New York: Routledge, 1999), 55–65.

114. John W. Self, "The (not-so) Laughable Political Argument: A Close-Textual Analysis of *The Daily Show with Jon Stewart,*" in Goodnow, The Daily Show *and Rhetoric,* 71; emphasis added.

115. Julia R. Fox, Glory Koloen, and Volkan Sahin, "No Joke: A Comparison of Substance in *The Daily Show with Jon Stewart* and Broadcast Network Television Coverage of the 2004 Presidential Election Campaign," *Journal of Broadcasting & Electronic Media* 51, no. 2 (2007): 856–74.

116. Ibid.

117. Aaron Smuts, "Relief Theory," The Internet Encyclopedia of Philosophy, April 12, 2009, https://www.iep.utm.edu/humor/.

118. For more on how audiovisual texts can play into this process of emotional contagion, see Carl Plantinga, *Moving Viewers: American Film and the Spectator's Experience* (Berkeley: University of California Press, 2009).

119. Murray Smith, *Engaging Characters: Fiction, Emotion, and the Cinema* (New York: Oxford University Press, 1995), 6; emphasis in original.

120. Barbur and Goodnow, "The *Arete* of Amusement," 14.

121. Bernard Goldberg, "About Jon Stewart . . . ," BernardGoldberg.com, April 20, 2010, https://bernardgoldberg.com/about-jon-stewart/.

122. Barbur and Godnow, "The *Arete* of Amusement," 14.

123. Eve Kosofsky Sedgwick and Adam Frank, eds., *Shame and Its Sisters: A Silvan Tomkins Reader* (Durham, N.C.: Duke University Press, 1995), 45.

124. Massumi is quoted in Mary Zournazi, "Navigating Moments: A Conversation with Brian Massumi," in Zournazi, *Hope: New Philosophies for Change* (New York: Routledge, 2003), 216.

125. Benedict Anderson, *Imagined Communities: Reflections on the Origins and Spread of Nationalism,* rev. ed. (New York: Verso, 1991), 37.

126. Arjun Appadurai, *Modernity at Large: Cultural Dimensions of Globalization* (Minneapolis: University of Minnesota Press, 1996), 33, 195; emphasis in original.

127. "Third Month Mania," *The Daily Show,* Comedy Central, aired March 2017.

128. Three months later Comedy Central provided an opportunity for viewers to physically engage with one another and this material when they curated a three-day museum exhibition in New York City—only blocks from Trump Tower—featuring Donald Trump's tweets.

129. Alison Dagnes, *A Conservative Walks into a Bar: The Politics of Political Humor* (New York: Palgrave Macmillan, 2012).

130. For a discussion on the ways in which 4chan users employed humor as a strategy for political disruption during the 2016 election, see Jeffrey Hall, "Meme Warfare & Fake Hashtag Activism—4chan's Alt-Right Trolling Culture," in "Hashtag Activism Embodied, Emboldened, and Emblematized: Case Studies on Social Justice Movements across Sites and Disciplines," ed. Melissa Ames and Kristi McDuffie (forthcoming), chap. 10.

131. Oliver Morrison, "Waiting for the Conservative Jon Stewart," *Atlantic*, February 14, 2015, https://www.theatlantic.com/entertainment/archive/2015/02/why-theres-no-conservative-jon-stewart/385480/.

132. Rebecca Krefting, *All Joking Aside: American Humor and Its Discontents* (Baltimore: Johns Hopkins University Press, 2014), 23.

133. Postman, *Amusing Ourselves to Death*, 90.

134. Ron Lembo, *Thinking through Television* (New York: Cambridge University Press, 2000), 111–12.

135. Eron Berg and Louis Lippman, "Does Humor in Radio Advertising Affect Recognition of Novel Product Brand Names?" *Journal of General Psychology* 128, no. 2 (2001): 194–205.

136. MacMullan, "Jon Stewart and the New Public Intellectual," 58.

137. Sotos, "The Fake News as the Fifth Estate," 36.

138. Alison Flood, "'Post-Truth' Named Word of the Year by Oxford Dictionaries," *Guardian*, November 15, 2016, https://www.theguardian.com/books/2016/nov/15/post-truth-named-word-of-the-year-by-oxford-dictionaries; Jeff Grabmeier, "Partisan Media Can Influence Viewers to Reject Facts," *Ohio State University News*, August 10, 2016; Kristiina Cooper, "The Psychology of Voting: An Emotional Matter?" *BBC News*, May 6, 2015, https://www.bbc.com/news/election-2015-32537661.

4. "All the Best Cowboys Have Daddy Issues"

1. Luigi Zoja, *The Father: Historical, Psychological and Cultural Perspectives*, trans. Henry Martin (Philadelphia: Brunner-Routledge, 2001), 9.

2. Andrew Samuels, ed., *The Father: Contemporary Jungian Perspectives* (New York: New York University Press, 1985), 4.

3. Ibid.

4. Ibid., 23.

5. Ibid., 24.

6. Ibid., 2.

7. Carl G. Jung, *The Collected Works of C. G. Jung* (London: Routledge, 1983), 17.

8. Ibid.

9. Jung is quoted in Samuels, *The Father,* 49.

10. W. Ralph Layland, "In Search of a Loving Father," in Samuels, *The Father,* 156.

11. Michael Bader, "The Psychology of Patriotism," *Phi Delta Kappan* 87, no. 8 (2006): 582.

12. Ibid.

13. Ibid.

14. Samuels, *The Father,* 3.

15. Ibid.; emphasis in original.

16. Zoja, *The Father,* 9.

17. Ibid., 225.

18. Ibid.

19. Ibid.

20. Roland Barthes, *The Pleasure of the Text,* trans. Richard Miller (New York: Hill and Wang, 1975), 10.

21. Jason Bainbridge, "Blaming Daddy: The Portrayal of the Evil Father in Popular Culture," https://researchbank.swinburne.edu.au/file/ee01d987–547f-4728–9d33–290ff48be8ce/1/PDF%20%28Published%20version%29.pdf, 1.

22. Daniel Dervin, "The Absent Father's Presence in Modern and American Gay Drama," *American Imago* 56, no. 1 (1999): 53.

23. Michael Zeitlin, "Father-Murder and Father-Rescue: The Post-Freudian Allegories of Donald Barthelme," *Contemporary Literature* 34, no. 2 (1993): 197.

24. Ibid.

25. Ibid., 198; emphasis in original.

26. Donald Barthelme, *The Dead Father* (New York: Farrar, Straus and Giroux, 1975), 5; emphasis in original.

Barbara Greenfield, "The Archetypal Masculine: Its Manifestation in Myth, and Its

27. Significance for Women," in Samuels, *The Father,* 204.

28. Bainbridge, "Blaming Daddy," 1.

29. Ibid., 8.

30. Ibid.

31. Rebecca Feasey, *Masculinity and Popular Television* (Edinburgh: Edinburgh University Press, 2008), 16.

32. Ibid., 36.

33. *Lost,* episode 1.11, "All the Best Cowboys Have Daddy Issues," ABC, aired December 8, 2004.

34. J. Wood, *Living Lost: Why We're All Stuck on the Island* (New Orleans: Garrett County Press, 2007), 23.

35. Samuels, *The Father,* 9.

36. Ibid.; emphasis added.

37. Ibid.

38. Holly Hassel and Nancy L. Chick, "'It Always Ends the Same': Paternal Failures," in *Looking for Lost: Critical Essays on the Enigmatic Series,* ed. Randy Laist (Jefferson, N.C.: McFarland, 2011), 155.

39. Ibid., 169.

40. Bainbridge, "Blaming Daddy," 1.

41. *Lost,* episode 1.5, "White Rabbit," ABC, aired October 20, 2004.

42. Ibid.

43. Ibid.

44. *Lost,* episode 4.9, "The Shape of Things to Come," ABC, aired April 24, 2008.

45. Feasey, *Masculinity and Popular Television,* 68–93.

46. *Lost,* episode 1.14, "Special," ABC, aired January 19, 2005.

47. David Magill, "The *Lost* Boys and Masculinity Found," in Laist, *Looking for Lost,* 137.

48. Ibid., 137, 141.

49. *Lost,* episode 3.18, "D.O.C.," ABC, aired April 25, 2007.

50. *Lost,* episode 3.21, "Greatest Hits," ABC, aired May 16, 2007.

51. Carl Jung, "The Significance of the Father in the Destiny of the Individual" (1949), in Samuels, *The Father,* 239–40.

52. Eva Seligman, "The Half-Alive Ones," in Samuels, *The Father,* 81.

53. Bainbridge, "Blaming Daddy," 3.

54. Bader, "The Psychology of Patriotism," 582.

55. John King, "Bush Calls Saddam 'The Guy Who Tried to Kill My Dad,'" CNN, September 27, 2002, https://www.cnn.com/2002/ALLPOLITICS/09/27/bush.war.talk/.

56. Ibid.

57. Ibid.

58. Zoja, *The Father,* 197.

59. Wood, *Living Lost,* viii–ix.

60. Ibid., ix.

61. Sarah Himsel Burcon, "*Lost* in Our Middle Hour: Faith, Fate, and Redemption Post-9/11," in *Time in Television Narrative: Exploring Temporality in Twenty-First-Century Programming,* ed. Melissa Ames (Jackson: University Press of Mississippi, 2012), 126.

62. Wood, *Living Lost,* 54.

63. Ibid.

64. Bader, "The Psychology of Patriotism," 584.

65. Ibid.

66. *Lost,* episode 1.2, "Pilot, Part 2," ABC, aired September 29, 2004.

67. Wood, *Living Lost,* 107–8.

68. Michael Newbury, "*Lost* in the Orient: Transnationalism Interrupted," in *Reading* Lost: *Perspectives on a Hit Television Show,* ed. Roberta Pearson (London: I. B. Tauris, 2009), 204.

69. Jesse Kavadlo, "We Have to Go Back: *Lost* after 9/11," in Laist, *Looking for Lost,* 232.

70. Wood, *Living Lost,* 121.

71. Ibid., 121–22.

5. The Trauma of Post-Apocalyptic Motherhood

1. This changes in seasons 5 and 6, when the main characters engage with people who have lived in a gated community where their lives—and therefore their family relations—have been largely unaffected by the reordered world they are isolated from.

2. Jonathan Maberry, "Go On: Bring a Zombie to Life," *Writer* 123, no. 10 (2010): 22–24.

3. Ibid.

4. Jen Webb and Sam Byrnand, "Some Kind of Virus: The Zombie as Body and as Trope," *Body & Society* 14, no. 2 (2008): 83.

5. Stephanie Boluk and Wylie Lenz, "Infection, Media, and Capitalism: From Early Modern Plagues to Postmodern Zombies," *Journal for Early Modern Cultural Studies* 10, no. 2 (2010): 127.

6. Dan Birlew, "Why Are Zombies So Popular?" September 15, 2010, http://www.danbirlew.com/why-are-zombies-so-popular/.

7. Gareth Schott, "Dawn of the Digital Dead: The Zombie as Interactive Social Satire in American Popular Culture," *Australasian Journal of American Studies* 29, no. 1 (2010): 61–75.

8. Adam Baker, "Blood Money: Why the Public Loves Zombies," *Huffington Post UK,* June 7, 2012.

9. Gerry Canavan, "'We *Are* the Walking Dead': Race, Time, and Survival in Zombie Narrative," *Exploration* 51, no. 3 (2010): 432.

10. Jeff May, "Zombie Geographies and the Undead City," *Social & Cultural Geography* 11, no. 3 (2010): 285–98.

11. Michael Newbury, "Fast Zombie/Slow Zombie: Food Writing, Horror Movies, and Agribusiness Apocalypse," *American Literary History* 24, no. 1 (2012): 87–114.

12. For an intersectional study of monsters in over seventy twenty-first-century horror narratives, see Natalie Wilson, *Willful Monstrosity: Gender and Race in 21st Century Horror* (Jefferson, N.C.: McFarland, 2020).

13. Jon Stratton, "Zombie Trouble: Zombie Texts, Bare Life, and Displaced People," *European Journal of Cultural Studies* 14, no. 3 (2011): 278.

14. Ibid.

15. An analysis of Facebook advertising released by President Trump's reelection campaign between January 2019 and August 2019 revealed over 2,000 instances of the word *invasion* in anti-immigration messaging. See Thomas Kaplan, "How the Trump Campaign Used Facebook Ads to Amplify His 'Invasion' Claim," *New York Times,* August 5, 2019, https://www.nytimes.com/2019/08/05/us/politics/trump-campaign-facebook-ads-invasion.html; and Ben Zimmer, "Where Does Trump's 'Invasion' Rhetoric Come From?" *Atlantic,* August 6, 2019, https://www.theatlantic.com/entertainment/archive/2019/08/trump-immigrant-invasion-language-origins/595579/.

16. See Jeff Birkenstein, Anna Froula, and Karen Randell, eds., *Reframing 9/11: Film, Popular Culture and the "War on Terror"* (New York: Continuum, 2010); Samantha Lynn Kolpin, "Fight the Dead, Fear the Living: Post-Apocalyptic Narratives of Fear, Governance and Social Control" (master's thesis, Wilfred Laurier University, 2014), https://scholars.wlu.ca/etd/1682/; Terence McSweeney, "Decade of the Dead: Zombie Films as Allegory of National Trauma," in McSweeney, *The 'War on Terror' and American Film: 9/11 Frames per Second* (Edinburgh: Edinburgh University Press, 2016), 157–74; Philip Simpson, "Sects and Violence: The Allegory of Sectarian Conflict in AMC's Zombie Apocalypse," in "*The Walking Dead Live*"*! Essays on the Television Show,* ed. Philip Simpson and Marcus Mallard (Lanham, Md.: Rowman & Littlefield, 2016); Stratton, "Zombie Trouble."

17. Will Nixon, "Are Zombies the Guilty Conscience of Post-9/11 America?" *SOP,* October 27, 2011.

18. Andrea Peyser, "America Is Being Bullied into Sympathizing with 9/11 Attackers," *New York Post,* September 11, 2015, https://nypost.com/2015/09/11/america-is-being-bullied-into-sympathizing-with-911-attackers/.

19. The notion of survival shifts for the first time in Season 6, when the group takes a more offensive versus defensive role in survivorship.

20. The *Walking Dead* Roundtable, "And Now: "The Walking Dead" as the War on Terror," *Atlantic,* December 3, 2012, https://www.theatlantic.com/entertainment/archive/2012/12/and-now-the-walking-dead-as-the-war-on-terror/265846/; *The Walking Dead,* episode 3.8, "Made to Suffer," AMC, aired December 2, 2012.

21. M. King Adkins, "The Walking Dead, Season 6, Episode 12—'Not Tomorrow Yet,'" *Pop Matters,* March 14, 2016, https://www.popmatters.com/the-walking-dead-s6ep12-2495444712.html.

22. *Walking Dead* Roundtable, "And Now."

23. Zach Beauchamp, "What 'The Walking Dead' Says about the War on Terrorism," *Think Progress,* December 3, 2012, https://thinkprogress.org/guest-post-what-the-walking-dead-says-about-the-war-on-terrorism-5dc0d45a6392/.

24. DJ Pangburn, "'The Walking Dead' Writers Show Just How 'Terrorist' Boogeymen are Created," *Medium,* February 20, 2013, https://medium.com/@djpangburn/the-walking-dead-writers-show-just-how-terrorist-boogeymen-are-created-12e4c72882c1.

25. Jeremy Egner, "'The Walking Dead' Recap: Has Rick Lost His Hold on the Group?" *New York Times,* February 22, 2015, https://artsbeat.blogs.nytimes.com/2015/02/22/the-walking-dead-recap-has-rick-lost-his-hold-on-the group/.

26. Ibid.

27. Philip L. Simpson and Marcus Mallard, introduction to Simpson and Mallard, *The Walking Dead Live,* xix.

28. Susan Faludi, *The Terror Dream: Fear and Fantasy in Post-9/11 America* (New York: Metropolitan, 2007), 20, 21.

29. Ibid., 20.

30. Charon is quoted ibid., 21.

31. Ibid., 26.

32. Ibid., 35–36.

33. Ibid., 93.

34. Kdaley, "The Fridging Dead: The Walking Dead's Patriarchal Problem," *Artifice,* December 5, 2014, https://the-artifice.com/the-walking-dead-patriarchal-problem/.

35. Simone is quoted ibid.

36. Ibid.

37. Sara Century, "Let's Talk about the Woman of 'The Walking Dead,'" *Bitch Media,* February 19, 2015, https://www.bitchmedia.org/post/lets-talk-about-the-women-of-the-walking-dead.

38. Laura Bogart, "If You Think Your Mom's Awful . . ." *Dame,* November 4, 2014, https://www.damemagazine.com/2014/11/04/if-you-think-your-moms-awful/.

39. *The Walking Dead,* episode 4.14, "The Grove," AMC, aired March 16, 2014.

40. Ibid.

41. Century, "Let's Talk about the Woman of 'The Walking Dead.'"

42. "The Rising 'Tough' Women in AMC's 'The Walking Dead' Season Five," *Bitch Flicks,* October 26, 2015, http://www.btchflcks.com/2015/10/the-rising-tough-women-in-amcs-the-walking-dead-season-five.html#.Xh-NP4UuY58.

43. *The Walking Dead,* episode 5.12, "Remember," AMC, aired March 1, 2015.

44. Rikke Schubart, "Age Anxiety, Television Horror, and Off-Script Femininity: The Middle Age Mother in *The Walking Dead, Hemlock Grove,* and *American Horror Story*" (paper presented at the Society for Cinema and Media Studies, Montreal, April 24–30, 2015), 12.

45. *The Walking Dead,* episode 5.13, "Forget," AMC, aired March 8, 2015.

46. *The Walking Dead,* episode 6.12, "Not Tomorrow Yet," AMC, aired March 6, 2016.

47. Ibid.

48. *The Walking Dead,* episode 3.4, "Killer Within," AMC, aired November 4, 2012.

49. *The Walking Dead,* episode 6.9, "No Way Out," AMC, aired February 14, 2016.

50. *The Walking Dead,* episode 7.1, "The Day Will Come When You Won't Be," AMC, aired October 23, 2016. For a long list of tragedies that befall mothers on this show, see Audre Az, "Does 'The Walking Dead' Hate Mothers?" *Mode,* February 24, 2016.

51. *The Walking Dead,* episode 6.13, "The Same Boat," AMC, aired March 13, 2016.

52. Athena, "Taking the Teeth Out of Carol: Motherhood and *The Walking Dead,*" *Necropolitan,* March 27, 2016, https://thenecropolitan.wordpress.com/2016/03/27/taking-the-teeth-out-of-carol-motherhood-and-the-walking-dead/.

53. Ibid.

54. Bogart, "If You Think Your Mom's Awful . . ."

55. Ibid.

56. Ibid.

57. Ibid.

58. For more on how zombie narratives have long been argued to be products of the crisis in masculinity both within and outside the United States, see Linnie Blake, "Zombies, Dog Men and Dragons: Generic Hybridity and Gender Crisis in British Horror of the New Millennium," in Blake, *The Wounds of Nations: Horror Cinema, Historical Trauma and National Identity* (Manchester, U.K.: Manchester University Press, 2008), 161–86; and Beppie Keane, "Meat, Masculinity, and Pathologized Adolescence in Michael Logan's *Apocalypse Cow* and Scott Westerfeld's *Peeps,*" *Jeunesse: Young People, Texts, Cultures* 6, no. 1 (2014): 13–35. For an interesting article on how contemporary zombie narratives comment on the decay of the family, see Sarah Baker, "The Walking Dead and Gothic Excess: The Decaying Social Structures of Contagion," *M/C: A Journal of Media and Culture* 17, no. 4 (2014), http://www.journal.media-culture.org.au/index.php/mcjournal/article/viewArticle/860.

59. For example, see Barbara Creed, *The Monstrous-Feminine: Film, Feminism, Psychoanalysis* (New York: Routledge, 1993); Marilyn Francus, *Monstrous Motherhood: Eighteenth-Century Culture and the Ideology of Domesticity* (Baltimore: Johns Hopkins University Press, 2012); and Jane M. Ussher, *Managing the Monstrous Feminine: Regulating the Reproductive Body* (New York: Routledge, 2006).

60. Rebecca Munford, "Daddy's Girls and the Gothic Fiction of Maternity," in Munford, *Decadent Daughters and Monstrous Mothers: Angela Carter and European Gothic* (Manchester, U.K.: Manchester University Press, 2013), 154–92.

61. See Sarah Arnold, *Maternal Horror Film: Melodrama and Motherhood* (New York: Palgrave Macmillan, 2013); Silvia Moreno-Garcia, "Mommy Dearest: Horror and Motherhood in Film," *Innsmouth Free Press Blog,* May 7, 2010, http://www.innsmouthfreepress.com/blog/mommy-dearest-horror-and-motherhood-in-film/; Tammy Oler, "The Mommy Trap," *Slate,* November 24, 2014, https://slate.com/culture/2014/11/horror-movies-about-mothers-and-children-the-babadook-lyle-and-other-films-by-women.html.

62. Rachel Elfassy Bitoun, "Maternal Horror Films: Understanding the 'Dysfunctional' Mother," *Artifice,* June 8, 2016, https://the-artifice.com/maternal-horror-films-dysfunctional-mother/.

63. For more on the importance of the body in zombie narratives, see Daniel Drezner, *Theories of International Politics and Zombies,* rev. ed. (Princeton: Princeton University Press, 2015).

64. Jessica Murray, "A Zombie Apocalypse: Opening Representational Spaces for Alternative Constructions of Gender and Sexuality," *Journal of Literary Studies* 29, no. 4 (2013): 1–19.

65. Baker, "The Walking Dead and Gothic Excess."

66. Stephen Joyce, "Eating Time: The Cultural Significance of the Zombie Apocalypse," *LiNQ* 41 (2014): 98–111.

67. Denise N. Cook, "The Cultural Life of the Living Dead," *Contexts* 12, no. 4 (2013): 54–56.

68. Shaunna Murphy, "Why Watching 'The Walking Dead' Might Be Good for You—Even If It Makes You Depressed," *MTV News,* February 25, 2015, http://www.mtv.com/news/2089247/walking-dead-psychology/.

69. Travis Langley, ed., *The Walking Dead Psychology: Psych of the Living Dead* (New York: Sterling, 2015).

70. Ibid.

71. Murphy, "Why Watching 'The Walking Dead' Might Be Good for You," citing Langley.

72. Langley is quoted ibid.

73. Joshua Rothkopf, "From Romero to 'Walking Dead': A Brief History of Zombies in Pop Culture," *Rolling Stone,* August 19, 2015, https://www

.rollingstone.com/culture/culture-news/from-romero-to-walking-dead-a-brief-history-of-zombies-in-pop-culture-173931/.

74. Ibid.

6. A Country (Still) Divided

1. Howard L. Malchow, *Gothic Images of Race in Nineteenth-Century Britain* (Stanford: Stanford University Press, 1996), 168.

2. Sara Libby Robinson, *Blood Will Tell: Vampires as Political Metaphors before World War I* (Brighton, Mass.: Academic Studies Press, 2011).

3. Nina Auerbach, *Our Vampires, Ourselves* (Chicago: University of Chicago Press, 1995), 145.

4. "Tea Party Channels the Confederacy with Reactionary Rhetoric," *Grio,* March 29, 2010, https://thegrio.com/2010/03/29/tea-party-channels-the-confederacy-more-than-founding-fathers/; Chris Matthews, "Tea Party Reminds Me of Confederates in Civil War," *Real Clear Politics,* August 2, 2012, https://www.realclearpolitics.com/video/2012/08/02/chris_matthews_tea_party_reminds_me_of_confederates_in_civil_war.html.

5. Christine Seifert, "Bite Me! (Or Don't): "Twilight" Has Created a New YA Genre: Abstinence Porn," *Bitch Media,* December 15, 2008, https://www.bitchmedia.org/article/bite-me-or-dont.

6. Thompson is quoted in Tom Alderman, "Vampires: Why Here, Why Now?" *Huffington Post,* November 10, 2009, https://www.huffpost.com/entry/vampires-why-here-why-now.

7. Thompson is quoted ibid.

8. Thompson is quoted ibid.

9. Karen Backstein, "(Un)safe Sex: Romancing the Vampire," *Cinéaste* 35, no. 1 (2009): 38.

10. For more on the sympathetic vampire, see Natalie Wilson, *Seduced by "Twilight": The Allure and Contradictory Messages of the Popular Saga* (Jefferson, N.C.: McFarland, 2011).

11. Backstein, "(Un)safe Sex: Romancing the Vampire," 39.

12. Alderman, "Vampires: Why Here, Why Now?"; Rodney Clapp, "Vampires among Us: Tales of Defeat and Redemption," *Christian Century,* February 9, 2010, https://www.christiancentury.org/article/2010–02/vampires-among-us; Patrick Pritchett, "On Vampires and 9/11," *Writing the Messianic,* January 22, 2010, https://writingthemessianic.blogspot.com/2010/01/on-vampires-and-911.html?m=0.

13. Rebecca Housel quoted in Tom Morris, "Interview with a Philosopher: On the Vampire," *Huffington Post,* June 10, 2010, https://www.huffpost.com/entry/vampires_b_604190.

14. Amy Jenkins, "Powerless in the Grip of Vampires," *Independent,* October 17, 2009, https://www.independent.co.uk/voices/commentators/amy-jenkins-powerless-in-the-grip-of-vampires-1804351.html.

15. Laura Westengard, "Vampire Fantasy: Terrorism, Trauma, and the Undead in Post-9/11 Popular Culture" (paper presented at the Pacific Ancient and Modern Language Association conference, San Diego, November 16, 2013).

16. Candace Benefiel, "Foreign Fangs, Domestic Defenders: The Americanization of the Vampire in the Contemporary Novel" (paper presented at the National Popular Culture Association conference, Washington, D.C., March 28, 2013).

17. Ibid.

18. *The Vampire Diaries,* episode 4.23, "Graduation," CW, aired May 16, 2013.

19. Ibid.

20. Ibid.

21. This film is an adaptation of Seth Grahame-Smith's 2010 novel of the same name.

22. Benefiel, "Foreign Fangs, Domestic Defenders."

23. There is, however, no racial consistency among the vampire hunters.

24. Sabrina Boyer, "'Thou Shalt Not Crave Thy Neighbor': True Blood, Abjection, and Otherness," *Studies in Popular Culture* 33, no. 2 (2011): 27.

25. Ibid., 29.

26. Ibid.

27. Ibid.

28. Natalie Wilson, "Civilized Vampires versus Savage Werewolves: Race and Ethnicity in the Twilight Series," in *Bitten by Twilight: Youth Culture, Media, and the Vampire Franchise,* ed. Melissa A. Click, Jennifer Stevens Aubrey, and Elizabeth Behm-Morawitz (New York: Peter Lang, 2010), 56.

29. Ibid.

30. Ibid., 61.

31. Ibid.

32. Ibid., 59.

33. Ibid. For more on the intersections between race, class, and gender in contemporary horror texts, see Natalie Wilson, *Willful Monstrosity: Gender and Race in 21st Century Horror* (Jefferson, N.C.: McFarland, 2020).

34. Jenkins, "Powerless in the Grip of Vampires."

35. Ibid.

36. Nicole Rabin, "True Blood: The Vampire as a Multiracial Critique on Post-Race Ideology," *Journal of Dracula Studies* 12 (2010): 2.

37. Ibid., 4.

38. Ibid., 4–5.

39. Ibid., 6.

40. *True Blood,* episode 1.1, "Strange Love," HBO, aired September 7, 2008.

41. Rabin, "True Blood," 7.

42. Boyer, "'Thou Shalt Not Crave Thy Neighbor,'" 36.

43. Ibid., 36–37. This scenario is repeated with some variation in season 5, when hate crimes against vampires and other supernatural beings become a major narrative focus. The perpetrators of these murders are all white men who, not unimportantly, carry out their attacks while wearing Obama masks—a fact that adds to the racial commentary present in the season.

44. J. M. Tyree, "Warm-Blooded: *True Blood* and *Let the Right One In*," *Film Quarterly* 63, no. 2 (2009): 32.

45. Housel is quoted in Morris, "Interview with a Philosopher."

46. Tyree, "Warm-Blooded," 32.

47. Boyer, "'Thou Shalt Not Crave Thy Neighbor,'" 37.

48. Ibid., 37–38.

49. Tyree, "Warm-Blooded," 34.

50. Ibid.

51. James Brady Ryan, "Vamp Stamp: What Is True Blood Saying about Women and Sex?" *Nerve,* July 14, 2009.

52. See Gina R. Dalfonzo, "In Love with Death: The *Twilight* of American Fiction," *National Review,* August 22, 2008, http://www.nationalreview.com/articles/2008/08/love-death/gina-r-dalfonzo/; Carrie Anne Platt, "Cullen Family Values: Gender and Sexual Politics in the Twilight Series," in Click et al., *Bitten by Twilight,* 71–86; Seifert, "Bite Me! (Or Don't)"; Sarah Seltzer, "'Twilight': Sexual Longing in an Abstinence-Only World," *Huffington Post,* September 9, 2008, https://www.huffpost.com/entry/twilight-sexual-longing-i_b_117927.

53. Platt, "Cullen Family Values," 83.

54. Ibid., 72.

55. Ibid., 72–73.

56. Seifert, "Bite Me! (Or Don't)"; Seltzer, "'Twilight': Sexual Longing in an Abstinence-Only World."

57. Platt, "Cullen Family Values," 72; Dalfonzo, "In Love with Death."

58. Rebecca Housel is quoted in Morris, "Interview with a Philosopher."

59. Tarah Scalzo, "Chivalry Is Undead: Bad Boy/Nice Guy Dichotomies in The Vampire Diaries or, What Does Elena Want?" *Hey, Sugar,* December 2, 2012, https://heysugarplum.wordpress.com/2012/12/02/chivalry-is-undead-bad-boynice-guy-dichotomies-in-the-vampire-diaries-or-what-does-elena-want/.

60. Ibid. .

61. Ibid.; emphases in original.

62. Ibid.

63. Susan Faludi, *The Terror Dream: Fear and Fantasy in Post-9/11 America* (New York: Metropolitan, 2007), 14.

64. Ibid.

7. Fictionalizing Ferguson in Prime-Time Dramas

1. See Mya Abraham, "How Black Lives Matter Is Penetrating Pop Culture," *BET,* June 9, 2016, https://www.bet.com/celebrities/news/2016/06/09/how-black-lives-matter-is-penetrating-pop-culture.html; Joshua Alston, "Why Scripted Television Is Ill-Equipped to Tackle #BlackLivesMatter," *AV Club,* July 21, 2016, https://tv.avclub.com/why-scripted-television-is-ill-equipped-to-tackle-blac-1798249601; Crystal Bell, "'Empire' Takes on 'Black Lives Matter' Movement with 'Born to Lose,'" *MTV,* September 24, 2015, http://www.mtv.com/news/2280930/empire-born-to-lose/; Gabrielle Gray and Kenneth Cooper, "Raising the Black Consciousness: How Black Television Elites Have Responded to the Black Lives Matter Movement" (paper presented at the National Conference of Black Political Scientists, San Diego, November 16, 2016); "'The Carmichael Show' Takes on Black Lives Matter in a Surprising Way," Media Research Center, 2016, https://www.mrc.org/cmi-tv-blog-post/carmichael-show-takes-black-lives-matter-surprising-way; Pilot Viruet, "Let's Talk about TV's Obsession with Police Violence and Black Lives Matter," *Flavorwire,* November 16, 2015, https://www.flavorwire.com/547060/lets-talk-about-tvs-obsession-with-police-violence-and-black-lives-matter.

2. Carolyn Steedman, "Enforced Narratives: Stories of Another Self," in *Feminism and Autobiography: Texts, Theories, Methods,* ed. Tess Cosslett, Celia Lury, and Penny Summerfield (New York: Routledge, 2000), 34.

3. Marie-Françoise Chanfrault-Duchet, "Textualisation of the Self and Gender Identity in the Life-Story," in Cosslett et al., *Feminism and Autobiography,* 70.

4. Jill Bennett, *Empathic Vision: Affect, Trauma, and Contemporary Art* (Stanford: Stanford University Press, 2005), 8; Dominick LaCapra, *History in Transit: Experience, Identity, Critical Theory* (Ithaca: Cornell University Press, 2004), 39.

5. Bennett, *Empathic Vision,* 10.

6. For scholarship on representations of black women and families on TV, see Beretta Smith-Shomade, *Shaded Lives: African-American Women and Television* (New Brunswick, N.J.: Rutgers University Press, 2002), and Melbourne S. Cummings, "The Changing Image of the Black Family on Television," *Journal of Popular Culture* 22, no. 2 (1988): 75–85). For scholarship on racial stereotypes on television across genres, see Julia M. Bristor, Renee Gravois Lee, and Michelle R. Hunt, "Race and Ideology: African American Images in Television Advertising," *Journal of Public Policy & Marketing* 14, no. 1 (1995): 48–59; Brian F. Schaffner and Mark Gadson, "Reinforcing Stereotypes? Race and Local Television News Coverage of Congress," *Social Science Quarterly* 85, no. 3 (2004): 604–23; Bryan Denham and Richelle Jones, "Survival of the Stereotypical: A Study of Personal Characteristics and Order of Elimination on Reality Television," *Studies in Popular Culture* 30, no. 2 (2008): 79–99; Delia Douglas, "Venus, Serena, and the

Inconspicuous Consumption of Blackness: A Commentary on Surveillance, Race Talk, and New Racism(s)," *Journal of Black Studies* 43, no. 2 (2012): 127–45; Elizabeth Monk-Turner et al., "The Portrayal of Racial Minorities on Prime Time Television: A Replication of the Mastro and Greenberg Study a Decade Later," *Studies in Popular Culture* 32, no. 2 (2010): 101–14; Ebony Roberts, "Through the Eyes of a Child: Representations of Blackness in Children's Television Programming," *Race, Gender & Class* 11, no. 2 (2004): 130–39; Robert Staples and Terry Jones, "Culture, Ideology, and Black Television Images," *Black Scholar* 16, no. 3 (1985): 10–20; Nicholas Valentino, Vincent Hutchings, and Ismail White, "Cues That Matter: How Political Ads Prime Racial Attitudes during Campaigns," *American Political Science Review* 96, no. 1 (2002): 75–90.

7. See Robert Entman and Andrew Rojecki, *The Black Image in the White Mind: Media and Race in America* (Chicago: University of Chicago Press, 2000); Karen Ross, "Viewing (P)leasure, Viewer Pain: Black Audiences and British Television," *Leisure Studies* 16, no. 4 (1997): 233–48; Carolyn Stoman, "The Socialization Influence of Television on Black Children," *Journal of Black Studies* 15, no. 1 (1984): 79–100; Max Weisbuch, Kristin Pauker, and Nalini Ambady, "The Subtle Transmission of Race Bias via Televised Nonverbal Behavior," *Science,* n.s. 326, no. 5960 (2009): 1711–14; Thomas E. Ford, "Effects of Stereotypical Television Portrayals of African-Americans on Person Perception," *Social Psychology Quarterly* 60, no. 3 (1997): 266–75.

8. Sasha Torres, *Black, White, and in Color: Television and Black Civil Rights* (Princeton: Princeton University Press, 2003).

9. Richard Breaux, "Review of *Black, White, and in Color: Television and Black Civil Rights* by Sasha Torres," *Journal of African American History* 89, no. 1 (2004): 88–91.

10. Mike Chopra-Gant, "The Law of the Father, the Law of the Land: Power, Gender and Race in 'The Shield,'" *Journal of American Studies* 41, no. 3 (2007): 660.

11. John Sumser, *Morality and Social Order in Television Crime Drama* (Jefferson, N.C.: McFarland, 1996).

12. Constance DeRoche and John DeRoche, "Black and White: Racial Construction in Television Police Dramas," *Canadian Ethnic Studies* 23, no. 3 (1991): 70; Staples and Jones, "Culture, Ideology, and Black Television Images," 10–11, point out that crime shows are not alone in frequently casting African Americans in criminal roles.

13. See Abraham, "How Black Lives Matter Is Penetrating Pop Culture"; and Mary Ann McGivern, "How Television Undergirds Racism," *National Catholic Reporter,* July 29, 2016, https://www.ncronline.org/blogs/ncr-today/how-television-undergirds-racism.

14. *The Good Wife,* episode 6.12, "The Debate," CBS, aired January 11, 2015.

15. Lauren Hoffman, "The *Good Wife* Did a Ferguson-Based Episode Last Night," *Vulture,* January 12, 2015, https://www.vulture.com/2015/01/good-wife-recap-season-6-episode-12-ferguson-states-attorney-debate.html.

16. Simon Howell, "The Good Wife, Ep. 6.12: 'The Debate' Bites Off More Than It Can Chew," *PopOptiq,* January 12, 2015, https://www.popoptiq.com/the-good-wife-ep-6–12-the-debate-bites-off-more-than-it-can-chew/.

17. *The Good Wife,* episode 6.12, "The Debate."

18. Hoffman, "The *Good Wife* Did a Ferguson-Based Episode Last Night."

19. Ibid.

20. David Sims, "*The Good Wife* Takes a Weak Swipe at Racism," *Atlantic,* January 12, 2015, https://www.theatlantic.com/entertainment/archive/2015/01/the-good-wife-stumbles-trying-to-confront-institutional-racism/384448/.

21. Sofiya Ballin and Molly Eichel, "When Ferguson Hits Primetime: How Shows Like 'Scandal' Handle Race," *Philly.com,* March 21, 2015, https://www.inquirer.com/philly/entertainment/television/TV-Ferguson-primetime-Scandal-race.html.

22. Hoffman, "The *Good Wife* Did a Ferguson-Based Episode Last Night."

23. Karen Fratti, "The Good Wife Recap: Too Soon for 'The Debate,'" *Huffington Post,* January 14, 2015.

24. Howell, "The Good Wife, Ep. 6.12: 'The Debate.'"

25. Nora Grenfell, "The Latest Episode of 'The Good Wife' Revisits Ferguson," *Mashable,* January 12, 2015, https://mashable.com/author/nora-grenfell/.

26. Sophie Gilbert, "*Scandal*'s Ferguson-Inspired Episode Was Extraordinary Television," *Atlantic,* March 6, 2015, https://www.theatlantic.com/entertainment/archive/2015/03/scandals-ferguson-inspired-episode-was-extraordinary-television/387106/.

27. Ibid.

28. Ibid.

29. Ibid.

30. Aisha Harris, "Why *Scandal*'s Ferguson-Themed Episode Was So Frustrating," *Slate,* March 6, 2015, https://slate.com/culture/2015/03/scandal-police-brutality-episode-the-lawn-chair-tackles-michael-brown-video.html.

31. Gilbert, "*Scandal*'s Ferguson-Inspired Episode." To some extent, there are some parallels here to the various criticisms President Obama faced for not focusing enough on racial justice during his presidency. See Nick Bryant, "Barack Obama Legacy: Did He Improve US Race Relations?" *BBC News,* January 10, 2017, https://www.bbc.com/news/world-us-canada-38536668.

32. Gilbert, "*Scandal*'s Ferguson-Inspired Episode."

33. Ibid.

34. Lauren Duca, "'Scandal' Takes on Institutionalized Racism and Police Brutality in Ferguson-Inspired Episode," *Huffington Post,* March 5, 2015.

35. Gilbert, "*Scandal*'s Ferguson-Inspired Episode."

36. *Scandal,* episode 4.14, "The Lawn Chair," ABC, aired March 5, 2015.

37. Gilbert, "*Scandal*'s Ferguson-Inspired Episode."

38. Ibid.

39. Michael Arceneaux, "Did Scandal's Ferguson-Inspired Episode Have Too Happy of an Ending?" VH1, March 6, 2015, http://www.vh1.com/news/89816/scandal-ferguson-episode/.

40. Gilbert, "*Scandal*'s Ferguson-Inspired Episode"; see also Brennan Williams, "'Scandal' Cast Share Their Reactions to Ferguson-Inspired Episode," *Huffington Post,* March 10, 2015, https://www.huffpost.com/entry/scandal-cast-share-reaction-ferguson-episode_n_6840280.

41. Gilbert, "*Scandal*'s Ferguson-Inspired Episode."

42. Harris, "Why *Scandal*'s Ferguson-Themed Episode Was So Frustrating"; emphasis in original.

43. Shannon Houston, "The Baltimore Uprising and How TV Dramas Can Make a 'Race' Episode That Works," *Paste,* May 5, 2015, https://www.pastemagazine.com/articles/2015/05/the-baltimore-uprising-and-how-tv-dramas-can-make.html.

44. Arceneaux, "Did Scandal's Ferguson-Inspired Episode Have Too Happy of an Ending?"

45. Ibid.

46. Gilbert, "*Scandal*'s Ferguson-Inspired Episode."

47. Ibid.

48. Duca, "'Scandal' Takes on Institutionalized Racism."

49. Rhimes amended her tweet seconds later to include the missing word *not.*

50. For additional collected viewer tweets gauging reactions to this episode, see Duca, "'Scandal' Takes on Institutionalized Racism," and Emily Orley, "People Had Very Mixed Reactions to the Ferguson-Inspired Episode of 'Scandal,'" *BuzzFeed,* March 5, 2015, https://www.buzzfeed.com/emilyorley/the-ferguson-inspired-episode-of-scandal-reactions.

51. Heywood quoted in Viruet, "Let's Talk about TV's Obsession with Police Violence and Black Lives Matter."

52. Houston, "The Baltimore Uprising."

53. Ibid.

54. Alston, "Why Scripted Television Is Ill-Equipped to Tackle #BlackLivesMatter."

55. Viruet, "Let's Talk about TV's Obsession with Police Violence and Black Lives Matter."

56. Ibid.

57. Ibid.

58. Houston, "The Baltimore Uprising."

59. Alston, "Why Scripted Television Is Ill-Equipped to Tackle #BlackLivesMatter."

60. Ibid.

61. Houston, "The Baltimore Uprising."

62. Ballin and Eichel, "When Ferguson Hits Primetime." For the roles that various aesthetic strategies can play in the "ethics of witnessing," see Ann Kaplan, *Trauma Culture: The Politics of Terror and Loss in Media and Literature* (New Brunswick, N.J.: Rutgers University Press, 2005), 122.

63. Greg Braxton, "ABC's 'American Crime' Series Pushes Hot Buttons of Race, Culture," *Los Angeles Times,* February 27, 2015, https://www.latimes.com/entertainment/tv/la-et-st-abc-american-crime-race-culture-20150301-story.html; emphasis added.

64. Ibid.

65. Cory Barker, "*American Crime* Review: A Series with Something to Say," *TV.com,* March 5, 2015, http://www.tv.com/news/american-crime-review-a-series-with-something-to-say-142543494524/.

66. Ibid.

67. Braxton, "ABC's 'American Crime' Series Pushes Hot Buttons."

68. Barker, "*American Crime* Review."

69. Ibid.

70. Brian Moylan, "American Crime: Could This Show Be the New Wire?" *Guardian,* March 5, 2015, https://www.theguardian.com/culture/2015/mar/05/american-crime-classy-drama-multiple-viewpoints.

71. *American Crime,* episode 1.1, ABC, aired March 5, 2015.

72. Keertana Sastry, "American Crime Season 1 Finale Recap: Episode 11," *Entertainment Weekly,* May 15, 2015, https://ew.com/recap/american-crime-season-1-finale/.

73. Braxton, "ABC's 'American Crime' Series Pushes Hot Buttons."

74. Libby Hill, "*American Crime:* Episode Eleven," *A. V. Club,* May 14, 2015, https://tv.avclub.com/american-crime-episode-eleven-1798183814.

75. Alston, "Why Scripted Television Is Ill-Equipped to Tackle #BlackLivesMatter."

76. Monk-Turner et al., "The Portrayal of Racial Minorities on Prime Time Television," 103.

77. In her analysis of literature and media, Ann Kaplan echoes the important cognitive elements of affect discussed earlier in this chapter and throughout this text. In fictional narratives, she argues, this type of "vicarious traumatization may be a component of witnessing" that—if done well—can move beyond "only intensifying the desire to help an individual in front of one" and lead to a "broader understanding of the *meaning* of what has been done to victims." See Kaplan, *Trauma Culture,* 123; emphasis added.

8. Live Tweets as Social Commentary?

1. Aletha Huston Stein, "Mass Media and Moral Development" (paper presented at the American Association of Elementary-Kindergarten-Nursery Educators Conference, January 1973), https://files.eric.ed.gov/fulltext/ED080175.pdf; Herbert London, "Television: What TV Drama Is Teaching Our Children," *New York Times,* August 23, 1987; Tim Dant, *Television and the Moral Imaginary: Society through the Small Screen* (New York: Palgrave Macmillan, 2012); Andy Dehnart, "Reality TV Presents Plenty of Moral Dilemmas," *Today,* December 16, 2008, http://www.today.com/id/27917852/ns/today-today_entertainment/t/reality-tv-presents-plenty-moral-dilemmas/; Richard Wilk, "'It's Destroying a Whole Generation': Television and Moral Discourse in Belize," *Visual Anthropology* 5, no. 3–4 (1993): 229–44.

2. Sidneyeve Matrix, "The Netflix Effect: Teens, Binge Watching, and On-Demand Digital Media Trends," *Jeunesse: Young People, Texts, Cultures* 6, no. 1 (2014): 119–38; Poncie Rutsch, "Does Binge-Watching Make Us Depressed? Good Question," *NPR,* February 4, 2015, https://www.npr.org/sections/health-shots/2015/02/04/383527370/does-binge-watching-make-us-depressed-good-question; "6 Physical Effects of Binge-Watching TV," *Fox News,* March 5, 2015, https://www.foxnews.com/health/6-physical-effects-of-binge-watching-tv; Alice Park, "This Is What Binge Watching Does to Your Health," *Time,* April 1, 2015, https://time.com/3767458/tv-binge-watching-health/.

3. "Twitter and Facebook Could Harm Moral Values, Scientists Warn," *Telegraph,* April 13, 2009, https://www.telegraph.co.uk/news/science/science-news/5149195/Twitter-and-Facebook-could-harm-moral-values-scientists-warn.html; Alice Walton, "Jealous of Your Facebook Friends? Why Social Media Makes Us Bitter," *Forbes,* January 22, 2013, https://www.forbes.com/sites/alicegwalton/2013/01/22/jealous-of-your-facebook-friends-why-social-media-makes-us-bitter/#1474d5f635cc; Damon Beres, "Heavy Facebook Use Makes Some People Jealous and Depressed: Study," *Huffington Post,* February 4, 2015, https://www.huffpost.com/entry/facebook-envy_n_6606824; Matt Stewart, "Facebook and Twitter Leading to Depression and Decreased Empathy," *Stuff,* December 8, 2015, https://www.stuff.co.nz/technology/social-networking/74854561/.

4. Fabio Giglietto and Donatella Selva, "Second Screen and Participation: A Content Analysis on a Full Season Dataset of Tweets," *Journal of Communication* 65, no. 2 (2014): 260–77; Lesley Goldberg, "'How to Get Away with Murder' Creator Breaks Down Shondaland's New Drama," *Hollywood Reporter,* September 25, 2014, https://www.hollywoodreporter.com/live-feed/how-get-away-murder-creator-730206.

5. Giglietto and Selva, "Second Screen and Participation," 261.

6. See "The Making of Social TV: Loyal Fans and Big Moments Build Program-Related Buzz," Nielsen, August 24, 2015, https://www.nielsen.com/us/en/insights/article/2015/the-making-of-social-tv-loyal-fans-and-big-moments-build-program-buzz/. Note that *Scandal* was ranked first and *How to Get Away with Murder* was ranked fourth.

7. Anna Everett, "Scandalicious: Scandal, Social Media, and Shonda Rhimes' Auteurist Juggernaut," *Black Scholar* 45, no. 1 (2015): 34–43.

8. Ibid., 34.

9. International Centre for Public Pedagogy, University of East London, 2019, https://www.uel.ac.uk/research/the-international-centre-for-public-pedagogy.

10. Michael Idato, "How to Get Away with Murder: Viola Davis Prefers Moral Ambiguity," *Sydney Morning Herald,* February 2, 2015, https://www.smh.com.au/entertainment/tv-and-radio/how-to-get-away-with-murder-viola-davis-prefers-moral-ambiguity-20150202–133tri.html; Tirdad Derakhshani, "Love Is Murderous in 'How to Get Away with Murder,'" *Philadelphia Inquirer,* November 22, 2015, https://www.inquirer.com/philly/entertainment/television/20151122_Love_is_murderous_in__How_to_Get_Away_with_Murder_.html.

11. *How to Get Away with Murder,* episode 1.1, "Pilot: It's All Her Fault, Part I," ABC, aired September 25, 2014.

12. Idato, "How to Get Away with Murder: Viola Davis Prefers Moral Ambiguity."

13. Ibid.

14. Discussions of the post-racial claim can be found in Ian Haney-López, "Is the Post in Post-Racial the Blind in Colorblind," *Cardozo Law Review* 32, no. 807 (2010); available at Berkeley Law Scholarship Repository, https://scholarship.law.berkeley.edu/facpubs/1816/; H. Roy Kaplan, *The Myth of Post-Racial America: Searching for Equality in the Age of Materialism* (Lanham, Md.: Rowman & Littlefield, 2011); Howard McGary, *The Post-Racial Ideal* (Milwaukee: Marquette University Press, 2012); Barack Obama, "America Is Not a Post-Racial Society" (transcript), *Guardian,* July 19, 2013, https://www.theguardian.com/commentisfree/2013/jul/19/america-not-post-racial-society-barack-obama; Nico Lang, "It's Time to Wake Up from the Myth of a 'Post-Racial America,'" *Daily Dot,* November 25, 2014, https://www.dailydot.com/via/ferguson-michael-brown-post-racial-myth/, Ta-Nehisi Coates, "There Is No Post-Racial America," *Atlantic,* July–August 2015, https://www.theatlantic.com/magazine/archive/2015/07/post-racial-society-distant-dream/395255/; Naomi Zack, *White Privilege and Black Rights: The Injustice of U. S. Police Racial Profiling and Homicide* (Lanham, Md.: Rowman & Littlefield, 2015).

15. See Roxane Gay "The Oscars and Hollywood's Race Problem," *New York Times,* January 22, 2016, https://www.nytimes.com/2016/01/24/opinion/the-oscars-and-hollywoods-race-problem.html, and Rebecca Keegan and Steven

Zeitchick, "Oscars 2016: Here's Why the Nominees Are So White—Again," *Los Angeles Times,* January 14, 2016, https://www.latimes.com/entertainment/movies/moviesnow/la-et-mn-all-white-oscar-acting-nominees-20160114-story.html. In her acceptance speech, Viola Davis drew attention to the entertainment industry's racial inequality, noting, "You cannot win an Emmy for roles that are simply not there"; see Michael Gold, "Viola Davis's Emmy Speech," *New York Times,* September 20, 2015, https://www.nytimes.com/live/emmys-2015/viola-daviss-emotional-emmys-acceptance-speech/.

16. Carita Rizzio, "Shonda Rhimes's Powerful Message on Receiving Her PGA Award: 'I Deserve This,'" *Vulture,* January 24, 2016, https://www.vulture.com/2016/01/shonda-rhimes-on-pga-award-i-deserve-this.html.

17. Ibid.

18. Michael Zimmer and Nicholas John Proferes, "A Topology of Twitter Research: Disciplines, Methods, and Ethics," *Aslib Journal of Information Management* 66, no. 3 (2014): 250.

19. Vincent Miller, "New Media, Networking and Phatic Culture," *Convergence* 14, no. 4 (2008): 387–400; Amanda Lotz, *Cable Guys: Television and Masculinities in the 21st Century* (New York: New York University Press, 2014); Jennifer Pozner, *Reality Bites Back: The Troubling Truth about Guilty Pleasure TV* (Berkeley, Calif.: Seal, 2010).

20. Jonathan Michael, "The Rise of the Anti-Hero: Why the Characters in TV and Movies We Love Most Are the Ones with Fatal Flaws," *Relevant,* April 26, 2013, https://relevantmagazine.com/culture/rise-anti-hero/.

21. Ibid.

22. Akash Nikolas, "Where Is the Female Tony Soprano?" *Atlantic,* June 27, 2013, https://www.theatlantic.com/entertainment/archive/2013/06/where-is-the-female-tony-soprano/277270/.

23. Meghan Gallagher, "Scandal's Olivia Pope and the Rise of the Female Antihero," *Artifice,* January 5, 2015, https://the-artifice.com/scandal-olivia-pope-female-antihero/.

24. Joanna Robinson, "How a Lifetime Show Gave Us TV's First Pure Female Antihero," *Vanity Fair,* August 3, 2015, https://www.vanityfair.com/hollywood/2015/08/unreal-shiri-appleby-rachel-female-anti-hero; emphasis in original. As Andrea Morabito discusses, these female antiheroes often provide interesting gender critiques: *Homeland*'s Carrie "is as reckless in her quest to fend off terrorists as she is disinterested in motherhood"; *The Americans* "delightfully flips the gender norms for its KGB spy couple by making Elizabeth . . . the more ruthless spouse, more purely committed to the cause than husband Philip"; and *Orange Is the New Black* "offers up an entire cast of flawed women who just can't seem to escape their checkered pasts." See Morabito, "Long Live TV's Female Anti-

heroes," *New York Post,* August 13, 2015, https://nypost.com/2015/08/13/long-live-tvs-female-anti-heroes/.

25. Meghan Gallagher, "Scandal's Olivia Pope and the Rise of the Female Antihero."

26. Eliana Dockterman argues that the presence of the antiheroes' traumatic backstory may be even more important in the case of female antiheroes since we seem to require an arc that starts with their being "likable women" who undergo a transformation because of some "unfortunate circumstances"; see "UnREAL and the Arrival of the Totally Dark, Utterly Irresistible Female Anti-Hero," *Time,* August 3, 2015, https://time.com/3982291/unreal-and-the-evolution-of-the-female-anti-hero/.

27. Jason Steward, "Tube Talk: TV's Female Anti-Heroes: A Trend for the 21st Century's Teen Years," *Critic Studio,* July 20, 2011.

28. Michael, "The Rise of the Anti-Hero."

29. Richard Keen, Monica L. McCoy, and Elizabeth Powell, "Rooting for the Bad Guy: Psychological Perspectives," *Studies in Popular Culture* 34, no. 2 (2012): 137.

30. Sophie Janicke and Arthur Raney, "Exploring How We Enjoy Antihero Narratives: A Comparison of Fans and Nonfans of *24*" (paper presented at the meeting of the International Communication Association, Boston, 2011), 5.

31. Michele Corriston, "HTGAWM's Charlie Weber on That Heart-Stopping Finale and Annalise's 'Crazy Little Family,'" *People,* November 20, 2015.

32. See Grace Bello, "The Likability Trap: We Like to Root for the Antihero, but Not the Antiheroine," *Bitch Magazine,* March 7, 2013, https://www.bitchmedia.org/post/complex-heroines-of-scandal-and-enlightened; and Duca, "Anatomy of the Female Antihero."

33. The prevalence of narratives that feature plots wherein a woman's love or friendship endangers a male hero has been well documented by scholars; for more on the female as temptress, see David Thorburn and Henry Jenkins, eds., *Rethinking Media Change: The Aesthetics of Transition* (Cambridge: MIT Press, 2003), 269. For more on the long-standing tradition of casting black actors as immoral characters, see Clint Wilson, Félix Gutiérrez, and Lena Chao, *Racism, Sexism, and the Media: Multicultural Issues into the New Communications Age* (Thousand Oaks, Calif.: Sage, 2013).

34. Michelle Juergen, "Why Critics Can't Handle the Female Anti-Hero," *Arts.Mic,* January 15, 2014, https://www.mic.com/articles/79047/why-critics-can-t-handle-the-female-anti-hero.

35. Lauren Duca, "Anatomy of the Female Antihero," *Huffpost,* July 13, 2015, https://www.huffpost.com/entry/anatomy-of-the-female-anti-hero_n_55a3c250e4b0ecec71bc684a

36. Ibid.

37. Juergen, "Why Critics Can't Handle the Female Anti-Hero."

38. Ibid.

39. Alyssa Rosenberg, "Why We'll Never Have a Female Tony Soprano," *Slate,* June 27, 2013, https://slate.com/human-interest/2013/06/james-gandolfini-and-the-male-anti-hero-why-well-never-have-a-female-tony-soprano.html.

40. Roxane Gay, "Not Here to Make Friends: On the Importance of Unlikable Female Protagonists," *BuzzFeed,* January 3, 2014, https://www.buzzfeed.com/roxanegay/not-here-to-make-friends-unlikable.

41. Messud quoted in Jason Bailey, "Why There Are So Few Female Antiheroes on Film," *Flavorwire,* June 21, 2013, https://www.flavorwire.com/399697/why-are-there-so-few-female-antiheroes-on-film.

42. Jessica Valenti, "She Who Dies with the Most 'Likes' Wins?" *Nation,* November 29, 2012, https://www.thenation.com/article/she-who-dies-most-likes-wins/.

43. E. Keating, "Once upon a Time and the Villainization of Women," *Artifice,* January 7, 2015, https://the-artifice.com/once-upon-a-time-villainization-women/.

44. Gallagher, "Scandal's Olivia Pope and the Rise of the Female Antihero."

45. Ibid.

46. Natalie Abrams, "*How to Get Away with Murder:* Viola Davis Does Not Wear a White Hat, *Scandal* Fans," *TV Guide,* July 15, 2014, https://www.tvguide.com/authors/natalie-abrams/3/; Goldberg, "'How to Get Away with Murder' Creator Breaks Down Shondaland's New Drama"; Brian Cantor, "'How to Get Away with Murder' Gets Away with Risky Character," Headline Planet, September 25, 2015, https://headlineplanet.com/home/2014/09/25/abc-takes-character-risk-get-away-murder-review/.

47. Goldberg, "'How to Get Away with Murder' Creator Breaks Down Shondaland's New Drama."

48. Cantor, "'How to Get Away with Murder' Gets Away with Risky Character"; emphasis in original.

49. Ibid.

50. #HowToGetAwayWithMurder is the second-most popular hashtag associated with the program; the most frequently used is #HTGAWM. Many of the tweets in this data collection used both hashtags, but not all did. This is true of tweets using #HTGAWM as well. This means that this study cannot claim to have collected all the live tweets connected to this show during the nine-episode period; rather, it collected a subset of them.

51. This study's focus on "critiquing" posts would align with what D. Y. Wohn and E. K. Na call "opinion" posts in their AEIO analytical model for mapping the type and flow of content found in social media threads. In studying the live-tweeting practices of television viewers watching two nonscripted television

programs (a reality television live competition show and a live political speech), Wohn and Na determined four main kinds of posts made by viewers: attention-seeking posts, emoting posts, informational posts, and opinion-based posts; see Wohn and Na, "Tweeting about TV: Sharing Television Viewing Experiences via Social Media Message Streams," *First Monday* 16, no. 3 (2011). Fabio Giglietto and Donatella Selva also studied the prevalence of tweets that express opinions. In their study they found that 59 percent of tweets served this purpose; see "Second Screen and Participation."

52. Zimmer and Proferes, "A Topology of Twitter Research," 256.

53. A. Bruns, J. E. Burgess, K. Crawford, and F. Shaw, "#Qldfloods and @QPSMedia: Crisis Communication on Twitter in the 2011 South East Queensland Floods," report, Media Ecologies Project, ARC Centre of Excellence for Creative Industries and Innovation (January 2012), 13, http://eprints.qut.edu.au/48241/1/floodsreport.pdf.

54. It should be noted that these figures actually underrepresent the number of tweets that focused on Annalise, as this count includes only correct spellings of her name and omits indirect references to her.

55. The tweets pertaining to Annalise's appearance could be disregarded as just one-off opinions about trivial things such as costuming. However, often these comments attended to the stylized racialization of her character, indicating that viewers were picking up on the program's purposeful attention to race.

56. Jessica Rawden, "How to Get Away with Murder Review: A Frantic Pace and Viola Davis Are Reasons to Watch," *CinemaBlend,* September 24, 2014, https://www.cinemablend.com/television/How-Get-Away-With-Murder-Review-Frantic-Pace-Viola-Davis-Reasons-Watch-67487.html.

57. Ibid.

58. Alicia Edison, "The Impact of the Media on Biracial Identity Formation" (master's thesis, University of North Texas, 2007), 53.

59. This corresponds with a recent research study by University of Sussex that determined that women are as likely to be harassed online by other women as they were to be harassed by men; see "Women Troll Each Other Online: How Females Are Just as Likely to Be Abused by Their Own Sex as by Men," *Daily Mail,* May 14, 2014, https://www.dailymail.co.uk/news/article-2628755/Women-troll-online-How-females-just-likely-abused-sex-men.html.

60. Jennifer Kowalski, "Stereotypes of History: Reconstructing Truth and the Black Mammy," *Transcending Silence* (Spring 2009).

61. Even viewers who were somewhat critical of Annalise's behavior seemed to believe it stemmed from her having "the weirdest mothering instincts," as @emeraldnocturne observed on October 22, 2015.

62. Gilligan's distinction is explored in Jenefer Robinson and Stephanie Ross, "Women, Morality, and Fiction," *Hypatia* 5, no. 2 (1990): 77.

63. Ibid.

64. *How to Get Away with Murder,* episode 2.7, "I Want You to Die," ABC, aired November 5, 2015.

65. Sarah Appleton Aguiar, *The Bitch Is Back: Wicked Women in Literature* (Carbondale: Southern Illinois University Press, 2001), 65.

66. *How to Get Away with Murder,* episode 2.4, "Skanks Get Shanked," ABC, aired October 15, 2015.

67. Ibid.

68. Melissa Ames, "Sex Undoes Her: What the Fall Premiers of How to Get Away with Murder, Scandal, & Grey's Anatomy Reveal about the Effects of Sexualizing Strong Female Characters," *Small Screen Scholar,* September 30, 2014, http://smallscreenscholar.blogspot.com/2014/09/sex-undoes-her-what-fall-premiers-of.html; Chuck Wendig, "How 'Strong Female Characters' Still End Up Weak and Powerless ('Or, Do They Pass the Action Figure Test?')" *Terribleminds,* February 16, 2015, http://terribleminds.com/ramble/2015/02/16/how-strong-female-characters-still-end-up-weak-and-powerless-or-do-they-pass-the-action-figure-test/.

69. Keating, "Once upon a Time and the Villainization of Women."

70. Gallagher, "Scandal's Olivia Pope and the Rise of the Female Antihero."

71. Kayla Kumari Upadhyaya, "Everyone Is Pretty Casual about Murder on *How to Get Away with Murder,*" *A. V. Club,* October 2, 2015, https://www.avclub.com/c/tv-review/how-to-get-away-with-murder/season-2.

72. *How to Get Away with Murder,* episode 2.2, "She's Dying," ABC, aired October 1, 2015; *How to Get Away with Murder,* episode 2.8, "Hi, I'm Philip," ABC, aired November 12, 2015.

73. Upadhyaya, "Everyone Is Pretty Casual about Murder."

74. The idea that Twitter provides users with an imagined community is well documented in scholarship; see Gina Masullo Chen, "Tweet This: A Uses and Gratifications Perspective on How Active Twitter Use Gratifies a Need to Connect with Others," *Computers in Human Behavior* 27, no. 2 (2011): 755–62; A. B. Gruzd, B. Wellman, and Y. Takhteyev, "Imagining Twitter as an Imagined Community," *American Behavioral Scientist* 55, no. 10 (2011): 1294–1318; Xu Huimin and Yan Ruoh-Nan, "Feeling Connected via Television Viewing: Exploring the Scale and Its Correlates," *Communication Studies* 62, no. 2 (2011): 186–206; Steven Harrington, Tim Highfield, and Axel Bruns, "More Than a Backchannel: Twitter and Television," in *Audience Interactivity and Participation,* ed. José Manuel Noguera (Brussels: COST Action IS0906 Transforming Audiences, 2012), 13–17.

75. On tracking cultural sentiment, see N. A. Diakopoulos and D. A. Shamma, "Characterizing Debate Performance via Aggregated Twitter Sentiment," in *Proceedings of the SIGCHI Conference on Human Factors in Computing Systems,* ed.

Elizabeth Mynatt and Association for Computing Machinery (New York: ACM, 2010): 1195–98. On the performative nature of Twitter, see Michael A. Stefanone, Derek Lackaff, and Devan Rosen, "The Relationship between Traditional Mass Media and 'Social Media': Reality Television as a Model for Social Network Site Behavior," *Journal of Broadcasting & Electronic Media* 54, no. 3 (2010): 508–25; Paul Booth, "The Television Social Network: Exploring TV Characters," *Communication Studies* 63, no. 3 (2012): 309–27; Lin Qui, Han Lin, Jonathan Ramsay, and Fang Yang, "You Are What You Tweet: Personality Expression and Perception on Twitter," *Journal of Research in Personality* 46 (2012): 710–14. Although not prominently displayed for *HTGAWM,* live-tweeting practices for other fictional television programs have involved even more explicit performances wherein viewer engagement has involved setting up and maintaining social media accounts for fictional characters and posting as those characters; see Harrington et al., "More Than a Backchannel," 13. This, along with the ways in which viewers conflate characters with actors who play them, further indicates that live tweets concerning fictional programs are probably not ideal for determining actual user sentiments.

76. Avery Holton and Seth C. Lewis, "Journalists, Social Media, and the Use of Humor on Twitter," *Electronic Journal of Communication* 21 (2011): 6. In regard to humor, the following posts represent the type of comedic tweets found in the data collection. On October 15, 2015, Tznya L. Pinchback (@Tznya) wrote: "Frank's LinkedIn profile: The reaper for top ranked boutique law firm." On October 8, 2015, Trishelle Cantz (@TrishelleCantz1) tweeted: "Asher is so oblivious and unimportant to the group he is like beige or the yellow starburst." And on October 29, 2015, @lavallaispics posted: "When all of your friends are murderers, you need to reevaluate your life."

77. *How to Get Away with Murder,* episode 2.1, "It's Time to Move On," ABC, aired September 24, 2015.

78. *How to Get Away with Murder,* episode 2.5, "Meet Bonnie," ABC, aired October 22, 2015.

79. Michaela Meyer, "The 'Other' Woman in Contemporary Television Drama: Analyzing Intersectional Representation on *Bones,*" *Sexuality & Culture* 19, no. 4 (2015): 904.

80. Ibid., 911.

81. Brennan Williams, "Shonda Rhimes Says She Isn't 'Diversifying' Television, She's 'Normalizing' It—There's a Difference," *Huffington Post,* March 20, 2015, https://www.huffpost.com/entry/shonda-rhimes-diversity-normalize-television_n_6878842; emphasis in original.

82. Megan M. Wood and Linda Baughman, "*Glee* Fandom and Twitter: Something New, or More of the Same?" *Communication Studies* 63, no. 3 (2012): 340.

83. Wood and Baughman also attend to the ways in which live-tweeting fans "become a source of free marketing labor," serving to reinforce traditional live broadcast viewing since their tweets are best understood if read while watching the program in real time. Encouraging this type of viewing consequently makes it more likely that fans are being exposed to the commercials that the producers and advertisers intend them to see; ibid.

9. Defending *The Bachelorette*

1. Jennifer Pozner, *Reality Bites Back: The Troubling Truth about Guilty Pleasure TV* (Berkeley, Calif.: Seal, 2010), 17.

2. Ibid., 17.

3. Ibid., 53.

4. Ibid., 55.

5. Ibid., 72.

6. For more on the problematic "sexual ethos" of the program, see Willa Paskin, "Finally, a *Bachelor* Contestant Exposes the Show's Weird Sex Issues," *Slate*, February 4, 2014, https://slate.com/culture/2014/02/the-bachelor-clare-sleeps-with-juan-pablo-exposes-the-shows-weird-sexual-issues.html.

7. Emily Yahr, "'The Bachelorette' Reveals Slut-Shaming Attacks against Kaitlyn While Never Actually Using the Word 'Sex,'" *Washington Post*, July 21, 2015, https://www.washingtonpost.com/news/arts-and-entertainment/wp/2015/07/21/the-bachelorette-reveals-slut-shaming-attacks-against-kaitlyn-while-never-actually-using-the-word-sex/.

8. Jennifer Gerson Uffalussy, "The Slut-Shaming on The Bachelorette's 'Men Tell All' Episode Was a Disgrace," *Guardian*, July 21, 2015, https://www.theguardian.com/tv-and-radio/2015/jul/21/the-bachelorette-kaitlyn-bristowe-slut-shaming-cyberbullying.

9. Emma Gray, "'The Bachelorette' Proved We're Still Scandalized by Women Who Have Sex," *Huffington Post*, June 23, 2015, https://www.huffpost.com/entry/the-bachelorette-sex-kaitlyn-bristowe-nick-viall_n_7642118.

10. Ibid.

11. Amanda Michelle Steiner, "*The Bachelorette*'s Kaitlyn Bristowe: I Was Judged for Having Sex with Nick Viall 'Because I'm a Woman,'" *People*, June 25, 2015, https://people.com/tv/bachelorette-kaitlyn-bristowe-on-sex-with-nick-viall-slut-shaming-sexism/.

12. Uffalussy, "The Slut-Shaming on The Bachelorette's 'Men Tell All' Episode."

13. Ibid.

14. Yahr, "'The Bachelorette' Reveals Slut-Shaming Attacks against Kaitlyn."

15. D. Y. Wohn and E. K. Na, "Tweeting about TV: Sharing Television Viewing Experiences via Social Media Message Streams," *First Monday* 16, no. 3 (2011).

16. Since the majority of the tweets analyzed in this chapter were posted during the June 22, 2015, episode, dates are omitted unless an example is pulled from a different period.

17. Studies continue to find evidence of a cultural double standard pertaining to acceptance of male versus female sexual activity; see Derek Kreager and Jeremy Staff, "The Sexual Double Standard and Adolescent Peer Acceptance," *Social Psychology Quarterly* 72, no. 2 (2009): 143–64, and Zhana Vrangalova, "Is Our Sexual Double Standard Going Away?" *Psychology Today*, March 3, 2014, https://www.psychologytoday.com/us/blog/strictly-casual/201403/is-our-sexual-double-standard-going-away.

18. This, of course, assumes that the profile pictures and names used are an accurate representation of users' gender.

19. Megan Gibson, "Study: Women Slut-Shame Each Other on Twitter as Much as Men Do," *Time*, May 21, 2014, https://time.com/107228/women-misogyny-twitter-study-demos/. Interestingly, a recent study has found that even women who identify as sexually permissive are likely to criticize another woman's sexual activity; see Zhana Vrangalova, Rachel E. Bukberg, and Gerulf Rieger, "Birds of a Feather? Not When It Comes to Sexual Permissiveness," *Journal of Social and Personal Relationships* 31, no. 1 (2014): 93–113.

20. See note 75 in chapter 8.

21. Avery Holton and Seth C. Lewis, "Journalists, Social Media, and the Use of Humor on Twitter," *Electronic Journal of Communication* 21, nos. 1–2 (2011): 1–21.

22. See note 74 in chapter 8.

23. Despite—or perhaps because of—being one of the most disliked contestants on the show, Nick was brought onto two seasons of the spin-off show *Bachelor in Paradise* and then became the bachelor himself in 2017. His continued place in the reality television spotlight showcases the different ways in which men and women are treated for their so-called sexual transgressions.

24. As chapter 10 will discuss, this aligns with the long history of women being judged on the basis of the behavior of their male romantic partners. Consider, for example, the ways in which Bill Clinton's infidelity was used to criticize Hillary Clinton during the 2016 presidential campaign.

25. Studies have found that Twitter, like most online platforms, reinforces cultural norms concerning identity construction; see Roopika Risam, "Toxic Femininity 4.0," *First Monday* 20, no. 4 (2015), https://firstmonday.org/article/view/5896/4417.

26. This type of feminist digital activism appears to be more common within program-specific Twitter threads. A recent example is the ways in which female fans of *Dr. Who* pointed out the sexism in complaints by male fans after the announcement about casting of the first female Dr. Who; see Oliver Gettell, "Merriam-Webster Shuts Down Trolls Complaining about Female 'Doctor Who' Casting," *Yahoo Finance,* July 17, 2017, https://finance.yahoo.com/news/merriam-webster-shuts-down-trolls-020121861.html.

27. Jessalynn Keller, "Making Activism Accessible: Exploring Girls' Blogs as Sites of Contemporary Feminist Activism," in *Girlhood and the Politics of Place,* ed. Claudia Mitchell and Carrie Rentschler (New York: Berghahn Books, 2016), 266.

28. André Brock, "From the Blackhand Side: Twitter as a Cultural Conversation," *Journal of Broadcasting & Electronic Media* 56, no. 4 (2012): 535.

29. Hemant Purohit, Tanvi Banerjee, Andrew Hampton, Valerie Shalin, Nayanesh Bhandutia, and Amit Sheth, "Gender-Based Violence in 140 Characters or Fewer: A #BigData Case Study of Twitter," *First Monday* 21, no. 1 (2016).

30. Tanja Carstensen, "Struggling for Feminist Design: The Role of Users in Producing and Constructing Web 2.0 Media," in *Feminist Media: Participatory Spaces, Networks and Cultural Citizenship,* ed. Elke Zobl and Ricarda Drüeke (Bielefeld, Germany: Transcript, 2012), 170–81.

31. Rosemary Clark, "'Hope in a Hashtag': The Discursive Activism of #WhyIStayed," *Feminist Media Studies* 16, no. 5 (2016): 789.

32. Rosemary Clark, "#NotBuyingIt: Hashtag Feminists Expand the Commercial Media Conversation," *Feminist Media Studies* 14, no. 6 (2014): 1109.

33. Kira Cochrane, "How to Set Up and Run a Successful Feminist Campaign," *Guardian,* January 6, 2014, https://www.theguardian.com/lifeandstyle/2014/jan/06/how-to-run-a-successful-feminist-campaign.

34. Meghan Murphy, "The Trouble with Twitter Feminism," *Feminist Current,* December 18, 2013, https://www.feministcurrent.com/2013/12/18/the-trouble-with-twitter-feminism/.

35. Michelle Goldberg, "Feminism's Toxic Twitter Wars," *Nation,* January 29, 2014, https://www.thenation.com/article/feminisms-toxic-twitter-wars/; Suey Park and David J. Leonard, "In Defense of Twitter Feminism: Call-Out Culture, Gentrification on Social Media and the Politics of Feminist Discourse Online," *Model View Culture,* February 3, 2014, https://modelviewculture.com/pieces/in-defense-of-twitter-feminism; Risam, "Toxic Femininity 4.0."

36. Jessie Daniels, "The Trouble with White Feminism: Whiteness, Digital Feminism and the Intersectional Internet," in *Intersectional Internet: Race, Sex and Culture Online,* ed. Andre Brock, Safiya Noble, and Brendesha Tynes (New York: Peter Lang Digital, 2016), https://academicworks.cuny.edu/cgi/viewcontent.cgi?article=1212&context=gc_pubs; Risam, "Toxic Femininity 4.0."

37. Daniels, "The Trouble with White Feminism."

38. Murphy, "The Trouble with Twitter Feminism"; emphasis in original.

39. Helga Sadowski, "From #aufschrei to *hatr.org:* Digital-Material Entanglements in the Context of German Digital Feminist Activisms," *Feminist Media Studies* 16, no. 1 (2016): 55–69.

40. Ibid.

41. Tierney Bricker, "Ben Higgins Defends Saying I Love You to Two Women on *The Bachelor:* 'I Didn't Know There Were Rules to This,'" *E!News,* March 1, 2016, https://www.eonline.com/fr/news/744940/ben-higgins-defends-saying-i-love-you-to-two-women-on-the-bachelor-i-didn-t-know-there-were-rules-to-this.

42. Ibid.

43. Yahr, "'The Bachelorette' Reveals Slut-Shaming Attacks against Kaitlyn."

44. It should be noted that the 2020 Bachelor, Peter Weber, the contestant whom Hannah admitted having had sex with (three times—in a windmill), faced a similar situation: he was given an ultimatum by one of his final women, Madison Prewett. Leading up to the fantasy suite episode, she revealed her religious decision to remain abstinent until marriage and said she would probably not be able to continue if he was intimate with any of the other women.

45. Emily Yahr, "'I Have had Sex . . . and Jesus Still Loves Me': How 'The Bachelorette' Had a Rare Moment of Sex-Positivity," *Washington Post,* July 15, 2019, https://www.washingtonpost.com/lifestyle/2019/07/16/i-have-had-sex-jesus-still-loves-me-how-bachelorette-had-rare-moment-sex-positivity/.

46. Ibid.

10. "I'm (Not) with Her"

1. The first televised presidential debate, held on September 26, 1960, between John F. Kennedy and Richard Nixon, is credited with starting the era of the medium's influence on politics; see Kayla Webley, "How the Nixon-Kennedy Debate Changed the World," *Time,* September 23, 2010, http://content.time.com/time/nation/article/0,8599,2021078,00.html.

2. A survey conducted by the American Psychological Association indicates that more than half of American citizens consider the 2016 presidential election to me a major stressor in their lives; see American Psychological Association, "APA Survey Reveals 2016 Presidential Election Source of Significant Stress for More Than Half of Americans," October 13, 2016, https://www.apa.org/news/press/releases/2016/10/presidential-election-stress.

3. Of course, the entertainment industry has long been credited with having a liberal bias, so perhaps these developments are not that surprising. For a look at the ways in which conservatives, in particular alt-right communities, co-opt popular culture for their own political purposes, see Sean Milligan's analysis of

how the animated character Pepe the Frog was appropriated as a symbol for white nationalism: "A Rhetoric of Zaniness: Trolling, the Alt-Right, and Pepe the Frog," in "Hashtag Activism Embodied, Emboldened, and Emblematized: Case Studies on Social Justice Movements across Sites and Disciplines," ed. Melissa Ames and Kristi McDuffie (forthcoming), chap. 11.

4. See, for example, Anna McCarthy, *Ambient Television: Visual Culture and Public Space* (Durham, N.C.: Duke University Press, 2001).

5. For more on how the Internet is helping reconfigure what we call television, see Marie-José Montpetit, "The Internet Is Changing the Definition of Television," *Guardian*, June 10, 2014, https://www.theguardian.com/media-network/media-network-blog/2014/jun/10/internet-changing-definition-television.

6. Media scholars and laypersons have been debating the shifting nature of "water-cooler" conversations about television with the rise of alternative viewing platforms and niche programming. Some land on more optimistic sides of the spectrum; see Nolan Feeney, "Netflix and On-Demand Aren't Killing 'Water-Cooler TV'—They're Saving It," *Atlantic*, September 30, 2013, https://www.theatlantic.com/entertainment/archive/2013/09/netflix-and-on-demand-arent-killing-water-cooler-tv-theyre-saving-it/280113/.

7. For studies on the live tweeting of televised current events and current affairs programming, see Evelien D'heer, Pieter Verdegem, and Cédric Courtois, "Audiences as Publics: Tweeting with the Television On," *Selected Papers of Internet Research* 14, no. 1 (2013): 1–3, and Peter Dahlgren, *Media and Political Engagement: Citizens, Communication, and Democracy* (New York: Cambridge University Press, 2009).

8. Deborah Carr, "Gender Politics," *Contexts* 7, no. 4 (2008): 58–59.

9. Ibid., 59.

10. Kathleen Dolan, "Gender Stereotypes, Candidate Evaluations, and Voting for Women Candidates: What Really Matters?" *Political Research Quarterly* 67, no. 1 (2014): 104; emphasis added.

11. Kira Sanbonmatsu and Kathleen Dolan, "Do Gender Stereotypes Transcend Party?" *Political Research Quarterly* 62, no. 3 (2009): 490.

12. Jeffrey Koch, "Do Citizens Apply Gender Stereotypes to Infer Candidates' Ideological Orientations?" *Journal of Politics* 62, no. 2 (2000): 426.

13. Virginia Sapiro, Katherine Cramer Walsh, Patricia Strach, and Valerie Hennings, "Gender, Context, and Television Advertising: A Comprehensive Analysis of 2000 and 2002 House Races," *Political Research Quarterly* 64, no. 1 (2011): 111.

14. Ibid., 116.

15. Jessica Grose, "There's No Such Thing as 'Voting with Your Vagina,'" *Lenny Letter*, February 3, 2016, https://www.lennyletter.com/story/theres-no-such-thing-as-voting-with-your-vagina.

16. Kathleen Dolan, "The Impact of Gender Stereotyped Evaluations on Support for Women Candidates," *Political Behavior* 32 (2010): 87. These findings extend to first ladies as well. A study examining evaluations of Hillary Clinton and Laura Bush during their tenures as first ladies produced similar results; see Valerie Sulfaro, "Affective Evaluations of First Ladies: A Comparison of Hillary Clinton and Laura Bush," *Presidential Studies Quarterly* 37, no. 3 (2007): 507.

17. Dolan, "The Impact of Gender Stereotyped Evaluations," 87.

18. Brian Schaffner, "Priming Gender: Campaigning on Women's Issues in U. S. Senate Elections," *American Journal of Political Science* 49, no. 4 (2005): 815.

19. Melissa Ames and Sarah Burcon, *How Pop Culture Shapes the Stages of a Woman's Life: From Toddlers-in-Tiaras to Cougars-on-the-Prowl* (New York: Palgrave Macmillan, 2016), 152.

20. Rebecca Traister, *Big Girls Don't Cry: The Election That Changed Everything for American Women* (New York: Free Press, 2010); Beverly Guy-Sheftall and Johnnetta Betsch Cole, eds., *Who Should Be First? Feminists Speak Out on the 2008 Presidential Campaign* (Albany: State University of New York Press, 2010); Regina Lawrence and Melody Rose, *Hillary Clinton's Race for the White House: Gender Politics and the Media on the Campaign Trail* (Boulder, Colo.: Lynne Rienner, 2009); Kristina Horn Sheeler and Karrin Vasby Anderson, *Woman President: Confronting Postfeminist Political Culture* (College Station: Texas A&M University Press, 2013).

21. Dolan, "Gender Stereotypes, Candidate Evaluations, and Voting for Women Candidates," 96.

22. Emily Douglas, "Sexism, Racism, and Hillary," *Women's Review of Books* 28, no. 2 (2011): 6.

23. Joseph Uscinski and Lilly Goren, "What's in a Name? Coverage of Senator Hillary Clinton during the 2008 Democratic Primary," *Political Research Quarterly* 64, no. 4 (2011): 884.

24. Ibid., 892.

25. Barbara Burrell, "Likeable? Effective Commander in Chief? Polling on Candidate Traits in the 'Year of the Presidential Woman,'" *Political Science and Politics* 41, no. 4 (2008): 751; Uscinski and Goren, "What's in a Name?" 892.

26. Megan Haines, "Woman Hating," *Off Our Backs* 37, no. 4 (2007): 10.

27. Thrity Umrigar, "Bernie Bros Made Me Finally Recognize Misogyny in America," *Huffington Post,* May 5, 2016, https://www.huffpost.com/entry/bernie-bros-sexism_b_9847092; Sally Kohn, "I Felt the Bern but the Bros Are Extinguishing the Flames," *Time,* May 18, 2016, https://time.com/4339865/bernie-sanders-supporters-violence/.

28. Jessica Valenti, "It Will Be Hard to Get Over What Happened to Elizabeth Warren," Gen/Medium, March 4, 2020, https://gen.medium.com/it-will-be-hard-to-get-over-what-happened-to-elizabeth-warren-4b2e11b71a4b.

29. Rebekah Tromble and Dirk Hovy, "These 6 Charts Show How Much Sexism Hillary Clinton Faces on Twitter," *Washington Post,* February 24, 2016, https://www.washingtonpost.com/news/monkey-cage/wp/2016/02/24/these-6-charts-show-how-much-sexism-hillary-clinton-faces-on-twitter/.

30. Ibid.

31. Ibid.

32. Ibid.

33. Ibid.

34. To be clear, his sexism was on full display long before this debate. Daniel Bush details many of Trump's forms of hostile sexism in the election: insulting the appearance of the Republican contender Carly Fiorina ("Look at that face. Would anyone vote for that?") and attempting to undermine the Fox News host Megyn Kelly because of her gender ("she had blood coming out of her wherever"); see Daniel Bush, "The Hidden Sexism That Could Sway the Election," PBS, June 15, 2016, https://www.pbs.org/newshour/politics/the-hidden-sexism-that-could-sway-the-election. And, of course, there was that time when Trump suggested that "Second Amendment people" might be able to do something to get rid of Clinton; see Nick Corasaniti and Maggie Haberman. "Donald Trump Suggests 'Second Amendment People' Could Act against Hillary Clinton," *New York Times,* August 9, 2016, https://www.nytimes.com/2016/08/10/us/politics/donald-trump-hillary-clinton.html.

35. Brian Stelter, "Debate Breaks Records as Most-Watched in U. S. History," *CNN Money,* September 27, 2016, https://money.cnn.com/2016/09/27/media/debate-ratings-record-viewership/.

36. Admittedly, this is a rather small amount; at the peak, nearly 2.5 million tweets were being generated per hour during the debate. With approximately 5 million tweets produced between 9 and 11 P.M. EST, this represents merely .26 percent of the communications.

37. Stelter, "Debate Breaks Records as Most-Watched." When indirect references (e.g., pronouns) are taken into consideration, the proportion of references to Trump over Clinton increases. Since such indirect references can be ambiguous, however (i.e., use of the word *he* in this debate could have referred to Trump or the moderator, Lester Holt, in some instances), these figures were omitted.

38. Animalistic language (references to her "claws") was also present, which reinforces the age-old metaphor of women as being "catty."

39. Ames and Burcon, *How Pop Culture Shapes the Stages of a Woman's Life,* 217.

40. Simple word counts for such derogatory slurs were not useful in this analysis, as a subset of the tweets using such terms were actually directing them at Trump rather than Clinton (e.g., "Hillary Clinton stood tall in front of the bully, and he's acting like a bitch. #debatenight #debates2016," Aqua174, 10:37 P.M.).

41. Of course, her campaign pointedly embraced this critique throughout the campaign by building on Clinton's applauded response to Trump's making this very claim: "Well, if fighting for women's health care and paid family leave and equal pay is playing the woman card, then deal me in."

42. Ames and Burcon, *How Pop Culture Shapes the Stages of a Woman's Life,* 152, 218.

43. Laura Bates, "Hillary Clinton Presidency: Donald Trump Tweet Shows Scale of Sexism Blighting Hillary's Campaign," *International Business Times,* April 21, 2015, https://www.ibtimes.co.uk/hillary-clinton-presidency-donald-trump-tweet-shows-scale-sexism-blighting-hillarys-campaign-1497593.

44. As I discuss throughout part III of this book, the inability to determine authorial intent is always going to be a limitation of Twitter if one is studying it to determine digital activism. Take, for example, this tweet: "Hillary is not nice. That's my next president. #debatenight" (ty1errichardson, 10:38 P.M.). Taken out of context, which is easy to do in an overpopulated Twitter thread, this tweet is hard to decipher. Is it a criticism of Clinton (it states that she "is not nice")? And if so, does the follow-up statement, "That's my next president," refer not to her but to Trump? Or is this tweet meant to serve as social commentary indicating that a woman need not be nice in order to serve in the office as the president? Does the juxtaposition of these seemingly incompatible sentences actually reveal that the user appreciates Clinton's rejection of the feminine mandate to act "nice"?

45. See Robbie Couch, "Donald Trump's Major Fat-Shaming Problem Was on Full Display at the Debate," *Upworthy,* September 27, 2016, https://www.upworthy.com/donald-trumps-major-fat-shaming-problem-was-on-full-display-at-the-debate; Lucia Graves, "Alicia Machado, Miss Universe Weight-Shamed by Trump, Speaks Out for Clinton," *Guardian,* September 28, 2016, https://www.theguardian.com/us-news/2016/sep/27/alicia-machado-miss-universe-weight-shame-trump-speaks-out-clinton; Françoise Moulty, "Donald Trump Is Barry Blitt's 'Miss Congeniality,'" *New Yorker,* September 29, 2016, https://www.newyorker.com/culture/culture-desk/cover-story-2016–10–10; Katie Zezima and Jose DelReal, "Donald Trump's Weight Problem: He Can't Stop Talking about 'Fat' People," *Washington Post,* September 28, 2016. Commentary arose in all forms of media and from various people. For example, Claire McCaskill, then a Democratic senator from Missouri, tweeted: "The D women Senators have talked & we're concerned about Donald's weight. Campaign stress? We think a public daily weigh-in is called for" (September 28, 2016, 3:10 P.M.).

46. Emily Crockett and Sarah Frostenson, "Trump Interrupted Clinton 25 Times in the First 26 Minutes of the Debate," *Vox,* September 26, 2016, https://www.vox.com/policy-and-politics/2016/9/26/13068010/presidential-debate-2016-trump-clinton-interruptions; emphasis in original.

47. For a scholarly analysis see Ezra Klein, "The First Debate Featured an Unprepared Man Repeatedly Shouting over a Highly Prepared Woman," *Vox,* September 26, 2016, https://www.vox.com/policy-and-politics/2016/9/26/13067798/trump-clinton-first-debate. For satire see Alexandra Petri, "Last Night's Debate, or the Mansplaining Olympics," *Washington Post,* September 27, 2016, https://www.washingtonpost.com/blogs/compost/wp/2016/09/27/last-nights-debate-or-the-mansplaining-olympics/; and "Viewers Impressed by How Male Trump Looked during Debate," *Onion,* September 26, 2016, https://politics.theonion.com/viewers-impressed-by-how-male-trump-looked-during-debat-1819579276. For listicles, see Jessica Samakow, "10 Times Women Wanted to Throw Things at the TV during the Debate," *Huffington Post,* September 27, 2016, https://www.huffpost.com/entry/11-times-women-wanted-to-throw-things-at-the-tv-monday-night_n_57e9b311e4b082aad9b6545f, and Elana Sztokman, "10 Emotional Abuse Tactics That Trump Blatantly Used in the First Debate," *Everyday Feminism,* September 27, 2016, https://everydayfeminism.com/2016/09/trump-emotional-abuse-tactics/.

48. Annalisa Merelli, "The First US Presidential Debate Will be Shown in Gender Studies Classes for Years to Come," *Quartz,* September 26, 2016, https://qz.com/792389/tonights-us-presidential-debate-between-donald-trump-and-hillary-clinton-will-be-shown-in-gender-studies-classes-for-years-to-come/. During the debate users kept tally of how many times Clinton was interrupted (e.g., "@HillaryClinton has been interrupted 40 times so far during tonight's presidential debate. #DebateNight," voxdotcom, 9:54 P.M.), and many wrote about how this reminded them of encounters they had had with men in professional work spaces.

49. Petri, "Last Night's Debate, or the Mansplaining Olympics."

50. Emma Gray, "Donald Trump Couldn't Stop Interrupting Hillary Clinton on Debate Night: This Is What 'Manterrupting' Looks Like," *Huffington Post,* September 26, 2016, https://www.huffpost.com/entry/donald-trump-couldnt-stop-interrupting-hillary-clinton-on-debate-night_n_57e9ca11e4b024a52d2a0e26.

51. Alexandra Svokos, "Hillary Clinton's Debate-Winning Shoulder Shimmy Is the New 'Bye Felicia,'" *Elite Daily,* September 26, 2016, https://www.elitedaily.com/news/politics/hillary-clinton-debate-reaction-donald-trump/1624484.

52. Dee Lockett, "Billy Bush Responds after Getting Routed on Social Media for Encouraging Donald Trump's Sexism in New Tape," *Vulture,* October 7, 2016, https://www.vulture.com/2016/10/billy-bush-under-fire-for-lewd-remarks-trump-tape.html; David Fahrenthold, "Trump Recorded Having Extremely Lewd Conversation about Women in 2005," *Washington Post,* October 8, 2016, https://www.washingtonpost.com/politics/trump-recorded-having-extremely-lewd-conversation-about-women-in-2005/2016/10/07/3b9ce776-8cb4-11e6-bf8a-3d26847eeed4_story.html.

53. Jeannie Ludlow, "I'd like to suggest that there is a better way . . ." October 15, 2016, 9:50 A.M., Facebook.

54. Jessica Valenti, "A lot of women watching are going to recognize the way that he's interrupting her & yelling #debatenight." October 14, 2016, 9:08 A.M., Twitter.

55. Jenavieve Hatch, "18 Pieces of Merch for the Nasty Woman in All of Us," *Huffington Post,* October 20, 2016, https://www.huffpost.com/entry/18-perfect-pieces-of-merch-for-the-nasty-woman-in-all-of-us_n_5807c5c4e4b0b994d4c3705c.

56. Madeline Berg, "How Donald Trump Accidentally Created the Nasty Woman Economy," *Forbes,* October 21, 2016, https://www.forbes.com/sites/maddieberg/2016/10/21/how-donald-trump-donald-trump-accidentally-created-the-nasty-woman-economy/#48a6237e55ca.

57. Chris D'Angelo, "Trump Supporters Are Peddling Disgustingly Sexist Anti-Hillary Clinton Swag," *Huffington Post,* May 3, 2016, https://www.huffpost.com/entry/deplorable-anti-clinton-merch-at-trump-rallies_n_572836e1e4b016f378936c22; Claire Landsbaum, "The Most Misogynistic Gear Spotted at Trump Rallies," *New York Magazine,* October 12, 2016, https://www.thecut.com/2016/10/the-most-misogynistic-things-people-wore-to-trump-rallies.html.

58. Melanie Eversley, "Post-Election Spate of Hate Crimes Worse Than Post-9/11, Experts Say," *USA Today,* November 14, 2016, https://www.usatoday.com/story/news/2016/11/12/post-election-spate-hate-crimes-worse-than-post-911-experts-say/93681294/; Southern Poverty Law Center, "Update: Incidents of Hateful Harassment since Election Day Now Number 701," *SPLC Hatewatch,* November 18, 2016, https://www.splcenter.org/hatewatch/2016/11/18/update-incidents-hateful-harassment-election-day-now-number-701.

59. Louise Liu, "Here's How Nate Silver Thinks the US Election Map Would Look if Just Men Voted," *Business Insider,* October 12, 2016, https://www.businessinsider.my/this-is-what-the-election-map-would-look-like-if-just-men-voted-on-election-day-2016-10/.

60. "Exit Polls," *CNN,* November 23, 2016, https://edition.cnn.com/election/2016/results/exit-polls.

61. Joan C. Williams, "What So Many People Don't Get about the U. S. Working Class," *Harvard Business Review,* November 10, 2016, https://hbr.org/2016/11/what-so-many-people-dont-get-about-the-u-s-working-class; Mark Lilla, "The End of Identity Liberalism," *New York Times,* November 18, 2016, https://www.nytimes.com/2016/11/20/opinion/sunday/the-end-of-identity-liberalism.html.

62. Max Weiss, "Things I Blame for Hillary Clinton's Loss, Ranked," *Huffington Post,* December 5, 2016, https://www.huffpost.com/entry/things-i-blame-for-hillary-clintons-loss-ranked_b_58459894e4b0496fbcb0c26d.

63. L. V. Anderson, "White Women Sold Out the Sisterhood and the World by Voting for Trump," *Slate,* November 9, 2016, https://slate.com/human-interest

/2016/11/white-women-sold-out-the-sisterhood-and-the-world-by-voting-for-trump.html; Dahleen Glanton, "White Women, Own Up to It: You're the Reason Hillary Clinton Lost," *Chicago Tribune,* November 18, 2016, https://www.chicagotribune.com/columns/dahleen-glanton/ct-white-women-glanton-20161118-column.html; Phoebe Lett, "White Women Voted Trump. Now What?" *New York Times,* November 10, 2016, https://www.nytimes.com/2016/11/10/opinion/white-women-voted-trump-now-what.html; Katie McDonough, "The Quiet Racism behind the White Female Trump Voter," *Splinter,* November 17, 2016, https://splinternews.com/the-quiet-racism-behind-the-white-female-trump-voter-1793863796.

64. Laura Turner, "When National Turmoil Becomes Personal Anxiety," *Atlantic,* November 1, 2016, https://www.theatlantic.com/health/archive/2016/11/election-anxiety/505964/.

Conclusion

1. Daniel Holloway, "ABC Shelved 'Black-ish' Political Episode over 'Creative Differences,'" *Variety,* March 9, 2018, https://variety.com/2018/tv/news/abc-shelves-blackish-political-1202722980/.

2. *Grey's Anatomy,* episode 4.19, "Beautiful Dreamer," ABC, aired April 12, 2018.

3. *13 Reasons Why,* seasons 1–3, Netflix, aired starting March 31, 2017, May 18, 2018, and August 23, 2019. Besides these themes, the third season also tapped into current cultural fears by including a story line involving an ICE deportation.

4. *Roseanne,* episode 10.1, "Twenty Years to Life," ABC, aired March 27, 2018.

5. John Koblin, "After Racist Tweet, Roseanne Barr's Show Is Canceled by ABC," *New York Times,* May 29, 2018, https://www.nytimes.com/2018/05/29/business/media/roseanne-barr-offensive-tweets.html. The show was later rebranded and aired as *The Connors;* Barr's character was written out of the narrative.

6. For an in-depth discussion of this, see MJ Robinson, *Television on Demand: Curatorial Culture and the Transformation of TV* (New York: Bloomsbury, 2017).

7. See Nabeel Gillani et al., "Me, My Echo Chamber, and I: Introspection on Social Media Polarization" (paper presented at the International World Wide Web Conference, Lyon, France, April 23, 2018).

8. See Melissa Ames, "Feminism, Postmodernism, and Affect: An Unlikely Love Triangle in Women's Media" (Ph.D. diss., Wayne State University, 2007).

9. Jennifer Pybus, "Accumulating Affect: Social Networks and Their Archives of Feelings," in *Networked Affect,* ed. Ken Hillis, Susanna Paasonen, and Michael Petit (Cambridge: MIT Press, 2015), 239.

10. Susanna Paasonen, "A Midsummer's Bonfire: Affective Intensities of Online Debate," in Hillis et al., *Networked Affect,* 31.

11. Morten Bay, "Weaponizing the Haters: *The Last Jedi* and the Strategic Politicization of Pop Culture through Social Media Manipulation," *First Monday* 23, no. 11 (2018), https://firstmonday.org/article/view/9388/7603.

Index